The House of

From its foundation to the end of

the eighteenth century

Lady Newton

Alpha Editions

This edition published in 2019

ISBN : 9789353977573

Design and Setting By
Alpha Editions
email - alphaedis@gmail.com

THE HOUSE OF LYME

FROM ITS FOUNDATION TO THE END OF THE EIGHTEENTH CENTURY

BY THE LADY NEWTON

ILLUSTRATED

NEW YORK
G. P. PUTNAM'S SONS
1917

TO MY HUSBAND

PREFATORY NOTE

A LOCAL antiquary of considerable learning, W. Beamont, printed in 1876, I believe for private circulation, " A History of the House of Lyme." Although the present work is the result of researches which are entirely independent, I have not scrupled to avail myself of Mr. Beamont's monograph, which was dedicated to my father-in-law, the late William John Legh, M.P. for South Lancashire and East Cheshire, afterwards first Lord Newton, whenever we were dealing with the same documents. I have to thank the executors of the late Mrs. Beamont for permission to quote from this work, and from her husband's " History of Warrington " (1849).*

I have to thank Mr. F. Madan and the authorities of Brasenose College, Oxford, for permission to quote from Mr. G. H. Wakeling's " History of Brasenose College, 1603–1660." Mr. Madan has also given me very kind help in other ways. The Master of St. John's College, Cambridge, and Dr. J. Bass Mullinger have very courteously examined for me the records of their college.

My thanks are also due to Mr. John Henry Master, who is a direct descendant of Elizabeth Legh, Lady Master, for permission to quote from some of the papers in his possession, and Major Darby Griffiths—a descendant of the Chicheleys—has kindly allowed me access to his family papers.

I am indebted to the Dean of Manchester for kindly granting me permission to make the necessary transcripts from the Raines MSS. in the Library of Chetham's Hospital, and

---

* " Warrington in 1465," printed for the Chetham Society, 1849. Edited by W. Beamont.

vii

PREFATORY NOTE

to Mr. C. W. Sutton and the authorities of the Chetham Society for a similar service.

The Rev. Edwin Bedford, Rector of St. George the Martyr Church, Queen Square, has courteously examined for me his parish registers.

From my friends the present Lord Egerton of Tatton and the Duchess of Buckingham and Chandos I have received kind help which is acknowledged in the text.

To my brother-in-law, Sir Edward Ridley, I am indebted for advice in dealing with the very early history.

Last, but by no means least, my most sincere thanks and gratitude I owe to my good friend Mr. Edmund Gosse. Without his never-failing help and encouragement this history would scarcely have been begun, and would certainly never have been completed.

E. N.

Lyme, Christmas, 1916

CONTENTS

CONTENTS

ILLUSTRATIONS

ILLUSTRATIONS

† By permission of the Editor of *Country Life*.

INTRODUCTION

THE idea of writing the history of this wonderful old house and its owners came to me after the discovery which I made some years ago of a large quantity of papers tied up in bundles labelled "Old Letters" in a fireproof cupboard, the existence of which was unknown or had been forgotten. The letters were arranged in no sort of order or sequence, and although they had evidently been examined after a fashion, they had lain where I found them for upwards of forty years. Many of them were almost undecipherable from damp, much of the paper had been gnawed by rats or mice and occasionally, as I untied the bundles, the contents fell to pieces in my hands. I was then unfamiliar with Court hand, consequently many of the letters were quite unintelligible to me, but with patience and a certain amount of wear and tear of eyesight, I mastered the difficulties of Elizabethan writing until I found it as easy to read as that of the present day. It took me many months of work to sort out and classify these letters, and to arrange them chronologically, and then I began the even longer task of copying. I have done this almost entirely with my own hand as I found copyists inaccurate, and the amount of time and patience required for the work could, I felt, only be given by some one as deeply interested in the letters as I was myself, The writing was so faint as to be often almost illegible, and it took me sometimes half an hour, using a strong magnifying glass, to decipher a single word.

Although this is only the history of a private house and family, the domestic details of three hundred years ago will, I hope, interest, if not the public at large, at any rate a section of it. There is so much even in private letters which throws

INTRODUCTION

a sidelight upon the history of the time that it seems to me
to be a duty to publish these records of bygone centuries,
without considering the possible success or failure of my
enterprise.

We can hardly realize as we gaze at the rather wooden faces
of the early portraits that these were once living men and
women of flesh and blood, very similar to ourselves but for
their different conditions of life and surroundings ; and in the
case of these early Leghs they had this characteristic—if one
may call it so—which they share with their descendants, the
intense love of their home which shows itself in each succeeding
generation. "Dear Lyme," "Sweet Lyme"—they call it by
no other epithet ; their longing to get back to it when absent,
their joy at their return to what for them is the only spot on
earth, is apparent through hundreds of years.

I have grown to know and love these dear dead people with
whose characters and handwritings I am now so familiar, and
who are as real to me as living beings of to-day, even as I love
every stone of the grand old house that has seen the passing
of so many of this long line. I touch with reverent hands
things fashioned by fingers long since turned to dust, and
tenderly I handle objects that were the joy and pride of those
who created them centuries ago ; and as I sit in the old
rooms I can people them with these figures from the dim
past, who seem to glide before me—a silent procession of
shadows.

I see the first Sir Piers, a faint and distant outline in his
heavy armour, grim and determined ; the knight and priest
with his tonsured head, in vestments and chasuble, coming
into bolder relief. Next advances, plainer and more distinct,
the seventh Sir Piers, builder of the house, with his ascetic
face and bright red hair ; and clearer still and more distinct
comes the ninth and last Sir Peter, his ruddy weather-beaten
countenance and silvery white hair standing out plainly
before me ; his Margaret passes, wan and delicate, followed
by Dorothy, shrewd, capable, and precise. Then Francis, tall
and shambling, an invalid almost from his birth, the

xiv

INTRODUCTION

erudite Dr. Thomas, who much resembles his great-grand-father Sir Piers, having the same sharp features and bright red hair, so characteristic of the race, his faithful Lettice and all her merry little ones. Now advances my special beloved, the tall and stately Richard, resplendent in the satin and lace of Charles II's day, the full wig framing his handsome face with its chiselled features and beautiful large dark brown eyes; beside him his Elizabeth, his " dearest Heart," fair and comely, and all his " dear brats." I seem to hear their little feet pattering over the old boards. Next comes Peter, small and slight, and Frances, his fond and devoted wife, and finally Peter, last of his name, with his shrewish Martha, her character warped and soured by grief at the loss of two precious boys. And so the procession passes into the shadows.

There has always been to me a pathetic interest in the lives of those who have been before us within these same walls, who have lived and loved, and suffered and died, who have had their successes and failures, joys and sorrows, hopes and disappointments so like our own to-day; who have looked out on these same hills with the eyes of youth, full of joy and courage and anticipation, or with the sickness of hope deferred, and in the shadow of some grief too deep for tears. These records tell us of noble deeds, brave exploits, and high aspirations, of troubles borne with resignation and of lives of uncomplaining self-sacrifice, helped and sustained by simple faith and belief and trust, undisturbed by the doubts and questions of the religion of to-day.

I long hesitated whether or no to publish the letters of Richard Legh to his wife as being too sacred for the cold eye of criticism or the garish light of day, but I decided that this picture of ideal married happiness should be commemorated, together with the record of a noble life which shines like some bright jewel in the setting of those callous pleasure-loving days.

To the best of my ability I have tried to render a faithful picture of the time, contemporary with each individual as I describe him or her. I have endeavoured, without drawing too much upon my imagination, to give the dead bones life and to make my figures speak and move.

To those of my readers who have the patience to wade through the many pages of this record, I tender my apologies for its length, while craving their indulgence for its many imperfections. If I have painted my subject in too glowing colours, and in my enthusiasm have given a semblance of bombast to my descriptions, I must plead in excuse my great love of the old house and its traditions.

E. N.

CHAPTER I

THE EARLY HISTORY OF THE LEGHS

THE House of Lyme has its origin in the person of Peter or Piers—afterwards Sir Piers Legh—eldest son of Robert Legh of Adlington—and a descendant of the Leghs of Booths—by his second wife Maude, daughter and heiress of Sir John Norley. This Sir Piers Legh married, in 1388, Margaret, daughter and heiress of Sir Thomas Danyers, the owner of a small domain or manor called Bradley within Appleton, in Cheshire—and widow of Sir John Savage—and founded the family of Legh of Lyme.

The absence of any letters earlier than the sixteenth century makes it impossible to give more than a short chronological account of these very early Leghs, whose history has been gleaned chiefly from old deeds and pedigrees pieced together with occasional references to them found in the chronicles of the time.

The Sir Piers Legh of whom we write—the first of a long 1346 succession of Sir Piers, is the subject of a much-disputed controversy as to whether it was he or his father-in-law, Sir Thomas Danyers (a Cheshire Knight who fought for Edward III in France), who rescued the Standard of the Black Prince at the battle before the gates of Caen and took prisoner the Constable and the Earl of Tancarville.* Tradition ascribes the honour to Sir Piers, but Froissart makes no mention of either Sir Thomas or Sir Piers, and names Sir Thomas Holland " in company

---

* Jean, Vicomte de Melun and Comte de Tancarville, valiant French soldier, created hereditary Chamberlain of Normandy by King Jean le Bon, captured at the battle of Caen but released, captured again at Poitiers, died 1382. The Seigneurs de Tancarville were great supporters of the Kings of France, and determined enemies of England.

with 5 or 6 other Knights " as the hero of the capture. The existence of letters patent of Richard II which recite the grant made by the Black Prince to Piers Legh and Margaret his wife, of the land called Hanley, or Lyme Hanley—given for services rendered—and Sir Thomas Danyers' services being therein specified and recognized, seems to place the matter beyond all doubt. For this service rendered to the King by Sir Thomas Danyers, he was to receive forty marks a year from his manor of Frodsham in Cheshire, and the ground before mentioned, within the forest of Macclesfield, to continue to him and his heirs for ever. There still seems, however, to have been much dispute about the question. A pedigree by one Sampson Yeardswicke dated April 24, 1576, makes mention of

"Piers Leghe Esqr Justice Steward of Macclesfield and ye forest thereof . . . to whom King Richard II gave Hanley—not only for ye Relevinge of his father's Standard at the battle of Cressay,* but also for ye Manfull takinge of ye Earle of Tankerville at the same Battale as apereth by Letters patent of the same Kinge Richard II for whose cause and for that he fully and faithfully pued [proved ?] him he was after on St Lawrence daie beheaded at Chester by King Henry 4 in A.D. 1400."

In Holinshed we find the following description of the battle before the gates of Caen :

"When the Constable [of France] saw their good willes, he was contented to follow their desire [to go forth and fight the English outside the town] and so forth they went in good order, and made good face to put their lyues in hazard but when they sawe the Englishmen approach in good order deuided into three batteils, & the archers readie to shoote, which they of Caen had not seene before, they were sore afrayde and fled away towards the towne without any order or array, for all that the Constable could doe to stay them. The Englishmen followed and in the chase slew many, and entred the towne with their enemies. The Constable and the Earle of Tankeruile tooke a Tower at the bridge foote, thinking there to saue themselves, but

* There appears to be some confusion between the two battles, the Battle of Crécy and the one fought before the gates of Caen, which are referred to as if they were one and the same, whereas the two places lie widely apart.

2

perceyuing the place to be of no force, nor able long to holde out, they submitted themselues unto Sir Thomas Hollande.*

" But here whatsoever Froissart doth report of the taking of this towne and of the yeilding of these two noble men, it is to be proued the sayde Earle of Tankerville was taken by one Ligh—anncester to Sir Peter Lighe now liuing whether in the fight or within the Tower I have not to say ; but for the taking of the sayde Earle, and for his other Manlike prowes showed here and elsewhere in the iourney King Edward in recompence of his agreeable seruice geve to him a Lordship in the Countie of Chester called Hanley which the sayde Sir Peter Lighe nowe liuing doth enjoy and possesse as successor and heire to his anncester the foresayd Ligh to whom it was first given."

From the same historian we get a further account :

" King Richard beying in the Castell of Conway sore discomfited, and fearing least he should not remaine there long in safetie, uppon knowledge had by his trustie friendes John Pallet and Richard Seimoure, of the dealings and approach of his aduersaries, sent the Duke of Exeter † to talke with the Duke of Lancaster,‡ who in the meane while, had caused one of King Richards faithful and trustie friends Sir Peers a Legh, commonly called Perkyn a Lee, lose his head and commanded the same to be set up, uppon one of the highest turrets aboute all the Citie, and so that true and faithful Gentleman, for his stedfast faith, and assured loyaltie to his louinge soueraigne, thus lost his life."

The account given by Holinshed is thus in conflict with that given by Froissart. We must remember, however, that Sir Piers Legh, according to the account accepted by Earwaker (" East Cheshire," vol. ii, p. 291 *et sqq.*), had not been born at the date of the battle of Caen. If that is so, then the controversy is really between the name of Sir Thomas Holland on the one hand and that of Sir Thomas Danyers on the other. The grant was to Sir Thomas Danyers, and it was as his son-in-law that Piers received the benefit of it. It might be suggested that

---

* Sir Thomas Holland, first Earl of Kent of the Holland family; soldier; captain-general in France and Normandy 1359; died 1360.

† John, Duke of Exeter, third son of Sir Thomas Holland, first Earl of Kent (1352 ?–1400), half-brother to Richard II.; married Elizabeth, daughter of John of Gaunt.

‡ The son of John of Gaunt, and afterwards King Henry IV.

3

in which they are spoken of by the early writers. Like all his other favourites they obtained a complete ascendancy over him, and indulged in great freedom of speech towards him ; a specimen of which the ' Chronicle of Kenilworth ' gives in the original dialect, In tantam familiaritatem domino regi annectebantur, ut idem in materna lingua audacter confabularentur; ' Dycon slep sicury quile we wake, and dread nougt quile we lyve seftow ; ffor zif thow haddest weddet Perkyn, daughter of Lye, thow mun halde alone day with any man in Chesterschire in ffaith ! ' This provincial discourse being turned into pure modern English may stand thus : ' Richard, sleep soundly, while we watch, and fear nothing while we lie beside thee, for if thou hadst married the daughter of Perkyn of Lye [Sir Piers Legh of Lyme, near Macclesfield, beheaded by the Duke of Lancaster], thou mightest have kept Hallowtide * with any man in Cheshire.'

" The head of poor Sir Perkyn [commonly called Perkyn a Legh] was ordered by Henry IV to be set upon one of the loftiest towers of Chester."

A grant of arms was given by King Richard II in 1397 to this Sir Piers—first of his name—viz. gules a cross engrailed argent, and the crest, issuing from a ducal coronet or, a ram's head argent, attired or, holding in its mouth a laurel sprig proper, with the grand motto *En Dieu est ma foi.* This was confirmed by Norroy in his visitation of Cheshire in 1575, with an additional grant of an escutcheon of honour or shield of pretence—sable, within an orle of estoiles argent, an arm couped, embowed and armed proper, holding a pennon argent. In the patent express mention is made by the herald of its being granted for the services rendered by the first Sir Piers at Crécy. The official record of the first grant is not to be found, but is referred to in that of Elizabeth, and is further confirmed on April 8, 1665. Casts made from seals on old deeds prove that no other arms have been used by the family since the original grant in 1397.†

* " Keep Hallowtide "—*i.e.* " Be as good and substantial as any in Cheshire."
† In connexion with this grant a wonderful discovery may here be mentioned, which was made when the present owners came to Lyme, sixteen years ago, namely, that of a rose-water dish and ewer, parcel gilt and in delicate workmanship of the finest kind. The dish is of the date of Queen Mary, 1556 ; the ewer, eighteen years later—1574. Both are in splendid preservation and seem, fortunately, to have been hidden away for many years and never used. The dish and ewer were exhibited in London at the Fine Arts and other exhibitions, and the late Mr. Cripps was very much interested in the discovery of this almost unique piece of plate, and thought

EARLY HISTORY OF THE LEGHS

With the eldest son of the first Sir Piers, Peter Legh of 1403
Lyme and Haydock, afterwards Sir Peter—began the Lancashire
connexion, he having been married about 1403 when a child,
as was so much the fashion in those early days, to Joan, daughter
and heiress of Sir Gilbert de Haydock. Through her the Legh
family became possessed of very large estates in both Lancashire
and Cheshire, and the young couple, at the consummation of
the marriage, took up their abode in Lancashire at Bradley
House, the ancient seat of the Haydock family, leaving the old
Cheshire home of the Danyers—another Bradley. At Bradley
House, Lancashire, the Leghs continued for many generations,
adding to their estates by marriages with successive heiresses,
which resulted in a great portion of Cheshire and Lancashire
being owned by the family. Henry V, when Prince of Wales,
was often in Cheshire, and on one of his visits made this Peter
Legh (afterwards Sir Peter) a grant of a piece of land called
Heghleghfield within the forest of Macclesfield with the office 1411
of forester of that forest for the term of his life.

Following the example of his father, Sir Peter Legh threw
in his lot with his sovereign and accompanied King Henry V
on his expedition to France. He is mentioned in Sir Harris
Nicolas' * " History of the Battle of Agincourt " and appears to
have been a person of much importance in the King's army,
being styled Monsieur Piers de Legh † in the Battle Roll, with
his retinue, Robert and Hugh de Orell, Thomas Sutton, John
Pygott, and George de Ashley, who were probably all archers.
He was made knight banneret on the field of Agincourt and 1422
died in Paris in 1422, presumably from the result of wounds
received in battle. His widow married secondly Sir Richard
Molyneux.‡

it must have been made commemorative of the grant of arms, as the shield of pretence appears to have been stamped down over the other arms, which are beautifully
executed in coloured enamels.

* Sir Nicholas Harris Nicolas (1799–1848), antiquary; author of many valuable
works, including "The Battle of Agincourt," which he wrote in 1827.

† Monsr. Piers de Legh, or sa Retenu, etc.

‡ Richard Molyneux, served under Henry V in the French wars, and specially
distinguished himself at Agincourt, after which battle he was knighted. By his
second wife, Joan, widow of Sir Piers Legh, he had eight sons and three daughters.

During practically the whole of the fifteenth century England was being decimated by the Wars of the Roses, in which the Legh family took no small part. Peter the third (son of Sir Peter Legh last named) succeeded his father at the
1430 age of seven or eight. He was married when only sixteen to Margaret Molyneux, the daughter of his stepfather, Sir Richard Molyneux, by Ellen, daughter of Sir W. Harrington of Hornby. At her death, shortly before June 28, 1428, when the writ of *diem clausit extremum* issued, Peter Legh married, secondly, Elizabeth, daughter of Edmund Trafford and widow of Sir John Pilkington. He joined the Yorkists at Sandal Castle, and was made knight banneret at the Battle of Wakefield; it is not known whether he was at Blore Heath, where his brother-in-law, Sir Richard Molyneux * and so many Lancashire and Cheshire men were killed. On May 10, 1461, Edward IV appointed Sir Peter Legh Governor of Rhudlam Castle, and he was present at the Battle of Towton in 1461 and joined the King's expedition towards Scotland in 1462.

1465 A curious MS. comprising 333 pages all written in Latin is attributed to this Sir Peter Legh. It is a register of his large estates in Cheshire and Lancashire, and deals minutely with every particular of the rents of his possessions, but unfortunately it contains no mention of any of the stirring events of the time, nor does it give even a passing reference outside the subject on which the author writes. The book is a small folio, and is bound in a strong binding, probably of the eighteenth century. It is written throughout in the same hand, which is legible and distinct. From the fact that reference is made to " the said Peter " or " the said Peter Legh " without the knightly prefix, it seems possible—though hardly probable—that Sir Peter himself, and not one of the two chaplains whose names occur, might be the author. But the knights of those days were handier with the sword than with the pen, and although Sir Peter might have desired, after his long and arduous labours in the field, to devote the remaining years of

* Sir Richard Molyneux, soldier, son of the above, Constable of Liverpool, 1446; sided with Henry VI in the Wars of the Roses; fell at Blore Heath, 1459.

8

his life to literary work, it is very doubtful whether he possessed the requisite knowledge or skill to do so.

In the first page we learn that the work was begun on the third Tuesday in Lent (March 19), in the year 1465, the sixth Edward IV. From a translation * made by the late Mr. W. Beamont, the antiquarian, we get the following curious description of Bradley House, the ancient seat of the Haydock family, which Sir Peter had inherited from his mother, and where he was living at the time the MS. was written.

> " The aforesaid Peter Legh holds the manor of Bradley in the vill of Burtonwood within the parish of Werrington to himself his heirs and assigns for ever, that is to say, a new hall with three new chambers and a fair dining room, with a new kitchen, bakehouse, and brewhouse, and also with a new tower built of stone with turrets, and a fair gateway, and above it a stone ' bastille ' well defended, with a fair chapel, all of the said Peter's making, also one ancient chamber called the Knyghtes chamber, all which premises aforesaid, with other different houses, are surrounded by a moat with a drawbridge, and outside the said moat are three great barns, namely, on the north part of the said manor house with a great shippon and stable, with a small house for the bailiff, and a new oven built at the eastern end of the place called the ' Parogardyne,' with all the members and demesne lands to the said manor house belonging or appertaining, with one large orchard, enclosed with hedges and ditches on the south part of the said place called the ' Parogardyne,' with an enclosed garden beyond the old oven."

From this we gather that Sir Peter practically rebuilt the house, only the " Knyghtes ancient chamber " remaining of the original building. All that is now left of what must have been an imposing structure is the moat and a ruined portion of a gateway. The house, which is now a farm, contains some fine old doors clamped with iron and studded with huge nails : also some beautiful large oak beams. We get besides from this book a curious description of Lyme as it then existed, which will be quoted in a later chapter ; many of the old names of fields, woods, and enclosures can still be traced.

From Mr. Beamont's translation we learn that fencing and

---

* "Warrington in 1465."

enclosing of fields and hedges prevailed to a considerable extent at the date of the MS., and the mode of cultivating the soil appears to have been by burning the turf or surface of the fields, which are called " brandearths." The " pratum " or meadow, the " terra arabilis " or ploughed land, and the " terra fisca " or fresh land are all mentioned. There was no uniform system of measure, says Mr. Beamont, quantity was estimated " according to the working of the plough and not by measure " ; and the author speaks of " an acre of land according to the measure of Makerfield." This was probably the Lancashire measure of seven yards to the rod. The trees mentioned in the MS. are the " alnus " or alder, the ash, birch, " salix " or willow, the " quercus " or oak, the " tremula " or aspen, the elder, thorn, bramble, rose, woodrose, holly, blackberry, crab-tree, cherry-tree, broom-heath, and arbutus. One is disposed to wonder whether the climate can have been more genial in the fifteenth century than it is at the present day, since the arbutus will now only flourish in protected situations, and would certainly not grow at Lyme, at the elevation of 800 feet. Grains and roots named in the MS. are corn, wheat, barley, pease, vetches, kale, and flax ; and among plants, fern, thistle, dock, and moss. Amongst birds the crow, hawk, lark, sparrow, snipe, woodcock, drake, hen, goose, and swan occur ; and among the edible animals are the " porcus " or hog, the cow, sheep, deer, hind, roe, and cony, while the fox is often mentioned ; but among reptiles we find only the adder. One curious instance is met with where the wolf seems to have become recently extinct in the neighbourhood of Lyme, when the MS. was written.

Though pit-coal was not unknown in the middle of the fifteenth century, nothing occurs in the MS. about coals or coal-houses, which seems strange in such a district.

Among the trades named are le nayler, milward, mason, smith, fisher, miller, thatcher, swain, glover, and webster, while the " presbyter " or priest, the " capellanus " or chaplain, and the " aquaebajulus " or clerk have to do with the religious duties. The " jurisperitus " or lawyer is mentioned, while the glover, webster, " sowter " or shoemaker, and the fuller have reference to clothing. The cook, fisher, and miller may come under the heading of food, and the species of recreation indulged in by the family may be inferred from the mention of the " citherator " or harper, and the " piper."

> " The holdings by which the tenants held their lands under Sir Peter [says Mr. Beamont] were various. Some of them held their lands by knight's service, which bound them to perform service in war and subjected them to homage, relief, and various other feudal claims, but left them in other respects almost absolute owners of the land. It was the most onerous but at the same time the most honourable species of tenure."

This Sir Peter Legh died at Bradley in 1478 at the age of sixty-three, and his eldest son, also a Peter, the fourth of his name, married, about 1449, Mabell, the heiress of the Crofts. She leaves a very curious will, dated 1474, in which there is mentioned an indenture of the 8 of July, 14 Edward IV, by which " Dame Mabell Lye, widow of Peres Legh," provides for her three younger sons, Hamond, James, and John, with 100 shillings yearly during their lives, the money " if they be evil deposit or wrong gydit " to go to her eldest son " Peersher," *i.e.* Piers or Peter. One hundred shillings would be equivalent to about £80 of the money of the present day ; but this would not appear to be a very munificent portion even for a younger son.

This Peter dying in the lifetime of his father, the estates devolved, at the death of Sir Peter in 1478, on his grandson, Peter the fifth, generally called Piers, born in 1455, and married in 1467 when a child to Ellen, daughter of Sir John Savage. This Piers kept up the family traditions, he served with Lord Stanley's * force in the Scottish expedition under the Duke of Gloucester,† and won his spurs and was made a knight banneret at Hutton Field at a great review of the forces. Richard III granted him £10 a year for life in consideration of his services, and is supposed to have been his guest at Bradley. A very curious old oak bed is the only remaining relic left at Bradley

marginal notes: 1478   1482   1 Richard III

---

* Thomas Stanley, first Earl of Derby (1435?–1504), succeeded his father as second Baron Stanley, 1459; held commands in France, 1475, and Scotland, 1482; married Margaret Beaufort, Countess of Richmond, mother of Henry VII. He was created Earl of Derby by that King.   † Afterwards Richard III.

(now a farm-house). It has four low bedposts, and is put together with wooden pegs—which were used before nails or screws. The bed is undoubtedly of the fifteenth century; it goes by the name of "The King's Bed" and may well have been occupied by Richard III during his visit to Bradley.

1505   It is unknown if Sir Piers was at Bosworth. He received from King Henry VII the much-coveted office of Steward of Blackburnshire, Tottington, Rochdale, and Clitheroe in consideration of services rendered.

The parish church of Disley was built in 1524 by this Sir Piers Legh. He desired to place in it three priests and two deacons, but he died before endowing it. He also erected on one of the highest points of the park a building which has always gone by the name of " Lyme Cage "; it is quadrangular in shape, with four towers, and was probably originally intended as a watch-tower; and, Lyme being part of a royal forest, was perhaps later on used as a place of detention for prisoners awaiting their trial at the assizes at Chester. It is marked on all the old maps, and is a prominent landmark for many miles round. The present building was altered by Giacomo Leoni, a well-known Italian architect, in 1726.

By his wife Ellen, Sir Piers had four sons. and three daughters. His second son, Gowther, gave £10 a year towards a free school at Winwick, Lancashire (one of the oldest parts of the Legh property), which fact is notified by a brass on the school building erected by Gowther's great-nephew, Sir Peter Legh, in 1618, who augmented the grant by another yearly sum of £10, " for his zeal to God's glorye and his love to the parish of Winwick and common good of the country."

An interesting episode relating to Gowther Legh appears in the " Pleadings and Depositions of the Duchy of Lancaster in the time of Henry VII and Henry VIII." *

1517   " To the Right Hon. Sir Henry Marney, Knight.
" Gowther Legh complains that whereas he dwells in a tenement in Wynwhyck [Winwick] in the county of Lancaster, and has there a

* By the kind permission of the editor, Lieut.-Col. Henry Fishwick, F.S.A., I am allowed to publish this extract.

chest containing a gold ring price 26/8, and certain evidences and
other Juelles . . . on the 30th day of October last [1517] in the
eventyde after the sonne sett, certain riotous persons [specified by
name] with 20 others broke into the plaintiff's said house, he being
then away in Cheshire, and carried away with them in a weyne
[waggon] the said chest, which they still wrongfully detain ; " adding
that if he or his wife had been in the house at the time, they would
have been in danger of their lives. He prays therefore for " Privy
Seales."

He makes a further complaint to Sir William Fitzwilliam,*
and this time it appears to be against his brother, Peter Legh
of Bradley, that on December 21, about eleven o'clock at night,
at the command of the said Peter, certain persons whose names
are given

"'entered the said park of Wonewycke [Winwick], with bows, arrows   1517
&ct and shot many and dyverz arroys at William Haughton, servant
to the plaintiff and keeper of the said park, who was walking about
within the pale of the same, and who was in such danger of his life
that he was glad to flye out of the park to plaintiff's house.' Haughton
then called up certain of the plaintiff's servants ' then beyng at rest
in their beddes ' and they all went to the said park where they found
the said persons had pulled down the stakes set there for the ' save-
gard ' of the deer, 'but how many deer they had killed in the meantime plaintiff does not know.' "

Haughton thereupon arrested the leader of the marauders.
Peter Legh then commanded certain of his retainers to lie in
wait upon the highway between the plaintiff's house and
Latham, where

" the plaintiff was then waiting upon the Earl of Derby † his master,
to murder the plaintiff and such of his servants as should carry Peter
Nailor [the ringleader] to the manor to be examined, whereof plaintiff
and his servants are in danger of their lives and cannot go about
their business. Prays for letters of privy seal."

* Sir William Fitzwilliam, Earl of Southampton, Lord High Admiral, wounded
in action off Brest 1513; knighted at Tournay; Chancellor of Duchy of Lancaster,
1529; intimate friend of Henry VIII, whom he served both at home and abroad.
Died 1542.
† Thomas, second Earl of Derby, succeeded his father as tenth Lord Strange in
1497, and his grandfather as Earl of Derby in 1504. He married Anne, daughter
of Edward, Lord Hastings, and died in 1521.

Winwick ranked among the most extensive of the Lancashire parishes, comprising as it did an area of 20,000 statute acres, containing ten townships and furnished with a living of the value of from £7000 to £10,000 a year. This was divided in 1845, and the parish was cut down to two townships and the living to £1500 a year. It is supposed, from its name, to have been the seat of one of the twelve Saxon chiefs who founded their establishment in South Lancashire before the formation of parishes, and is said to have been the favourite residence of Oswald, King of Northumbria, patron saint of the church. Oswald was killed in battle on August 5, A.D. 642, at a place called by Bede Maserfelth, thought by many authorities to be Makerfield in the parish of Winwick. A very ancient inscription is upon the upper part of the wall on the south side of the church—three lines of which have been transcribed. They run as follows :

> " This place of old did Oswald greatly love
> Who the Northumbers ruled, now reigns above,
> And from Marcelde did to Heaven remove."

A pig roughly cut in stone on the front of the church tower is supposed to be a further sign of its great antiquity. A story is told that at the first choosing of the site a heap of stones was deposited in one particular spot, preparatory to the commencement of the building. During the night a pig took the stones and placed them higher up the hill, repeating this performance —whenever the stones were replaced—three times in succession. This was taken to be a sign that the church was not intended to be built where the first site was chosen, and the building was therefore erected at the place where the pig deposited the stones, the animal being commemorated on the wall of the church. There is a local tradition that the name " Winwick " is derived from the grunt or squeal of the pig, " Win-week-week."

The church consists of a tower, nave, side aisles, a chancel, and two chapels, Legh and Gerard. The former contains a curious brass, described later, and some monuments, but it has suffered much from restoration. The church stands on a small knoll from which a fine view of the country round is obtained, the Cheshire hills being plainly visible.

In 1491, Sir Piers Legh lost his wife, to whom he was devotedly attached. She was buried at Bewgenet, in Sussex, but there is no record to show what took her there. Her husband, who never ceased to mourn her loss, retired from the world at her death and became a monk, probably influenced by his brother-in-law, the Archbishop of York.* He died at Lyme in 1527, and is buried at Winwick, the burial-place of the Legh family for many generations. Unfortunately the parish registers there only begin with the year 1563, so there is no mention of this Sir Piers Legh—Knight and Priest—as he is always styled, but he is commemorated in the church by a very curious and probably almost unique brass, which represents him dressed as a knight in armour, with a sword and spurs, while his bare head shows the priestly tonsure. Over his armour he wears a chasuble. Between his hands, which are raised as if in prayer, lies his shield of six quarterings, the colours of which appear to have been enamelled, which is repeated on another part of the brass. By his side is placed the effigy of his wife, with the Danyers and Savage arms upon her robe. She wears a head-dress coming into a sort of point over her forehead, with two lappets which hang down on each side of her face; round her waist hangs a broad girdle clasped with three roses, and suspended from the girdle is a pomander (a small, round, perforated box which contained a perfume-ball or perfumed powder, worn as a charm). Her bare hands are clasped against a large cross which falls from her neck.

Small figures of his four little sons are at the feet of Sir Piers, three little daughters being at the feet of their mother.

At the four corners of the brass are emblems of the Evangelists, and this inscription is engraved upon it :

Orate pro animis probi viri, dni Petri Legh, militis, hic tumulati, et dnae Elenae, ux ejus, filiae Johis Savage, militis, cujus quidem Elenae

---

* Thomas Savage, Archbishop of York, brother of Sir John Savage, politician and soldier, who fought for Henry of Richmond at Bosworth. The Archbishop died 1507.

Corpus sepelitur apud Bewgenett 17° die Mensis Mai, anno Domini Millesim CCCCLXXXXJ.

Idem Petrus, post ipsius Elenae mortem i. Sacerdotium Canonice, consecrat obiit apud Lyme i. Hanley XI die Augusti ao di MVCCXXVIJ.

The translation runs as follows :

Pray for the souls of the excellent man Sir Peter Legh, knight, here buried, and of the Lady Elena, his wife, daughter of John Savage, knight, the body of which Elena was deposited at Bewgenett, 17th May, A.D. 1491. The same Peter, after the death of this Elena, having been consecrated to the priesthood, died at Lyme in Hanley, 11th August, 1527.

Three wills were made by this Sir Piers Legh, the first and second dated respectively February and December 1522, in which he makes mention of all his lands, and states his wishes as to the disposal of them ; the last will, bearing the same date as the second, December 14, 1522, is most interesting and instructive. He begins by bequeathing his soul to Almighty God, Our Lady, and all the Saints in Heaven, and his body to be buried in the Trinity Chapel of Winwick. He specifies that his body shall be laid " afore the myddst of the Altar " there, that the priest shall " alwaies at the tyme of consecration stand ever over and upon my harte." In the event of his dying more than twenty miles distant from Winwick, his remains are to be placed upon a horse litter to be borne thither with his servants and " other Christian people," the horses to be covered and craped with black " and myn Armes to be sett on every side of the litter." His standard banner and complete armour to be carried before his body " in such condicon as shalbe thought most convenient." Out of his " goods and catalls " forty gowns of black cloth are to be divided amongst " persons as be of my howse & in my wages & other my frends. And these and euery of them to go abowte my body," and out of the proceeds of the same " goods and catalls " twenty-four white gowns are to be bought and given to twenty-four of the poorest of his tenants, every one of whom is to bear a torch in his hand and " beyre them aboute my body till I come to the

16

church to be buried." After the ceremony the trappings and torches are to be divided between the said Chapel of Winwick and the Chapel of Our Lady at Disley.

One tries to picture this funeral, and to wonder how the immense distance—about thirty miles—was accomplished, as all those attending cannot have been mounted. The coffin on its horse litter, followed by the weird procession of monks and priests and black- and white-robed figures, all bearing torches, chanting their solemn dirges, stumbling along the weary distance on the heavy tracks that stood for roads in those early days, the procession ending in the little Lancashire village, passing through the rows of gaping villagers to the church. All this pomp and ceremony must have been strangely incongruous in the midst of such quiet and prosaic surroundings.

Sir Piers further directs that out of the issues and profits of the said goods and chattels, £20 be " disposed for my Saule the day of my burial in Massez and other Almez at the Church," and that within a month of his decease one hundred priests are to say one hundred Masses, viz. twenty Masses of IHS, twenty of the five wounds, twenty of Our Lady, twenty of the Holy Ghost, and ten of the Trinity and ten of the Reginum. And every priest to have for the same, four pence, and every priest to " get him a Clerk to helpe him say dirgs and Massez and every of thame to have two pence." And at every Mass one penny is to be offered for him at the laudatory. He desires also that his executors should buy an " overlay " of marble " and lay upon me with a picture after me and my Wieff and our Armes to be set in eithere of our Coots " and a superscription is to be set on the said " overlay " with their names and the day and year of their decease.

Further he desires that out of the proceeds of the sale of the goods and chattels, on every Good Friday for seven years after his death, two shillings and sixpence shall be distributed amongst the poorest of his tenants in Warrington and Winwick parishes, and for five years after his death, every evening of Our Lady, fourpence is to be given to each of the five poorest of his tenants, each of whom should be required to " knele upon thar knees within the said Trinite Chapell the said evens and every of thame to say a Lady Sauto^r for my Saule."

Each gentleman of his household is to receive; beside his wages, thirteen shillings and fourpence, every yeoman six shillings and eightpence, and every labourer three shillings and fourpence " and to kepe thame and every of thame together upon my cost a Moneth after my decease if they will abyde." His son Peter to have all the residue of his goods not bequeathed by writing " nor by mouthe afore Recorde," and the strictest injunctions are given that all his instructions are to be carried out without delay or " prolonginge of tyme," and his " especial good Lord Cuthbert, now Bishop of London, and Sir William Molyneux* and Sir William Stanley of Hooton " are appointed executors.

" In Witness whereof I the said Sr Peris hereunto haue sett my Seale of Armes And subscribed the same with my hande the day and yere afore said

In an Indenture made October 7, 1522, between Sir Piers Legh, Knight and Priest, of the one part, and Piers, his eldest son and heir, of the other, he charges his said son most solemnly to carry out his wishes respecting the building and endowment of Disley church.

Some ten years later an inquiry was held before certain commissioners on behalf of Sir Piers' executors, and the various witnesses to the signing of the said Indenture were called and sworn. Amongst them was Gowther Legh, son of Sir Piers, who declared that his father, being at the point of death in 1522 (as a matter of fact he did not die till five years after) had answered in response to a question put to him by Gowther " that he was in full mind to have a foundation of a chapel at Disley " and that the foundation should be made by the advice of his executors. Being asked " whether should my

---

* Sir William Molyneux (1483–1548), soldier; a leader at Flodden Field, 1513, where he took two Scottish banners.

brother Perys intermeddle there anent or not ? the said Sir
Perys to him then said ' What else, he must be the head, for it
must be his deed and not mine.' " Another witness swears
that he had heard Sir Piers declare that he would have three
priests and two clerks in the form rehearsed.

At a survey made in 1548, the yearly value of Disley was
stated to be £21 13s. 4d. ; plate and jewels eight ounces, goods
and ornaments there 32s. 8d. ; lead and bells 4s. " Note that
the said value of xxj^{li} xiij^{s} iiij^{d} [£21 13s. 4d.] was presented for
the king by oon [one] of the incumbents then at the fyrst survey
made in the xxxvijth [37th] year of the late Henry VIII
[1545–6], and now at this last survey oon Sr Peter Legh knight
denyeth the king's interest therein and claymeth the same to
be parcel of his inheritance."

The church stands on a hill overlooking the village. It
consists of a tower, nave, and side aisles (added at the beginning
of the nineteenth century). The East window contains some
very fine old glass, probably German, which was placed there
about a hundred years ago, when the Elizabethan heraldic
glass was removed to Lyme. The church has been much
restored, and has lost a good deal of its interest and character.
The churchyard has some fine old trees.

This Sir Piers—a very remarkable man in his way—was
succeeded by his son, another Peter, sixth of his line, who had
reached the age of forty-eight at his father's death. He was
twice married, first to Jane, daughter of Sir Thomas Gerard,
and in 1510 to Margaret, daughter of Nicolas de Tydesley, by
whom he had one son, born in 1513. It is quite possible that
he may have fought in the Battle of Flodden Field. A curious
copy of a ballad describing the battle is among the Legh papers.
It is written by a Legh of Baguley on six narrow strips of
parchment, and is in a very good state of preservation, only
a portion of the beginning being undecipherable. Many of
the names of those taking part in the battle are mentioned :
" Surrey * that sure Earle," " Buckingham † that bolde Duke,"

* Thomas Howard, first Earl of Surrey and second Duke of Norfolk of the
Howard house (1443–1524), warrior and statesman ; Lieutenant-General of the
North in the attack against James IV of Scotland at Flodden Field, 9th September,
1513.   † Edward, third Duke of Buckingham (1478–1521).

1513   " and of Derby * that deare Erle," the names of Sir Thomas Gerard and Sir William Molyneux † also occur, but we look in vain for Legh of Lyme.

The author states the fact that :

> " Lancashire like lyons
> layden them aboute,"

the last few lines are given as a specimen of this very curious ballad, which was sent some years ago at the special request of the authorities of the Bodleian Library for their inspection.

> " Then the Erle of Surrey himself
> calleth to him a heralde
> bad him fare into frannce
> wth theis faire tithandes (tidings)
> commende me to o^r Kinge,
> theis comfortable wordes
> tell him I haue rescowed his realme
> so right required
> The King of Scots is killed
> wthall his cursed lordes
> when the Kinge his kindnes
> heard theis wordes.
> he saith I will singe him a son. . . . .
> wth the sound of my gunnes
> such a noyse to my name
> was never heard before.
> for there was shott at a shotte
> a thousand at ones.
> that all rang wth that Rowte
> Rocher and other.
> Now is this fierse seilde ‡
> foughten to an ende
> many a wee wanted his horse
> and wandered home one fote

---

* Thomas, second Earl of Derby, succeeded his grandfather in 1504. Attended Henry VIII on the French expedition and was present at the Battle of Spurs, 18th August 1513, so it is difficult to see how he could also have fought at Flodden Field on September 9 of this same year.

† Sir William Molyneux flourished under Henry VIII ; performed signal service at the Battle of Flodden Field, where he and Sir Edward Stanley (first Baron Monteagle) commanded the rear, and with his own hands took two standards of arms from the Scots. He married, first, Jane, only daughter and heiress of Sir Richard Rugge of Shropshire, secondly, Elizabeth, daughter and heiress of Cuthbert Clifton.

‡ I think this must mean "attack." Halliwell gives the word *seilinge*—assault, attack.

all was long of the murch men
a mischieffe them happen
He was a gentilman by Jesu
that this Jest made
wch said but as ye see
for soth and no other
   At Baguley that burne
his biding place he had
his anncestors of long tyme
haue yerded their longe
before William conqueror
this Conntrey Inhabited.
Jesue bring them to thy blisse
that brought us forth of bale
that haue hearck^d me here
and heard well my tale."

Finis.

This Peter Legh was supposed to have been afflicted with lameness, whether from a wound received at Flodden or no does not appear; very little is known about him, and he seems to have led an uneventful life, dying at Bradley in 1541, at the age of sixty-two. He was apparently of a somewhat quarrelsome nature, and figures as defendant in two suits brought against him in 1538 before the Court of the Star Chamber. The account of the trial * gives a vivid picture of the manners and customs of the time. The plaintiff was one Roger Jodrell of Yeardsley, Peter Legh's nearest neighbour, and the suits refer to the rights of pasture. In the second of these, Peter Legh repudiates certain imputations brought against him by Jodrell, alleging that " It is untrue that Peter Legh commanded that, if they could take one Roger Jodrell, gent, they should cut in sunder the legs and hock sinews of the said Jodrell, and pull his dwelling house down."

The descendants of the same two families are still near neighbours, and meet every year on the same ground for the prosaic purpose of grouse shooting, and the feuds of 370 years ago are happily things of the past.

* "Lancashire and Cheshire proceedings in the Star Chamber (*temp*. Henry VIII)," published by the Record Society.

CHAPTER II

THE HISTORY OF THE HOUSE

1465 ALTHOUGH we know nothing about the first building of Lyme, there is evidence of the existence of a house in the beginning of the fifteenth century, but it was not until the middle of the sixteenth that the Sir Piers Legh, seventh in succession, who succeeded his father in 1541, built the present house and made his principal abode in Cheshire. Before dealing with his life it may perhaps be as well to give here some description of the house and park as they existed in the fifteenth and sixteenth centuries.

Of the actual building of the present Lyme we have very scant knowledge. In the MS. volume referred to in the preceding chapter there is the following description of the house as it was in 1465 :

> "One fair hall with a high chamber, kitchen, bakehouse and brewhouse, and a fair park, surrounded with a paling, and divers fields and heys contained in the same park with the woods, underwoods, meadows, feedings and pastures thereto belonging, which are worth to the said Peter X[1] a year."

Other lands are described as belonging to the estate, with rents amounting to the sum of £42 9s.

We have therefore knowledge of the existence of an impaled park as early as the middle of the fifteenth century. It was surrounded by a wall at the beginning of the seventeenth in pursuance of a licence from Queen Elizabeth, who also granted permission to its owner to have free warren within it and the adjoining lands. Its extent is about 1500 acres ; it has at the present time a circumference of about nine miles ; the scenery is wild and picturesque, and the mixture of moorland, wood,

22

and water all combine to form enchanting views that meet the eye on every side.

In the fifteenth century it must have been a wild and desolate region, part forest, part moorland, the house two miles distant from the village of Disley or Distelye, which at that time can have contained only a few houses.

Some rather quaint names, dating from the earliest times, are given to different woods and enclosures in the park, of which the following are a few instances: the Knight's Low, the Sponds, Calf Croft, the Purse Fields,* Turfhouse Meadow, the Elmhurst, White's Mead, Hey's Bank, the Hampers and Clowes Hey.

Two very curious stones or crosses are placed at the top of one of the highest points of the moor which forms part of the park and are called the Bowstones. The use to which these stones were put has hitherto baffled all geologists and antiquarians, though all are agreed as to their great antiquity. They consist of two circular pillars fixed into sockets hewn in rough stone, one being slightly higher than the other, measuring about four feet in height with a circumference of four feet at the base, tapering to two feet at the top. Various theories have been put forward to explain the existence and use of these stones, some antiquarians having thought that they may have been used for human sacrifices, but the more prevalent idea is that they were probably meres or boundaries of the districts of the forest, similar ones occurring on the opposite Derbyshire hills, within the verge of the ancient forest of Peak.

The hill on which these stones lie commands an almost boundless view over the plain of Cheshire on the one side and the Derbyshire hills on the other, and has an elevation of about 1200 feet above the sea.

Near these pillars are two gravestones, said to cover the

* In the "Survey of Crown Lands" taken in 1650, reference is made to a certain property "scituate & adjoyninge to Lincolns Inn Fields, alias Pursefeild." In the "Survey of London," St. Giles, Part II, Purse Fields is stated, in 1590, to have been part of High Holborn between the Turnstiles.

remains of people who died of the plague. On one is the following inscription :

> John Hampson and his wife
> and three children left this life
> 1646.

On the other :

> Think it not strange our bones ly here
> Thine may ly thou knowest not where
> Elizabeth Hampson.

Poor bones ! Though not in hallowed ground, they lie there more peaceful and undisturbed than in some crowded churchyard.

A plague decimated some of the villages of Derbyshire in the seventeenth century, Eyam for example, where practically the entire population was wiped out, and where to this day annual services are held to commemorate the deliverance of the village from this scourge of 300 years ago, the sermon being preached from the open-air rock pulpit which was used at the time to minimize the risk of infection.

Lyme is situated at an elevation of 800 feet above the sea, on a spur of the Peak between the forests of Peak and Macclesfield, and is on the borders of Cheshire, Lancashire, and Derbyshire, hence its name Lyme, from *limes*—a border. Being part of a royal forest it may well have served in very early days as a hunting-lodge for the reigning king, and it is probable that there was an even older house than the one existing in 1465.

Certain it is, however, that the " one fair hall with its high chamber," etc., did not meet with the requirements of Sir Piers Legh, who constructed all the earliest portion of the present building, which has been altered and added to by each successive owner.

The house is built of grey stone, no doubt obtained from the quarries in the park, round a courtyard or quadrangle, and was, at the time of its first erection in the middle of the sixteenth century, purely Elizabethan, with the characteristic mullioned windows. It is almost square, the four corners cor-

LYME : NORTH FRONT

responding as nearly as possible to the points of the compass, and has at the present time a frontage of fifteen windows. The approach from the park is through a fine gateway leading into a large outer quadrangular courtyard, enclosed in former days by a wall which was replaced in the eighteenth century by the present iron railings. The gateway is flanked by two watch-towers, in each of which is a tiny room with leaded windows on the outer side, and doors on the side of the quadrangle. Couchant lions—two each side lying back to back, one thus facing both ways—form the tops of the towers, while an arch with an urn upon it spans the space between, thus connecting both towers.

The centre portion of the north front of the house, which has fortunately been left untouched with the exception of the windows in the subsequent alterations, is ascribed to that shadowy personage John of Padua. It has a curious arrangement of columns and small windows—originally mullioned—crowned by a pediment on which is a small shield displaying the Legh arms and quarterings and flanked by niches. There are four tiers of columns, Doric, Ionic, and Corinthian, graduating in size to the top, the centre part being occupied by a clock, the whole surmounted by a seated figure of Minerva. This figure was added by Leoni.

About 1676 some alteration was made in the windows, directions being given in a letter of the time for " the height and wideness of Mrs. Legh's closett windows "—a diagram accompanies the letter with measurements. Lead rain-water pipes of a beautiful design, bearing the Legh and Chicheley arms and with the monogram $\frac{E}{R\ L}$ and an arrangement of flourishes and the date 1676, are evidences of the work being carried out at this time.

Later on, in 1726, Giacomo Leoni, the Italian architect who did so much work in England at this period, faced the whole of the south front and built a fine Ionic portico projecting twelve feet and reaching to the top of the house The roof of the portico rests on six columns of stone springing from a balcony on the first floor, surrounded by a massive stone balustrade, while its lower part is supported by arches of rusticated stone. Leoni also added a covered gallery round the courtyard reaching to the second floor, giving access to the rooms on the first floor, which formerly all opened one into the other and had no separate entrances except at the two ends. The gallery is supported by arches of rusticated stone forming cloisters.

A double flight of steps with an iron railing leads from the inner courtyard into the entrance hall, the whole much resembling an Italian palace.

Lead figures of Neptune with his trident, Venus with her cestus, and Pan with his pipes, ornament the house on the south side, while on the east side are similar figures of Diana with her stag and bow and arrow, and Actæon and his dog.

A curious old octagonal lanthorn-shaped tower, formerly on the top of the house, was taken down and built up in a wood near by when the final additions were being made by Sir Jeffry Wyatville * in 1810, who replaced the lanthorn by a square tower, providing the house with some much-needed bedrooms.

In the "Vale Royal of England," published in 1656, by Daniel King † who also executed the engravings, we find the following passage relating to Lyme, written about 1600 by one William Webb, M.A. :

> "And when we have cast our eye upon Whealey bridge the utmost Confines and Passage into a part of Derbyshire and Distley, we turn us almost full West again to come to Lime; the stately seat and scituation whereof, with the large and spacious Park richly stored with Red and Fallow Deer, with all other fitnese for Lordly delights, may well shew the worthy discent of that great Family and name of the Leighs of Lyme, of whom, though there have been many famous Knights, and renowned Owners, yet none more compleat and accomplished in generous and heroical vertues, then Sir Peter Leigh, now the Possessor thereof, a noble Gentleman, and of great respect."

No mention is made in the fifteenth-century MS. of the red

---

* Sir Jeffry Wyatville (1766–1840), architect. His work was considered very superior to that of his uncle James Wyatt, who has often been styled the "execrable James."

† Daniel King, engraver; died about 1664.

deer or wild cattle. These wild cattle which were supposed to be indigenous to the place were similar to the breed at Chillingham—that is to say, they were white with large wide-spreading horns, black muzzles, and pink inside the ears, and were distinct from the Hamilton and Ferrers breeds. Up to the middle of the nineteenth century there were still several remaining, but from want of fresh blood and other causes they gradually died out and are extinct at the present day.

The red deer, which have roamed the park for upwards of five hundred years, have always been famous for their size and fierceness : many stories have been told of hairbreadth escapes of luckless individuals who chanced to cross the path of a beaten stag.

In connexion with these deer a very curious custom prevailed at Lyme from earliest times, namely, the driving of the stags at midsummer across a pond, called the Stag Pond—now no longer in existence. This performance was attended by a certain amount of ceremony, it formed a species of entertainment, and neighbours and friends from a distance were invited to be present and to take part in the chase. Vivares,* in a print after a picture by T. Smith,† still preserved at Lyme, represents the stags swimming across the pond, those in the foreground emerging from the water and fighting with their forefeet, the horns being in velvet : in the background are the ladies and gentlemen following the hunt on horseback, dressed in eighteenth-century costume. The print is inscribed :

A View in Lyme Park
With that extraordinary Custom of driving the Stag,
the property of Peter Legh Esqr
to whom this plate is inscribed by his most humble
servant T. Smith
Published Aug: 17. 1745.

* François Vivares (1709–1780), a French landscape engraver; came to London 1727; kept a print shop, 1750–1780.
† Thomas Smith, styled "Smith of Derby," one of the first of English artists to explore and display the charming scenery of his native county. He painted many picturesque views in the Peak, forty of these engraved by Vivares were published collectively by Boydell in 1760. He died 1769.

THE HOUSE OF LMYE

There is an interesting account given by Arthur Wilson,* the historian and dramatist, of a visit which he paid to Lyme as gentleman-in-waiting to Robert, third Earl of Essex, about 1620. The following is the account of Wilson's adventure which appears in Peck's " Desiderata Curiosa," xii, 10 :

> " Sir Peter Lee of Lime in Cheshire invited my lord one summer to hunt the Stagg. And having a great Stagg in chace, & many gentlemen in the pursuite, the stagg took soyle. And divers (whereof I was one) alighted, & stood with Swords drawne, to have a cut at him, at his coming out of the water. The Staggs there, being wonderful fierce & dangerous, made us youthes more eager to be at him. But he escaped us all. And it was my misfortune to be hindred of my coming nere him the way being sliperie, by a fall. Which gave occasion to some who did not know mee, to speak as if I had falne for feare which being told mee, I left the stagg, & followed the Gentleman who (first) spake it. But I found him of that cold temper, that it seemes, his words made an escape from him, as by his denyall & repentance it appeared. But this made me more violent in pursuite of the Stag to recover my reputation. And I happened to be the only horseman in, when the dogs sett him up at a bay ; & approaching nere him on horseback, he broke through the dogs, & run at mee, & tore my horse's side with his hornes, close by my thigh. Then I quitted my horse, & grew more cunning (for the dogs had sett him up againe) stealing behind him with my Sword, & cut his ham-strings ; & then got upon his back & cut his throate. Which as I was doing the Company came in and blamed my rashness, for running such a hazard."

This incident is mentioned in the notes to the " Lady of the Lake," by Sir Walter Scott, who visited Lyme when writing his history of " Peveril of the Peak."

In connexion with these stags mention may here be made of a remarkable personage, one Joseph Watson, who was keeper at Lyme for seventy years. Born in 1648, he lived in the reigns of no fewer than seven sovereigns of England, namely, Charles I, Charles II, James II, William and Mary, Anne,

---

* Arthur Wilson (1595–1652), gentleman-in-waiting to Robert Devereux, third Earl of Essex.

George I, and George II. The following curious obituary notice is quoted in all Cheshire histories : *

" Buried at Disley Church In Cheshire
June 2d, in the year of Our Lord 1753.

" Mr. Joseph Watson in the 105 Year of his Age, he was born at Moseley Common in the Parish of Leigh in the County of Lancaster and Married his Wife from Eccles nere Manchester in the said Country —the [they] were an happy Couple 72 years. She died in the 94 Year of her Age. . . . He was Park Keeper to the late Peter Leigh Esqr of Lyme and his Father before him 64 years. And while he lived he showed the Red Deer to most of the Nobility and Gentry in this Part of the Kingdom to a General Satisfaction to all who ever saw them for he had Driven and Commanded them at his pleasure as if the [they] had been Common Horned Cattle—In the Reign of Queen Ann Esqr Leigh was at Macclesfield in Cheshire in company with a Number of Gentlemen. Amongst them was Sir Rodger Mason who was then one of the Members for the said County—the [they] being Merry and free Esqr Leigh said his Keeper should drive 12 Brace of Stags to the Forest of Windsor a Present to the Queen so Sir Rodger Opposed it with a Wager of 500 guineas that neither his Keeper nor any Other Person could Drive 12 Brace of Stags from Lyme. Park to Windsor Forest on any occasion So Esqr Leigh Accepted the Wager from Sir Rodger and Immediately sent a Messenger to Lyme for his Keeper who Directly Came to his Master who told him he must Immediately Prepare himself to Drive 12 Brace of Stags to Windsor Forest for a Wager of 500 Guineas so he gave the Esqr his Master this Answer—At his Command he [would] Drive him 12 Brace of Stags to Windsor Forest or to any other part of the Kingdom by his Worships directions or he would lose his life and fortune. He accordingly undertook and accomplished this most astonishing performance, which is not to be equalled in the annals of history. He was a Man of low stature, not bulky, of a fresh complexion and pleasant countenance, and he believed he had drunk a Gallon of malt liquor one day with another for about sixty years of his time, and at the latter end of his life he drank plentifully, which was agreeable to his constitution and agreeable to himself. He was a very mild-tempered man, he knew behaviour was cheerful Company, and was allowed by all who knew him to be as fine a Keeper as any in England."

* It appears in a slightly varied form in all the Cheshire histories, but it has been found impossible to trace its origin.

THE HOUSE OF LYME

There are two full-length portraits at Lyme of Joseph Watson, both in hunting dress, signed " Jo^n Slack pinxt, 1750." The following inscription is on one :

> " Jo Watson who in the 26th Year of his Age Anno 1674 commenced Keeper at Lime Park : In wch Service he Continued 70 yeares and anno 1750 In the 102nd Year of his Age He hunted a Buck a Chase near Six hours Long at wch Hunting one gentleman was present whose Ancestors he had Hunted with for four generations before & He being the fiveth Generation he had hunted with."

The drinking propensity of this ancient retainer is alluded to in several of the old letters, his excesses being much deplored.

CHAPTER III

THE BUILDER OF THE HOUSE

THE Sir Piers Legh, seventh of his name, builder of the present
house, was born in 1513, and was married when only five years
old to Margaret, daughter of Sir Thomas Gerard of the Bryn.
The Church's dispensation was necessary as they were cousins ;
this seems to have been obtained and they were married the
same year, 1518.

Nothing is known of the early youth of Sir Piers. He
succeeded his father in 1541, and in 1544 he formed part of the
expedition to Scotland under Lord Hertford,* an expedition
attended with a certain amount of danger, which was undertaken with the idea of affording support to the party of Scotch
reformers.

Sir Piers took part in the storming and burning of Edinburgh
and Leith, and was knighted on May 11 of that same year, 1544.
The following is from the State Papers at the Record Office :

" 1544, Sunday 11th of May at Leith

"Knights dubbed in Scotland by the Earl of Hertford the Kings
Lieutenant, 36th Henry VIII, at the burning of Edinburgh Leith
and others, viz. the Lords Clinton and Conyers etc. etc.

" Peter Lee "

" 19th May Expedition against Scotland.

"Hertford's warrant to Sadler to pay Sir Edw: Warner Capt: of 100
Men 20. days Wages at 4/ for himself, 2/ for his petty Captain and
6d a Man from 29. April to 18. May, deducting £25. 2. 3. for victuals
had out of the King's provision.

" Berwick, 19th May 36. Henry VIII signed "

* Edward Seymour, first Earl of Hertford and Duke of Somerset (1506–1552),
the Protector ; brother of Jane Seymour, third wife of Henry VIII ; Lieut.-General
in the North, 1544 ; pillaged Edinburgh.

" Receipt signed the same day by Warner's servant, Albane Bampton "

" The like for John Preston, deducting £32. received by himself "

" The like for Sir Piers Lighe, deducting £30. 9. 9. Received by Ligh's servant Piers Hey X "

" The same day (19th May) two similar warrants for conduct money, viz :
Sir Piers Legh for 100 Men to Warrington, Lancashire, 140 miles Received by himself."

(Each warrant is written on one side of a separate piece of paper.)

In a letter* from the Earl of Hertford to Henry VIII, written about May 18, 1544, he mentions

" those who have don Your Highnes right honest and paynful service in this journey I thoughte it also my parte to signifie the same to Your Majeste if it might please the same to remember them with Your Majestes condign thanks it would be much to theyre comfortes "

then follow the names, which include that of " Master Legh." Sir Piers Legh (not yet knighted) was evidently the messenger sent with this letter, as Lord Hertford adds :

" Fynally Mr. Lee who I assure Your Majeste hath served in this journey both honestly and willingly, doth bring unto Your Highnes a platte [a map or plan] of Legh [meant probably for Leith], and Edenburgh so as Your Majeste shall perceyve the scituacions of the same which is undoubtedly set fourth."

1545   In the York Herald's account of the second Scotch campaign under Lord Hertford which took place in September and October of the following year, 1545, which was little more than a border foray on a large scale and the destruction of many monasteries and castles, the name of Sir Piers a Ligh appears with many others present in the " battaill " before the Abbey of " Chelsse."

1550   In 1550 we find Sir Piers was made High Sheriff of Lancashire, and in 1585 he was appointed Provost-Marshal for Lancashire, Cheshire, and Chester, a post which carried with it much responsibility.

* State papers (Record Office).

THE BUILDER OF THE HOUSE

It is difficult to form an opinion of his character as very few of the letters written to him remain, and of his own writing there is only one letter to be found. He was evidently a person of importance, keeping quite a little court at Lyme, where he was visited by Leicester, Essex, and by many others of the great people of the day. Mary, Queen of Scots, is known to have been a visitor on her way either to or from Buxton, where she went several times during her captivity to drink the waters, as she was a great sufferer from rheumatism. No documentary proof of her visit is to be found, but the bed she slept in remains —now, alas, sadly mutilated—a grand arrangement of pillars and columns, ornamented with the fleur-de-lis inlaid in satin-wood in the oak. Small wooden statues of angels and the evangelists stood round the original bed, the whole being an imposing structure hung with curtains of the blue and green needlework of the period.

A beautiful little reliquary in coloured wax and needlework —said to be Queen Mary's own handiwork—was presented by her at the conclusion of her visit, and remains to this day a cherished and precious heirloom.

There is a tradition that Queen Elizabeth also visited Lyme. The drawing-room, a beautifully panelled room, happily untouched during the alterations, has a fine chimney-piece with the royal arms, which may have been erected at the time of her visit, if it ever took place. The remains of a bed traditionally said to have been the one slept in by Queen Elizabeth are of a later date.

It must have been no easy task to steer a clear course through all the reign of terror that held England during the years that immediately followed the Reformation when the sway of Thomas Cromwell was at its height ; and at the time when Sir Piers succeeded his father in 1541, the monasteries had all been swept away and the reforms of the New Learning were being rapidly carried out. The air was thick with plots and conspiracies, spies were everywhere and the very walls had ears. Men's hearts must indeed have quaked with fear, for not only was " thought made treason, but men were forced to give expression to their thoughts for fear of their silence being misinterpreted." *

Sir Piers had been brought up in the faith of his forefathers, but he probably thought it wisest to conform, and at his instance the church at Disley, built in 1524 by his grandfather the " Knight and Priest," was in 1558 consecrated for Protestant worship. Probably a recusant, he was in 1580, under the persecutions of Elizabeth suspected of holding Mass in his own house, which in his position as a Justice of the Peace and with the Test Act in full force would lay him open to the charge of high treason. In vol. 27 of the Callender of State Papers for the year 1580 (Record Office) we find the following significant notice :

1580   " 1580. Names of 12 Gentlemen and 1 lady in Cheshire whose houses are greatlie infected with Popery & not loked unto . . . Sir Piers leighe a Justice, never communicateth his famylie greatlie corrupteth, & come not at churche, & is a Cherisher of Masse prestes and suche others."

Happily no punishment seems to have followed this accusation, and Sir Piers was probably let off with a warning or the payment of a fine.

Among the earliest documents found at Lyme, irrespective of deeds and wills (the deeds go back to 1247), is a curious paper of directions dated 1534, addressed to Sir William Fitz-William,† afterwards Earl of Southampton and Chancellor of the Duchy of Lancaster, and the Justices of the Peace of the county of Lancaster, also the oath to be sworn by them, directing them to

" beyre faythe trauthe & obedience alonly to the Kings Majestye, And to his Heyres of his bodye. And of his most dere & entyreley beloued Wiefe Queene Anne begoten and they should obserue kepe mainteyne & defende the saide Acte of succession & all the hoole effects & contents thereof."

The very curious will of Jane, Lady Gerard (one of the sisters of Sir Piers Legh), dated November 20, 1575, is preserved

* Green's " History of the English People."
† See note p. 13.

SIR PIERS LEGH, 1572
Builder of the House
From a Portrait at Lyme

among the Legh papers. This lady was married about 1518 to Sir Thomas Gerard of the Bryn, a connexion of the Gerards of Bromley. By him she had one son, Thomas, afterwards High Sheriff of Lancashire, and two daughters, Catherine, married to William Tarbocke, and another daughter married to Robert Charnocke.

Sir Thomas was by no means a faithful husband, and gave his wife a good deal of trouble as we gather from the following interesting document.*

"1 June. XXXV. Hen. VIII. 1543.

" At which daye forasmoche as it appearyd to ye Kynges Comissoners that Thomas Gerard of the Bryne hath kept a Concubyne and lyved in Adulterye. And that the disagreement betwyxt him and hys wyfe hath bene the cose and originall grounds thereof. And yt further appeareth to the s^d Comissioners that by medyacion of fryndes and for desyr to plese god the same Thomas and hys wyfe wyll cohabyt and gree agayne togeder : It is Ordered that from hensforth the sayd Thomas Gerard of th' one ptye and Jane Gerard and Peers Legh her brother [who had also married Margaret daughter of Thomas Gerard of the Bryn] of th' other ptye shall not only be faythfull loving and harty fryndes together But that also the said Thomas and Jane shall forget and forgive all fawtes trespasses and offences by hys sayd wyfe heretofore comytted and ye sayd Thomas in lyke maner, and they shall knyt in hartys wth faythfull love a new and pfecte Matrymonye. And the said Peers Legh and his wife Margaret and the sayd Jane Gerard the iii. daye of Julye next comyng shall lovyingly with free and gentle harts come together to Wyndlishaw and there Hunt and make merry with the said Thomas Gerard and his frynds and that the morrow after that is to say the iiii. daye of July the said Thomas Gerard and Jane his wyfe shall goe agayne to Hunt and make merry with the sayd Peers Legh at Bradley and then return with his sayd wyfe to the Bryn, or whither him pleaseth, and cohabit with his sayd wyfe. . . . And if any breach or disagreement doe chaunce again betwixt the sayd Thomas and his wyfe they shall upon proofe thereof immediately pay to the sayd Peers Legh vi^l. xiii^s. iiii^d. for costs and charges he hath sustayned heretofore. And above all, the Commissioners doe order that from hensforth the sayd Thomas shall kepe no carnal accompayne with hys olde Concubyne

---

* Printed in vol. lxxv of the Chetham Society's publications ("Lancashire Funeral Certificates," edited by L. W. King).

nowther take no newe one unto him. And that the Penanuce for his misdemenors heretofore due and condygne shalbe further respettyd tyll tryall of his Amendment."

This well-meant attempt at effecting a reconciliation between the two was not productive of much result, for in the 38th Henry VIII, Lady Gerard and her brother Sir Piers Legh charged her husband Sir Thomas Gerard with "incontinence, assault, and imprisonment"; this probably led to her divorce four years later, November 27, 4th Edward VI, 1550.

In 1574 Sir Piers Legh is mentioned as a mourner at the gorgeous funeral of Edward, third Earl of Derby.* He appears to have ridden with seven others "being assistants to the Chief Mourner [Henry, 4th Earl], their hoods over their shoulders and heads and their horses trapped with fine cloth to the ground." †

1580   The earliest letter found at Lyme is one from Henry, 4th Earl of Derby,‡ to Sir Piers Legh, and is dated 1580. The letter is an unimportant one, merely giving directions for the restitution of one John Potte to a copyhold tenement within the forest of Macclesfield from which he appears to have been evicted. Sir Piers in his capacity of Deputy Steward of Her Majesty's forest of Macclesfield was to carry out this order. The Earls of Derby were seneschals and master foresters of the forest, and had under them officials and guardians sworn to preserve the game and report on any stealing or infringement of the laws. Besides these officials there were eight "foresters in fee" who held their office by payment of a small fee farm rent to the crown, and the owner of Lyme was always included among these. The letter in question is addressed "to my faithfull servant," and is signed "your louing Master."

At no time was rank so much considered and thought of as in the cultured times of Queen Elizabeth; class distinctions

* Edward, third Earl of Derby (1508–1572), signed petition to Pope Clement VII for Henry VIII's divorce; Lord-Lieutenant of Cheshire and Lancashire, 1569.

† Collins' "Peerage," ed. 1812, vol. iii, pp. 73–78.

‡ Born 1531, son of Edward, third Earl; hostage in France 1550; gentleman of the privy chamber to Edward VI; married Margaret Clifford, daughter of Henry, Earl of Cumberland, and granddaughter of Mary Tudor, sister of Henry VIII.

were greater then than they have almost ever been before or since, and what we should now call a snobbish or servile spirit was considered to be the proper way in which to approach persons of high and exalted rank. The Earls of Derby were small sovereigns in their way in Lancashire and the Isle of Man, where they had ruled as kings from 1404–5 till after 1504, when the title was renounced by Thomas, second Earl.

Henry, Lord Derby, was on terms of great intimacy with Sir Piers Legh, with whom he corresponded, asking his advice and opinion on many matters of local interest; it is also evident that he visited at Lyme, one of his letters ending with thanks for " the greate good cheare and entertaynment you latelie made me." He is anxious, however, to remind Sir Piers of his importance, and his letters never end with any other signature than that of " your loving Master." The following letter from him to Sir Piers gives some idea of the system of extorting payment in those early days.

" After my verie hartie commendacons

" Understandinge that at sundrie Courte heretofore holden at Macclesfeilde certeigne fynes haue bene imposed uppon trespasses committed, the which being negligentlie passed over, and not regarded as was meete, have growne unto a larger Somme then the parties are able to answere : albeit I ame informed there be manye of that poore sorte by whom more is due unto me, then can be hadde of them, by means of their povertie, I would have you deale with them by composicon and punishment as you yourself shall thinke good.

" And soe doe bidd you hartelie farewell

" Yo^r assured loving M^r

" H. DERBY."

" Post Script

" My meaninge [nevertheless] is that noe fynes be remitted to anye of those, who are of hibilitie [*sic*] to annswere the same."

The letter is addressed :

" To my right trustie and righte welbeloved servante
Sr Peeter Leighe Knighte
my Deputie Stewarde of Macclesfeilde."

Meantime everywhere abroad was war and rumour of war. Spain was at the height and zenith of her power ; enriched by the discoveries of Columbus in the West, she was now adding to her conquests the best and most fertile of the districts of Italy, and the commercial wealth of the Netherlands, and Philip was boasting that he had no rival, and was preparing himself for his final triumph—the conquest of England.

1585   In 1585, the Low Countries, maddened by his cruelties and oppression, had risen in open revolt, and Elizabeth, who had been secretly helping them, sent the Earl of Leicester with a force of 5000 men on his disastrous expedition by way of coercing the Netherlands into accepting the terms offered by their aggressor—that is to say—a restoration of their constitutional privileges on their submission to the Church. There had been a call for volunteers, as the following letter from Lord Derby will show :

" After my verie hartie Commendacons

" Where I ame required amonge my owne Tenants and frenndes psentlie to furnishe and put in A readiness A certeigne Nombr of stronge hable and tale Archers to be ymployed in her Matys service in the Lowe Contries under my verie good Lorde and Cosin the Erle of Leicester and the same to be in A readiness to sett forwards uppon Warninge the seconde of November nexte I have alreadie taken order throughout all my Landes on the Northe side Trente for A Nombr to be furnished and because the same dothe not Amownt unto and reache the Nombr expected nowe at my hands, the wch yf I should whollie require of myne owne would extende to A Grete charge. I ame therefore boulde as wth other my frends and svants accordinge to the direccon Geven me, thereby to Charge you with the Chusinge, and furnishinge amonnge yor Tenants of one verie sufficiente and stronge Archer suche A one as shalbe serviceable and of good government not Inclined or geven to dronkennes or any Notorious Vice. And soe note dowbtinge of yor full and due regarde hereunto in all respects as may stande wth myne honor and yor owne creditt.

" Newpke my house this XXIIIth of Octobr 1585
" Yo^r assured loving M^r
" H. DERBY."

" To my righte trustie and right Welbeloued Snnte
Sr Peeter Leighe Knighte my
Provoste Marshall for Lancashire Chesshire and Chester."

THE BUILDER OF THE HOUSE

The expedition proved a disastrous failure. Leicester was 1585-6 welcomed and acclaimed by the Netherlanders, and was in January 1585-6 offered by a deputation from the States-General the absolute government of the United Provinces ; but as a general he showed himself hopelessly incompetent, and after a series of reverses (in one of which the gallant Sir Philip Sidney * was killed), hampered by a total want of supplies, he brought his inglorious campaign to a close and returned to England in 1587. The following year England was threatened by the invasion of the Spanish Armada, and Sir Piers Legh subscribed £100 (a very large sum in those days, equal to about £1600 of our money) towards the fitting out and equipment of our opposing fleet.

By his wife Margaret Sir Piers had five sons and two daughters. His eldest son, Peter, born about 1540, married Katherine, daughter of Sir Thomas Venables, Baron of Kinderton, and died in the lifetime of his father, leaving issue three sons and one daughter. There is no record of Katherine his wife ; it is therefore to be presumed that she died also at an early age, as the children were brought up by their grandfather.

Sir Piers Legh's eldest grandson, Peter, aged at this time about twenty-one, was probably sent with Leicester's expedition, but no mention of his name occurs among the lists of volunteers in Leicester's train. Negotiations had been proceeding between his grandfather and Sir Gilbert Gerard,† Master of the Rolls, regarding the marriage of young Peter with Margaret, daughter of Sir Gilbert. In two very interesting but almost undecipherable letters from him to Sir Piers Legh— the first bearing date November 23, 1584, he speaks of the latter's want of liberality towards his heir, and complains of the terms of the marriage settlement, and of his being tied down to so hard a bargain :

" for if I shuld follow the verie letter of the Articles (as you doe) & not shewe any more liberalitie then the words of the Articles doeth

---

* Sir Philip Sidney, soldier, statesman, and poet (1554–1586).

† Knighted 1579; Master of the Rolls, 1581; M.P. for Lancaster, 1584; married Anne, daughter of Thomas Radcliffe of Wimersley. He died 1593

bynde me unto, then truly the yong folks might thynke they were hardly used . . . but I dyd thynke that there shuld not have bene founde any disposicon eyther in you or in me to see theyme wantt of any thynge Convenyent for theyme, & therefore for my pte I haue hetherto ben at a grete deale more charge then ys expressed in any of my Articles, & there hath Comen nothyng from you more then the letter of the Articles . . . . . . (which argueth that you haue but smalle affeccon to yor Cosyne) otherwise then fr. some profit to yor selff by the Bargane."

1584-5   This must have been about the time of the marriage; the second letter, dated January 30, 1584–5, was after the marriage had taken place, and is in the same strain.

"I haue borne all chargs for the tyme past but thereof I make no accompt, yf yt may turne you to some gayne fr that wyll please you best, yet truly yff I hadde thought to haue found you soe harde & unwyllyng to doe fr yor heyre as I nowe see you arre I wold not haue taken hym of geft at yor hands,"

ending, however, with the pious wish: "God kepe you in helth & welth."

The term "cosin" appears to have been used for any degree of relationship.

The conditions of the marriage settlement are peculiar—to say the least. The ceremony was to take place within three years from the date of the said agreement, the articles being dated June 1, 1579 (21st Elizabeth). If during the interval the said Peter Legh were to die, his next brother, Edward, was to marry the said Margaret, " or ells suche other of the daughters of the said Gilbert Gerrarde and wthin suche convenyent tyme as the said Gilbert shall appoynt." And if the said Edward were to die before the marriage was consummated, Margaret was to be passed on to the next brother. The sum of £40 yearly was to be subscribed by Sir Piers towards the maintenance of the young couple, " from and after suche tyme as the said daughter shall accomplish the age of 12 years," Sir Gilbert Gerard was to " fynd them and any issue it myght please God to send them, competent apparell, meate, drynke, lodginge and other things necessary and Requisite for them at all times," and was to assure to Sir Piers Legh certain lands in Lancashire for the term of his natural life. If it should happen that Sir Piers should be appointed to serve Her Majesty or her heirs or successors in any of their wars, he reserved to himself the right, in the event of his being taken prisoner, to sell land not exceeding the yearly rent of £40, " for his delyuerance." Sir Piers was also to have the liberty to assure out of the rent of his lands £20 a year for the keeping up of a school at Disley, and also of a priest " for the doing of divine service."

One cannot help feeling that Sir Piers got the best of the bargain, and that Sir Gilbert Gerard was justified in his complaint.

If Peter Legh did accompany Leicester in his expedition to the Low Countries he must have done so immediately after his marriage, probably returning, as so many others did, the following year. In the letter from Sir Gilbert Gerard just mentioned, there is a passage in which he speaks of " some dannger uppon Casualties that myght haue happened & nowe thankes be to God that ys past " ; this makes it appear probable that Peter took part in the campaign.

In connexion with the Earl of Leicester,* a charming letter written by him to Sir Piers Legh is here given in full :

" Sir Piers Leighe
" Ffor yor hounde and for yor hynde, sent me by yor Servante, I 1584
do right hartely thank you ; I perceyve you will not forget me and
assure yor selfe that as occasion shall serve, I will not be unmyndefull
of yor Continewall remembrance of me. And so praying you to
make assured accompt, wth my right harty commendacons, and
lyke thankes, I bid you ffarewell
          " ffro the Courte the XIXth
          of November, 1584.
               " Yor very louinge frend
                    " R. Leycester.

" I thanke you very hartiley Sr Piers for yor hounde and will requyte
you the loose of him wth as good a thinge."

          " To my very louinge frend
          Sr Piers Leighe Knight."

* Robert Dudley, first Earl of Leicester of the fourth creation (1532 ?–1588), Queen Elizabeth's favourite.

THE HOUSE OF LYME

The hound mentioned in the letter was no doubt one of the celebrated Lyme mastiffs, now, alas, threatened with extinction. This breed has existed at Lyme for generations; the dogs are noted for their immense size, being almost as large as donkeys. They are of a pale lemon colour, with gigantic heads somewhat resembling bloodhounds, black ears and muzzles, immensely broad chests, and soft brown eyes. Tradition states that the second Sir Piers had one of these dogs with him at the Battle of Agincourt, and mention is made of them in many of the old letters.

That they were much thought of in the sixteenth and seventeenth centuries is apparent from the fact that in Stowe's "Annals" we find mention of a pair among the propitiatory gifts sent in 1604 by James I to Philip III of Spain, when the Earl of Nottingham * went on his embassy to Madrid, carrying with him the Oath for the Confirmation of the Articles of Peace at the close of England's war with Spain. The following is from the text :

> "At the deliuery of the presents by Thomas Knoll Esquier, the King and Queen Came in person to View & receive them with a very kind and princeley acceptation.
>
> "The presents were
>> "Sixe stately Horses, with saddles and saddle clothes very richly and curiously embroidered, that is to say three for the King and three for the Queene Two Crosse bowes with Sheffes of Arrowes Foure fowlling pieces with their furniture very richly garnished and inlaid with plates of gold A Cupple of Lyme hounds of singular qualities."

In the great picture by Velasquez of the children of Philip IV, the *Las Meniñas*, which hangs in the Gallery at Madrid, a large mastiff is seen in the foreground, one of the children rubbing its back with his foot. The dog is precisely the same as the Lyme mastiffs of the present day, having all their characteristics, and was no doubt a descendant of the pair presented by James I to Philip III in 1604.

Sir Piers Legh, besides doing good service as a soldier, was

---

* Howard Charles, first Earl of Nottingham (1536–1624).

THE BUILDER OF THE HOUSE

for his time a cultured man ; he was a lover of music and of
the drama, patronizing the itinerant actors of the day and
keeping his own band of musicians and troupe of players ;
and dramatic performances seem frequently to have been given
at Lyme for the entertainment of his guests and neighbours.
He was also a great lover of heraldry, and was visited in 1575
by William Flower, Norroy king-of-arms, who granted the shield
of augmentation mentioned in a former chapter.   A beautiful
little manuscript book of drawings on vellum of the numerous
coats of arms belonging to the Legh family is still preserved
amongst the heirlooms.   It bears date 1575, and contains the
following dedicatory notice on the front page :

> "The names, Armes, Etymologies and Blazon, of euery Coate, apper-
> taining unto his especiall good frende Mr Peter Legh Esquier, both
> in Englishe & Latyn."

On the last leaf it is signed

> "Frortunato. M.P."

and it is thought that these are the initials of Mercury Patten,
Blue Mantle herald, its copyist.   The "Mr Peter Legh Esquier"
must have been Peter Legh, then about twelve years old.

The only letter to be found written by Sir Piers Legh is
dated January 22, 1584–5, and is addressed in somewhat
indignant terms to Robert Glover, Somerset Herald, who
conducted visitations in Durham in 1575, Cheshire 1580, and
Yorkshire in 1584.*   One sentence is reproduced :

> "I do not perceave by yr letter that you allowe me my Cosyn Legh
> of the Boothes his Armes yf you deale so hardly as not to allowe
> theis Armes Then you force me to seeke to the Erle Mrshall whoe I
> trust will allowe me that of Right I ought to have. But my trust
> is you wilnot put me unto that shefte for this matter & that although
> you have my money aforehande payd you will use me well."

The letter is beautifully written on large paper with rough
edges, the ink is still quite black and the handwriting—for that
of the period—is clear and distinct.

* Thinking it might interest the gentlemen at the Herald's College I sent this
letter for their inspection, and was told that it was very much the kind of letter
they were in the habit of receiving at the present day.

It is a curious fact that the clipping and misplacing of h's is not by any means peculiar to modern times. Many instances of this prevail in letters of the Elizabethan and Jacobean period, though as a rule both writing and spelling were better in the sixteenth than in the seventeenth century, when the writing, particularly that of the women, was atrocious and the spelling purely phonetic. One gathers from this phonetic spelling that the pronunciation of people of the upper classes must closely have resembled the dialect of the country people of to-day, they write " me broother," for instance, for " my brother," " coom " for " come," etc. Mary, Queen of Scots, spoke broad Scotch, and so did James I.

The writers were very long-winded, and, time having no value, they entered into long explanations, protestations, and diatribes, taking several pages to express what might have been said in a few lines. An instance of this may be seen in two letters of stupendous length written by Ferdinando, fifth Earl of Derby, to Robert, second Earl of Essex, copies of which had evidently been sent to Lyme. The letters contain nothing but reproaches to Lord Essex for taking into his service a certain Richard Bold, afterwards connected with the Leghs by marriage, who had previously been in Lord Derby's service and had left him, probably with a view to bettering his condition. Lord Essex writes excusing himself in a letter nearly as long, but evidently did not succeed in propitiating Lord Derby.

A portrait of Sir Piers Legh said to have been painted in 1572, when he would have been fifty-nine, represents him wearing a black satin doublet with a small white ruff, and trimmed with sable. On his head is an Edward VI bonnet bordered with roses and worn slightly over the right ear. The hair and the short pointed beard are red, characteristic of the race, and the face, much lined, is stern and resolute, with thin firm lips and a very decided chin.

There is also a portrait of his wife, Margaret, by an unknown artist, painted in her ninetieth year. She is dressed in what must evidently have been widow's weeds with a large black hood lined with white coming over her head and face, and a

MARGARET LADY LEGH

Widow of Sir Piers Legh, with her great-granddaughter Anne Legh,
afterwards Mrs. Bold, 1595

From a Portrait at Lyme

little white ruff at her chin. In her arms she holds her great-grandchild, aged one year. The child is dressed in a long white robe of lace, much resembling some old point lace of the Elizabethan period, still preserved among the Legh heirlooms. On her head is a little close-fitting white cap, round her neck is a coral necklace, and hanging from it a silver and coral rattle, and in one little hand she holds a red flower.

Over the old woman is inscribed, " Aetatis suae 90.* A. 1595 Domini 1595. Sir Piers Leghs Lady." Above the child's head is " Anno Primo after marryed to Bold."

Except in one letter of Peter Legh's in which he sends a message to " my good old grandmother " there is no mention of or allusion to Dame Margaret Legh. The women of that period led—with few exceptions—colourless lives, hampered and tied in by the conditions of the time in which they lived. Lady Legh survived her husband several years, living, as has been seen, to a great age. She must have had her sorrows, her fears, and anxieties for her husband's safety during his absence at the wars, and the knowledge of his infidelity, which we gather from his will.† The face in her portrait shows signs of suffering and the eyes have shed many tears, but she lived to see her children's children grow up around her, and she may have found comfort and consolation in watching the growth and development of their little lives.

Sir Piers made his will in 1587, in a document of stupendous length. It bears evidence of the influence of the Reformation, for there is no mention of " Our Lady " or the saints. He bequeathes his soul into the hands of Almighty God, the Creator and Maker of the whole world, and of Jesus Christ his Saviour, and his body to be buried " in my Chapel situate in the parishe Churche of Winwicke in the Countie of Lancaster where now my ancestors doe lie. Also for my Corsepntet ‡ or mortuarie I will accordinge to the lawes of this Realme." To

---

* She must, therefore, have been married at the age of thirteen, her husband being five years old.

† A bequest to his " base daughter " Jane.

‡ Corse-present—a mortuary fee.

his wife he leaves " the full thirde parte of all my goodes and catalls accordinge to the laudable Anciente Custome."

After providing for his sons and other relatives he leaves to Henry, fourth Earl of Derby, " my beste guilte Bowle of Silver with the Cover thereunto belonging in token of my verie faithfull goodwill towards him and his house which I have ever loved and honored." To Lord Derby's eldest son, Lord Strange, afterwards Ferdinando, fifth Earl, he bequeathes " all my hawks of what kynde and sorte soever they bee, And all my houndes of siche and every sorte, a smale guyfte wherein in tymes past I have had singuler good likeinge " ; and at the same time he prays Lord Derby and his son to " bestowe the Office which I nowe possesse and enjoy here in this Countrie Upon Peter Legh my Cosyn and heire male trustinge he will faithfully use and execute the same to their honors likeing." What the office was is not certain, it was probably that of Captain of the 1587 Isle of Man, which office Peter Legh was holding in 1593. Sir Piers also expresses a wish that " my poore house might ever contynewe and remayne to the house of my Lord and his posteritie for ever . . . and in case my posteritie should not appertaine and Retain to their honors and their posteritie (as I and my predecessors ever heretofore have don) if a Dead-man might have knowledge thereof and receive and take grief thereat there could not be any greater grief unto me then that in all this worlde."

Numerous bequests and annuities are left to the parsons and poor of the different parishes, and all his cousins and servants are remembered, no one apparently being omitted.

1590 Three years afterwards, on December 6, 1590, Sir Piers Legh died peacefully at Lyme at the age of seventy-seven, having lived longer than any of his predecessors ; his remains were taken to Winwick, the family burial-place in Lancashire, where they were interred on January 10, 1590–1, more than a month after his death.

His life is a very fair specimen of that of an English country gentleman of the sixteenth century. There are perhaps no great deeds of valour to recount, no list of honours to enumerate, but he faithfully served his sovereign and country; he filled the posts he occupied with honour and distinction; he was loved and respected by his friends and neighbours, he was a friend and benefactor to the poor; and though he may have had his faults, he did his duty according to his lights, and the good in his life predominates. No brass or stone marks the place of his burial, but he lives in the records of his ancient house, and his works have followed him.

CHAPTER IV

THE LAST SIR PETER AND HIS HOUSEHOLD

PETER LEGH—ninth Peter in succession, and last of the Sir Peters—was born in 1563, and would therefore have been about twenty-seven years of age at the time of his grandfather's death in 1590. His father and mother having died young, he and his two brothers, Edward and Thomas, and their sister Elizabeth, were brought up by their grandfather and grandmother. It is not known whether Peter Legh was sent to the University; his brother Edward matriculated at Brazenose College, Oxford, on May 31, 1581, at the age of sixteen, and took his B.A. degree on October 31, 1583. The younger brother, Thomas, matriculated there the same year as his elder brother, at the age of fourteen, and took his B.A. degree also in 1583.

University life began very early for the youth of the Elizabethan era. They were sent out to face the world when they were still mere children, and although more supervision seems to have been exercised over them than is the case in the colleges of the present day, considering the difficulties and dangers of travelling, the mothers of that time must have suffered even more—one would imagine—at parting with their sons than do the fond mothers of these more coddling days.

In 1584, Henry, fourth Earl of Derby, went on a mission to France to convey the garter from Queen Elizabeth to Henri III. A Mr. Peter Legh is included among his gentlemen-ushers or train-bearers. Though we have no documentary proof, it seems not unlikely that this may have been our Peter Legh—always supposing that he did not go with Leicester's expedition to the Low Countries, for he could scarcely have

SIR PETER LEGH

As a young man.   Painted on a panel by a French artist, 1591

From a Portrait at Lyme

done both—as his grandfather may have thought this a good opportunity for him to see something of the world under such good auspices. He appears to have entered one of the Inns of Court, probably with a view of obtaining some experience of the duties of a magistrate and justice of the peace, becoming an inmate of Gray's Inn in 1585—the year of his marriage. On March 16, 1591, we find a receipt for the sum of £5, signed by one Thomas Tyldesley at the hands of James Hey for Peter Legh " to be paid by mee to Hierome Pecocke of Graies Inne Gent for the use of the said Peter Lighe." In 1586 and 1590 he was M.P. for the borough of Wigan, and in 1595 he was Deputy Lieutenant, Justice of the Peace, and High Sheriff of Cheshire, and was in 1597 elected M.P. for the county of Chester, having as his colleague Thomas Holcroft of Vale Royal. He is then for the first time described as Sir Peter Legh, though it is said that he was not knighted until 1598, when Queen Elizabeth conferred that honour upon him at Greenwich at the close of Essex's two expeditions to Spain—in both of which Sir Peter took part.

1591

The first expedition (1596) was undertaken with the object of checking the advance of the Spaniards, who—encouraged by the failure of Drake's last campaign—were likely, it was feared, to give support to the disaffected in Ireland. They had already captured Calais, and Henri IV was imploring help from England. Essex set sail from Plymouth on June 1, 1596, with ninety-three ships and nearly 13,000 men, his colleague being Sir Walter Raleigh, and entirely defeated the Spanish fleet drawn up in Cadiz Bay. The town surrendered and the whole campaign proved a brilliant success. Essex returned in July, the hero of the hour, and a Thanksgiving Service was held in St. Paul's Cathedral.

In spite, however, of this defeat, the Spaniards prepared a fleet the following year to advance upon the English coast. Essex went on a second expedition to intercept it and to seize the Azores, but a terrible storm practically destroyed the Spanish fleet, and the English ships were so disabled and scattered as to have the greatest difficulty in reaching port with the capture of only a few Spanish treasure ships. Queen Elizabeth, though seriously annoyed with Essex for his failure, ultimately made him Earl Marshal, bestowing honours and rewards also upon his followers, Sir Peter Legh amongst their number.

In 1599, when all Celtic Ireland rose in support of Hugh O'Neill * who had instigated a rebellion against the oppression of the English settlers, Essex was sent by Queen Elizabeth to quell the revolt, and there was a general muster. We find † among the names of the gentlemen who were to furnish horse for Ireland that of Sir Peter Legh, viz. " Chester—Sir Peter Legh, 1 horse."

A well-executed portrait of him on a panel, thought to be by a French artist, and probably painted during his absence abroad, represents him as a young man dressed in a black satin doublet with wide puffed sleeves, a black cloak over his left shoulder. His right hand rests on his hip, and his left hand clasps the hilt of a sword which hangs from a silver belt. The face is large and massive, with a heavy square-set jaw, grey eyes, and chestnut hair parted on the left side and hanging in curls. Inscribed on the picture is :

Aetatis suae 28. Ivsqves A Lors:

Sir Peter Legh Knight.

There are two good miniatures of him. An early one painted in oils before water-colour miniatures came into fashion, gives him a moustache and short square beard, a large white linen collar falling over his armour. The other miniature, painted in 1631, when he was sixty-eight, depicts him in armour with very thick white hair, a moustache and short pointed beard— a vigorous-looking old man. Another portrait of him, about the same date as the early miniature, shows him in typical Elizabethan dress wearing a very beautiful sword, only part of the hilt of which is still in existence.

In 1593 we find Peter Legh discharging the duties of Captain

* Hugh O'Neill, third Baron of Duncannon, and second Earl of Tyrone (1540 ?–1616).

† From the "Acts of the Privy Council for 1599–1600" (Record Office).

50

of the Isle of Man, to which post Lord Derby had appointed him at the earnest request—specified, as we have seen, by his will—of his grandfather, Sir Piers, who had held the post himself for many years before his death. An interesting paper of the accounts for 1593 names all the charges of the Receiver, the Water Bailiff, and other officials, and gives one some idea of the difficulties the newly appointed Captain must have had to contend with in dealing with procrastinating officials who evidently tried to impose upon the young man and take advantage of his youth and inexperience. They were, however, soon to find that he was not to be trifled with. The Receiver being called upon to produce his accounts, answered that he had not yet received all from the different parts of the country, but the Captain would listen to no reasons or excuses, and insisted that all sums were to be brought in before his departure from the island. The Receiver complaining that he had been overcharged £5, the Captain remarked " he hath as yet shown me no reason." In this Peter showed early in life the careful and businesslike turn of mind which was so strong a feature of his character. Of great piety, shrewd, capable, far-seeing, with a very strict sense of duty, he had many good qualities, but his was not a lovable nature, and there was a vein of hardness which appears in his treatment of his children, whom he thwarted in what seems to have been an objectless and needless fashion.

He was accompanied on these expeditions by his wife, Margaret (thus they were another Peter and Margaret), a daughter, as we have seen, of Sir Gilbert Gerard, Master of the Rolls.

A journey to the Isle of Man in those days was somewhat of an undertaking, and can only have been accomplished with a certain amount of difficulty and no small danger, but Margaret, undaunted, followed her husband through storm and stress—a faithful and devoted wife.

In a very long letter addressed to her by Henry Sumner, chaplain to Sir Peter Legh, the date of which is missing, he gives a sort of lecture on the duties of marriage, and dwells particularly on Margaret's devotion to her husband:

" I will not now speaks of yor willingnes to learne & readines to performe these holy coniugall Duties. Yor voyage with yor husband
into the Isle of Manne, through the raginge waves of the surginge
seas (the most unrulie creature that ever was made the powers of
Hell except) the which you endured with more then womanlie bouldnes,
the faythfullnes of a wife embouldeninge the fearfulnes of a woman,
doth sufficiently speake for me. The which Dutie so well begonne
was as well contynued to yor great commendacon, in that all those
manie sweete delights which deare kynsfolkes & desyred Countrie
can afford, could not move yor heart to retourne from thence, tyll
you might retourne accompanied as you came. A notable argument
of that holie stryfe which is betweene yor kyndest husband & you :
stryvinge (not as do manie, whether may be frowarder,) but whether
in kyndnes may excell other."

Margaret can only have been fifteen or sixteen at the time
of her marriage in 1585, and barely twenty, but already the
mother of one or two children, when she started the cares and
responsibilities of housekeeping at Lyme. The house was not
even finished ; there were workmen to control and supervise,
and the provisioning of and catering for a household the size
of Lyme must have required more knowledge and experience
than poor Margaret can have possessed.

The good old grandmother, Margaret Lady Legh, was living
—as we know by her portrait in 1595—and no doubt helped
the young couple with her sage advice and counsel, and with
the bringing up of part of their large family of seven sons and
two daughters. After the old lady's death, however, Margaret
must often have been left alone during her husband's absence
at the wars, or in London—where Sir Peter had to go to
attend to his parliamentary duties—to cope with the worries
and anxieties of a large family and household, as we see from
the following letter from Dorothy, Lady Halsall,* one of the
few of Margaret's letters that have survived, written during
the absence of both their husbands with Essex's expedition :

" Cousine Leighe, Your seconde selfe, beinge so farre absent as he is,
and myne owne, noe nearer home, at this instant : I coulde not

* A natural daughter of Henry, fourth Earl of Derby, by Jane Halsall of Knowsley.
she married Sir Cuthbert Halsall, who dissipated the whole of his large fortune and
died 1631.

MARGARET GERARD
First wife of Sir Peter Legh of Lyme
By MARCUS GHEERAERTS

From a Portrait at Lyme

wthout injurie to your good nature, and impeache to myne owne affection, but performe this smalle kindnes, in sendinge to see you; hartely wishinge you woulde solace your selfe, wth the hope of their happie, and hastie retorne. Untill when and ever God keepe you, in asmuche health, and happines, as I wishe to myne owne selfe. And yf you heare anie thinge from them [before they come] I praye you ptake yt; for that nothinge can come unto me more welcome, or wished for, save themselves. And so with manie Commendacons, I commit you to God.

    "Halsall. This 12th of Marche, 1596.

     "Your louinge Cousine and so assured

             "DOROTHIE HALSALL."

In spite of her assertion that she writes to obtain news of   1596 her dear cousin, the very obvious reason for her letter appears in the postscript:

"Cousine I pray you sende me the oyle of Almondes you pmised [promised] me by this berrer.

    "To my verie louinge and beloued good Cousine

     "Mris Margaret Leighe at Lyme her house hast theise."

A full-length portrait of Margaret Legh, painted about 1600, by Marcus Gheeraerts gives one a charming conception of her. She wears a yellow silk gown with green horizontal stripes, the dress standing out from her slight figure in the grotesque fashion of the period, with very high lace ruff, and large puffed sleeves, terminating in lace cuffs at the wrist. On her head is a curious kind of aigrette, almost like a crown, with two ornaments which fall from each side. Her dark hair is drawn very high above her lovely and pathetic face with its small delicate features and dark blue eyes. Round her neck is a double row of small pearls, below this another necklace in a design of points, also of pearls; hanging from her bodice is a necklace of four rows of large pearls—alas, no longer in existence. Over her whole dress there falls a sort of transparent material almost resembling chiffon, and from her shoulders and falling to the ground a cobweb-like cloak sewn with large pearls. In her right hand she holds a fan, hanging by a ribbon from her waist. Her left hand, which rests on the front of her gown, shows no wedding-ring, but on the third finger is what appears to be a thin silken string, knotted and crossed over the back of the hand and disappearing into the cuff.* The picture is inscribed : " Sir Peter Legh's first Lady, Thomas Lord Gerard of Bromley, Master of the Rolls his daughter." A lovely little miniature of Margaret, said in the catalogue to be by Cornelis Janssen, but with the blue background very characteristic of Oliver, shows her wearing a huge lace ruff, small gold rings in her ears, a necklace of pearls and gold, and a small aigrette in her hair.

It is rather difficult to picture to oneself what the interior of the house was like at the period of which we write, each succeeding generation having made important structural additions and alterations. The drawing-room has fortunately been left untouched and is practically as it was when built—a splendid example of Elizabethan art—the date probably about 1580. The whole room is panelled from the floor to within four feet of the ceiling with oak inlaid with satinwood in a design of panels arranged in arches with small pillars and a pattern of carving made to resemble brickwork in between, ornamented with raised diamond-shaped squares of oak and satinwood and a series of grotesque heads. Above the panelling is an elaborate plaster frieze divided into panels—each of a different design— supposed to be the work of Italians, who were largely employed in the decoration of English houses of this date. The ceiling is very elaborate in plaster strapwork with bosses and pendants. A stone and coloured plaster chimney-piece reaches from the floor to the ceiling, a double set of columns supports the lower part, the centre having the arms of Queen Elizabeth with the lion and griffin instead of unicorn, as used before the union with Scotland, the whole being surmounted by a crown. Flanking the arms are four caryatides—two on each side, having on their heads baskets of fruit richly gilt, as are also the arms and quarterings, the colours of which are painted.

Succeeding generations have left their mark in this beautiful room, as one may see by the Chippendale mirrors and carved

* I have seen this curious feature in other pictures of the same date, but have never been able to ascertain what it means.—E.N.

LYME : PART OF THE DRAWING-ROOM

wood and gilt chandelier, which though perhaps not strictly speaking correct in an Elizabethan room, still give a touch of life and colour to the somewhat sombre walls. The basket-grate is a fine example of diamond-cut steel in an Adam design, with very elaborately worked fender and fireirons.

A bay window to the east is filled with coloured glass, originally placed by this Sir Peter Legh in the east window of Disley Church, and moved to its present position about a hundred years ago. The centre portion of the bow is all heraldic glass (surrounded by a border of a symbolical series of the months of the year) representing the Legh coats of arms in successive marriages, Sir Peter Legh's portrait being placed conspicuously in the centre. The two side portions of the bow are occupied by shields of the arms of Knights of the Garter and Earls of Chester of Elizabeth's time, and are of a rich and beautifully mellow colour ; the doors and window-shutters of the room are of delicate workmanship. Three windows to the north have in each five small panels of coloured glass. These are arranged in the shape of a cross, a coat of arms forming each panel. The centre of the middle window is filled with a large ram's head, holding in its mouth a sprig of laurel and issuing from a ducal coronet—the Legh crest. The dates on the coats of arms vary from 1586 to 1661, which last is placed over the Legh arms quartered with the Chicheley.

Recent researches at the British Museum have resulted in the discovery of some drawings of the Legh coats of arms, signed Randle Holme,* 1630, and with this inscription : " Thus made in glass for Sr Peter Lighe—1630." This coat is in the centre window just below the ram's head.

On the south side of the room is a secret opening in the panelling, revealing a recess behind the back of a full-length portrait of the Black Prince hanging in the Hall below, the floor of which is about twelve feet lower than that of the drawing-room. The picture slides to one side on a cleverly

* There were two Randle Holmes, father and son, who died within four years of each other. The father was Deputy to the College of Arms for Cheshire, Shropshire, and South Wales, and died in 1654 ; the son was a genealogist who added to the Holme MSS., and died in 1659 (" Dictionary of National Biography ").

contrived hinge and can be opened and shut at pleasure. It is said that Sir Walter Scott visited Lyme when writing " Peveril of the Peak," and that he was so delighted with this curious feature that he made use of the idea in "Woodstock," where there is an incident of a picture opening in very much the same way and serving as a hiding-place. A beautiful red lacquer clock with brass mounts, the face inscribed Claude Viet, London, is also in this room; the clock plays fourteen different tunes, mostly Jacobite airs, some of the names of which are given as follows: " Gigue Lelebolere," " Gauoat Nameless," " The Eunuch Song," " The Granaderes March," " Trumpet Tune " and " Trumpet Menuet," and " Joy to Great Cæsar." Here are also pieces of old Jacobite and Italian glass, incised lacquer cabinets and Oriental china, Elizabethan, Charles II, and Chippendale chairs, all fine specimens. Fastened on to the panelling of the bay window are six curious and well painted portraits on panel and unframed; they represent Mary, Queen of Scots, James I, Charles I, Charles II, William III, and Queen Anne; other portraits in the room include one of James, seventh Earl of Derby, beheaded in 1651, and his wife Charlotte de la Trémouille, renowned for her defence of Lathom House, replicas (except that they are not full lengths) of the ones at Knowsley.

Opening out of the drawing-room is a room called " the Stag Parlour " of a rather later date than the drawing-room, having the arms of James I over the chimney-piece flanked by small figures of " Peace " and " Plenty " executed in coloured plaster. Above the Jacobean chimney-piece is a curious bas-relief of the house, showing it as it was in old Sir Piers Legh's time, with the mullioned windows and small lanthorn tower. Round the house a stag hunt is depicted, horsemen in top-boots and hats somewhat resembling the round hats of the present day, all executed in coloured plaster and grotesque in scale, the stags reaching up to the roof of the house, the horses and dogs not very much smaller. A bas-relief in medallions of coloured plaster runs round the entire cornice, representing different episodes in the life of the stag.

LYME: THE STAG PARLOUR

With bas-relief showing the house as it was before the alterations

THE LAST SIR PETER

Here are kept relics of Charles I : his gloves, his agate-handled dagger, with " Carolus " on the blade, and the remains of his cloak, cut up by some vandal to cover six very fine early Chippendale chairs, which were evidently made for the cloak, as they have the initials C R intertwined in the backs. A curious portrait of Charles I, said to be by Edward Bower,* though not signed, hangs in this room. The King is represented in a black cloak and Roundhead hat, seated in the chair he occupied at his trial ; in one hand he holds a cane, in the other a paper—supposed to be his death-warrant —the beard is grey, the hair much darker than in most of his portraits. The picture is said to be one of the " Black Charles," of which there are only a very few known ; they were painted for and presented to devoted adherents in memory of their martyred King. The room is hung with English tapestry.

These two rooms are the only ones on the first floor that are of Elizabethan or Jacobean date ; there is another oak-panelled room on the ground floor called the " Stone Parlour," which has a large stone and plaster chimney-piece with the Molyneux arms and quarterings in the centre.

The Hall, which is hung with Mortlake tapestries, signed with the initials F. C. (Sir Francis Crane, the first director of the factory), is of a much later date. The Saloon, with its beautiful carvings by Grinling Gibbons, and the library, which has antique Greek " stelæ " and bronzes, and the dining-room, a comparatively modern room, will be described later on.

Upstairs on the second floor is the Long Gallery, such a feature of every Elizabethan house. It is 120 feet long by 18 feet broad, with a floor of sycamore wood, the boards laid across the room and very uneven ; the oak panelling is inlaid with satinwood in the same design as that in the drawing-room, part of the woodwork being only grained and painted. A coloured plaster chimney-piece similar to the one in the drawing-room, also having the arms of Elizabeth, occupies the centre of the east

* A portrait-painter of the time of Charles I. He painted John Pym, General Fairfax, and Lord Fairfax, the two last engraved by Hollar.

side of the room, and there is a large bow window—anciently termed a " compass window "—on the same side of the room at each end.

It is always a question as to what use these galleries were put—they were certainly much used as living-rooms ; we find Sir Peter Legh seated in the " compas window of his gallerie," hearing the claims and complaints of his tenants and paying the wages of his retainers. Here again the theatrical performances so often mentioned must have taken place, the " musicians " delighting their audience with their old-time airs, the fool with his jests filling up the interludes. Many a scene of mirth and revelry have these old walls witnessed, and many a dance, from the courtly pavane and minuet to the barn dance of our own prosaic times.

Opening formerly out of the gallery but now divided from it by a passage is the room occupied by Mary, Queen of Scots, with a small dressing-room attached ; here is still what remains of the bed she slept in, which has been already described ; the stone and coloured plaster chimney-piece reaching from floor to ceiling like those in the other rooms has in the centre the arms and quarterings of the Gerards of Ince. The ceiling is in raised plaster-work in which the fleur-de-lis figures conspicuously; there is also a plaster frieze. In the floor of this room there is a small secret chamber or priest-hole in which it is said the skeleton of some poor forgotten priest was found many years ago, and this has given rise to the tradition that the room is haunted. It has always borne the name of the " Ghost Room," but no supernatural visitor has ever been seen ; a secret passage is supposed to lead from it to the " Cage "—the tower in the park described in a former chapter.

It seems strange that Queen Mary should have been put into so small and unimportant a room, as other larger bedrooms are on the first floor ; but this was no doubt done with a view to keeping the poor Queen better guarded, her jailors being probably put in the gallery adjoining.

In these times of luxury and self-indulgence it is difficult to realize how life can have been possible in those early days.

THE LAST SIR PETER

The deadly cold and discomfort of the houses, where there can have been no heating apparatus apart from fires ; the darkness and gloom of the rooms, oak panelled and hung with heavy arras, lit only by candles. It is small wonder that one reads of the " agues " and " feavors " in so many of the letters of the time. Before the reign of Elizabeth, except in the houses of the great, there were no chimneys, the smoke being allowed to escape through a hole in the roof ; there was little or no glass to the windows, the substitute being horn or parchment let into the shutters. During the first half of the fifteenth century, stools or benches with loose cushions were all people had to sit upon, chairs were seldom seen and were used only by the master and mistress of the house, or given to an honoured guest, upholstery being practically unknown before the seventeenth century. Beds were mere pallets stuffed with straw, often with nothing but a log of wood for a pillow, it being a common saying that pillows were fit only for sick women.* Until a very recent period the beds in the older part of Lyme had one mattress—as hard and stiff as a deal board—laid over laths of wood, the bed being considerably more uncomfortable to sleep on than the bare floor would have been.

From old inventories one gathers that there can have been very little furniture of any description in houses of the Elizabethan and Jacobean periods. Unfortunately no inventory exists at Lyme earlier than one made in 1642 (which will be quoted later on), after the death of one of the owners, when the contents of the house appear to have been valued. What must have been one of the best bedrooms contained little beyond a bed, some " orras hangings " and a chest and cushions ; the servants' rooms contained apparently only beds.

Before the sixteenth century nothing but wooden platters were used, pewter and tin being then introduced ; forks were unknown till late in the seventeenth century, " fingers were made before forks," and people must have used their fingers freely to tear their food with the help of knives.

Privacy there was none, rooms all opened one into the

* Gardiner's " History of England."

59

other, for passages did not exist, and it was necessary to pass through a whole suite of bedrooms before going from one end of the house to the other. The four-post beds, with their curtains closely drawn, were no doubt the only means people had either of keeping out the piercing draughts from badly closing doors and windows, or of obtaining some semblance of decency and privacy. Washing was sparsely indulged in, even in palaces these arrangements—up to the eighteenth century—were of a very primitive description. In some of the state rooms at Hampton Court, one can see what stood for a bathroom and was probably considered a great luxury, a kind of marble alcove containing a sort of basin in which it was just possible to stand, a tap being provided for the necessary ablutions.

The dirt must have been indescribable, and the habits of both the gentlemen and ladies of the time seem to our modern ideas absolutely uncivilized. In the days of powder, ladies used to sleep for weeks together without taking down their hair; the condition of the heads, with all the grease and necessary appliances for stiffening and maintaining the huge erections they wore, is easier to imagine than to describe.

Life for the women must indeed have been of a dreary monotony. Left alone for weeks and months together in the absence of their lords on warlike expeditions, they were dependent on any chance messenger or visitor for news of the outer world. There were, of course, no regular posts, no newspapers, the books of the pre-Elizabethan time were chiefly in Latin and devotional, and there were few histories. There was nothing to relieve the deadly monotony of their lives but the care of their children and household, in which every lady, however exalted her rank, took a practical and personal interest.

One marvels how they can have dressed for outdoor exercise; the dresses seem principally to have been cut low in the neck, and this fashion and the voluminous skirts do not suggest the possibility of walking in snow or bad weather. They probably seldom went out in winter, taking their exercise in the long galleries that formed a part of the houses of that period. Women of every degree travelled on horseback, the state of the roads making any other means of progress impossible; light luggage was carried on " pack horses."

There appears to have been in every house a number of poor lady relations, who helped to a certain extent in the cooking and housework in return for their keep, assisting also at all the family interesting events and writing the gossip and news of the day. The beautiful pieces of needlework and embroidery that remain testify to the industry of these ladies of a bygone age, and must have whiled away many of their weary hours; thus they lived their patient gentle lives, and knowing nothing better were content and perhaps even happy.

The country houses of the period were all self-contained, everything being, as it were, done on the premises. The slaughtering, baking, brewing, cheesemaking—a very important art in Cheshire then as now—the stillroom work with its pickling, preserving, candying, and the dairy and syllabubs, in which the ladies of that time took so keen a part and interest, must have kept them fully employed.

The household at Lyme was composed of a very large 1607 number of menservants as compared with the women; the names of thirty-eight menservants are given in an account book for 1607, their wages varying from 5s. to 20s. a quarter, headed by the steward, who kept all the accounts, paid all the wages and rode on horseback to the different towns to order provisions and to buy and sell the stock. " For my dinner in Manchester and my horse when I went to paie Mr George Tippinge xl^{lb} [£40]—viii^d [8d.], Spent on John Gaiskell, Turner ye Shephard and myselfe when we went to sell sheepe viii^d, Spent on John Gaiskell and myselfe and o^r horses at Warrington faire, xx^d [1s. 8d.]."

Only five or six women's names appear, each receiving 5s. a quarter, the total of wages averaging about £20 to £25 the quarter. Thus there can have been no fewer than from 80 to 100 people—or even more—to be fed every day, and this without counting the visitors and their attendants who seem to have been very frequently entertained.

THE HOUSE OF LYME

The difficulty of feeding and keeping large quantities of animals through the winter was so great that much of the meat was salted down, and for a young housewife the task of providing variety for the daily bill of fare must have been no easy one. To judge from the account book there seems to have been good food and plenty of it, though evidently the resources of the establishment were inadequate to cope with the demand, as a great deal appears to have been bought.

Besides beef, mutton, lamb, veal, and pork, mention is made of turkeys, geese, ducklings, chickens, capons, rabbits, woodcocks, snipe, partridges (killed on August 20), wildfowl, plover, curlew, lapwing, fieldfares, and even blackbirds and sparrows, with, of course, plenty of good venison always obtainable from the deer in the park. The fish they had, a great deal of which came from Warrington, includes salmon, trout, eels, sparlings (the old name for smelts, still in use in this part of Cheshire and in the north), sturgeon (bought in kegs), lampreys, skate, carp, herrings, lobsters, crabs, oysters, mussels, and cockles. The fruit mentioned includes strawberries, cherries, quinces (preserved in barrels), prunes, plums, apples, pears, walnuts, almonds and raisins, and currants ; some of the prices are as follows :

For a yoke of Oxen . . .	ix^{lb} x^s [£9 10s.]
A fat Cowe . . .	iv^{lb} iii^s iv^d [£4 3s. 4d.]
One Oxe bought to feed .	iiii^{lb} [£4]
For halfe a lambe and the head .	iiii^s vi^d [4s. 6d.]
For a lambe . . .	iii^s iv^d [3s. 4d.]
For a fatte Caulfe . .	viii^s viii^d [8s. 8d.]
A pige	ii^s vi^d [2s. 6d.]
A quarter of mutton . .	iii^s [3s.]
Breast and neck of mutton .	ii^s ii^d [2s. 2d.]
A chicken . . .	ii^d [2d.]
A goose	iiii^d [4d.]
A Turkey . . .	xx^d [1s. 8d.]
A duckling . . .	iiii^d [4d.]
A woodcock . . .	ii^d [2d.]
A curlew	xiv^d [1s. 2d.]
6 dozen sparrows . .	vi^d [6d.]
A salmon	viii^s [8s.]

A carp	.	.	.	.	x^d (10d.)
A skate	.	.	.	.	x^d (10d.)
200 oysters	.	.	.	ii^s iiii^d [2s. 4d.]
200 lampreys	.	.	.	xvii^d [1s. 5d.]
For Crabs and lobsters	.	.	iiii^s [4s.]
To a Stranger for foure score and				
thirteen sparlings	.	.	.	xii^d [1s.]
1 lb. of currants	.	.	.	vi^d [6d.]
1 lb. of prunes	.	.	.	iv^d [4d.]
1 lb. of cherries	.	.	.	xi^d [11d.]
Almonds and raisins	.	.	.	iiii^s [4s.]

Four hundred walnuts cost 2s. 3d., 612 eggs were bought for 2s., sugar cost 1s. 4d. the pound and was bought in large quantities. Three shillings were paid for three couple of rabbits; we must suppose this was for the trouble of catching them, as there must have been plenty in the park then as now. Churning, which was done by a man who was paid 4d. a day, is seldom mentioned, butter was bought by the gallon, costing about 2s. 6d., and occurs more frequently than any other item; there were three prices, 10d., 11d., and 1s. the quartern—this last probably for salt butter.

No mention is made of vegetables; potatoes had been 1607 imported into England from Virginia, it was said, by Sir John Hawkins in 1563, and again by Sir Francis Drake in 1596, but they were looked upon as curiosities and do not seem to have been cultivated as food for many years afterwards. There is no mention of them in the Legh letters before 1675, when Mrs. Richard Legh writes thanking her husband for the potatoes "which are very good, & if they be not deare if one knew how to kepe them any time they would be a good desh when wone has company." The item " Sallet oyle," costing 1s. the pint, occurring from time to time shows that there must have been some variety from a diet of meat.

Pastry is mentioned, " cap-paper " (a coarse sort of brownish paper), being bought " for the use of the Cooke in the pastrie."

Claret cost £7 10s. the hogshead; there was also white wine at 6d. the quartern, " a Rundlett of Sacke and the carriage, xxxix⁹, viᵈ " (£1 19s. 6d.), and " Wormwood Ale " besides the ordinary home-brewed.

There is mention made of " Cole pitts " about this time, but this was probably " crop coal," that is to say, coal which came up to the surface, the collier being paid 1s. the quarter for getting it : " For setting down an eie in the Colepitt," and " for getting of coles wʰ was behind ye ould kichine—iiiˡᵇ 3ˢ " (£3 3s.). Coal being everywhere in this part of the world, it was actually dug out from under the house up to about a hundred years ago. Charcoal was made from timber in what were called " Cole pitts," and we find an entry of 18s. paid to " the Charcole man " for twenty-eight days and nights.

The different kind of work was apportioned to special individuals ; thus we find there were brewers, spit-turners, glaziers, " tincklers," mat-makers,* tailors, marlers, dawbers,† gutterers, panners,‡ mole-catchers, and rat-catchers, all forming part of the establishment and paid by the piece. Labourers were paid at prices varying from 5d., 6d., 8d. and 9d. a day according to the class of work they did. Tree-felling was paid at 6d. a day, the men being " tabled " ; if at their own finding, 9d. a day was paid them. They appear to have worked quickly and well by an entry of 2s. 8d. having been paid for the " falling of 12 trees." Bricklayers got 8d. a day, carters and hewers 6d. and 8d., and thatchers 8d. ; these last receiving rather more than the wages of the ordinary labourers in consideration, probably, of their more skilled labour. " Dawbers " (plasterers) were paid wages varying from 3d., 4d., and 6d. a day ; the glazier was paid 30s. a year for keeping all the windows in repair. The chimneys were all swept for 8s.

Such trifles as " removing the hyll behind the mounte " were soon got over, at a cost, however, of £4. " For holding downe the plow foote 6 days," a man was remunerated with 1s., " mowing rushes in the Queen's Mead, viiiˢ 10ᵈ." " To John Smith for evening Copps and riddings in the Gallowtree

* Carpet-makers.   † Plasterers.
‡ Makers of cloth, baize, etc., not weavers.

hand Meadow, vii^s." *   Two men were paid 3s. 4d. for breaking
30½ loads of limestone.

A great deal of building was going on in the latter years of
Elizabeth's and the early years of James I's reign at Bradley
in Lancashire, where Sir Peter still kept up his house. The
following verse is still to be seen cut in raised letters on an old
beam in one of the upper rooms of Bradley Hall, now a farm-
house :

"The Master doth and Mistress both Unite with one Accorde
With Godly mindes and zealous hartes to Serve the livinge Lorde.
                                        "Henry Wesley, 1598."

The "Stag Parlour" at Lyme was no doubt in process of
construction about this time, and Sir Peter was also restoring
the Legh Chapel in Macclesfield Church, and new-roofing the
church at Disley.

A new boat-house and pigeon-house, "arbours in the
garden" and "quicksetts for the new poole" all appear in
1609, the sum of £62 5s. having been paid for building alone
from April to November, the housekeeping expenses for the
same period totalling £144 18s. 3d.

A somewhat original entry occurs in April 1608, when a   1608
man was paid 1s. "for keeping a Caulfe 9 daies which was
tyred in driving from Lyme to Worsley"; the distance being
twenty miles or more, the result is perhaps scarcely surprising.
Oxen were used as beasts of burden and were shod like horses
at regular intervals. At the end of the account book are
particulars of the stud, showing that Sir Peter bred horses.
Sir Richard Molyneux † writes, "I have sent your Mare to
Diamonde for he is at Tarbocke, and I hope he will get you a
seconde Jynette to winne Houlte Cuppe as before."

Soap and candles were also manufactured on the premises.
"The Sope man" was paid regularly about 8s. at a time, and

* I have tried, unsuccessfully, to discover the origin of this name; there can be
no doubt that executions must have taken place there.

† Sir Richard Molyneux, knighted by Queen Elizabeth in 1596; married
Frances, daughter of Sir Gilbert Gerard, Master of the Rolls, and a sister therefore of
Margaret, Lady Legh.

the Candlemaker fetched hastily from Congleton on one occasion, a distance of sixteen miles, to make " 6 odd dozen of Candles— 6s." the messenger being paid 4d. for his trouble.

When visitors came to Lyme, cooks from the neighbouring houses came in to assist although there seem to have been no fewer than three men cooks kept. On the occasion of Sir John Egerton's * visit " my Lady Bentley's Cooke " was paid 5s.— " the ould Cooke which came from Tatton," on the other hand, receiving only 2s., in consideration, we will suppose, of 1609 his age and failing powers. Great preparations appear to have been made for the visit of Sir John Stanhope † in August 1609, " a Cople of Turkies—iii^s iv^d," (3s. 4d.), 24 chickens at 2d. a piece, " 4 hennes " costing 2s., a quarter of veal, 2s., a pig 1s. 8d., eggs 8d., with " Ale possets for the house iiii^d," (4d.) and " the hyre of ii garnishes of pewter iii^s " (3s.), " a woman harp " being provided at a cost of 6d. for the entertainment of the company.

Besides hawking and the hunting of the stag which has been mentioned, in which friends and neighbours were invited to take part, cock-fighting seems to have been a very favourite amusement ; frequent mention is made of " Cokes " being taken from Lyme to different places to take part, no doubt, in matches. A letter from Sir Anthony St. John, younger brother of Bolingbroke, to Sir Peter Legh, bearing no date, says :

" We are here very bussy with our Cokes but the mach them [they match them] slowly—there are as yeat but thirteen battells made whereof there are eight of them played yesterday and our Country men have gott fower [four] battells clept [called—a term used in a

* Sir John Egerton, created in 1617 first Earl of Bridgewater, married Lady Frances Stanley, daughter and co-heiress of Ferdinando, 5th Earl of Derby. Lord Bridgewater died 1649.
† Sir John Stanhope, first Baron Stanhope of Harrington (1545 ?–1621), appointed treasurer of the chamber and knighted, 1596 ; had some influence at Court which Bacon sought to enlist in his favour. One of his daughters married Robert, Viscount Cholmondeley, afterwards Earl of Leinster, who became connected with the Legh family through the marriage of his niece, Lettice Calveley, with Dr. Thomas Legh, the father of Richard.

66

game], I can not wright by reason of ower eagernes in following the
teaint [a term used at tilting or hawking] whilst it is whot [hot]."

There is something very attractively human about this letter,
the excitement of the young man at the prospect of the match
preventing him from writing properly to his friend. A letter
from Thomas Legh of Adlington—written in somewhat churlish
terms—is also on the same subject ; he appears to find difficulty
in arranging a match :

"We commend your care but conceave the Conditions you tender
to be somewhat Incompetent for besides that the weather may be
toe warme for us to sende our Cockes so farre at the season you
specifie . . . twoe of our chiefest Cockers, viz Sir Thomas Beaumont
& Mr Thomas Burdett are *Vice-Comites* and Jure Officii aboute St
James syde [&] must serue Kinge James In their own Shires."

The letter ends with

"unlesse you will be pleased to dispence with our cominge Into your
cuntrey untill next yeare, there is noe possibilitie of our giving you
satisfaction."

Sir Richard Molyneux also talks of seeing Sir Peter " after
the cockinge at Lyme." In connexion with cock-fighting
mention may here be made of two old blue silk bags, beautifully
embroidered in gold and silver with the Legh crest and motto,
which were found at Lyme very many years ago. The silk of
which these bags were made was much worn, and it being not
known to what use these interesting relics were put, the work
was removed and was converted into banner screens. It was
only after this irreparable damage had been done that it was
discovered that these bags had been used to convey the cocks
from one place to another during the " cocking season."

Sir Peter, like his grandfather, was a book-lover and a man
of letters. His name appears as an acrostic in " The Golden
Mirror," a volume of poems of some note published in 1587 or
1589 by one Richard Robinson, a native of Cheshire or Staffordshire, who is said to have formed part of the household of the
Earl of Shrewsbury, and to have assisted in keeping watch
over Mary, Queen of Scots, during the time that she was in

Lord Shrewsbury's custody. The acrostic is in eighteen stanzas of six lines each, which take the following eighteen letters, Peter Leigh Essqvyer (written, of course, before the death of his grandfather). The verses have no allusion to the person to whom they are addressed beyond the dedicatory notice, " Verses penned vpon the Etimologie of the name of the right worshipfull Maister Peter Leigh, heire apparent to the valiaunt Gentleman, Sir Peter Leigh of the linne, Knight." The poetry is not conspicuous for the beauty or symmetry of the metre, as the last verse will show :

> " Revenge from skies with fiery flames
> Shall now at hand devour and wast
> All mortall men unto their shames
> Except where grace and vertue's plast
> Those that believe, and God doe feare,
> As Angels then shall straight appeare."

It would seem as if the last two lines might be intended as alluding in a complimentary manner to Peter Legh. The acrostic is one of several appearing in the same volume and addressed to different Cheshire and Lancashire magnates, such as Ferdinando, Lord Strange, afterwards fifth Earl of Derby, Lady Julian Holcroft of Vale Royal, Thomas Legh of Adlington, and Peter Warburton of Arley.

1590   In 1590, Sir Peter was adding to the library at Lyme. Writing to his chaplain, Henry Sumner, he names some books he desires to acquire, " Opera Bernard Scapuli," * " Jerome Molleyne's Homelyes," " Thomas Aquynus † upon the Scruples . . ." " Fulke ‡ upon the Revelation & two other mallengly [melancholy] bookes." He is also anxious to provide suitable literature for his relations : " I wold very gladly yf you can convenyently bestowe a Sermone on my two Brothers-

---

* Bernard Scapuli, one of the most illustrious Christian teachers and representatives of monasteries in the Middle Ages, born at Fontaines near Dijon, 1091, died 1155.

† Aquinas on the Scruples upon the Revelation. Div : Thomas Aquinatis in B. Joannis Apocalypsim expositio, 1549 ? (British Museum.)

‡ William Fulke, 1538–1589, puritan divine, deprived of his fellowship at St. John's College, Cambridge, for preaching against the surplice, published astronomical and theological works (" Dictionary of National Biography ").

in-law wch be nowe in the Country, for soe muche I promised theym." The two brothers-in-law whose sojourn in the country was to be cheered and enlivened in this fashion were probably Sir Richard Molyneux, married to Frances, sister of Margaret, Lady Legh, and Sir Thomas Gerard, her brother, afterwards created Lord Gerard of Bromley.

Among the books that must have formed part of the Lyme library at this date is one of the most precious of the Legh heirlooms, namely, a Caxton of very early date, the earliest known impression of the Sarum Missal, printed in Paris for Caxton in 1487.*

* The discovery of this volume was made in 1873, and it was then taken to the British Museum for the inspection of Mr. Rye, keeper of the Printed Books, and other authorities, who pronounced it to be unique. By their advice the book, which was in a very bad state, was entrusted to Bedford, the celebrated bookbinder, by whom it was very carefully mended and bound. Only one of the old covers is in existence ; it is on wood covered with leather stamped with fleurs-de-lis. An account of this book appeared in the *Athenæum* on March 21, 1874, written by Mr. William Blades, from which I quote the following extract :

" The book is entirely unknown to bibliographers, and is in folio, double column, black letter. It is noteworthy in two aspects :

" 1. It is the earliest known impression of the Salisbury Missal, and has a plain colophon, dated Dec. 4. 1487, which is about five years earlier than the celebrated Rouen edition, dated October 1, 1492, hitherto looked upon as the *editio princeps*.

" 2. It gives a new fact in the typographical history of England's proto-typographer, William Caxton, having been printed for him at Paris by William Maynyal, to whom Caxton must have lent his large device, which appears prominently at the end of the volume. That Caxton's successors employed foreign printers to assist them is well known ; but it was not suspected until now that Caxton had initiated the custom."

This was the first book in which Caxton's mark was used. The following is the colophon :

" Missale ad vsum Sar*um* cunctitene*n*tis dei dono magno conamine elaboratum finit feliciter. Exeratum Parisi*us* [*sic*] impensa optimi viri Guillermi Caxton. Arte vero et industria Magistri Guillermi Maynyal. Anno domini M.cccc.lxxxvii., iiij Decembris."

On June 5, 1896, Mr. Edward Scott, Keeper of the MSS. and Egerton Librarian, M.R.A.S., of the British Museum, wrote the following in the *Athenæum* :

" This volume was exhibited at the Caxton Exhibition in the year 1877, but from that day to this no other copy has appeared, nor has any allusion to such an edition of the Sarum Missal been found. But a few days ago in cataloguing the unpublished inventories among the Westminster Abbey muniments I found in one dated November 10th, 12 Henry viii [A.D. 1520], containing the articles kept in the shrine of Edward the Confessor, this entry : ' Item, a paper masse-boke of Salisburys vse of William Caxton gyffte.' . . . There is no direct

An additional interest is given to the book by some marginal notes in handwriting of the sixteenth century, in which the name Richard Mody twice occurs with contemptuous epithets attached to it :

" Rychard Mody & pater Batson had gyffen yem gud hesse (?) the " and " I otterly Beshrew Rychard Mody wt all my hert & a peyse of my stomycher for he is a knave for the nonesset fare yow well wt."

A Richard Moody was Rector of Standish in Lancashire at the beginning of Queen Elizabeth's reign, and conformed to the religious changes ; it may therefore be concluded that he had acted as priest to old Sir Piers Legh (then living in Lancashire before the building of Lyme was completed) and that upon changing his religion he had relinquished his post, leaving behind him his missal, which has remained in the possession of the Legh family ever since. The indignant lady who was ready to part with a piece of her stomacher to see him punished was no doubt Dame Margaret, wife of old Sir Piers Legh.

Like his grandfather also, Sir Peter was a great lover of music, keeping his own " pyper," who was fitted out from time to time with a " jerkin and hose and a hatte " ; but he does not seem to have kept the band of " Musicians " which formed so important a part of the establishment of old Sir Piers. Francis Pilkington, lutenist and musical composer, and in 1624 minor canon and chaunter of Chester Cathedral, in 1624 dedicated to him a volume of madrigals ; and he was on intimate terms with Henry Lawes, the great musician who wrote the music for Milton's " Comus."

On grand occasions when visitors of importance came to Lyme, music and theatricals were provided for their entertainment and amusement. Many of the great houses kept their own private bands of musicians and troupes of actors, and these seem to have been procurable when required. " Given

evidence in the volume to connect it with Westminster, as unfortunately the first leaves of the Calendar and of the Missal are missing, and the MS. notes at the end are only instructions to the priest for the service of St. Thomas of Canterbury, as the leaves in the body of the work which originally contained it have been abstracted."

SIR PETER LEGH

From a Portrait at Lyme

in reward to 4 Trumpetters of my Lo: of Pembrookes—
...... iii^s iv^d " (3s. 4d.). " Given in reward to a piper of Sr Thomas Smith, i^s." " To my Lo: Chaundos his players, given in reward, 3 plaies—xxvii^s viii^d " (27s. 8d.). " To my Lo: of Darbis players, xx^s." " Given in reward to my Lo: of Lincoln's players, xl^s " (40s.). There appear also to have been variety entertainments : " To the man with the dancing horse v^s " and " To the Tomboleres [dancers] v^s." A shilling was paid for " a set of tablemen," " tables " was a form of backgammon, anciently played in different ways, and was no doubt a great solace on long winter evenings.

Sir Peter kept his own " fool " or jester, who was clothed and fed at his master's expense, and who doubtless made the old house ring with laughter at his wit ; should we have understood and appreciated his jests ? Hardly more, I fear, than we should have done his language.

In 1611 appears an entry of 4d. for the carriage of tobacco 1611 from London. Sir Walter Raleigh is always supposed to have been responsible for the importation of tobacco into this country, but although he may have had much to do with its popularity, he was not its introducer. Sir John Hawkins * first brought it into England in 1565, where it was being successfully cultivated—as also in Scotland—in 1571.

James I disliked smoking extremely,† denouncing it in 1604, in his famous " Counterblaste to Tobacco," and describing it as " A Custom loathesome to the eye, hateful to the nose, harmful to the lungs, and in the black stinking fume thereof nearest resembling the horrible Stygian smoke of the pit that is bottomless." In spite, however, of his disapprobation, plantations sprang up all over the country and smoking continued to be popular. In an undated letter written to Francis Legh by a lady named Marie Savage, she mentions a " candle " she is sending him

" to tok tobacco, yet I trow I would not have you take too much to doe yourself harme, for they saie it doth many men harme, they never

---

* Sir John Hawkins (1532–1595), naval commander ; Treasurer and Comptroller of the Navy ; introduced many improvements in shipbuilding.
† " Chambers's Encyclopædia."

live so long as they were wont to doe—I warrant you my husband would not take a pype of tobacco yf a man would geve a gould angle." *

In 1614 a tax was set upon tobacco by the Star Chamber, and so much was smoking regarded as a noxious and pernicious habit that in respect to responsible appointments one of the qualifications of a teacher was that he should be no "puffer of tobacco." Charles II ultimately forbad its cultivation in England and placed a duty on the imported article. It is a curious fact that no mention of smoking occurs in any of Shakespeare's works.

Housekeeping in the seventeenth century was not unattended by domestic worries, and these occasionally assumed alarming proportions. In 1611 a serious brawl took place between Edward Thorniley, steward to Sir Peter, and a certain Ratcliffe, whose name appears in the list of domestic servants in September and December 1611. The outcome of the brawl was the probable death of, or at any rate severe injury to, Ratcliffe. An inquiry was held on March 23, 1611–12, before three magistrates, Sir Urian Legh, Sir Peter Legh, and Sir William Davenport of Bramhall, and the following facts were ascertained.

Thorniley being in the kitchen at Lyme on March 2, "after one of the clock," Ratcliffe entered, and in abusive language accused Thorniley of having stolen all his "bandes, my shertes, stockinges, bootes, bootehose, bookes and my chamber ript and all that I have is gone," desiring Thorniley to accompany him to his chamber and see for himself. The dairywoman interposed, "What haste, let him eate his Meate before he goe." Thorniley, however, "not thinking any harme (as the Lord knoweth)" repaired with Ratcliffe into the latter's chamber, who forthwith proceeded to bolt the door and drawing a sword, heaped abuse upon Thorniley, calling him a cowardly rascal and villain. "This sword," he cried, "shall cut thy flesh and this rapier shall run thee through, for thou hast told thy Master I have stolen xxtie staves." Thorniley protested he had never done him any harm all the days of his life, but Ratcliffe bade him

* Angel—a gold coin, varying in value from six to ten shillings.

72

hold his peace and meet him under the Cage to fight it out. This Thorniley declined, giving as his reason that God had visited him in one of his hands, and that he could not hold a sword. " Then," said Ratcliffe, " thou coward, seeing thou refuses to meet me under the Cage, nor will appoint noe other place, betake thee to God, thy life is near an end." Thorniley begged for his life, being unarmed, as he pointed out, and was finally allowed to leave the chamber, being admonished by his assailant to " tell neither Master nor Lady, for if thou do I will kill thee wherever I meet thee ! " Thorniley thereupon went into his own chamber and took " a staffe about two yeardes and a quarter longe with two blunte pykes in " and went off to Disley on some business for his master. Ratcliffe appears to have followed him, for Thorniley, " looking by ye way saw Ratcliffe come running towards him and when he came about xii roodes from him, he put off his gowne and layd it downe and drew his weapons and layd the scabarde with his gowne and soe comes running at this Examinent, and sayd A, cowardly Rascall I shall soon dispatch thee, and soe desperately ran at him, and then this Exam^t for safeguard of his life did defend himself."

We do not learn what the sequel was, but it seems evident that Thorniley's " visitation in his hand " did not prevent him from defending himself to some purpose, and Ratcliffe may possibly have received his death wound. His name certainly disappears from the account book after December 1611, but Edward Thorniley continued in Sir Peter's service for some years.

Christmas at Lyme was kept in good old-fashioned style, the sum of £4 3s. 6d. being expended for spice alone ; the poor were not forgotten, and presents were sent to friends and neighbours. " To John Rowson for the carrying of a Woodcock pie—waight 44 lbs.—iii^s viii^d " (3s. 8d.). One would almost think that the messenger deserved a higher remuneration.

Writing paper is mentioned frequently, and cost 4d. the quire. Some rather quaint entries include the following : " To an ould woman for hekchellng [egg shelling] vii daies—

x^d." "For a bell for the tame deer i^s," "For stufe to dress the mastiv—vi^d." "Given to a poor preacher at Disley i^s." "To Thomas Smith for wine bought for the Communie iii^s iii^d" (3s. 3d.). "The 3d of August for getting awaie the bees in the ould parlour end one daie and a halfe—i^s." "For Katten meat—ii^d." In a household the size of Lyme one would have thought that scraps for the cat might have been found without buying special meat. "For ii chains for the Monkey—xii^d" (1s.). Monkeys were kept as pets as we now keep dogs, and are mentioned in the Legh letters for many generations. These fetched large prices. We read of £60 being given for a monkey in 1660. Among the entries is the charge of 5s. for an operation performed on the monkey.

The children were now growing up. Piers, the eldest son, who was to incur his father's lasting displeasure by making a marriage Sir Peter disapproved of (though for no reason that can be discovered); Francis, the second son, tall and lanky and outgrowing his strength, and Thomas, number three, destined for the Church, though much against his will, were all at school, though where we do not know; it is possible that they may have been sent to the school at Winwick, founded by Sir Peter's great-uncle Gowther Legh. Up to this time the boys had been instructed by Henry Sumner, chaplain to Sir Peter. They and their two sisters, Anne and the baby Katherine, had to be frequently supplied with clothes—principally boots, as we find by entries in the account-book: "For a pear of shoes for Mris Anne—ii^s ii^d" (2s. 2d.). "For the mending of a pear of bodes [boots] for Mris Anne—xx^d" (1s. 8d.). "Mending two pair of shoes v^d; For a pare of showes for Mris Katteren—iii^s; For lacing and furniture for Mris Kattie—xvii^s [17s.], For a pare of stockings for Mris Anne—iii^s iv^d [3s. 4d.]; for a pare of gartteres for her—io^d. For a pare of gloves for Mris Anne—6^d. To John Collier for making a gowne for Mris Kattie v^s, To him more for gladen for Mris Kattie for a Wastcote—ii^s io^d—For 2 gardels for the boys—vii^d; To Katherine Allinew for washing Mris Anne's gowne and finding soape—iiii^d" (4d.). This must have been something special as a laundry-maid was kept—a whisket (basket) being provided " for her to carry clothes in." " For a pare of stockings for the foole, iii^s [3s.] ; For a pare of hose for the pyper and foole, ii^s x^d " (2s. 10d.) ; and the grim entry— " For iiij [four] yards of cloth for lying forth littell pyper, ii^s " (2s.).

Now and then appears the item " Medicine for Mris Anne " or " Mris Kattie," as the case may be, and nux vomica is once mentioned as being bought, but we are not enlightened any further as to what species of decoction was being administered to the unfortunate child. Doctors' remedies in those early days were of a terribly drastic kind : " blood-letting " was their one idea, whether for a fever or a decline ; wounds were dressed with butter, and the patients were left more or less to take their chance—it being a case of the survival of the fittest.

Sir Peter had a house at Fulham in 1600. His elder sons had been sent to school, having been taken from the sheltering care of Henry Sumner, who appears also to have discharged the duty of parson at Disley Church in addition to being Chaplain to Sir Peter. A letter dated April 2, 1602, in the form of a petition with four signatures, prays that

"Mr. Sumner may come downe into the Countrye and remayne at Dyslye where he hath done much good in tyme past & where he is greatlye missed at thys present. He is very much desyred of your neighbours that bee of good disposition about Dyslye who are very willing to heare him to their comfort as they have done many tymes heretofore. Yt may therefore please you to satisfye there godlye and earnest desyre by bringinge him downe with you when you come and by leavinge him in the Countrye when you shall returne."

The letter is addressed :

" To Sr Peter Legh at hys house in Frulham neere to London."

It was at his house at Fulham in the following year—1603, 1603 the year that saw the death of Queen Elizabeth—that there came to Sir Peter the first great sorrow of his life, for here, on July 3, he lost his gentle Margaret, his faithful and devoted wife, who died, probably at the birth of her youngest child, leaving him with six surviving children, lonely and desolate to mourn her loss.

Margaret, Lady Legh, makes a very short and fleeting appearance upon our stage; she passes across without even a speaking part (not a morsel of her handwriting even remaining), a lovely and rather pathetic figure with her sweet pale face and delicate hands. Too fragile and tender to bear the storm and turmoil of those rigorous days, she faded out of her husband's life as she fades out of this history, and remained but a memory. Sir Peter erected a most beautiful monument to her, which is still in the chancel of All Saints Church, Fulham, and is supposed to be one of the finest specimens of Jacobean art existing. It represents her effigy in pink-veined marble almost resembling alabaster, rather below life-size, seated in a niche between two pillars with gilt capitals; one hand is on her breast, the other clasps a baby, while another child is placed beside her. She wears the full wide skirt of the period, the same dress apparently as that in which she appears in her full-length portrait, a large hood with a Marie Stuart point coming over the front of her head; an hour-glass is by her right side and above her head are the Legh and Gerard arms and quarterings. Below is the following touching inscription:

"To the memory or what dearer remaineth of that vertiouce la: Lady Margaret Legh daughter of him yt sometime was Sr Gilbert Gerard Kt and Master of the Roles in the High Cort of Chancery wife of Sir Peter Legh of Lyme in the county of Cheshire Kt. & by him the mother of seven sons Piers, Francis, Radcliffe, Thomas, Peter, Gilbert, John with 2 daughters Anne and Keterine of which Rat: Gilb: and John deceased infants ye rest yet surviving to the happy increas of their house, the years that she enjoyed the world was 33 that her husband enjoyed her 17 att which period she yeilded her soul to the blessedness of long rest and her body to this earth Jul: 29, 1603.

"This inscription in the note of her piety and love by her sad husband is heare devoutedly placed."

TOMB OF MARGARET, LADY LEGH
In All Saints' Church, Fulham

CHAPTER V

LYME UNDER DOROTHY LEGH

ALAS for the inconstancy of man! Poor Margaret was hardly cold in her grave before Sir Peter was thinking of replacing her. In a will, afterwards cancelled, dated August 20, only a little more than six weeks after her death, while still in all the exaltation and exuberance of his grief, he admits the falling into temptation, bemoans his many sins and transgressions, and acknowledges himself a miserable sinner, but still feels assured that by his true repentance he will receive a " very blessed and everlasting life in heaven." He then proceeds to dispose of his earthly possessions; his lands, etc., he leaves to his " heyre," and bequests to his other children, whom he relegates, in the event of his death, to the care and guardianship of his mother-in-law, " the Lady Anne Gerard, widow." In a codicil dated December " secundo " of the same year, 1603, when his tears appear to have dried, he bequeathes " unto my Cosin Dorothie Brereton off Worsley (in regard of her assured affection and true friendship) my best Juell off diamonds." This lady he 1604 had married before March 2 of the following year, 1604.

There is much to be said for Sir Peter's marrying again, though he certainly might have shown a little less indecent haste. Left in the prime of life—barely forty—with a family of six young children to look after, the eldest boy sixteen, the youngest girl a babe a few weeks old, he must indeed have felt the want of a woman's help and influence, and perhaps he was paying Margaret the compliment that a widower is always said to render to his first wife by replacing her as soon as possible with a second.

His choice in this case was singularly fortunate. Clever,

shrewd, capable, and businesslike, Dorothy Brereton was well qualified to undertake the duties of stepmother to a young family and of châtelaine to a large establishment. A daughter of Sir Richard Egerton of Ridley, and therefore a half-sister of the distinguished Sir Thomas Egerton, afterwards Lord Ellesmere, Lord Chancellor of England, she had been married in 1572, when only twelve years old, to Richard Brereton, Lord of the Manor of Worsley, near Manchester, the marriage being celebrated apparently without licence. There was one child only of the marriage, a daughter, who died in infancy, and Richard Brereton, before his death in 1598, settled his Cheshire and Shropshire estates on his wife's half-brother, Lord Chancellor Ellesmere ; the Lancashire property he left to his widow for her life, to go at her death to Lord Chancellor Ellesmere. From a worldly point of view, therefore, Sir Peter's marriage with Dorothy was a prudent one ; she brought him large possessions—in which, of course, she had only a life interest— but her jointure and the Worsley rental made a substantial addition to Sir Peter's already comfortable income.

At the time of her second marriage she must have been about the same age as her bridegroom, to whom she made an admirable wife, and to his motherless children she proved a kind stepmother. Piers, the eldest son, who was already at Cambridge, writes her the following letter, which is undated but which must have been written soon after the marriage had taken place. It was evidently done very quietly and looks rather as if Sir Peter felt that he was acting too precipitately.

"GOOD MADAME,—although I haue much desired before this time to haue professed my dutie, and love unto your Ladyshippe, yet was I hindred till now by wante of a convenient messenger and besides had not (ye ?) true relation and that full understanding of the happy mariage betwene my father and your selfe, as of late I have been informed by some kynde freindes, whose commendations of you together with the greate love and care of my father towardes his children shewed in this match, doth much comfort me, and I doe hereby promise to you, as his seconde selfe all dutie and obedience, and do beseach God to continue you both longe to our comfort. I have received your kinde remembrance by my Cosen Collier which

I take in so kinde manner, as I can not in a sheetes Compasse expresse, and Good Madame continue your love and favour to mee, as I shall deserue. And so desiring you to remember mee in your dayly praires, I will craue pardon for this trouble, and pray the Lord to preserve you.

"Cambrideg this xxviith of November

"Your loving and obedient sonne,

"PEIRES LEGH.

"I pray you Madame, as your leisure will permitt you, let mee receave from you some fewe lynes which wilbe not a little welcome to me."

A handsome and generous letter from a son of an age to feel the loss of a beloved mother, and who would be supposed, rightly, to resent her place being so soon occupied by a stranger. Poor Piers ! He was shortly after to incur his father's serious displeasure, which we learn by a letter from Sir Peter to Henry Sumner, his chaplain and great friend and confidant :

"GOOD HARYE,—I am enforced with greefe to take my Sonne from 1605 Cambridge and send him home, the bearer can tell you more off the Cause then I am willing to committ to paper only this now because I am in hast (even as you love me wch I know you doe & haue euer faythfully donne) lett not yor eyes looke off him till I see you, wch God willing shalbe soone, and use the matter soe now att . . . [word missing] as he may respect you more then he doth his teacher ; I wold faine haue him to haue learning & understanding, and if he will nott, I must be sory for itt now, & he heareafter. And so I commend me & committ you to God.

"Yor assured loving frend

"P. LEGH."

The offence does not appear ; it was probably something very trivial and may have had to do with want of application. He was, however, in disgrace for a time, and we hear nothing more of him for some years.

The relations between parents and children in former days were very different from those existing in these happier times. Children lived in awe and almost terror of their parents, whom they addressed as "sir" and "madam," and in some cases never spoke to them except upon their knees. No child ever dreamt of sitting down in his father's presence, the slightest faults were magnified into heinous crimes and were visited with the harshest punishment; the rod was not spared, and though the child might be spoilt it was never from want of corporal punishment. Poor little children of long ago! To look at their sad and solemn faces one would scarcely imagine that they could have played or romped as do the children of to-day. The elaborate samplers with their quaint verses and the name and age of some poor mite are silent evidences of the martyrdom of these small babes. What weary hours they have spent seated on some hard stool, bending over the stitches with tired eyes and little hot fingers. Far better would they have been out in the sweet sunshine chasing butterflies or gathering daisies for a chain!

> " Children shall weep in after years
> Far fewer tears—far softer tears."

With the beginning of the new reign Sir Peter thought it wise to sue for a general pardon, an old custom which brought in fees to the Exchequer and was supposed to clear off all sins of omission or commission and to give people a clean slate with which to enter upon the new regime. Taxation appears to have been heavy; there was the King's rent to pay and subsidies, and Sir Peter was required to furnish " at any muster " the following : " one demi-lance, one light horse, six corselets, three muskets, and two calivers " (a large pistol or blunderbuss).

He and his Dorothy were now settled down to a comfortable family life. He was adding to his property, which he increased and improved by judicious acquisition of land, and although he was spending a considerable sum of money on his building and various schemes, and was entertaining on a very large scale and keeping practically open house, he succeeded by careful management in leaving his children well provided for and his estate unencumbered at his death. Dame Dorothy was an excellent and practical housekeeper. Besides the establishment at Lyme she had her own property at Worsley to look after ; this comprised a large estate as well as a beautiful black-and-white house where she and her husband spent a

DOROTHY BRERETON

Second wife of Sir Peter Legh of Lyme

1615

By MARCUS GHEERAERTS

From a Portrait at Lyme

ÆTATIS·SVÆ·52
AN·DŌNI·1615
SIR·PETER·LEGH
SECOND·LADY

Dorothie Legh

portion of each year. From the account book we gather that Dame Dorothy took a very keen part and interest in the farming of her estate and in buying and selling of stock. In this respect she was, no doubt, of more practical help to Sir Peter than his poor Margaret can have been with her perpetually increasing family and consequent incapacity for exertion.

A beautiful " kit-cat " portrait of Dorothy Legh painted by Marcus Gheeraerts in 1615, one of the finest pictures in the Lyme collection, represents her in a black gown and ruff trimmed with gold and silver lace similar to some still existing, lace cuffs, and with two gold and jewelled bracelets. She wears rings on the third finger of each hand, and a gold ring resembling a wedding-ring on the first joint of her left thumb ; in her left hand is what appears to be a fan. Round her neck is a tight collar of four rows of pearls divided by gold slides, and falling to her waist is the beautiful pearl necklace that we see in Margaret's portrait, but there are five instead of four rows, the necklace falling only to the waist instead of to the knees as in Margaret's portrait. On her head is a curious black steeple-crowned hat with a band of gold and pearls in a Holbein design, and fastened to the left side of the hat is a brooch in the same design with three large pearl drops. On a little table in front of her sits a small monkey. From letters of a later date we read of " my Lady Brereton's breed of monkies," which were, no doubt, of a special kind. The Egerton and Brereton arms are painted in the left-hand corner, and on the right side of the picture is the following inscription : " Aetatis sua 52, An. Dom. 1615. Sir Peter Legh second Lady." The face is clever and comely and she does not look her fifty-two years.

Another portrait by Zuccaro, said in the catalogue to be the Queen of Bohemia, is obviously an earlier one of Dorothy, painted probably during her first widowhood. She wears a black dress with a small white ruff and lace cuffs ; on her head is the same curious steeple-crowned hat, but with no jewellery attached, as befits her condition ; the face is sad and pinched, and lacks the prosperous and happy expression that we see in her later portrait.

1606   In September 1606 Sir Peter had the misfortune to lose his old friend and chaplain Henry Sumner, who died and was buried at Disley, Sir Peter commemorating him in a brass which is placed in the church close to the pulpit. The inscription opens with the following : " In piam Memoriam Henrici Sumneri optimi et fidelissimi hujus Ecclesiæ Ministri, Petrus Legh miles posvit."

Of Sir Peter's daughters, Anne and Katherine, we hear very little at this time. Anne, the baby painted with her great-grandmother in 1595, would have been about thirteen at this date (1607), and appears to have been somewhat precocious for her years. Her father's clerk, John Bullinge, writes to her on October 6, 1607, from Hallom, Lancashire, where her Uncle Thomas lived, thanking her for her

> " kynde token and letter, sore doe I desire to see you yett God knowes I cannot performe my sore longing. Good Mris, do not condemn me of anie forgetfulness of you, nor blame me not, I pray you, for presuming to write unto you for it is all I have left to comforte my self withall in absence of my friends."

Of Katherine, the youngest of Sir Peter's children, we hear nothing beyond an occasional reference to her in the account book; the only other mention of her is in the Disley Parish Register for the year 1617, September 14, when her death is recorded.

Sir Peter's brother Edward, who had adopted the law as a profession, was in failing health about this time. He writes to his brother on January 21, 1607 :

> " If you come in companie with anie phisician or others of Judgement I pray you learne what course were best for me to hold to restore this my decayed sickly body if it be God's holie will, Mr Doctor Barrowe * lyeth every terme in Graies Inne at his son-in-law Mr Cotton's chamber, he is holden both in Cambridge and London little inferior to Mr. Butler,† I wish you would know his opinion."

* Philip Barrow or Barrough, a native of Suffolk, flourished 1590 ; medical writer, practised his profession in London. Author of " The Method of Phisicke," which he dedicated to Lord Burghley in 1590, and which reached its seventh edition in 1652.

† William Butler (1535–1618), physician ; born at Ipswich ; educated at Clare College, Cambridge, of which he became a Fellow. He attained to great eminence in his profession ; was summoned from Cambridge in 1612 to attend Henry, Prince of Wales, in his last illness.

He ends with hopes of a joyful meeting " heare or in Heaven," 1608
and his forebodings were realized, as he died the following year,
1608. They were fatalists in those early days, taking strangely
little heed or trouble to obviate what threatened, but bowing
to the inevitable whether of good or evil, assured that whatever
it brought them must be for the best.

The other brother, Thomas, who lived at Hallom, Lancashire,
and was in receipt of an annuity from Sir Peter of £15 a year,
is described as " One of His Majesty's Carvers in Ordinary,"
and was a personage of some importance at Court. He held
a post in the household of Prince Henry, for whom that most
beautiful of all the stately homes of England—Bramshill in
Hampshire—had been intended, but whose young life, full of
hope and promise, was so early cut off. Had he lived to be
king, England might have been spared all the catastrophes
that happened, and the disasters and bloodshed of the Civil
War might have been averted.

Thomas Legh is referred to in a letter written to Sir Peter
in 1635 from Parahiba, Brazil, by one John Harrison, Envoy to
Barbary and author, in which he speaks of having been " fami-
liarly acquainted with your brother Mr. Thomas Legh at Court
in the golden daies of Prince Henrie." King James did not
always remember his old servants. In a petition, bearing no
date, Thomas Legh humbly begs that

> " whereas yor Majesty about 6 years since bestowed on him [the
> petitioner] £2000, to be had and taken out of the forfeitures unto
> your Highness from Recusants in the Counties of Norfolk, Suffolk,
> Essex and London, about 4 years past the Lords Commissioners took
> that gift from him and in lieu thereof procured him yor Majesty's
> privy seale for £150,"

pointing out at the same time that other claimants placed
like himself have all long since been satisfied. He therefore
humbly prays that he may be paid without further delay
" that he may be in(h)abled to wayte in his place upon your
Majesty." Whether he ever received the money or no does
not appear. He died in 1626, and from an inventory of his goods
taken at his house in Watling Street, London, he seems only

to have been possessed of " one velvet ould cloake," valued at £2, and " one ould payre of breeches—10s.," which does not look as if he was in very affluent circumstances at the time of his death. His will, dated October 12, 1623, names his " most choice beloved nephew Francis Legh " his sole executor ; " to him I give all my leases, goods and chattells." To his brother Sir Peter Legh, " whom I much respect," he leaves the velvet cloak above mentioned.

Sir Peter's only sister, Elizabeth, was married in 1587 to Richard Lathom of Parbold, Lancashire, and had with other children a son, Edward, who is mentioned from time to time. Both Mr. and Mrs. Lathom were dead before 1624, and Edward was left to the guardianship of his two uncles, Sir Peter and Thomas Legh, and " two other gentlemen," who endeavoured to oust Thomas Legh from his position of guardian. He had evidently appealed to the great Duke of Buckingham,* who writes on November 3, 1623, to the Earl of Middlesex,† Lord High Treasurer of England and Master of His Majesty's Court of Wards and Liveries :

> " I understand by this gentleman Mr. Thomas Leigh that upon a Petition delivered unto you your Lordship was pleased to commit the wardship of a Nephew of his, one Richard ‡ Latham unto Sr Peter Leigh this gentleman and two others ; since which time some of those who had the said grant doe use meanes to put out Mr Leigh and to have the same wholly to themselves. My desire unto your Lordship is, that you would make good your own Act and doe him all the favor therein that you may, that he who hath been his Majestys ancient servant and one that I doe well respect may not receive any disgrace thereby. Which I shall take as a curtesie from your Lordship And ever rest
>
>   " Your Lordships faithfull friend and kinsman
>
>   " G BUCKINGHAM."

The letters, which up till now have been few and far between, become, from this period, more numerous, making the task of selection a difficult one.

* George Villiers, first Duke of Buckingham (1582–1628), Court favourite ; assassinated by Felton, 1628.

† Lionel Cranfield, first Earl of Middlesex (1575–1645) ; charged with corrupt practices as Master of Court of Wards and condemned, 1624 ; pardoned, 1625.

‡ ? Edward.

DOROTHY BRERETON

During her first widowhood

Afterwards second wife of Sir Peter Legh of Lyme

By ZUCCARO

From a Portrait at Lyme

LYME UNDER DOROTHY LEGH

As we have seen, there was a constant interchange of civilities between Sir Peter and his even distant neighbours. He was on the same friendly terms with the Derby family as his grandfather, and by his second marriage he was brought into nearer connexion with the families of Brereton and Egerton, and was on affectionate terms with all his new wife's relations as well as with his own. The Gerards and Molyneux were constantly writing to him for advice, and he had numerous god-children who always address him as " father " and write in language of the deepest respect as well as in that of genuine affection.

Henry Cavendish,* eldest son of Sir William Cavendish † and " Bess of Hardwick," was also an intimate friend ; writing to Sir Peter on March 14, 1608–9, he speaks of the first formation of a deer park at Chatsworth, which was to be partly stocked with red deer from Lyme :

> " WORTHIE SIR PETER—Whereas I purpose to make a smale red deare parke near unto my house att Chatsworth and Cannot furnish it with that game so speedilie as I would, my request is that you would be pleased to make exchange with me between a gallant Stallion and some of your red deare about Michaelmas and what you shall think meete I will stand to yor Cortesie for. My wief and I would be very glad to see you and yor good Ladie att Chatsworth anie tyme this Summer when it shall please you where wee will be very glad of you. If it please you to Like of the notion the horse shall be ready att an hours warning whensoever you shall send for him."

Much of this letter might have been written at the present day.

* M.P. for the County of Derby, married Grace, third daughter of George, sixth Earl of Shrewsbury, fourth husband of "Bess of Hardwick." Henry Cavendish died s.p. in 1616.

† Sir William Cavendish (1505 (?)–1557), second son of Thomas Cavendish of Cavendish, Suffolk, Clerk of the Pipe, bought the estate of Chatsworth, which he began to build in 1553. He married in 1547, as his third wife, Elizabeth, daughter and heiress of John Hardwick of Hardwick, Derbyshire, and widow of Robert Barlow of Barlow, Derbyshire. By this lady he had issue three sons : Henry, above mentioned ; William, afterwards first Earl of Devonshire ; and Charles, who settled at Welbeck, and was the father of the first Duke of Newcastle ; and three daughters : Frances, married Sir Henry Pierrepont of Holme Pierrepont, Nottingham, and was ancestress of the Dukes of Kingston ; Elizabeth, married Charles Stuart, Earl of Lennox, and was the mother of Arabella Stuart ; and Mary, married Gilbert Talbot, son of her stepfather, the Earl of Shrewsbury.

1607–8   In January 1607–8, Sir Peter's second and third surviving sons, Francis and Thomas, were admitted students at Brasenose College, Oxford, being aged eighteen and fourteen respectively; both matriculated the following year, in November 1609. They appear to have been under the care of a tutor, one Ralph Richardson, a native of Lancashire and a Fellow of the College, who accompanied them on their journeys to and from Lyme, and who kept a careful watch over them whilst they were in residence. From a series of letters written to Sir Peter by the Vice-Principal, Richard Taylor, between the years 1607 and 1611–12 we are given an interesting picture of the University life of the time, and we also realize the extraordinarily small amount of liberty that was enjoyed by the undergraduates, who were not even allowed pocket-money of their own.

From the pen of Mr. G. H. Wakeling,* M.A., Fellow of the College, we get the following description of Brasenose as it was in the early part of the seventeenth century :

> " It requires some effort of the imagination to picture the appearance of the College at the opening of the seventeenth century. It consisted solely of the present old quadrangle, divested of the gables and attics, Citizens' houses ran along the High from St. Mary's, while the place now occupied by the Library, Chapel, Cloisters and new buildings held a few old Halls. Some of these were connected with the College, and formed a residence for Tutors or scholars. It comes as a shock to be told, in the famous Census of 1612, that into these narrow confines were packed no less than 227 Brasenose men ! These numbers are twice our own, and the available space was scarcely half."

Upon investigation the census was proved inaccurate, the numbers being two hundred. Mr. Wakeling goes on to say :

> " This figure is sufficiently astonishing, and would still be inexplicable but for the system under which they lived. The large rooms, each of which is now a man's sitting-room, were then bedrooms. Each was used by one Fellow or senior member, and several of his ' schollars ' slept in truckle-beds in the same ' great chamber.' The present bedrooms were ' studies.' This solves the mystery of space, and that of comfort remains."

* " Brasenose Quatercentenary Monographs," vol. ii, Oxford, 1909.

LYME UNDER DOROTHY LEGH

Every pupil was compelled to have a tutor, of necessity one of the Fellows, who had the absolute control of his life, settled his work, and paid all his expenses with the sum of money allowed by his parents. Each tutor had his set of pupils, called a " compenie," who lived together almost like one family. Life was strenuous.* There were no comforts ; even a fire was seldom allowed and had to be paid for. The undergraduates were required to rise in time to attend chapel at 5 A.M. in summer and 6 in winter, and there was no cup of hot coffee or tea ; the most they can have had to begin the day upon would be a pint of ale or sack, and probably not that. They worked from 6 until 10 or 11, when dinner was served in Hall. A lugubrious meal this must have been, as all conversation had to be carried on in Latin. Supper took place at 5 P.M., immediately after evening chapel. After dinner came " disputations" from 1 to 3, then some form of recreation, but this was very restricted. Riding was allowable if the students could afford it ; fishing was looked upon as childish ; bathing was forbidden ; and if a walk was taken it could only be in company, for no one was allowed to walk out into the country unattended. Till late in the sixteenth century football was much looked down upon as being an " insolent " game, though in James I's reign it was regarded in a rather better light. Games of ball were strictly forbidden, though in 1608 there seems to have been an idea of establishing a tennis-court, but this was abandoned probably through want of funds. The students were required to be in college by 9 P.M. under peril of a beating, but impositions and fines seem to have been the more usual form of punishment.

Even allowing for the difference in the value of money then as compared with the same amount now, it seems almost incredible that Sir Peter should have considered that £30 a year apiece was enough to maintain his two sons at the University, but this was certainly his idea, and the two young men arrived with that sum, which was handed over to the college authorities on January 17, 1607–8, by one Thomas Eden, who probably had accompanied them there. That this allowance

* " Brasenose College " (Mr. Wakeling).

was considered inadequate we gather from the letters of Richard Taylor, who is constantly making applications for more. In his first letter, dated Brasenose, November 30, 1608, he says :

> "Your sonnes I thanke God are both well, and do follow their business orderlie and with good commendation, but the great dearth of all things, especially in this place, have raised their expences in short time so much, that the money wch I have received wch was just three score pounds in the whole, was neere quite ended in Michaelmase last, & yet I am sure their is none of their rank wch have lived so thriftelie as they have done. When it shall please you to send up any money, if you have not a convenient messenger to send it up the next way, you may send it, to be delivered in London to Mr William Singleton at his house the sign of the Windmill in the Pultrye, & thence I can have it returned within a short time after, so that I have notice in wrytinge what sum is sent from time to time."

1609   Oxford had suffered from frequent visitations of the plague, and there was an outbreak in 1609 and two deaths in the college. The drainage system was probably answerable for these epidemics.* It consisted of a huge pit beneath the ground where the Antechapel now stands. The pit was emptied every five or six years at a cost of £30. This outbreak must have added greatly to Richard Taylor's responsibilities and have caused him much anxiety. Writing to Sir Peter on June 7 of that year, he says :

> "There hath been some danger of ye sickness here in Oxford, but the fear of it as I take it, was greater then the danger, although I confesse the danger was very great unto some few. . . . I thanke God, I saw the danger, where it was, at the first, & took order accordinglie, that we mixt not our selves with any who were within the suspicion thereof. My purpose was, & so I had provided a house to have gone to Ensam & there to have lien together with my company, but the very day I was about to remove, word was brought me, that the sickness was in the town, whereupon I sent a messenger presently into Sussex with letters to three or four gentlemen, whose sons are likewise with me & to my brother Leigh for horses, & the gentlemen have sent horses for Francis and Thomas, & God willing I will bring them into Sussex & stay there with them some four or five days, and then will returne to Oxford again for I doubt not but our college is

---

* "Brasenose College" (Mr. Wakeling).

now very safe, to such as are not dainted with over much fear. I received by the London carrier for your sonnes use the fifteen pounds which your man sent this last term from London, and likewise a coople of cheeses wch my Lady your bedfellow sent to your sonnes and me self, we thank her Ladyship for them."

Francis and Thomas remained in Sussex with their tutor for about six weeks, returning at the end of that time to Oxford. Richard Taylor writes on July 18 :

"Your sonnes, our whole college and all the university I thanke God are well ; and it hath fallen out no otherwise then I conjectured in my last letter. Mr Richardson and your sonnes returned out of Sussex the last weeke, and our company doth increase dayly, and exercise is kept as before. No man hath been sick, since I writ ; three only (who were one man's scholars) had the sicknes, neither hath any one of their keepers, or such as kept company with them before caught the infection."

Though there were no fixed holidays, probably on account of the expense and length of time occupied by the journeys, the youths appear to have gone home once a year, and Richard Taylor seems to have visited at Lyme in August 1609, having probably accompanied the two young men on their return to Cheshire. His next letter, dated September 26, gives " humble thanks for your great kindness at my late being with you." He then goes on to say :

"The sicknes here in Oxford, I trust in God, is quite ceased, but I am certified from your nephew, Mr Edward Lathom this last week, that in London it is much increased ; and that there died the week before of the sicknes two hundred and ten . . . your sons are both well, I thank God, and so are the rest of the students, the number of whom increaseth dayly, the Lord bless their good endeavours . . . two of your nephews Sir Richard Molyneux * his sons, do come to our college about a fortnight hence to Mr Radcliffe † my honest countryman."

With the approach of winter the plague seems to have died out, and we hear no more of it.

* Sir Richard Molyneux, knighted by Queen Elizabeth, 1596 ; married Frances, sister of Margaret, Lady Legh, and a daughter of Sir Gilbert Gerard, Master of the Rolls.

† Samuel Radcliffe, a native of Lancashire, born 1580 ; matriculated at Brasenose, 1597 ; Fellow, 1603 ; Principal, 1614.

The following January, 1609–10, there came more applications for money :

"The sum I have received in all with the last ten pounds, comes to £130, out of wch sum sixteen pounds being deducted, wch is your sett allowance for two years already ended, there remains only ten pounds. Now your worship was pleased, that fifteen pounds should be for discharging their admission & makeing their gowns at the first, so that there is £5, according to this reckoning, to be received by me, for the evening of my accounts untill Christenmasse. But the truth is, I have already now before Christenmasse disbursed for them in all since their first coming, £139. 5. 2. as will appeare at any time by the particulars in my booke. Neither can I possibly keepe your elder son Mr Francis Legh within the compass of thirty pounds. For since August I was with your worship, of purpose I have set down their expences apart either by himself, & I find their is almost three pounds difference in this short time, neither can I impute it to any thinge but his height wch is extraordinary for his age, viz : full six foote and two inches. In mine opinion your worship may do well to allow him, ten pounds more by the year, and the rather by cause his cosins Sir Richard Molyneux his sonnes do live at a far higher rate. Besids both he and his brother will be able, & shall if your worship approve it be presented batchelars of the arts either in Michaelmas terme nexte, or just this time twelmonth wch I hope will be no way prejudicial unto them, but rather incourage them to apply their studies the harder, & make them more carefull and studious of manlike behaviour."

Richard Taylor had a hard man to deal with. Sir Peter was careful almost to the extent of being miserly, and was not to be persuaded by any suggestions that Francis, by reason of his great height, should require more money than his brother, or by any hint of his sons not making as good an appearance as their Molyneux cousins, to increase the very meagre allowance which he considered to be sufficient for their wants. He seems to have visited them himself at Oxford in May 1608, bringing with him the £15 which was to last till August.

He commissioned Richard Taylor to provide him with a chaplain, no doubt to replace Henry Sumner, and his views on the subject of a stipend appear to have been as limited as those he held with regard to his sons' allowance. He was holding out against having to pay as much as £20, although Richard Taylor assures him

> " I could not provide you of a preacher so well qualified, as in reason he should be for your house after the rate your worship desired me, and the reason is because it is not unusual in our South Countreys to have twenty pounds yearly & diet, in so much that two batchelars of the Arts of our house who indeed are good scholars & preachers do enjoy the like places & have done for two or three years together."

Ultimately he and "Mr. Principal" seem to have found a suitable man who was to come for a time on approval, "a Master of Arts of our own College one Mr Harison," whom he thoroughly recommends as having lived

> "honestly, civilly, & studiously as befitted one of his place. He hath since for two years or thereabouts exercised himself in the ministrie & taken good paines therein & received deserved commendation for the same . . . he is contented to be with you upon likeing for a time and after to know his allowance when sufficient trial & proofe hath been had of him."

Richard Taylor renews his application for an increased allowance on May 21, 1610 :

> "Let me know your worships pleasure concerning your sons, I pray you ; and namely for their proceeding wch will require some charges extraordinary, and whether your pleasure be, to make your elder son somewhat better allowance, for surely I cannot draw it out to serve him in any good sort, and I am loth often to trouble your worship in this argument."

Both young men took their B.A. degree on November 29 of this same year, 1610, and their allowance seems to have been slightly augmented in view of their new dignity. Richard Taylor on December 8, 1610, acknowledges the receipt of £35, their expenses in one quarter with " their apparell, & charge of proceedinge & some formalities for your younger sonne " amounting to £26, "or very near their abouts . . . your younger sonnes expences here, will not be lesse then tenne pounds a quarter, besides the charge of determininge in Lent."

Interesting particulars are given as to their gowns and hoods :

"The cloth for your sonnes gown and hood, which should be five yards I would willinglie have sent up, that the same might be made up before Christenmasse."

On January 8, 1610–11, he writes :

"I have received your worships letter of the 22th of December, and the cloath for your sonnes gowne, and the money likewise. What cloath shall be wanting I will provide, as reasonablie as I can, and will be as careful, that your money be not misspent as I coulde, if I shoulde pay it out of mine owne purse."

Taking a degree meant very serious application and the attending of constant lectures.* All examinations were oral and entailed a great strain upon the mind and attention, and when one considers the amount of work that had to be got through upon a very inferior and scanty supply of food, it is not surprising that this should have told upon the health of two growing youths whose constitutions were none too robust. Francis, as we have seen, was outgrowing his strength, measuring six foot two at eighteen, and Thomas, though of more sturdy build, was evidently in bad health at this time, as we learn by the following letter written to Sir Peter by Dr. Thomas Singleton, Head of the College and Vice-Chancellor in 1611 :

"Sir,—Your sonne Thomas havinge spent his spirites, and tired his boddy with sundry conflictes in the heat of disputations especially this hungry tyme of Lent, wee resolved upon mature deliberation, yt for the refreshinge of the man and recoveringe of his decayed strength, a journey in to Lancashire would prove his best phisique ; especially havings soe good company as Mr Vice-Principall [Richard Taylor], whoe will be carefull to see him conducted unto you, as alsoe in safety yt he be returned unto us agayne, to whom he shall be hartely welcome, as nowe I trust unto yourselfe, and more then ys [this] (wch I wish) moste kindly cherished for he well deserveth."

Thomas left Oxford for Lancashire accordingly with Richard Taylor, and appears from an entry in the account book to have actually been given ten shillings pocket-money on this occasion. In June we find him back at Oxford, where Francis had also returned, unexpectedly and unwelcome, it would seem from the following letter of Taylor's to Sir Peter dated June 17, 1611 :

* "Brasenose College" (Mr. Wakeling).

92

"I am sorry I heard not of your worships purpose to returne your sonne for Oxford before he came. And surelie had an other gentlemans sonne bene commended unto me, I shoulde have given him but small intertainment, neither can I tell well, how to provide for him, without displacing of some other. Besids my chamber & rooms above it, are all open, and I am more then a little troubled to get places for such as I have already charge of, until mine owne rooms can be made fitt for them againe, which will be both troublesome & chargeable. But howsoever, upon condition your sonne will be careful to do himself good & to winne againe your worships favour, I shall be content to do him what kindnes I may."

He goes on to speak about their gowns:

"I dare not take upon me to maintaine them for all necessaries in any reasonable sort here, (had the other a scholars gowne & a suite of apparell first provided) under tenne pounds by the quarter, nor the younger (who deserves more) under nine pounds quarterlie . . . how be it I cannot buy a gowne a civil hood & cappe, befittinge a bachelar of the Arts & large enough for your sonne, not much under six pounds."

We find by an entry in the account book that £10 13s. 8d. was spent on "clothes for the young gentlemen" in 1612, so that they cannot have been quite as badly off for garments as was made out. Although Francis must have been twenty-two years old in 1612 and Thomas eighteen, neither of them was given any money of his own, and this seems—and not unnaturally—to have been a cause of great annoyance to Francis, who protested against the practice. Oddly enough, Sir Peter was not disinclined to make him some small allowance, but Richard Taylor highly disapproved:

"Your elder sonne thinks he should keepe his owne money wch I hold highly inconvenient, for experience hath taught me that some young gentlemen can hardly be kept in anie order, let them but have an angell or two in their purse. . . . Nowe whereas your worship did insinuate in your letter, that your sonnes should keepe their owne money, give me leave to answer plainlie & truelie, that I thinke there is so manie inconveniences therein, that your worship well consideringe the same, will easily be of an other mind; as first it will not be in my power, on Fridays & Satterdays suppers to keepe them out of the towne, as nowe I do, nor at many other times to keepe them out of the worser & unthriftier sort of gentlemens company, if they be knowne to have money in their owne custodie. Nay, they should loose the favour & likeing of some of their friends, if they would not lend them money at their need, & if they lent it they would be in danger to loose their money, besids it would breed me a great trouble with the rest of my scholars & bring such an ataxie [disturbance] & disorder amongst them, that I could not easily remove. Howsoever if it be your worships pleasure to have it so, whensoever any money comes before hand unto me (which usually hath not happened) [this was evidently meant for a cut at Sir Peter] I shall deliver such sums unto them as your worship shall appoint, fitting for their apparell."

In 1611 Francis Legh was trying for a fellowship at All Souls, and this was made an excuse for writing to require for him

" a gowne, a civil hood, a cappe & an habit, a suite of apparell & divers other things which he wants, or else he will not be thought fitt by many to become a suiter for a fellowshippe in All Soules."

Francis was unsuccessful, although he had the support of the Bishop of Oxford, Sir Peter's brother Thomas, and Sir John Egerton, afterwards first Earl of Bridgewater, a nephew of Dorothy, Lady Legh. Mr. Thomas Singleton, Vice-Chancellor, also helped him by trying to persuade one of his kinsmen who held a fellowship to resign and make room for Francis; " but the truth is," said Richard Taylor, " his kinsman's benefice is litigious wch was a sufficient cause for him to keep his fellowship."

The demands for money recur with wearying reiteration. Granted that Sir Peter was a skinflint, which seems not improbable, it was a case of " diamond cut diamond," and Taylor was determined to get all he could and to lose nothing for want of asking, or even of threatening. An upper story was being added to the college in 1611, and on October 22, 1611, he begs for help towards the furnishing of the room that was to serve for himself and the two young Leghs and " others I have charge of," and endeavours to screw £10 out of Sir Peter, but in this, as in all other money transactions with the obstinate old knight, he was unsuccessful, and he had to be contented with less than half the amount.

94

LYME UNDER DOROTHY LEGH

As a last resource Richard Taylor suggests that the money Sir Peter sends does not always reach his hands!

> "Give me leave to answer your worship, that of the forty shillings sent before, twenty shillins onlie came to mine hands. . . . I hope your worship will easilie pardon this and my former bouldnes, by cause I have writ nothinge but that which I have bene urged unto, unlesse I shoulde take upon me the faulte of others, I meane of some of your officers, who doubtlesse have sometimes bene more careles in sending up your sonnes appointed allowance, then you yourselfe have knowne of or woulde have permitted had you formerlie bene made acquainted with the same."

This letter, written on January 14, 1611–12, is the last of 1611–12 the series, but there must have been many others, for although Francis left Oxford soon after this date, his age being now about twenty-two or twenty-three, Thomas was living there up to 1624. From the Brasenose Register we find that he became a Fellow (Frankland) on May 10, 1614; M.A. on July 7 of the same year; Resident Fellow in 1621; B.D. 1624, and D.D. in 1634. He also tried, but unsuccessfully, for the Proctorship, and was canvassed for several years.

Thomas had always been destined by his father for the Church, but it was much against his own wish, though he had to submit in this, as in all other things, to his father's iron will. Although he loved his children in his rough, uncouth fashion, Sir Peter would never brook the slightest deviation from his own wishes. He considered that it was for him to dispose of the lives of his children at his discretion, and that whatever he settled for them was for the best and must be acquiesced in by them with unfaltering obedience. Any sign of opposition on their part was certain to increase his fixed determination to carry his point at whatever cost it might be to them. Thomas tried his utmost to influence his father, but in vain.

> "Neither is there anie defect or want of willingnes in mee towards ye profession of it [divinity], but imperfections and disabilities towards ye performance of it doe discourage mee to take ye orders, as lacke of audacitie and boldnes as I think it is not unknowne to yourself (I presume to speak it boldly) yt we are all of us bashfull."

95

In a later letter he refers to the beautiful mother, of whom he probably had some dim recollection, begging to know if this desire of his father's were " with her consent and purpose," as " it would content me very much to know." Meantime he begs that he may be spared " from taking the orders of Ministry upon me, till such time as your disposition of me otherwise then where I now live [Oxford] shall occasion them. In the meantime I shall prepare my readiness for God's service therein as well as I can."

1619   His father was probably not more generous in his allowance than he had been when his sons first went into residence, though Thomas must have had his own pittance, whatever it was, as a Resident Fellow. In a letter dated July 21, 1619, he begs that he may be given

" out of that portion which my grandmother left me, 20¹, to furnish my studie with divinity bookes [acknowledging at the same time with humble thanks the last Midsummer quarter]. Mr Principal purposeth towards September or the later end of the Vacation to see Lyme and requesteth my company which I have halfe promised ye rather to confirm him in his intended journey, [but he has to obtain his fathers permission to return home before deciding], as I hear from you I shall resolve. A nagg I am provided of the same my Brother bestowed on mee the last year, which I keep—though but a sorrie one in hopes you will be pleased to better him. Thus not doubtful of your good health whereof would my Bro : Franke afford a little paper and paines I should be glad to hear more certain news then flying reports which ever speak the worst. But my prayers will ever continue for you— for myselfe to Remaine

" Yr humble obedient sonne

" THO : LEGH."

Sir Peter carried his point, and Thomas preached his first sermon in Disley Church—at the age of about thirty—on August 22, 1624, this red-letter day in the Disley annals being commemorated in the parish register for that date as follows :

" Mr Thomas Legh, son to Sir Peter Legh preached the same day at Disley, and it was the first time that he preached. Aug : 22. 1624."

Both young men kept up their interest in their old college and friendship with its officials to the end of their lives, and although Francis left the University long before his brother, we find him frequently paying visits there and writing for news of its inmates. His health had always been delicate, and on this account, probably, we do not hear of his following any profession.

A great event took place at Lyme on January 3, 1612–13, 1612-13 namely, the marriage of Sir Peter's eldest daughter, Anne, with Richard Bold of Bold, a wealthy Lancashire squire. This match was evidently in accordance with her father's wishes, and he made quite a handsome settlement. Anne must have been about eighteen at this time. Unfortunately no portrait of her exists other than the one painted of her, a chubby baby of a year old, in her great-grandmother's arms.

Bold, near Prescot, Lancashire, and within easy reach of Bradley, Sir Peter's Lancashire home, was rebuilt by this Richard Bold in 1616. It has now fallen into ruin, but was no doubt an imposing building, surrounded by a moat. A portion of a gable is still standing. It is composed of rich red sandstone, with mullioned windows, and the old doorway is still existing, over which are the initials and date, " R. B. 1616, A. B." The moat remains with part of the drawbridge, and two handsome stone gateposts with niches on the inner side, somewhat resembling the small watch-towers that flank the gateway at Lyme. One can see portions of a wall which no doubt surrounded the park at this date. Collieries and hideous chimneys have taken the place of the fine old timber and have defaced the charming rolling country, and these and noxious vapours from chemical and other works have laid waste what was once a smiling land.

In the parish registers of Farnworth Church, near Bold, a fine church dating from the twelfth century, we find the following notice :

" Richardus Bold de Bold Armiger et Anne filia venerabilis viri Petri Leighe de Lyme Militis Nupsere in domo eiusdem Petri Leigh e Magistrii Gerrard Rectorem Ecclia de Stopford 3. Jan: 1612."

by which we may infer that the marriage took place in the house at Lyme, the ceremony being performed by Richard

Gerard, who was Rector of Stockport at this time. He was a first cousin of Sir Peter's first wife Margaret, and was presented to the living of Stockport by his uncle, Sir Gilbert Gerard, Master of the Rolls.

1614   Richard and Anne had three sons and nine daughters; their eldest child was born at Lyme, as we find in the account book on December 16 of the year 1614, or 1615, the following entry:

> "To Larrance wyfe for ale when Mris Bold lay in Childbed— xiii^s vi^d" (13s. 6d.).

These interesting family events were always made the occasion of much drinking, carousing, and merrymaking, which must have been of a doubtful benefit to the mother and babe. Among the treasures discovered at Lyme about forty years ago were two coverlets in rose satin much discoloured with age, one large and one small, bordered with very fine silver guipure lace of the Elizabethan period. These coverlets were used on the bed of the mother and the cradle of the child when caudle cup was given to friends and gossips in the bedchamber after an interesting event, and had no doubt adorned the bed and cradle of Mistress Bold and her babe on this historic occasion, as they had probably done those of her mother and herself in days gone by.

CHAPTER VI

A LOVE TRAGEDY

We come now to a dark page in the annals of Sir Peter Legh, 1614 namely, his treatment of his eldest son, Piers. The young man had, as we have seen, been removed hastily from Cambridge for some offence which does not appear. He was, however, though possibly under a cloud for a time, not banished from his father's presence, as we hear of him at Lyme soon after his sister's marriage, when he writes to his brother Francis, possibly in connexion with horse-racing of some kind:

> "You write to me to know what success you have had in your horse money, which hath not bine so good as I could wish, for they like Poynton men which shall never be trusted again by me. My sister Bold sayeth she counteth to Whitsuntide, shee is wonderful great, pray God send her good lightening. My father is not yet come home but we every day expect him. You write to know what case your black nagge is in; our Spring this year hath bine so backward that he will not be in any case to be taken up till the later end of May though he hath all the helpe that can be for every other day my brother Peter or I give him a dishful of oats. My own nagge is so poore that I cannot take him up till towards the later end of June. We remembred you when the noble knight was over at Lyme at whose parting out of the cuntrey there was a foolish business fell out betwixt Dick Holland and my brother Peter, but God be thanckt there was no hurt done."

Those were days when a hasty word meant the drawing of swords and bloodshed. None waited to hear reason; a wrong was a wrong and must be wiped out at once at the sword's point, explanations—if such there were—might follow after. Peter was the youngest of Sir Peter's sons, and his age at this time would be about eighteen.

Piers had a warm-hearted, generous, and loving disposition, with high aspirations and a desire to learn and improve himself. He was devoted to his brothers, to whom he was always ready and willing to do any kindness, and the few letters of his that exist contain constant references to gifts bestowed upon them, though he can have had very little money to spend, as we do not gather that his father allowed him more than £20 a year.

As early as the year 1610, being then aged about twenty-two or twenty-three, he had formed an attachment for a certain Mistress Morley, of whom we know nothing beyond that from sentences in the various letters we gather that her portion was not large enough to satisfy the insatiable greed of Sir Peter, who flatly refused to consider the match at all. Various members of the family were called in to help in persuading Piers to give up the lady, which he finally agreed to do provided his father would allow him his own choice of a wife upon a future occasion, and would not force any one upon him against his inclination. He on his part undertook that the lady of his choice should be suitable both in birth and position as well as portion. He was anxious to be allowed to travel to open and improve his mind, and also as a means of distraction from the grief of his disappointment; but although the extent of his "travel" was only to be a visit to France (no doubt then considered a very dangerous expedition), Sir Peter refused his consent to this modest request, though for what reason except that of wishing to make himself thoroughly disagreeable it is impossible to conjecture.

Piers begged his aunt, Lady Molyneux (one of his mother's sisters), to intercede with his father on his behalf and allow him to go abroad.

" Good Brother [she writes to Sir Peter], At my Nephews request, I moved you that you would be pleased to let him travel, and you took tyme to consider of it, hee doth still importune mee to be a means to you for the effecting of the same desire, in respect he hopeth to better himself and his experience by that course, and that he is

much wearie of that hee now leads his life in, I know though I wish
his good to my uttermost, yet his proceeding and welldoing concerneth
you most neerly, yett I hope hee shall find that from you that his
desert and nature binds you to, I refer all to your discretion and
fatherlie care, who best know what is fit."

After some time Lady Molyneux seems to have persuaded
the young man to give up the idea of travelling :

"I have been in talke with my nephew Piers about the gentlewoman
he was in lykeing with, which is now married, (Mris Morley) and
likewise about the humour he hath to travell, I find he hath great
scorn of her course, and partly ashamed of his owne constancie to her,
I have disuaded him from the thought of travel and I find him sylent
in y^t, and not much to mislike of my perswations, and I doubt not
but whollie to alter that determination in him, if you like of it, for
my part I think y^t is the unfittest of all courses he can take."

Whether there was some evil influence at work against
poor Piers it is impossible to find out. Lady Molyneux seems
to suspect this, however, by a subsequent letter in which she
speaks of

"great discontentments you had conceaved against your son and
of some unnatural affection you conceive he had against you and
your courses, I protest unto you I both believe and hope you shall
never have any such occasion, and am afraid some ill mynd doth
worse offices betwixt you. [She finds] great willingness in him to
perform all dutie that a loving and obedient child ought to his Parent,
so far is he both by his protestations and oathes from any desire
of the matter you taxe him with, that as soon would he desire his own
ill or death as yours."

She ends, begging Sir Peter

"will be a kynde father to him for his mothers sake, who I am assured
you much loved, and I doubt not you shall find him a dutiful child."

Sir Richard Molyneux adds his remonstrances in the same
letter :

"Your sons desires (in my opinion) are very reasonable and so I think
you will conceve of them."

Some two years after breaking off his engagement with
Mistress Morley, Piers fell desperately in love with Anne,

daughter of Sir John (afterwards Lord) Savile * of Pontefract, Yorkshire, a lady in every way suitable but for the unfortunate fact that her family held different political views to those of Sir Peter, and that her portion was not sufficiently large to make her welcome as a daughter-in-law. Sir Peter therefore again refused his consent in most peremptory terms ; nor would he listen to the entreaties of Piers, nor to the remonstrances of his brothers- and sisters-in-law, who implored him not to deal thus harshly with his son, " and such a son," and pointed out that he was breaking his sacred word of honour :

> " I protest I utterly dislike of your resolution [writes Lord Gerard †], upon my fayth I wryte not this at Any instance of my nephews. But the love I beare to you and your house causeth yt, and if I might prevayle so mutche I earnestly desire yt."

Nothing, however, seemed to make any impression. John, first Earl of Bridgewater, son of Lord Chancellor Ellesmere and a nephew of Dorothy, Lady Legh, writes very strongly in support of Piers and adds his entreaties to the rest of the family that Sir Peter will not break his promised word :

> " You have ever bene noted firme of your worde and promise, let not your sonne be the first with whom you breake it. Good Uncle be content with that which is past to use the power of a father to the correction and strayne it not to the confusion of a sonne an eldest sonne and such a one as I dare undertake will be a loving and dutyfull sonne. [He ends very diplomatically :] I protest I write what I thinke, and what I write I would have forborne if I did not hope that it shoulde tend to yᵉ good and the manifestation of my love towardes you ; for in the worde of an honest man, Sʳ P. Legh alone is more in my affection then Piers Legh and all his endes and alliances."

These letters all show the most intense sympathy with Piers and appreciation of his character, which was in every respect estimable and lovable, and one can only marvel at the harshness and bitterness with which his father treated him.

---

* First Baron Savile (1556–1630), politician ; M.P. Lincolnshire, 1586 ; Comptroller of the Household, 1627 ; created a baron, 1627.

† Thomas, first Lord Gerard, eldest son of Sir Gilbert Gerard, Master of the Rolls; brother-in-law of Sir Peter Legh. He married Alice, daughter and heiress of Sir Thomas Rivet, and died 1618.

A LOVE TRAGEDY

The following letters passed between father and son during the year 1617, Piers being now aged about thirty and having implored and entreated for seven weary years :

Sir Peter Legh to his son Piers :

" How frowardly and stubbornly you have demeaned yourself (for these many yeares) unto me God and your Conscience knoweth. The breach of this 5th Commandment is held by all honest and Godly men to be very dangerous, yet I pray you may never feel punishment for it.   I know you have not forgotten our last parting at this howse ; in ye beginninge of the last Sommer when you made desire to goe unto London unto [word missing] I was unwillinge and wolde with too much myldnes faine have otherwise perswaded you, but received from you soe sower and Grumbling Answere as I layed my fatherly Command upon you to staye, and alsoe sent unto you (for that purpose) by our own two messengers but you observed neither me nor them, but went on thither, and at this unfit time I was moved by my Lord Gerard to perswade with me to geve way unto this your unadvised entendment, but I was sore greeved and perplexed with the first as I protested and vowed against ye last, wch vowe I must observe and will keepe.   Now for that I heare you Continue Constant unto yor former willfull frowardnes and doe egerly pursue this business (though in despight of my hart) I will once more advise you (though my Advice by you have ever bin contemned) unless you may by this match Compass unto you self more meanes then my poore meanes is, withdraw your fancie and proceede not with it, for beleeve me yt if you doe, and be very well assured you must expect noe more from me then a yonger brothers Annuitie.

> " And soe beseechinge God to blesse you with his holy and heavenly Grace I leave and Rest . . ." [no signature].

Piers Legh's answer to his father's letter :

" S^r
> " My humble dutie remembred, with desire of your blessings health and praiers.

" I have received your letter which still augmenteth my further miseries : Not in that I have no desyre to receive any letter from you.   Which God knoweth I much wish, yet more desyre to see you, and be yours in all love and duty.   But to receive such a letter wherein I am charged with such deepe and undutifull demeanours towards you (wherein my conscience telleth me I am not altogether faultie, and your continuance in those conjectures) is that which most greeveth me. Ffor whereas you charge me; first with the neglecte of my duty, for those many yeares, I can not tell rightly wherein I should deserve such a censure; because my dutyfull love hath ever desyred to show itselfe to your content. Howsoever it pleaseth you to thinke the contrary.

"Concerning owre last parting at Lyme. I well remember that I did not grumble in my answere to you; for I gave none at all to my knowledge. But in that I broke your commandement when you gave it me and sent it me by Henry Bradshaw, I must and do acknowledge.

"Yet it may be pardonable, if it please you to consider my affection at that tyme, and ever since towards Mris Anne Savile: setled above two yeares before, and my promis then passed to come to London; that both (especially the first) forced me to that breach.

"Uppon your debarring me the company of Mris Morley, and my earnest entreaty thereuppon by Henry Bradshaw for my going into Ffrance, you promised me before Sr Thomas Gerard my Lady Moloneux and my Lady Gerrard, that if I would obey then your command, I should take my owne choyce for a wife, which I have thereuppon to my owne lyking made choyce of.

"How I was dealte with concerning Mris Morley, God and you know; yet I am perswaded you entended all for my good. But where you say shee refused me first, I can (if please you geve me leave) resolve you to the contrary, As well by certaine letters from Sr Thomas Earlsfield as others since my refusall.

"It greeveth me much that my fortunes are so contrary to urge you to such a vowe as to gainesay this my affection, and that my vowe and promis to God to be hers in life or Death should be so opponent for my perpetual misery.

"God is my judge; I nether do, nor would do anything in despite of your harte. But this I know, although I ought to be youres in all deuty, yet it is saide fathers ought not to be too greevous to there children. And wherein can they be more than in this breache of affection.

"Ffor the wealth or portion I should receive by this match, I verily thinke you will judge it too meane; yet a yonger brothers portion wilbe lesse welcome. But lett the will of God be fullfilled. I intend to have nether (if uppon these conditions) But will rather pursue the fortunes of my miserable estate and life to be hers in death.

"Good Sr, if it lye in your powre, or that you can be resolved anyway to dispence with your contrariety to me, I beseech you with teares and uppon the knees of my soule to compassionate your distressed sonne, and lett your tender and deare love yeeld your consent, liking and receiveing of me into your fatherly protection, and not to pursue my ruinn with too much violence in debarring of that I have, do, and ever will desyre ; which if it shall please you to mitigate the first and grant the last, I will make a new vowe to God ever to be

"Your obedient sonne

"PEIRES LEGH."

To this touching letter Sir Peter returned answer that unless Piers chose to dispense with his " rashness and stubbornness " he should become " a mere stranger to me and myne."

This cruel letter was answered by Piers in one of the most pathetic ever written, which ends with the following touching appeal :

"Therefore O father, if not for my owne, yet for my mothers sake, who onst was deare unto you, and in her name, I once more begge, with my teares, your fatherly consideracion, and that I may go on herein. Allthough you make me and command me to be a stranger to all Christendome. And so humbly craving pardon for all my offences, resting betweene hope and despaire ether to be by you fully comforted or by you for ever undon. In which estate I now remaine

"Your woefull and distressed Sonne

"PEIRES LEGH."

But all in vain ! Nor entreaties nor persuasions nor tears had the slightest effect. The bitter struggle had continued for all these seven weary years, till at length, tired out by the hopelessness of making any impression upon the senseless obstinacy of his father, Piers took the law into his own hands and married Anne Savile about the end of 1617 or the beginning of the following year. In a letter, undated, from Sir Peter to his brother-in-law, Lord Gerard, he announces the unwelcome fact, and from the contents one would imagine that he was the aggrieved party :

"MY NOBLE GOOD LORD, As it hath been my hard hap hearetofore   1618 to suffer a great crosse by yᵉ long continued obstinacie of my eldest sonne wherewith yoᵘ Lordship hath bin both acquainted and many times troubled (and wch had not bin yf your good Advice to him had taken place) so now he hath showed forth ye fruictes of his disobedience and smale respect of me, in marynge himself without my consent or privitie (yea even in despight of my hart and mynde) to a daughter of Sir John Saviles, who hath lately sent me a strange message (to mocke me as I suppose) to crave my consent to a motion of a mariadge betwixt my Sonne and his daughter, and to have a meeting about it, it beinge past and donne some two moneths before he sent me this message, by which your Lo : may perceive how I am used and dealt withal by them.

"Had not my Lord of Rutlande * comen to me on Tuesday night last I had waited on you at Holmes Chappell to have imparted this unto you out of ye fulness of my true greeues hart and mynde wch I hop and assure me your Lo : will never Augment by giving way to any persuasions or desires that may be used unto yr Lo : by any that shall seeke to make you their meanes unto me for this unhappie business."

From that day to the day of Piers' death, in 1624, there is nothing to show that his father forgave him or that he ever saw his face again. Stern, relentless, unforgiving, it is almost impossible to understand such a character. The letters from Piers to his father are among the most pathetic ever written, but they made no more impression upon that adamantine heart than did the wind beating upon the hard grey walls of Lyme.

Some provision he did make for the maintenance of the young couple, who appear to have resided at Bradley, Lancashire. "I am contented to give them her marriage portion without intermedling with anie of it," he states in a paper of "Remembrances" that must have been drawn up about this date. He assures all his lands descended to him from his ancestors to his heir male ; failing issue in the direct line, his lands to go to his younger sons, "that my sonne (in case hee have no issue male of his owne bodie) cannot put the inheritance from the next heire male." He also assures a "reasonable jointure to my sonne's wife—the same not to take effect untill after my decease." With characteristic prudence and forethought he also reserves to himself the liberty—in the event of his surviving his wife Dorothy—to make "a reasonable jointure for anie wife which I shall hereafter marie."

---

* Francis, sixth Earl of Rutland (1578–1632), took part in Essex's plot, 1601 ; Admiral of the Fleet to bring home Prince Charles from Spain, 1623.

A LOVE TRAGEDY

What was the attitude of Dorothy, Lady Legh, during all these years? It is impossible to find out whether she tried to influence her husband in favour of her unfortunate stepson, or whether—as Lady Molyneux seems to hint—she fanned the flame. There could be no apparent reason for her doing so. She had no children who could benefit by Piers' disinheritance, and even if this were so, Sir Peter had other sons who would have a prior claim. Piers had given her no cause for dislike, as he had shown himself well disposed towards her from the first. One can therefore only conclude that her influence in her stepson's favour—if she used it at all—was of no more avail than was that of his other relations. She was on excellent terms with all her stepchildren, constantly writing to Thomas, still at Oxford, whom she addresses in various ways—" Mr. Thomas," " Tom Legh," and " Good Tom "—and sending him " tokens " and cheeses. She wishes these may prove well in eating, " that you may make merrie with them amongst your friends." She sends " the best our barren countrie can afford, entreating you and them to whom they are sent to take them in good part, and I wish with all my heart that they were ten times better then they are for your sakes."

The last letter from Piers, which must have been written 1624 not long before his death in 1624, is addressed to his brother Thomas at Brasenose, and shows his usual kindness and thoughtfulness for others in the midst of his own misfortunes. With his customary generosity he had sent Thomas a dog: " I percyve you received the greyhound I sent you which I wish may prove as good as may geve you the best content." His youngest brother he also remembers : " I pray you tell my brother Peter that though I am long in sending him a sword yet he shall find me sure." He begs Thomas not to stand out against his father's wishes that he should take Holy orders, but to be warned by his own sad experience :

" Your letter made me very glad and very sorry, glad in regard you were well and that since I could not see you so oft as my heart desyreth yet that I might heare from you in writinge w^h I desyre may be as oft as you can, sorry because I perceyved by your letter how unkindly my father dealeth with you, but I hope I may well be an example to you to beare all crosses and miseries that can happen you patiently."

By his wife Anne Savile Piers had four children, three daughters and one son, born August 12, 1623, who can have been barely a year old at the time of his father's death. When this took place we have no knowledge. There is no record of Piers's last illness, nor are there any letters mentioning the fact of his death or the date ; he seems to have been dead to his father from the moment of his marriage. Remorse the old man must have felt, for by a petition to the Court of Wards and Liveries signed by him in November 1624, we gather that he was anxious to secure the custody of the infant boy.

Under the existing laws the king had power over all minors. One of the feudal privileges which had come down to James I from the Middle Ages, to which he tenaciously held, was his right to the wardship of young heirs and the marriage of heiresses, and this privilege was considerably abused and was made a means of fiscal extortion.

The first intimation we get of the death of Piers is from a petition addressed by Thomas, brother of Sir Peter Legh, on November 7, 1624, to the King :

"The humble petition of Thomas Legh your Majesty's ould servant, prays that whereas the petitioner's nephew being his father's eldest son, marryed without his consent and died in his displeasure leaving one only son an infant, the body of the said infant might be granted to the petitioner who only desires it in order that the grandfather's favour may be procured towards the infant, hoping that he will estate the Inheritance upon him when hee seeth that hee may dispose of his education and mariage at his pleasure, which may recompense his father's offence and keepe the lands in the right course of descent, and which the Petitioner only desireth for the love hee bore to his said Nephew."

Armed with his petition Thomas Legh went off to Royston, where the King and Court were in residence. We learn that

"His Majesty is graciously pleased to grant this petition if it be not contrary to the instructions given to the Courte of Wardes, and to that purpose requires the Master of the Wardes to consider of it and certifye his opinion to his Majesty."

There were, however, many difficulties to be got over. Red tape played as important a part in the seventeenth as it does in the twentieth century, and although the King seemed willing enough, his sanction did not appear to be sufficient without the concurrence of the sacred Master of the Court of Wards and Liveries. This was probably subterfuge on the part of James, for Thomas Legh was told that "where the King intends a denial he puts it off to his officers." A letter addressed to Sir Peter Legh (who seems to have concurred in the sending of Thomas's petition) from Peter Daniel of Over Tabley, one of the Knights of the Council in the Parliament of 1625, mentions that

> "The same day y^t your man arrived in London your brother came. I spoke to him and y^t day he intended to goe towards Royston. Since then I heard not from him how he speedeth. Ye Court is soe farr remote at Royston y^t we can have noe entercourse by letters."

The village of Royston was no further remote than Cambridgeshire. Here James I had built himself a house which he used principally for purposes of hunting and hawking, and here he was staying with his favourite, the Earl of Somerset, when he received the news of the murder of Sir Thomas Overbury. Lord Somerset, who was suspected of complicity in the crime, was arrested in the King's presence, and it is said that James, who a moment before had been leaning on his favourite's shoulder, said coolly as soon as he had been removed from the apartment, "Now the de'el go with thee, for I will never see thy face any more."

Another of James I's favourites who got into trouble about this time was Archibald Armstrong,* his "fool" or jester, who afterwards gained great social distinction and made a large fortune. A curious proclamation addressed to the High

---

* Archibald Armstrong, known as "Archie," jester to James I and Charles I; supposed to have been a sheep-stealer; gained social distinction at Court; credited with having written "A Banquet of Jests," which appeared in 1630; died 1672.

Sheriff of Cambridge and Huntingdon, written from Royston and signed " James Rex," is preserved at Lyme. It states the King's pleasure that the body of his " sometyme fool Archibald Armestrong " having been received into the custody of the said High Sheriff " for some thefts by him annciently committed, Our pleasure is that forthwith he receive his tryall according to law and justice for malefactors in that case provided. And this shall be your sufficient warrant." He was ultimately expelled from Court in 1637 for insulting Archbishop Laud.

To revert to the petition. Apparently there was the usual delay in matters of this kind. Thomas Legh returned from Royston with the Earl of Anglesey * and together they waited upon Sir Robert Naunton,† whose answer was that he would confer with Sir Walter Pye,‡ "who was his director" and would give them his reply at a future date. Thomas Legh, however, was determined to get the matter settled as soon as possible, and begged Peter Daniel to accompany him to Sir Walter Pye; Daniel advising his friend to " spare no money in fees and bribes," otherwise, even with the King's sanction, he would obtain nothing. Thomas must " fee ye Attorney well," he writes to Sir Peter, telling him of their intended visit, " with 10 pieces or 5 at ye least, ye rest would follow, when he had a good reference he must to Court again, get ye King's hand to it and then bring it to ye priuie seale, and then to ye Kinge to signe, and then bring it to ye Great Seale and soe he makes it perfect. I am a little practised in these things," he adds, alluding no doubt to former experiences of his own, " and parsimony doth much hinder a business. This is a golden age." They went accordingly to Sir Walter Pye with the information that they had the King's sanction—subject to that of the Court—but Thomas Legh, who evidently had a private interview, seems to have

* Kit Villiers, first Earl of Anglesey (1593–1630), younger brother of Buckingham.
† Sir Robert Naunton (1563–1635), politician ; Master of the Court of Wards, 1623–35.
‡ Sir Walter Pye (1571–1635), lawyer ; a favourite of Buckingham, who procured his nomination as Attorney of the Court of Wards and Liveries in 1621.

met with little or no success. Peter Daniel writes to Sir Peter that "Mr Attorney told him plainly yt he would be against it yt it was against ye King's profit, it would overthrow his Courte yet yt he knew you [Sir Peter] and he thought another course would be as effectual." Their next step was to approach Sir Humphrey Davenport, serjeant-at-law and judge, who gave it as his opinion that a second petition must be framed, this time from Sir Peter Legh himself and to be addressed to the Court of Wards and Liveries, nominating certain gentlemen by his writing and under his hand, and stating that to these and none other should the body of the ward be granted. Accordingly a rough copy of a second petition, drawn up in practically the same words as the first, was forwarded to Sir Peter for his approval and sanction, Daniel begging that if there be anything offensive in this or in his letters Sir Peter will " bury it in your love, it is want of judgment." He gives directions that a space may be left at the top of the paper " yt we may give them their due stile."

From a subsequent letter, dated Gray's Inn, December 10, 1624, written from Peter Daniel to Sir Peter, we learn that " ye petition had no good conclusion, yet at hap nab it was delivered." Mr. Attorney promised to do his best, but it was evidently a question of how much greasing of palms there was to be. The official was reported to have " acted his part," and Daniel advises that as " he hath delt so freely and carefully in ye penning of it you may, (if you thinke soe fitt) augment ye bountie."

Ultimately the matter was settled, and Sir Peter, who is described as " a gent of greate antiquity and of greate worth in the Counties of Cheshire and Lancashire," was granted the custody of the infant with the joint guardian-ship of the following four gentlemen : Sir Richard Molyneux, Sir Charles Gerard, Peter Daniel, and the said Thomas Legh, " at such price and Consideration to be paid to his Majesty as they and the Court should decide." What the sum was does not appear.

The boy must from this time have been taken from his

mother and removed to Lyme.   He is frequently referred to in the letters as " little Peter," but there is no mention of Sir Peter's extending his forgiveness to his daughter-in-law, though she apparently visited at Lyme in after years.   She was allowed to see her son at stated intervals.   Writing to her brother-in-law Francis from Newton, Lancashire, where she seems to have removed after her husband's death, she hopes they are all well at Lyme,

> " and littell Peter, pray send me word if he learne his Booke well, say his prayers dayly, please his grandfather and carry himself to all as is fitting, which I shall be glad to heare of him—may God bless him."

She evidently saw very little of her only son—poor soul. " Sometyme this summer I purpose if it please God to see him," she writes to Francis, " but the time when I cannot yet set downe."   Parting with her precious only boy must have wrung her heart with anguish, but she may have comforted herself with the thought that it was necessary to put her own feelings on one side and do what was best for the boy ; she writes gratefully, " beholden for your kindness to my dear Jewill." None of the family, except perhaps Francis and Thomas, seem to have been very kind to her.   Anne Bold, writing to her father, alludes to her sister-in-law in somewhat scathing terms : " Sir Thomas Savile is come home and made a Lord * and my sister is com a widow as she went."   In a letter written in 1635, before the death of Sir Peter, she speaks of a visit to Lyme, so her company was probably tolerated for short periods.

* Lord Savile of Pontefract.

CHAPTER VII

SIR PETER AND HIS FRIENDS

LYME must have been completed by this date and was evidently 1623 looked upon as a show place and was being much talked about. " My stay in these parts," writes Sir Thomas Savage * in 1623, " by reason of my enjoyned attendance att London falleth out to be so shorte, that by no meanes I shalbe able att this tyme to see either you, as you request, or that place of yours that I have often hard off." Edward Kluttall, another correspondent, states that he was thirty miles on his way to visit Sir Peter, " but some speatiall (special) service of ye Kings in my office ffetched mee back againe otherwyse I hadde hadd a great hope to have injoyed soe much happines as to have kissed yor hand and to have seen Lyme."

Lord Herbert of Cherbury † thinks it is an age

> " since I have had the honner to see you, and more that no good occation gives me leave to send or inquire of your healthe. I am not in the number of those friends who delight in ye acquaintance only of kindred, or alliance, but with a further desire propose both to them & to myselfe such correspondency as may dayly make the bond more perfect."

Adding that when he is released from his engagements he will " presume to come and learne the way yt with lesse danger I may presume to be my wife's guide."

---

* Sir Thomas Savage, created Viscount Savage, 1626, was Chancellor of the Queen's Court at Westminster, 1634; died 1635; buried in the Savage chapel in Macclesfield church.

† Richard, second Baron Herbert of Cherbury, eldest son of Edward, first Lord, married Mary, daughter of John, first Earl of Bridgewater, nephew of Dorothy, Lady Legh. He was a great Royalist, performed many services for Charles I, and was chosen to conduct Queen Henrietta Maria from Bridlington to Oxford, 1643.

In 1626, Sir Richard Wilbraham * writes to excuse Lord Derby † from accepting the hospitality of Sir Peter,

> " hee wished me to let you know that you shall find him your feathfull frend to serve you, but desireth hee may be excused for coming unto you att this time from things falling cros to his intentions, butt this next summer hee will see you wth his Lady in his hand."

These letters, with many others, are abundant proof of the position that Sir Peter occupied, and of the affection and esteem in which he was held by all who knew him. Frequent communications were also passing between him and his relations. He was in constant correspondence with his wife's nephew, Sir John Egerton, afterwards first Earl of Bridgewater, who had married one of the daughters of Ferdinando, fifth Earl of Derby. On July 10, 1610, she writes that " Sans ceremonia " she must make bold again to intreat Sir Peter's " commiseration of this bearer, whose wrongs which he susteneth by rude and lawless fellowes is well knowen unto you," describing her protégé as " a pore Innocent lambe amongst a Number of Ravenous wolves," and beseeching her uncle to " patronize and direct him else his case will be worse."

Sir John Egerton writes in 1612 :

> " This Gent is so gladde that he hath furnisht you with Musicke this Christenmasse, [begging to know when he may enjoy the company of his respected uncle and aunt,] when you can come and will come you shall be hartely welcome. [He also sends his best thanks] for those Mastiffs which my Aunt and yourself sent me up, [adding,] I am turned Courtier more in a month of late then heretofore in a yeare, but neither Courte nor Country can make me other then
>   " Your most assured loving frend and respectfull
>   " Nephewe J. EGERTON."

Though the letters from his relations generally contain requests for money, venison, or favours of some kind, they bear strong evidence of the high respect and affection in which the

* Sir Richard Wilbraham of Woodhey, created Baronet 1621 ; married Grace, sister of Thomas, first Viscount Savage.

† William, sixth Earl of Derby, brother of Ferdinando, fifth Earl, said to have been a great traveller; married, 1594, Elizabeth, daughter of Edward Vere, seventeenth Earl of Oxford. He died 1642.

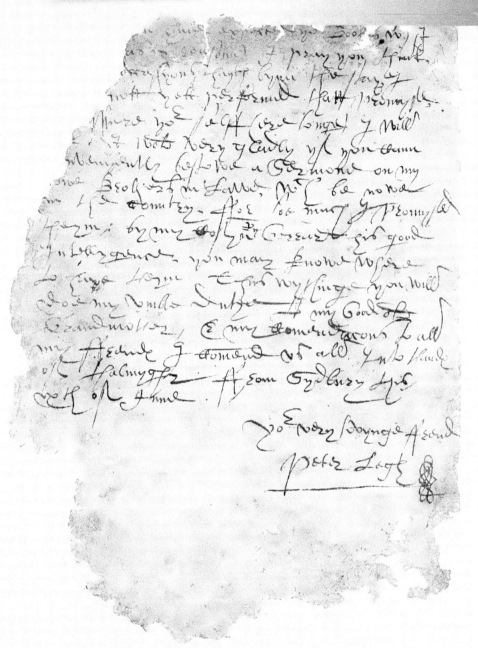

FACSIMILE OF A LETTER FROM SIR PETER LEGH TO HIS CHAPLAIN, 1591

. . haue expected y^e Bookes wch I . (as in reasonn) I pray you think . . occassyons hayth bynn the stay, I . . not yett performed thatt promyse, . . assure yor selff (ere longe) I will . . I wold very gladly yf you cann conveniently bestowe a Sermone on my towe Brothers in Lawe, wch be nowe in the Country—ffor soe much I promysed theym : by my Cosyn Rch : Gerrard his good Intellygence—you may knowe where to have theym. Thus wyshinge you will doe my vmble Dutye to my Good old Grandmother, & my Comendacons to all my ffrends I comend vs all into thands of thalmyghty. ffrom Sydbury this IXth of June.
                                                          Yo^r very lovynge ffrend
                                                                    PETER LEGH

writers held their august relative. He was a man of great strength of character and indomitable will, whose opinion carried much weight and was held to be of the highest value. Seldom did any family event occur amongst his even distant relatives, to whom he was constantly appointed guardian or trustee, without his help being solicited, his godchildren were innumerable, and he was generally looked up to as a personage of high worth and esteem. He was in advance of his times. His taste was good and refined, as we see by the additions he made to the house during his lifetime: the beautiful " Stag Parlour," for which he was responsible, which has already been described. His love of the arts, music, painting, and letters proclaim him to have been a man of cultivated tastes. He had inherited his grandfather's fondness for heraldry; he wrote a good and educated hand and his travels had broadened his mind and given him a polish that was not often found amongst his contemporaries. He was on intimate terms with all that was best in society, art, and letters. Essex, Leicester, Buckingham, the successive Earls of Derby and Rutland were all his friends, while his correspondents included such brilliant lights in the literary and musical world as Elias Ashmole and Henry Lawes. With John Bradshawe, the regicide judge, he was on the best of terms, though himself a staunch Royalist; a fortunate circumstance, which was to have good effect on the family fortunes in years to come during the Civil Wars, and probably saved the house from destruction or pillage.

His was a fine character, marred by intolerant harshness towards his children in matters connected with their lives and careers, which proceeded mainly from inordinate vanity —his besetting sin. He never conceived it possible that he could be mistaken ; any decision of his must be final, and must never be combated or questioned.

On the principle that " one good turn deserves another " Sir Peter was entreated by his brother-in-law, Lord Gerard,*

* Thomas, first Lord Gerard, eldest son of Sir Gilbert Gerard, Master of the Rolls; married Alice, daughter of Sir Thomas Rivet.

to use his influence with the latter's eldest son Gilbert,* knighted in 1611, at the creation of Henry, Prince of Wales. The young man appears to have given his father a good deal of trouble in 1614–15, and it was very much more serious trouble than that for which Sir Peter had solicited the help of Lord Gerard in his own case. Gilbert Gerard had married Elinor, daughter and heiress of Thomas Dutton of Dutton, who died in 1614, when Gilbert's wife succeeded to the estates and fortune, and Lord Gerard evidently considered that the young people were inclined to be wasteful and extravagant :

> " For my sonne Hee is yong and not Experyenced in courses of Land . . . I pray you both advyse and direct Hym in what is fytting. I wish my Syster Dutton " [the widow ; the respective fathers- and mothers-in-law immediately assumed this degree of relationship] " may keepe house and my Sonne and daughter to table with her."

The young man was anxious to obtain some appointment in the household of Charles, Prince of Wales, much against his father's wishes, who considered that his son's duty was to live on his estate and endeavour to improve his property :

> " I fear my Sonne's umour is too mutch bente for London and then I shall soone see what will come of Dutton. But as I have ever been most careful of his good so I protest to God if Hee will not be ruled by me and follow my directyons I will not only do Him what Hurte I can in my owne Estate but I will dash all Courses Hee shall runne both with the King and Prynce and turne my love to Hatred if Hee will not follow my directyons. . . . I cannot forget my brother Duttons wordes att the maryage, a Pygeon coming into the Hawle Hee says His House would be made a Pygeon Howse, for this I will disclayme before God and the world and if my Sonne uphold it not with Reputacon I wold Hee had never had it."

As will be seen from this letter and from those of Sir Peter Legh, the parents of those days continued to exercise absolute control over the lives of their children long after they had reached man's estate, and even middle age. Sir Peter was dictating terms to his son Piers after the latter had reached the

---

* Gilbert, eldest son of Thomas, first Lord Gerard ; married Elinor, sole daughter and heiress of Thomas Dutton of Dutton. She ultimately divorced her husband.

age of thirty, and Gilbert Gerard, although his father describes him as " yong," had been married some years when the letter from which we quote was written.

It is not surprising that Lord Gerard should have raised objections to his son's ambition to become associated with the household of Charles, Prince of Wales. The Court of James I was notorious for its profligacy and immorality and could boast of none of the grace and chivalry which had redeemed that of Queen Elizabeth. It had then been the centre of all that was noblest and best in society, art, and letters, but had now sunk to such depths of depravity that most of the self-respecting leading families had withdrawn themselves as much as possible from the capital. The King, surrounding himself with un-worthy favourites and pursuing his policy of the divine right of kings, attempting to rule without reference to the Constitution or consideration for the wishes of his people, was neither beloved nor respected by his subjects. He expected and exacted from them passive obedience to and humble acquiescence in all his wishes, and at home and abroad England had fallen from the high position she had occupied during the previous reign.

One does not hear of so many royal progresses as were made by Queen Elizabeth, who loved to honour her subjects with her presence at their country houses, but James must have descended upon them occasionally, an unexpected and somewhat unwelcome guest. Lord Gerard writes in a great flutter to Sir Peter on January 22, 1614–15, from Chippenham his house near Newmarket (which his wife had inherited from her father Sir Thomas Rivet, in 1582), bemoaning the fact that " the King being now so neere and every day expected heere, for so Hee tells me, and no place Hee hath to Hawke in but my Orchard poole."

Sir Peter evidently did his best with young Sir Gilbert Gerard :

" After my receipt of the first of your two last letters, [he writes to his brother-in-law] " I did shortly after go over to Dutton and because I had partly understood by some of my frends that my Nephew your sonne had a desire to bestowe himself for some tyme in the Prince's

Court, I did then of myself (out of my true love to him and respect to you, and yr house) endeavour myself to diswade him from that Course,"

taking the young man over with him to Croxteth * where Sir Richard and Lady Molyneux joined with him in their persuasions. Young Gilbert Gerard, however, though anxious to show all dutiful regard to his father,

> "seemed much greeved that you should so much oppose this his desire, yet wee cold not preceive but that he did still somewhat affect that course, howbeit he hath often protested unto me that he will live within his Compas, and proportion his means to answer his expences."

A contrite letter from the delinquent heartily thanks Sir Peter for his

> "worthye love and favours alwaies towards me showed, the which I shall more esteeme and prize then the greatest jewell, be it never of so great a value."

These were, however, mere words. After his father's death in 1618, he seems to have forced his wife to take some form of legal action, probably to prevent his dissipation of her entire fortune. Sir Peter, who was evidently a trustee, was doing what he could to help her.

Writing to his wife Dorothy from London in 1620, he alludes to "this poore lady's business," which he regrets has not progressed ; "I had much rather she sholde embrace peace (if with any indifferent means it will be gott) then extremitie wch is sure to beget much inconvenyencie and mischiefe." He arranges for a meeting between Lady Gerard and the great Duke of Buckingham, which he considers will be to the advantage of the distressed lady :

> "I have been often with my Lord of Rutland † whom I have fully acquainted with her miserie, and yesterday at his house dined his great son-in-law ‡ and his Lady wife, and his Lady Mother, and at after

* Croxteth, near Liverpool, the seat of the Molyneux family.
† Francis, sixth Earl of Rutland ; married, first, Frances, daughter of Sir Henry Knevet of Charlton, by whom he had one daughter married to George Villers, Duke of Buckingham.
‡ The Duke of Buckingham.

SIR PETER AND HIS FRIENDS

dinner I brought my Lady Gerard and her Mother and alsoe Sir Anth : * and his Lordship did nobly presnt them unto my Lord of Buckingham whoe hath promised to do her good."

Two years later, in 1622, Lord Gerard died and Elinor then 1622 married Lord Kilmorey, becoming stepmother to her son-in-law, Robert Needham, who had married her second daughter, Frances.

Among the numerous godchildren of Sir Peter Legh's we may here mention Thomas Cromwell, created, in 1624, Viscount Lecale, who, although an intimate friend and follower of Essex, remained faithful to the King during the Civil Wars. He writes frequently to his godfather, generally for money or excusing himself for non-payment of debts, and Sir Peter seems to have been very good to him :

" I am a child of yours [he writes to Sir Peter on January 22, 1622] who esteems himself most happy in your love."

In another letter he excuses himself for not repaying the sum of £50 :

" It is a hard time to get money and I am ashamed you have beene so long without your due, [adding with delightful candour his method for obtaining the money :] as concerning the money so nobly you lent me I will borrow it this next week of some frend, and present you with it and my service together."

Thomas Cromwell probably visited at Lyme with Lord Essex about this date, on the occasion of the celebrated stag-hunt described by Wilson the historian and mentioned in a former chapter.

As has already been said, Sir Peter counted amongst his intimate friends John Bradshawe, afterwards the regicide judge, whose signature heads the list of those who signed the death warrant of Charles I, and who presided at his trial. John Bradshawe was the third son of Henry Bradshawe " the elder," the descendant of an old Puritan family, hailing originally from Derbyshire and settled in Cheshire in the first years

* Sir Anthony St. John, second son of Oliver, Lord St. John of Bletsoe; married as his second wife (he being her third husband) Thomasine, widow of Thomas Dutton of Dutton, and mother of Elinor, Lady Gerard.

of the seventeenth century. His mother, who died in giving him birth, was the daughter and heiress of Ralph Winnington of Offerton. The home of John Bradshawe and his parents was at Marple, a beautiful old Jacobean house about five miles distant from Lyme. The house, which stands upon a rock of red sandstone, commands a splendid view over the valley of the Goyt and the surrounding hills, and is one of the most interesting in this part of Cheshire. It contains some priceless Gobelin tapestry, oak panelling, good pictures, and many other works of art.

It is believed that John Bradshawe was not born at Marple, but at " The Place," a smaller house in the neighbourhood. In the registers of Stockport parish church for the year 1602 appears the following notice : " December : 1602, the Sonne of Henry Bradshawe of Marple was baptized the 10th." In another hand the word " traitor " is added. At Marple is shown the room occupied by the regicide, which contains a splendid old oak bed, richly carved, and inscribed with curious mottoes. On the outside runs the following : " A man without Mercy of Mercy shall miss Bvt he shall have Mercy that merciful is." Round the inside : " Sleep not til V consider how V have spent the day if well thank God, if not Repent." Above the bed-head are the words : " Love God not Gold." The lattice window, which contains small panes of stained glass, is engraved with this verse :

> " My brother Henry shall heir the land
> My brother Frank shall be at his command ;
> While I, poor Jack, shall do that which all
> the world shall wonder at ! "

These lines, tradition states, were scribbled by President Bradshawe on a tombstone in the churchyard at Macclesfield, when he was being educated at the grammar school there. If this is so, they were strangely prophetic. Marple is said to be haunted by the ghost of Charles I, who walks on the terrace carrying his head in his hands.

A curious letter addressed by Bradshawe to Sir Peter about

this date gives much of the news of the day and is a vivid **1623**
picture of the life of the time. It is written from Gray's Inn,
where he was studying the law, and is in a very minute and
scholarly hand, most laborious to decipher. By the beginning of the letter we gather that he was having some dispute
with his father, who was dictating to his son and possibly
interfering with his work, and the future judge was soliciting
the help of Sir Peter Legh, thanking him at the same time for
past favours " in these my troublesome stormes, towards me
so meane and unworthy of the least expression of your love."
He promises at the same time " to wryte it with a pen of brasse
in the tables of my heart." He kept his word, for it was
certainly owing to his influence that Lyme escaped the fate of
other neighbouring houses, Bramhall, Adlington, and Wythenshawe, the two last of which were besieged and sacked during
the Civil Wars, the marks of the bullets in the walls being still
plainly visible.

The rest of the letter is as follows :

" Concerning my letter to my ffather I will onelie say thus much.
What ffruit that ffather may expect to come to his Sonnes studyes,
that wittinglie doth suppress the instrument of his labors & willinglie
keepe in ffetters the freedom of his mynd ?

" Ffor neglecting the Exercyses of the Howse, it is a fryvolous
objection. Himself hath been satysfyed in it & Mr Damport * will
justify me, knowing I never neglected but one Exercyse of myne owne,
wch was to argue a Case, wch according unto Course another should
haue done for me at my first Comming to the howse, & I by ffeeing
the Butler did of purpose neglect it, onelie deferring the tyme, that
after I had been heere a whyle, I might pleade the Case for my selfe.

" Ffor o^r domestique newes, I haue sent you the Cause of my Lo :
of Oxford † wch is to be heard this Terme, the plot it is thought hath
been, to terrifie him so from his Offyce, as to yeld his place of High
Chamberleyn of England to the swolne ffavoryte ‡ & his famylie, w^ch

* William Davenport, only child of Sir William Davenport of Bramhall, a beautiful old Elizabethan black-and-white house, still in existence, now the property
of Mr. Charles Nevill. Bramhall passed from the possession of the Davenport family
in the early part of the nineteenth century.

† Henry de Vere, eighteenth Earl of Oxford, 1593-1625; prisoner in the Tower in
1621 and 1623, through offence given to Buckingham.

‡ The Duke of Buckingham.

his great heart will never yeld to ;ʳ & therefor make him, if not depend-
ing, beholding to his greatest Enemie, it is lykelie, for his words he
shall be shrewdlie Censured, & so remayne in Durance, till Buckingham
returne from Spayne & gratify him wᵗʰ his liberte, & a Release of his
ffyne & so assuage his stomacke by this his plotted good turne. As it
succeeds, I will certyfie you. The Ships are yet on the Downs, hauing
been crossed & kept backe by contrary Wynds from their voyage.
We hears no newes from Spayne, nor haue not heard, this moneth,
onelie as it is suspected, the Princes Entertaynmᵗ continues not
so gloryous, as it hath been. It is hitherto a true observation,
that England hath been ffatall to Dukes, but aboue all most
omynous unto the Dukes of Buckingham, of wᶜʰ the Marquesse hath
the Tytle, & lykewyse Earle of Coventrie, & the Duke of Lenox *
is created, Duke of Richmond & Earle of Newcastle upon Tyne, &
more Dukes & Earles are expected to honor this liberall Age. Kit
Villiers † is made Earle of Anglesey in recompense of Barkshyres
escape, & to increase the kindred hath marryed with Shelton his
Mothers sisters Daughter, but we are so used to wonders, that this is
none at all. Lenox, Arundell,‡ Pembrooke,§ & some other Nobles, who
are styled the Lords of the Receptions, haue been at Southampton &
Portsmouth to prepare Royall lodgings & enterteynmᵗ for the Prince ‖
and his Bryde of Spayne, whensoever they arryue.

" To Conclude all my Relatyons, I will tell you of one mad prancke
that happened wᵗʰin theise two nights. Sr Thomas Bartley was
arrested hard by Grayes Inne, for 4000ˡ debt, & was carryed to the
higher end of Holborne, & Committed under Custody ; About 12 of the
Clocke at night, some Gentlemen of oʳ Howse & of Lincolnes Inne, met
together for his Rescue, broke downe the howse, took him away wᵗʰ
them, beat the Constables Sergeants & Watchmen, & though St
Gyles was raysed & almost all Holborne, yet they wᵗʰ their swords
& pistolls kept them of, & brought him along to Grayes Inne,
there were dyvers hurt wᵗʰ Halbreds, & about 200 swords drawne,
& at least 2000 people. There are 5 or 6 gents taken & sent
to Newgate, & wee heare that the Names of above 60 gents are gyven
up to the King, What will be done about it, we shall know in tyme.

* Stuart, second Duke of Lennox, and Duke of Richmond, 1574–1624 ; Steward
of the Household ; buried in Henry VII's Chapel in Westminster Abbey.

† Kit Villiers, first Earl of Anglesey, younger brother of George Villiers, first
Duke of Buckingham ; married Elizabeth Sheldon of Hooby, Co. Leicester.

‡ Thomas, second Earl of Arundel, 1586–1646 ; Earl Marshal, 1621 ; imprisoned
for hostility to Buckingham, 1626.

§ William Herbert, third Earl of Pembroke of the second creation, son of Henry,
second Earl, by his marriage with the sister of Sir Philip Sidney.

‖ Charles, Prince of Wales.

There are more Murthers, drownings, death & villaynies, then hath been knowne in London of long tyme before. I had almost forgot the Moderator, a booke uncerteyn whether wrytten by a Papist or a Statesman (for indeed they are now so lincked, as scarce can admit distinguishm^t) for preparing a way to Reconciliation, betwixt the Papists & us; howsoever, by whomsoever, or to what end soever it is penned, it is a treatise I am sure, excellently curious & Cauttlous,* and may stand our syde in much stedd, when they please to make use of it.

" I will now drawe to an end, intreating yor Worship not to mis-construe my forwardnes in taking notyce of theise things, for it agrees with my Genius to haue some smattering herein, neyther do they any Whyt hinder, but further my studyes & judgment.

" And so wth most humble thanks for all yor Worships favours, I remayne yor debtor for them, beseeching God Almightie to preserve & prosper you for the good of many, & my most specyll Comfort
" ever resting
" Yo^r Worships to dispose
" Jo : BRADSHAWE.

" Grayes Inne the First Day of the Terme."

The date of this letter is placed by experts at June 13, 1623, 1623 when the writer must have been nearly twenty-one years of age, Sir Peter being sixty. John Bradshawe was called to the bar in 1627, having previously served for several years as clerk to an attorney in Congleton, a town about twenty miles distant from Marple, where he also practised as a provincial barrister. He married Mary, daughter of Thomas Marbury of Marbury, Cheshire; she had no children, and at her death was buried in Westminster Abbey, but after the Restoration her remains were removed to the churchyard outside the Abbey.

It is said that John Bradshawe accepted very unwillingly the office of President of the Commission which sat at West-minster for the trial of Charles I. Be that as it may, his behaviour towards the royal prisoner was characterized by an overbearing brutality for which his memory is execrated, nor can any conscientious desire efficiently to discharge his duty excuse the coarse and gratuitous insults which he heaped upon his King.

* Cautelous—artful, artfully cautious.

CHAPTER VIII

THE HOUSE UNDER CHARLES I

On the accession of the new King, Sir Peter thought it prudent to sue for a pardon or bill of indemnity as he had done when James ascended the throne in 1603. This was obtained on February 10, 1626.

There were plenty of busybodies then as now, always ready to make mischief and stir up strife, and Sir Peter experienced this, as we gather by a letter from Sir Humphrey Davenport,* an eminent lawyer of the time, to the Archbishop of York. Representations appear to have been made to his Grace that Sir Peter had been defective in repairing an old ruined chapel within the limits of the parish church of Wigan. Sir Humphrey points out that this chapel has been in the same condition "tyme out of memorie," that the church of Wigan is complete without it and is more than sufficiently large for the attendance, "seldom a quarter of it is peopled at the time of divine service." He then proceeds to give a list of Sir Peter's good works :

> "The erecting a free school at Winwick in Lancashire and endowing of the same, in building a Chaple at Winwick aforesaid to his very great charges, and in rebuilding or re-edifying the Chappell of Disley and furnishing the same with foure bells, formall seats, and all fittinge ornaments, and maintaininge of a Curate and preacher ther uppon his owne charges. And likewyse in buildinge of a school house there wch hee intendeth to endowe wth landes to maintaine a Schoolmaster for the good of the Countrie there abouts."

He begs at the same time that Sir Peter may be left to himself for the performance of such pious acts "wherein he hath already made so good an entrance without any further

---

* Davenport of Bramhall (1566–1645); judge, King's Sergeant and adviser to Charles I.

or new trouble by way of suit to bee Inforced to this now Raised against him." Apparently the Archbishop was prevailed upon and Sir Peter was no more molested.

He got into further trouble, however, with his friends the Derbys, owing to mischief-makers :

> "According to your desire," writes Sir Roger Bradshaigh of Haigh, "I went to my Lorde * and found him hard by Litherland hawkeing where I did deliver your letter, he did take it, for anie thing I could discover, verie well and promised to make an atonement both there and in his owne chamber at Knowseley. I had an houre or two of conference with my Ladie in her bedchamber, where she did charge you with manie discurteous speeches that you should use against the house of Lathom. I did answere (soe farr accordinge to my rude manner) as except you make it good I shall be utterlie shamed or discredited there . . . I assure myselfe you have beene mightelie wronged to the Countesse."

Sir Peter thanks him gratefully for his " late paynes to my Lord and Lady of Derby and firme and friendly answers in my behalf," for which he assures his friend he shall receive " no manner of toche [blemish] or disparagement, for I knowe myselfe so cleare & Innocent as I shall be well able to answer anie acusation yt shall be brought before my face."

While everywhere abroad was war and strife, the family at Lyme was pursuing the even tenor of its way. Lady Legh was busy with her housekeeping, and was going backwards and forwards between Lyme and Worsley, Francis was helping his father with the care and management of the estate, Thomas was working hard at Oxford with occasional visits to Lyme, and little Peter, who had been provided with a tutor—a Mr. Woodcock—was growing up, learning his lessons and was endearing himself to his grandfather. A picture of a beautiful boy of about fourteen, in a green silk doublet slashed with white satin, hangs on the staircase at Lyme, and is probably a portrait of little Peter. It is inscribed " P. Legh," and bears the date 1636. We hear very little of Peter, youngest son of Sir Peter, but

---

* William, sixth Earl of Derby, born 1561 (or 1562), said to have been a great traveller. He married, in 1594, Elizabeth, daughter of Vere, seventeenth Earl of Oxford. He died 1642.

125

he was also living at Lyme up to the date of his marriage in
1631.

The building of Lyme was now complete, and beautiful
pieces of furniture were being acquired. The gradual rise in the
general standard of comfort which had begun in the reign of
Queen Elizabeth was continued in that of her successor. Inigo
Jones had returned from Italy full of enthusiasm for Palladio
and his school, and his influence was soon to be felt in the
interiors of English houses. Chairs and tables were made with
graceful spiral legs, and beautifully inlaid cabinets were taking
the place of the heavy, massive carved oak of the Elizabethan
period.*

A certain portion of each year Sir Peter had, of course, to
spend in London attending to his parliamentary duties. He
also visited Bath on several occasions to take the waters, and
was sometimes at Worsley, his wife's house in Lancashire, as
well as at his own Lancashire house, Haydock Lodge, Bradley
being inhabited by his daughter-in-law. During his absences
he was, however, receiving constant reports of what was going
on at Lyme from his agents and stewards. Dorothy, Lady
Legh, seems to have been more occupied with the selling
of her sheep and oxen than with the details connected
with the decoration of the house, which appear to have
been always settled by Sir Peter himself. Writing to Francis
Legh from Haydock, Lancashire, he says :

> " I pray you sell both woole and sheepe if possibly you can, and if you
> cannot sell as you wold then as you can. My wife hath sold for 15s
> a stone and makes 16 lb waight in a stone, and if you can sell me some
> sheepe I wold faine have Michell to varnishe the seeling in the parlor
> not with a light cullor, but lyke to this at Haydocke a sad cullor, and
> send to Manchester for what he shall direct ffor that purpose."

* A very fine specimen of a treasure chest and chest of drawers combined may
have been added to the furniture at Lyme about this period. The chest, which is of
satinwood, richly inlaid with ebony and heavily bound with brass, is fitted with
secret drawers, no doubt intended to contain money or important papers; the chest
of drawers is of walnut and satinwood inlaid with ebony, and has three long and
two small drawers with drop handles and richly chased brass locks. It is believed
that the combination of the treasure chest and chest of drawers is seldom seen.
Some spiral-legged chairs and tables belonging to the same period were probably
added at this date.

PETER LEGH, 1636
Killed in a duel, 1641–2
From a Portrait at Lyme

The British workman was apt to be slow and procrastinating in his work in the middle of the seventeenth century. " Send to the lame Richard in Macclesfield," writes Sir Peter, " to come presently and fall to his worke, or else he shall have noe more of my custome this year nor the next."

George Bowden, his agent, begs to know if he wishes to have any lay cattle in the park; 16s. a beast appears to have been the price obtained. Five of the servants have left, and

> " we doe stand in great nide [need] of a woman to searse [clean] the swyne and to doe anie drugeinge work there is nideful." The swine-herd, he writes, " is verie sorrie to go and saith he will do aniething that he may stay and will keep himself unpide [unpaid] until you come home."

A further letter from one servant to another speaks of their master being " evilly dealt withal both by the tenants swyne lying in the woods and by excessive gathering [gleaning]," the man complaining that one of the retainers does not report these abuses " or it might be as bad a tayle might be told against him . . . and he is content to wink or be silent "; the writer adding that there should be " restrayninge of such as wth gunes, boose & doges distroye the game before they be all kild up "; Sir Peter should be told of this, " and if hee will not cause these things better lookt unto hee will have the loose and you and others the shame."

In a family with such warlike traditions it seems strange that none of the sons should have been soldiers, fighting abroad at this time with so many of their countrymen; but Francis was no doubt incapacitated by ill-health from adopting an active profession, Thomas was in Holy orders, while Piers had died, as we have seen, in 1624, and Peter, the youngest, was destined for a parliamentary career. With him began the family of Legh of Bruch, a Lancashire property which Sir Peter acquired in 1622, and left to his youngest son. He had had difficulties connected with the transaction. His " unthankful Cousins (whom I have ever too much respected) ye Sonnes and daughters of Bruch," as he writes to his wife Dorothy in 1620, lodging " a verrie fowle and falce petition against me in the houses of parliament." The matter was settled, however, and the property duly acquired and entailed.

1630 Wedding bells were ringing at Lyme in 1630, Francis and Thomas both married that year, the former to Anne, daughter and heiress of Sir Edmund Fenner of Hamton Gey, Oxfordshire, whose acquaintance he probably made during the time he was at Oxford; the latter to Lettice, daughter and co-heiress of Sir George Calveley of Lea. Peter, the youngest son, married, probably the year following, Frances, daughter of Edward Bellot of Great Moreton, near Congleton. He was twice married, his second wife being Anne, daughter of H. Birkenhead of Chester.

Francis had been living at Lyme since his departure from Oxford, and after his Uncle Thomas's death in 1626, he seems to have helped in the management of the estate during Sir Peter's absence in London and elsewhere. His father writes to him frequently, giving directions as to the sheep and cattle and other farm details. Thomas, after his ordination, was living at Oxford, where he had been working very hard to obtain a Proctorship. "Make us happy with your good company," writes John Meredith to him on March 19, 1627, " the Proctering time Drawing on or rather your Proctering time will be a motive to hasten you. Dr Mansell * and Gil: Sheldon † kindly salute you." His friends were actively canvassing on his behalf, Sir Thomas Walmesley ‡ writing on February 10, 1628–9, to Mr. Lawrence Broadwood :

> " I am become a heartie sutor unto you in the behalfe of a deare frend of myne Mr Th : Legh fellow of your howse. I perceive his purpose is to stand for the Proctorshippe and is opposed by Mr. Worrall. I pray you lett me begg your voice and furtherance for Mr Legh whose good disposition I know will studdie & strive to requite you to the full."

* Francis Mansell (1579–1663), Principal of Jesus College, Oxford ; Fellow of all Souls.
† Gilbert Sheldon, afterwards Archbishop of Canterbury (1596–1677) ; Chaplain to Lord Keeper Coventry ; Warden of All Souls, 1626–45 ; prominent adviser of Charles II.
‡ Sir Thomas Walmesley, a Lancashire magnate, represented Clitheroe and Lancashire itself in Parliament ; died 1641–2.

Mr. Broadwood writes on the same subject to his son, a Fellow of Brasenose :

> " I am intreated by an old frend of yours & myne, Sr T. Walmesley, to move you by my letter for a kyndnes unto one of his frends and fellow of your howse, Mr Legh Junior. It is for your voice to make him Proctor."

Adding that his son owes his Fellowship to the good offices of Sir Thomas Walmesley,

> " who spake to your late Principal in your behalfe," begging that he will not be " branded with the marke of unthankfulness and deny the request of Sir T. Walmesley, your mother and me."

Thomas Legh was, however, unsuccessful in obtaining the Proctorship, which was given to Thomas Sixesmith, a Fellow of Brasenose and a holder of various college offices.

In 1632 he was presented by his cousin, Lord Molyneux, to the living of Sefton and Walton, a large parish near Croxteth, Lancashire, and here it was that he settled down with his wife Lettice after taking his degree, and here all his children were born.

His two elder sons' marriages must have been entirely to the liking of Sir Peter as the ladies were both heiresses. On April 12, 1631, he writes a very courteous letter to Lady Fenner, who had been visiting at Lyme not long after her daughter's marriage to Francis Legh :

> " Good Sister, I am sorrie you should conceive yor beinge here wth me to be a troble to me, wch I was so glad of as that I muste rather crave pardon of you for that I could not give you so good intertainment as you deserved & myself wished," reminding her at the same time, in his usual businesslike way, that she should " perform towards my son and your daughter the promises and agreements made . . . that there may be that kynd and good dealinge amongst us in all things that appertain to this matche alreadie by God's providence made between our children."

The married life of the young couple, though a happy one, was saddened by the ill-health of Mrs. Francis Legh, who seems to have been an invalid almost from the time of her marriage, and who died only three years afterwards, in 1633, leaving no children.

Lady Fenner was in constant correspondence with her son-in-law, with whom she appears to have been on the best of terms. Her writing and spelling are so atrocious that I have found it necessary to modernize the spelling to a certain extent in order to make the letters intelligible. " I have received your most welcom lines," she writes in December (no date), " wherein you give more thanks then so small a remembrance is worth," the present being two shirts. Francis had evidently returned the compliment by sending a present of venison :

> " You terme it a small trifle, I am of another opinion for I thinke there colde not be a better nor a greater made, and yourself and your wife weare often wished for at the eating of it, and I doe give you many thanks for it, but am angrye that you would not let me paye for the careg [carriage] of it."

She writes in great distress, her daughter, Mrs. Legh, having been taken seriously ill at Lyme :

> " I would to God you had let me know of it before I had gone into Harfordshire for I heare since my coming home that she was sick before I went, and though I doubt not of your care and love to hir, it would have given me a great deale of satisfaction to have bin with hir in hir sickness. I can hardly forbear coming to her now but that I must stay to provide things fit against your coming to Hampton, and I shall make redy the greate Chamber for you and my daughter and the litel chamber for your mayd, and I will make sum shift for your men. I am sorry to confine you to so litel roome, but I cannot tel how to helpe it."

Exercising the usual privilege of a mother-in-law, she was offering her advice and prescribing remedies :

> " You made no mention what her grefe was nether can I understand by Will Pickford [the carrier] what the docter saith it is. I have sent her some preserved burrig [burage] flowers which is a very good comfortable cordial thing, I pray make hir eate often of it. I have sent some allcermas which is a good comfort cordil to cheer the hart and sperets. If she be inclining to be hot then she may take it in a surrup of mulbres or lemons or vilets, but if she be not hot then she

may take as much as will lye upon a knives poynt of it selfe otherwise mingle it in a spone with surrup. I had sent sorup but I was
deseaued [deceived] so praying to God to bless hir and restore hir to
her former health I end with my prayers to the Almite God to blesh
you both

" Your euer louing Mother
" KATHERINE FENNER."

In 1631–2 her health was causing further anxiety : " Franc : 1631–2
Legh," writes his father from Woodhey, Sir Richard Wilbraham's, on March 5, of that year :

> " Since I heard of my daughter's good amendment I resolved to goe
> on my journey, otherwyse I had returned home. If she continue to
> recover, soe as you may well leave her, I shall be willing of your
> cominge into Lanc : accordinge as you wryte, but by anie meanes
> leave her not if it sholde please God that she sholde be worse againe.
> I perceive I shall haue much adoe to get hence and soe from the next
> house I goe to, but by God's help I hope to be at Bould* uppon Thursday
> or Frryday night next, and I purpose uppon Thursday."

On November 18 of the same year Francis gives a very bad
account of his wife, and assures his father that if it were possible
he would come to Lyme, but that if he did so now in his wife's
weak state " the clamerous people hereabouts would have but
too good cause to censure me," but that if she should
mend, he will come only too gladly, " as never man had lesse
comfort in living in any place then I have heere (God of
his mercy put an end to it)," ending with service to his father,
" and our good Lady and Mother your bedfellow, Yr dutiful and
most obedient sonne."

Thomas, in his character of parson, was preaching patience
to the poor afflicted husband :

> " Good Brother, I am hartily sorry to heare the ill news that you
> write to my father concerning yorself and my Sister, and my prayers
> to God shall bee to give a happie & speedie issue to all yor troubles. . . .
> I am now at Lyme, my arrant [errand] was a Communion sermon,
> where I thought there was much misse of you, but I truste in God
> wee shall live to have many of those meetings heere for a better lyfe
> heerafter."

* His daughter Anne's Lancashire home.

He was not always as sympathetic as he might have been. He was comfortably established at Walton, very happy with his wife Lettice, full of his work and interests, and so much taken up with his own affairs as rather to resent the attention 1632 that was bestowed upon poor Francis and his troubles. He writes to his father on November 25, 1632, delighted at the birth of his eldest son, Peter, named after his grandfather, who was also to stand sponsor :

> " Good Sir, My most humble dutie remembred & my wiffes, wth both our humble thankes for this greate favour that you haue done us. You haue encreased the number of yor Name by one more, & ye number of our joyes by manie more, in the midste whereof the very sight of my Brothers Letter is enough to take one off, being still a continuation of a tragicall subject ; the sweete Lorde of Heaven put an ende to his troubles. I am not able to advise what is best for him to doe in this Case of his wives extremity. All our hopes that I can thinke of are this, That God will give her some breathinge fitts of healthe, for otherwise hee cannot leave her wthout much clamour & evil rumours of her freinds and you neede not doubt but hee will take ye first opportunity of her beinge anie thinge well, to come see you," adding messages of thanks to Lady Legh " for her bountie likewise."

The Christmas season, always kept with much rejoicing and merry-making at Lyme, was, in 1632, destined to be a sad one. Mrs. Francis Legh, though slightly better, was still unable to be moved, and Anne Bold, who had hoped to spend it with her father, was prevented from doing so by her husband having a fit of the gout. Thomas and his wife were, however, at Lyme, she having made a great effort to come to please her father-in-law, though her baby was barely a month old. Writing to his brother Francis on St. Stephen's Day, Thomas Legh says :

> " I am exceedinge glad to heare by my father's letter of your own health & my Sisters amendment. I feare I shall not see you heere while I stay on this side, but I hope when you come over you will see Walton ere you returne backe, or if yor returne bee speedier Lett me know & I will come over to you hither to Lyme. My ffather was in a great perplex till hee received yor Letter which came not to him till Christmas Day. There never was a poorer Christmas for companie heere this many a day, my bro : Bold & sister were prevented by his

SIR PETER LEGH, 1631
From a Miniature at Lyme

Dr. THOMAS LEGH
By Hoskins, 1631
From a Miniature at Lyme

old gowtie disease, wch will not leave him for all of his old Coltes tooth. The hoswife is com to her owne home again. God hath blest me with a boye since I saw you, but my wiffe was faine (att my ffathers earnest request to her when hee was att Wallton last, to cast her counte so as to keepe her Christmas wth him) to come a fortnight or more before her time, she was delivered when I was last heere at Lyme, the same day or ye day after that I writ a letter to you. Wee are all ye guestes & my bro : Peters wiffe that are heere at Lyme, & my ffather & all in good health (God be thanked) and ye same to you from ye same bountiful bestower of all health. I pray you doe not overburthen yor minde wth too much thoughtfullnes."

What the mysterious illness was that she suffered from during those three years never transpires, but Mrs. Francis Legh died somewhere between the end of December 1632 and the end of March 1633.

Her daughter's death was a terrible grief to Lady Fenner. " Louing Sonne," she writes to Francis in March, 1633–4 :

" I am glad to see that some lines have found the way through your greifes for then I hope time may much lessen it. I could wish it might quite weare it away, I would be content since it hath pleased God to deprive us of our comfort we might now both of us forget the cause of it, but love and nature have made such an impression in both our hearts that cannot easily be done away. The meditation of the comfort we enjoyed in hir alive doth but increase the sorrow for hir losse. . . . I cannot forget those louing respects I received from you at your parting, and shall keepe them as remembrances both of your loue and hir that is gone."

She sends him a silver tankard " as an expression of my love to you," with a postscript stating that the carriage is paid.

Francis Legh, after his wife's death, returned to live at Lyme, much to his father's joy, who was never so happy as when he had his children round him. Lady Fenner continued to correspond with her son-in-law, to whom she seems to have been devotedly attached. Each letter contains advice in some shape or form ; he is to go on with his " diet drinke," which she is glad to hear has done him good ; she does not press him to come and see her, but when he can do so without fear of hurting himself she will be " most glad " to see him. She is much distressed to hear he has met with an accident, and deputes one of her cousins to write and sympathize in her name :

"Being casually at Hampton with my Lady Fenner," he writes, "she entreated me to let you know that she is heartily sorry for yr misfortune you had in putting yr arm out of joynt." She can't resist prescribing remedies: "If you think fit to apply a seercloth of your Paraceslain plaister to it, she is of opinion it will much comfort & strengthen the sineues & you will finde a greate deal of ease in it." She sends apologies for not writing herself by reason she is troubled with "a rheume in one of her eyes wch is very painful to her, and the lookinge steadfastly uppon any one object would, as I fear, increase the pain."

Again she writes, sorry to hear Francis has been so tortured with his leg :

"Good Sonne, have a care that you bruse it not againe when it is a litel well, I fear you will be too ventious [venturesome] on it for if you bruse it the dead flesh will grow againe. Keep it somewhat hard swathed continually, as well when it is hole as sore, for it will keep the humer from falling into it." She regrets being herself in the doctor's hands, "but I am troubled with my head sometimes with aking and continuall noyse in my head which is very troublesome to me."

She sends him half a dozen handkerchiefs, with the customary formula of her wish that the gift were more worth his acceptance.

Thomas Legh also had his correspondents, amongst whom was Richard Parr, afterwards Bishop of Sodor and Man, an old Brasenose friend, who writes at great length, his letters full of advice to the young Doctor of Divinity, and containing many scriptural quotations and hints for sermons. The plague was raging in the Isle of Man about 1630, Richard Parr describing the island as being "still under God's frowns and rods, death still sits on our threshalls, death comes into our windows and is entred into our palaces." One of his friends, he says, has been occupied in shutting up his neighbour's doors "to prevent ye spreadinge of a late breaking forth and ye fyringe of his owne house." Dentists were rare in those days ; he is sorry to hear that Thomas Legh's "swelling goome [gum] still waits on you ; can you neither kill it wth kyndnes, nor banish it wth harshnes ?" Much elated at his consecration, he describes a visit to his old college in 1635 : " I came downe by Oxon upon ye College solemn invitation, where ye Principall gave me Episcopall entertainment, seeminge to glorie much to see a Bishope of his college, though a poore." He regrets he cannot have the pleasure of christening one of Thomas's children, " desiring much to bestowe a Bishop's blessing on y^t tender babe." He hopes to be able to see his friends at Lyme some day, but begs only one thing, that if he *should* visit them, his new dignity may make no difference, but that he may be entertained " as an old servant and private friend and not otherwyse."

On Sunday, December 2, 1632, John Bradshawe, afterwards President Bradshawe, writes another of his interesting letters to Sir Peter. He begins by giving a long account of the war now raging abroad, and mentions the total defeat of the Elector Palatine, late King of Bohemia, with the news of his death, the battle having lasted a whole day, and 30,000 or 40,000 men being slain :

> " The tidings reached the English Court [states Bradshawe] about 8 of the Clock at night, which struck the King and the whole Court into a solemn dampe & spoyled a play which should have bene the Sunday night following."

Letters coming next day stated that the King was not dead but very dangerously wounded, but the first report, as it turned out, was the true one :

> " God grant [says Bradshawe] that the next intelligence Confirme or better this, ffor more sad or Heavie Tydings hath not in this Age bene brought since Prince Harrie's Death to the true Hearted English. What the Popishlie Affected make of it, it matters not ; Neither have they much cause to bragge, ffor if the King is dead, He is dead a Conqueror, having entred into a Covenant for the German Libertie wch he hath royallie kept & seal'd itt wth his Bloud."

In the light of subsequent events these sentiments from the future regicide seem a trifle inconsistent.

The letter goes on to say :

"Ffor domestique Businesse I doubt not but you haue heard how Affayres do stand. Marquis Hamylton * hath bene return'd these 2 months being received very graciouslie of the King & continued in former favour. Sr Harrie Vaux is lykewise back from his Negotiacon wth the Swede who will not be persuaded that the Emperor is able (his Armie being defeated) to levy 30,000 men throughout all his Dominions. Sr John Eliott † is languishing & drawing towards his last home lying a dying Man of an irrecoverable Consumpcon in the Tower: the Libertie of ffresher Ayre was deny'd him by the Judges upon motion, It being urged against him that though his Bodie was weake his spirit was strong & that if he would haue submytted, he might haue bene long since at large, wch unles he did, he must ly there still for them: that he will not yeeld unto, but assures his ffriends He shall dy a true Subject to the King & that he finds nothing in his Conscience or Judgm^t to checke himselfe for touching any thing wch he did or sayd in parliam^t. The Proclamations touching residence in London in Eating or dreshing of fflesh upon the Statute ffish dayes, are very sharplie look't unto: Palmer, a Somersetshire man, was ffyned in a 1000^l for his Abode in London contrary to the former proclamation, & many 100^ds are served wth p^tes out of the Star Chamber & Escheq^r to Answer the Breach of the lawe. There are divers Licences purchased for Eating of fflesh upon ffish dayes: yor Neighbour Mr Stanley of Alderley hath one & it cost him 7^l. Commissions for benevolence towards the Repaire of Paules are comming into all Counties; the very scaffolding whereof for that purpose is computed to amount to 20,000^l.

" Yo^r ever obliged

" Jo : BRADSHAWE."

"Congleton this Sunday the 2d of
December 1632."

This letter gives one some idea of the state of affairs existing in 1632. Parliament had been dissolved in 1629, and for eleven years Charles ruled without one. His intention never had been to establish a tyranny, but he hated parliaments and thought discussions dangerous things which led to insubordi-

---

* Third Marquis and first Duke of Hamilton in Scotch peerage; commanded British forces under Gustavus Adolphus, 1630–4; executed 1649.

† Sir John Eliot (1592–1632), patriot; imprisoned for conspiracy to resist the King's lawful order for the adjournment of Parliament on March 2, 1629, to calumniate the ministers of the Crown, and to assault the Speaker. Sentenced in 1630 to a fine of £2000; died in prison.

nation. Money, or the lack of it, was at the bottom of all his troubles. He had succeeded to his father's debts, and had no money with which to carry on the government of the country, so he resorted to the system of forced loans, benevolences, fines, and monopolies, and taxing the people without the authority of Parliament (which last had been abolished by James) in order to provide the necessary revenue. This system ended, of course, in abuses of the most violent kind. Trivial offences were punished by enormous penalties, fines of four and five thousand pounds were exacted for brawls, and extortion was practised on a more gigantic scale than had been seen before. We have an instance of this in the two cases mentioned by Bradshawe, the man Palmer being fined one thousand pounds for residing in London without giving due notice, and Mr. Stanley of Alderley being charged seven pounds for a licence to eat flesh upon a fast day.

The Star Chamber even was used for purposes of taxation. This tribunal had originated in early days out of exercise of jurisdiction by the King's Council, and in Tudor times had been of utility in bringing to justice the great nobles who would otherwise have had it in their power to set the law at defiance. The Star Chamber was independent of a jury. Treason, murder, and felony could be brought under its jurisdiction when the King chose to remit the capital sentence. It could apply torture and inflict any punishment short of death. Cases which ought to have come before the Common Law Courts were brought before it simply as a means of levying fines for the Crown. An instance of this was found recently at the Record Office, where among the papers dealing with causes specially appointed to be heard before the Star Chamber on October 31, 1635, was a charge against five men, John Barnes, John Wood, Henry Wood, James Kenion, and Edward Rowghley, the plaintiff being Sir Peter Legh. The offence was " ryotous huntinge and killinge the plaintiff's deere, assaulting his keeper, and other offences." On the 15th of November came the sentence : " The two Woods 100^l a piece to the Kinge, 7 yeeres bond to the good behaviour, three months imprisonment, acknowledgment to Sir Peter Legh at the Assizes." It is scarcely surprising that in 1641 the Star Chamber was abolished by act of Parliament.

1634-5 The winter of 1634-5 was one of exceptional severity. We read of " so grievous a snow as will deserve a future Kalender, seconded by extreme bitter stormes and more encrease of ye same snow that the memorie of man can hardly reporte ye like." From Haydock Lodge come accounts of terrible damage to the house.

> " The violence of the wyndes cominge together with the snowe [writes Sir Peter's agent, Greimsworth] did soe beat and drive into each particular false roofe in the house, they not being teared, that nowe at the thaw there is not one chamber free."

Sir Peter's own closet, Francis's chamber, the maids' and some part of Peter's escaped, and into these they carried the bedding.

> " Part of the upper roof of the Blewe Chamber is fallen, part of George Bowden's and part over the staires, and the Matted Chamber totally falne, which Matt I cannot for my life [writes Greimsworth] tell how to gett fourth, as fourth it must be taken, both in regard the Chamber may be anew drest at March, and the Matt new washt and preserved in the interim from rotting. I think it must be ript in many places, which if it be I know none (as some taylors I have had to see it) but Birchenough will undertake it againe. If circumspection or diligence could have prevented these inconveniences, I hope there is none will thinke but we did our utmost endeavours."

It will be noticed that much concern was being displayed over the damage done to the " Matt." The modern idea that tapestry was not much thought of in those early days is here proved to be erroneous.

During this winter many of the deer and sheep were lost, and even rabbits drowned in their burrows, " but God grant," says Greimsworth, " the violence of the floods doe our Milnes no harme."

Richard Molyneux,* second Viscount, writes to his great-

* Sir Richard Molyneux, second Viscount, eldest son of first Viscount. He fought in the Civil Wars, was with his brother Caryll at Oxford during its surrender, also at Worcester, but escaped; married Lady Frances Seymour, daughter of William, Marquis of Hertford.

138

uncle, Sir Peter, on January 23 of the same year, alluding to the difficulty of getting about owing to the floods :

> " Good Unckle, I haue maide boulde to sende my man for the tacking of those deare you pleased to bestowe on mee, wth netts, and I must entreate you to appoynte yor keepers to assiste him ; I haue tow [two] Cartes Maide of purpose, wch (by the grace of God) shalbee att Lyme uppon Twisday att night, I hadd sente them nowe, but that I feare they coulde not passe for waters, and besydes I knowe they will require sume tyme in tackinge, soe that I hope they will cum soone aenuffe ; I must render you Manie thanckes for all your noble ffauors, and will euer pray for yor health, esteeminge my selfe euer happie to remaine
> > " Yor assured louinge Nephew and Servante
> > > " RICHARDE MOLYNEUX."

Thomas Legh was finding his expenses at Walton somewhat heavy, a rapidly increasing family and the cost of living were proving too much for his slender purse, and he writes to beg help from his father :

> " For the surplusage of my Spirituall profitts I could never yet get one daie of paiment to bring in another by reason of ye excessive charge of many disbursements, the relation whereof would but trouble you, and the whole revenue perhaps not so greate as you esteeme it. You have many times askt me and merrily blamed me for want of a watch in my pocket ; I'le give you ye true answer now ; I can not well say that ever I was truly worth so much. An often Borrower I have beene and am still, but never yet a Treasurer."

He then proceeds to give an account of his finances :

> " eleven score pounds of my wife's portion still due to me and 100[1] legacy, the first I have good hopes of—the second, all I can say is It's welcome if it come."

He was hoping for seventeen score pounds more from a cousin of his wife's, and declares his anxiety to leave her

> " a Coat [cot] be it never so small to lay her head in after any occasion that by God's pleasure may befall me."

Sir Peter was constantly begged to arbitrate in matters domestic as well as legal or political, and to use his influence to smooth down an irate husband or to remonstrate with an unreasonable

1635 wife. A certain Mistress Goldsburgh begs that Sir Peter will persuade her husband to give his consent to the marriage of one of her sons. She does this through a third person, who states that " Mistress Goldsburgh thinks that if your worship would invite him to Lyme you might doe what you will with him." His Worship apparently complied with the lady's request, but received an excuse from the gentleman, who may possibly have had his suspicions of what the invitation meant. He pleads as a reason for his declining to accept Sir Peter's hospitality that " the waies are foule, and long withal, besides I have many businesses to dispatch with speed." He announces, however, that he will come next year and stay at Lyme " till you be weary of such a guest, and bring my heaviest burthen along with me, tho' it seems to live to Methusalem's age only in revenge of those that desires the contrary," by which we may infer that he was alluding in terms the reverse of complimentary to his better half.

The old tax of Ship-money, dating from Danish times, was revived in 1635. It had in those early days only been levied on seaport towns in time of war, but was now intended for the whole country in times of peace, and was to be a means of equipping a navy without cost to the exchequer. There were loud murmurings throughout the land ; petitions without end were signed and presented in protest against this imposition. An unknown correspondent, writing on November 8, 1635, mentions that the sheriffs of the different counties were refusing to make the assessments, Northampton, for example :

" In Gloucestershire they saie the Sheriff refuseth to execute the commission. Nothing at all is collected in Warwickshire, In Essex whole hundreds refuse to paie and they report here that at the Asises the Grand Juries offered to have presented the same to the Judges. The Earls of Essex, Hertford, Warwick, Lincoln, Bollingbroke, Cleveland, Tennet, Viscounts Mandeville and Lea, Lo : Brook, and ye Earl of Chesterfield and manie other Nobles, Knights and Gents in all the most Counties have declared that they will not pay."

It was the low rumbling of distant thunder before the coming storm.

CHAPTER IX

THE LAST DAYS OF SIR PETER

TIME and sorrow had laid chastening hands upon Sir Peter 1635
Legh. The fiery temper was now calmed, the indomitable will
and spirit were broken, the hard rough nature softened and
subdued. He was now, in 1635, 72 years old, but he was still
active and vigorous. Tortured by agonies of remorse, he
endeavoured to atone for the irrevocable past by a more humane
and enlightened treatment of those children who were left to
him, and whom in spite of all his harsh discipline he loved
devotedly. He clung to them more and more with advancing
years, and his chief happiness was to have them round him.

"Come as soon as you can and let me know when," he
writes to Francis on September 18, 1635. On the same day he
begs for news from Thomas of his wife and children, who had
been ill :

"Tom, It is now soe longe since I heard from you that this afternoone
I sente one to Bould to inquire of you, and he brought me such intelligence as gave me some comfort. My daughter * had entertained a
late messenger from Captaine Molyneux that brought her word of my
daughter [Thomas's wife, Lettice] and the children's somewhat recovery and being better. I pray you wryte though two lynes and tell
me if it be so, or howsoever it is with you. And so remembringe my
love to you, beseeching God bless you, my daughter and all your's,
I leave you to His goodness and mercie, in whose hands you and I
and all of us are

"Yr lovinge father
"P. LEGH."

"I would faine have you to come out of your phisicke and come
hither to me [he writes to Francis on September 30th of the same year

* Mrs. Bold.

141

from Haydock Lodge, Francis being at Lyme], for I both desyre to see you and have business with you. [And again in November:] If it shall fall soe out yt you can dispatch your busines yt you could come hither the latter end of this week or 2 or 3 daies in the beginning of the next I shold be glad to see you heare."

He had even relented somewhat towards poor Anne, his daughter-in-law, who was occasionally allowed to come and see her son Peter at Lyme. She writes to Thomas Legh on April 1, 1635, hoping he has recovered from the cold he had when he came to fetch little Peter, and like Lady Fenner, she is anxious to prescribe remedies of all kinds.

> "To satisfy myself the better I have sent this bearer to see you; and chiefly to bring you some Ellecompain * which is to be taken now at this time of the year. Summer is not so good by experience I have sene of meny who have used it; I thinke it is the best phisicke for fleame in the stomacke obstructions and to cause an appetite and good digestion that can be, many things more it is good for, ill in none that I know, and as far as I can conceive it cannot be better for anybody then for you, I wish it may doe you but as much good as I desier it may; take a spoonful every day first in the morning, fast an hower after it; I made shift to doe the best rootes I could get here."

She wishes to make him a present of a greyhound:

> "I have bred him at my own trencher purposely for you, because I desier you would sometimes take the fresh ayre and moderate recreation abroad, too much reading and studeing cannot but be hurtful for you; but take seasonabill wether, for I think you are subject otherways to take cold soune. . . . I mean if please God to see Petter this summer, and I should be very glad to meet you and my sister Bold at Lime, otherways I fear my stay in the cuntery will not be to see you which I much desier to doe. I hope Petter is well, learns his Booke, serves God and gives his Grandfather good content, pray God bless him and send me and all that loves him good comfort of him. [Subscribing herself] Your most affectionatt Sister and Seruant,
> "ANNE LEGH."

On April 4 of the same year she writes to Francis to beg that he will persuade her father-in-law to let her have "some

* Elecampane—the roots were used as remedy for a cold.

sheepe and Milke kine to stoke the grounds at Newton, my daughter and I cannot live upon it otherways to make any benefit of it." She adds, pathetically, that this is the first request she has ever made to Sir Peter for anything but " his blessing and love to me and mine which I hope in time when he pleasis he will make manifest to us all. I make no question but the Remembrance of him that is dead and gone hath so indeared your affection to his fatherles children whom he left behind him that in what you may you will be a father and a helper to me and them."

Sir Peter was beginning to fail. His handwriting becomes much less clear and distinct, and in some cases the letters have obviously been dictated, as, with the exception of the signature, which is very shaky and tremulous, they are in a different hand.

There are evidences of his having met with some kind of accident in January 1635–6; this may possibly have been a seizure.

> " Most Honoured S^r [writes one Ja : Anderton on January 12th], I did not heare of yor fall and hurte before y^t at ye same tyme I understood of yor recoverie and since now of yor wellbeing, whereof I had every wish yor happie continuance, and true prosperitie of you and yo^{rs} in this, and eternall happiness in ye life to come."

By February he was very seriously ill and his family were all summoned. Anne Bold came from Bold, her Lancashire home, Thomas from his rectory at Walton, and Francis and Peter were already at Lyme. Anne Bold had left her husband very ill in order to come to her father, bringing with her her two eldest daughters, Margaret and Mary.

> " Wee long to see you againe at Bold [writes James Hill, probably her chaplain, to her on February 6], the rather because Mr Bold is something weaker then hee was at your departure, & in regard of his weaknes keepes his chamber."

He much desires, therefore, that Mistress Bold should return to her husband " seeing your stay can doe Sr Peter little good." He tries to comfort her by reminding her that her father is already " full of dayes," that he has been blessed with long life, and that she must take heed lest she be " swallowed up with over-much sorrow and sin against your own selfe in weakening your body & hindring your owne health which you are bound by all meanes to further."

1635–6 Torn between her two duties, Anne returned to her husband, leaving her father, whom she knew well she would never see again. She writes on February 10 to her brother Francis for news of her father, and excuses herself for leaving him on account of her brother-in-law, Henry, who " hath reported that I care not for my husband because I staid soe long at Lyme."

In a postscript she says she is sending a bottle of " scurvie grease ale " * which nauseous decoction she prays may be given to her father " to drinke in a glase."

The old spirit was not dead. Peter Venables,† Baron of Kinderton, writes on the 11th of February to know

> " what rest he tooke this night, whether the payne he had be aswaged, and whether he yet incline to be ruled and aduised by the Doctors, retorne me this bearer earlie to-morrowe morning I praie you with two or three lynes how all thinges goe, I assure you Cosine there is non more sollicitous of yoʳ ffathers good health then I shalbe wch I hope in some good measure to heare of at this bearers retorne."

His Molyneux relations were also writing for news :

> " I am hartily sorrie for the weaknes of my Uncle yr ffather [writes Lord Molyneux ‡ on the 16th February], and as truly occasioned by many obligations to partake of that grieffe as any ffreind or kinsman of his whatsoever."

He died the following day, February 17, 1635–6, universally beloved, respected, and regretted.

His children mourned him with genuine sorrow. Lady Fenner writes beseeching her son-in-law not to be cast down with too much sorrow :

---

* Scurvy-grass ale.

† Peter Venables, Baron of Kinderton, cousin of Sir Peter; married, first, Mary, daughter of Sir R. Wilbraham of Woodhey ; secondly, Frances, youngest daughter of Sir Robert, afterwards Lord, Cholmondeley.

‡ Richard, second Viscount, great-nephew of Sir Peter Legh, was in the Civil Wars; died soon after the Battle of Worcester, in which he and his brother Caryll fought. Married Lady Frances Seymour, daughter of William, Marquis of Hertford, but left no children.

" Which may make you unfit for those many businesses that I am perswaded are layd upon you and I hope you will consider that hee was an olde man and that by corse of nature he could not liue long, and when your businesses are setled, if it please you to take my poore house for your home you shallbe most hartiely welcom to me."

Ralph Richardson sends his condolences to Thomas, his old pupil, much in the same strain :

" Let the greatest Monarch liue the yeares of Nestor or age of Methu-salem, at last he must descend into the grave, nothing can devert the evill of death ; [reminding Thomas that his father had died as he had lived] crowned wth honor heare in this world, & in full assurance of eternall happiness in the world to come."

He begs Thomas will look to his own health, as he hears that both he and Lord Molyneux have been

" dangerously sicke ; [praying for news] how it stands with yor health and my good little Lettice concerning her eye-sight & her good re-coverie, I had provided some small remembrance both for you and her, but these tymes are not for complements."

Sir William Brereton,* afterwards the head of the parlia-mentary movement in Cheshire, was an intimate friend and writes to Francis condoling and offering his services :

" Worthy S^r, As I cannot esteeme, of the performance of this service, any otherwise then as of the payment of a most due debt to my most worthy, faithfull freind yor Father, soe shall I bee of nothing more ambitious then of the Occasion whereby I may deserve to endeare my selfe in some measure unto yor selves, as much as I was sometimes obliged to the Person of yor Noble Father, the Memorie of whose Worthe will much survive the number of his Dayes : & in whose absence, if you please thereof to accept, I will make this tender of those services unto yor selves wch I owed unto yor Father, by virtue whereof you may att all times command him, who will in all conditions profess to remaine

" Yor most faithfull kinsman & Servant

" WILL : BRERETON.

" I will nott faile (if the Lord permitt) to bee in yor way or waite uppon you att Lyme."

---

* Sir William Brereton of Hondford (1604-1661); Parliamentarian commander; M.P. for Cheshire, 1628-1640.

Anne Legh, who could not be expected to feel her father-in-law's death very acutely, begs to know

"what he hath donn or left for me and the rest of my children besides Petter, whom you writ he hath made heire of his lands and fully if you will doe me the fauour to writ to me how and to whom he hath disposed both of his land and personall estat." She hopes Francis will not take this her wish to be satisfied on these points as being a "preduiuce [prejudice] to any that I know nor doe I dout you will make a worse construction of it then my meaning is: I have ever found love from you and my desier and hope is it will conting [continue]." She ends with her blessing to her "dear Jewill."

Sir Peter must have made his will a few days after he received his "fall and hurte," of which we get the first intelligence by a letter from James Anderton, written on January 12, 1635-6. The will is signed January 18, just a month before his death.

The document opens with the customary formula, the bequest of his soul into the hands of Almighty God, faithfully believing to be saved through the merits of his Saviour. He desires that he may be buried at Winwick, " neere unto the place where my father and forefathers weere interred," and he specially requests that no tomb shall be set over the place of his burial :

" But only a stone to cover it with some inscription of brass declaring the tyme of my lyfe and death, according to that which was laid over my greate greate grandfather, and desiringe alsoe that I may bee buried with little and small pomp and funerall charges, and that some fewe of my owne and my wyfes friends and kinsfoolkes shalbe invited thereto."

To his wife he bequeathes all the contents of Worsley and what will amount to a third part of his goods and chattels, and his children are all well provided for.

His grandson, Peter, he makes heir of all his estates, and his two sons, Francis and Peter, residuary legatees and executors of his will. Twelve grey coats he desires may be made and given to " twelve ould persons," such of his poorer neighbours as his executors shall select.

The funeral took place three days only after his death, a most unusually short interval, important personages being frequently not buried for quite a month after their decease.

The cortège set out from Lyme to Winwick, Lancashire, a distance of from twenty-five to thirty miles, and must have been composed of several hundred mourners. One is disposed to question how it was accomplished and what period of time was occupied by the journey. In the case of Sir Peter's great-great-grandfather the Knight and Priest, this must have been a matter of extreme difficulty, for there was far more pomp and ceremony attached, and the procession was probably a longer one.

As appears from a MS. in the British Museum, Sir Peter's funeral left Lyme in the following order :

The order of Sʳ Peter Leighes funerall from Lyme to Wynwyke

Tenants two and two
Gentlemens servants of blood and affinity in their liveries
The Barron of Kindertons in livery

Gawen Duncalfe	Jo : Duncalfe
John Carter	Rafe Carter
Mr Vernon	Mr Ouldfield
Mr Fenwick	Mr Owen

Here Sr R. Wilbraham's men
John Jenkyns the groome of Sr Peter

— Edelstone	Rich : Mostyn
Reginald Richardson	Sam Gasceyll
Jo : Osencroft	James Grimsworth
Robert Mather	Richard Legh
Peirs Gasceyll	Robert Gasceyll
Rafe Arnefeild	Wm. Swyndall
Tho : Patten	Mr Golbroch
Mr Legh	Mr Collier
Mr Hanmer	Mr Dunbabyn
Mr Brotherton	Mr Stoport

Mr Warren
Jo : Arnefeilde

THE HOUSE OF LYME

Mr Creswell his Taylor	Mr Woodcock his grand-child's tutor

Dr Nicholls

THE CORPS

Mr Peter Legh the heyre to his grandfather

Mr Francis Legh	Mr Tho : Legh
Mr Peter Legh	Mr Venables
Sr Anthony St John	Sr Geo : Booth

Sr Richard Wilbraham

A brass which marks the place of his burial is inscribed with these words :

"Here underneath this stone lyeth buried the body of Sr Peter Legh Kt who departed this life February 17, 1635,

Etatis suae 73."

Through all the troublous times and the many changes that had taken place in England during the devastating Wars of the Roses, through all the bloodshed and persecution of the religious upheaval and the unsettled state of the laws, the inheritance of Lyme had remained untouched by forfeiture or confiscation.

Ever since the estate was given by the Black Prince, except in two instances when the son had died before his father, and the succession had passed over one generation, it had descended in a direct unbroken line from father to son for nearly two hundred and fifty years. Many seasons had come and gone since the foundation-stone of the old grey house was laid. Many suns had risen and set, birth and death had taken place within its walls, generations had passed away, but still it stood, a monument of bygone times, crowned with the grand motto of its owners, " En Dieu est ma Foi."

From the time when the founder of the house had fallen, a martyr for his loyalty to his rightful sovereign, Richard II, and his son and successor had died of wounds received in the service of the son of the usurper, the owners of Lyme had, with few exceptions, taken their part and share in the fortunes of their country. Through evil repute and good repute they had served their successive sovereigns, and seeking no reward were content to live, and die if need be, in their King and Country's service.

Sir Peter had been the faithful subject of three successive sovereigns of England : Elizabeth, James I, and Charles I, all of whom he had loyally served.   He had seen England when she was at her greatest, in all the splendour and triumph of the closing years of Elizabeth's glorious reign.   Though he witnessed the beginning of the troubles, he was spared the horrors of the Civil War and the final tragedy which darkened the land and will remain a blot on the fair fame of England to the end of time.

With the death of the last of the Sir Peters, a great personality passed away.   His faults, and he had many, were the faults of his bringing up and of the times in which he lived, his virtues were his own.   Although his harsh treatment of his eldest son must ever tell against him, there were, perhaps, circumstances of which we know nothing which would explain or excuse what appears to have been heartless cruelty.   His piety, his charity, and many acts of kindness must count in his favour ; may the Recording Angel

> ". . . for the good man's sin
> Weep to record and blush to give it in." *

* " Pleasures of Hope," line 357 (Thomas Campbell)

CHAPTER X

A MINORITY AT LYME

1635–6 THE death of Sir Peter Legh was followed two days after by that of his son-in-law, Richard Bold, the husband of Anne. He had been in failing health for some years although scarcely past the prime of life, being aged only forty-seven at the time of his death. He made his will on the day that he died, leaving his property divided into three shares, one to go to his wife, one to his five surviving daughters, and the remaining share to his only son Peter.

The death of Sir Peter meant, of course, the entire break-up of the happy family life at Lyme. Dorothy, Lady Legh, seems to have removed to Worsley after her husband's death, but she only survived him three years, dying on April 15, 1639. Her will, a very long document containing some curious particulars, has been printed by the Chetham Society. It is dated February 8, 1638–9, and contains innumerable bequests. Her body she desires may be buried " with small pomp and funeral charges in the parish church of Eccles in that tomb which I heretofore made for my former husband Mr Brereton and myselfe to lye in." All her property to go back to her Egerton relations.

From the number of gowns bequeathed, her wardrobe seems to have been an unusually large one.

Bequests to all her distant relatives, servants, and dependents conclude this remarkable document, the poor of the different parishes being likewise not forgotten.

Francis Legh was beset with worries innumerable after his father's death. He and his youngest brother Peter—as guardians for their nephew " little Peter "—heir to his grandfather—were sued by Thomas Legh of Adlington for non-payment of tythe-herbage, he claiming at the same time one stag and one buck and one hind and one doe from the park. This was disputed by the Legh brothers, who carried the matter to the Consistory Court, but what the outcome was does not appear.

Immediately after Sir Peter's funeral Anne Legh claimed the wardship of her son Peter, then aged about thirteen, and carried matters with a very high hand. She also complained of not receiving her proper third part and took her grievances to the Attorney-General, Sir John Bankes,* who seems to have been a very intimate friend and to have taken the greatest possible interest in Anne and her children. In spite, however, of being much prejudiced in her favour, he took a very fair and unbiased view of the case.

> " For notwithstanding all her soliciting him by letters [writes a correspondent to Francis Legh] yet you see in what a fair manner he writes. I assure myself you shall find him a most honest and indifferent man. I pray you sett downe what kind respects you have showed to her both in actions as well as words and how strictly she hath used herself both to you and my cosen Peter."

Up to the time of the lawsuit the boy Peter seems to have continued at Lyme under the care of his tutor, Mr. Woodcock, and to have been kept somewhat strictly by his Uncle Francis. The latter refused to allow him to accept a visit to Dr. Legh at Walton, and the boy had evidently been much looking forward to this and to enjoying the companionship of his cousins, and was therefore proportionately disappointed at the invitation being declined.

> " Theise are to give you notice [writes Mr. Woodcock to Dr. Legh] that your letter to Pe : was received with great joy and expectation but is sure to be answered with as great excesse of sorrowe. For the

---

* Sir John Bankes (1589–1644), Attorney-General, 1637; represented the Crown against John Hampden, 1637. Married Mary, only daughter of Robert Hawtrey of Ruislip, Co. Middlesex, the representative of an ancient family of Norman origin. This lady is celebrated for her heroic defence of Corfe Castle during the Civil War. It had been purchased by Sir John Bankes about 1635, but he came originally from Cumberland. He is described as exceeding Bacon in eloquence, Chancellor Ellesmere in judgment, and William Noy in law.

request being denide wherin you proposed to my Mr (Francis Legh) how hainouslie it was taken of Pe : and with what malcontentednesse you may easilie coniecture : In short Sr because the bearer hastens mee, your resonable request is denied, and Pe : though extreamlie against his will, may not come. The reason wee know not, those wee suppose, my Mr his letter will afford you."

Anne Legh ultimately won her case, and obtained the ward-ship, custody, and marriage of her son upon payment of the large sum of £2000 to the King, and £200 a year rent.

"Having tried and observed the various opinions of lawyers, the corruptors of man [writes Francis to his brother Peter], and being well tyred with attending . . . I thought it best to accept thereof. Thereupon I condescended to let her have the wardshippe uppon some covenant that shee shall not bestowe her sonne in mariage without myne and your consent. And soe shee came to compounde her selfe, and the councell of wards assigned her to pay 2000[l] composicon and 200[l] a yeare rent, what abatance shee can get I knowe not. . . . For that done, I came imediately out of towne, glad I had noe more to doe with it."

In 1636 or 1637 young Peter was sent to a grammar school at Amersham, Bucks, founded by Dr. Robert Challoner, a former Rector in 1621, and this appears to have been a prepara-tory school for Oxford. One does not quite understand why he was sent so far from home, as there must have been good schools in Lancashire, to say nothing of the one at Winwick, built by his grandfather. Peter must have been aged about fourteen or fifteen when he was sent to Amersham. The pre-vailing system of strict supervision and no liberty seems to have been carried to excess in his case, and the high-spirited boy chafed greatly under the treatment. John Houghton, an official of Brasenose, Oxford, writes on November 30, 1638, to Francis Legh, having just seen young Peter :

"He was then in perfect health, and well in all things (as he told) except his imprisonment, for soe he term'd his staying at schoole ; for he was asham'd, he said, for one of his years and stature to be still an a–b–c–darian and a companion of children under the supercilious eye of a severe schoolmaster ; but he hoped the next Spring to see Oxon (if his Mother would be pleased to condescend to his wishes.)

A MINORITY AT LYME

[Houghton reports favourably on the youth :] I professe I like him passinge well ; he still stands faire in the esteeme of all yt live there abouts and knowe him ; I hope he will prove a true Legh."

The following year, in June 1639, the boy was visiting his 1639 Uncle Francis for a few days at Lyme, his mother, however, stipulating that he should return to her with as little delay as possible, " Friday or Saturday at furthest."

The habit of sending youths to the university at a very early age still prevailed, and Peter cannot have been more than sixteen at the outside when he matriculated at Oriel College, Oxford, on January 25, 1638-9.* Sir John Bankes, the Attorney-General, in his character of friend and benefactor to Mrs. Anne Legh and her children, made himself responsible for the boy's Oxford expenses and provided him with a tutor, though one does not quite make out the reason for this, as there was no relationship and Anne was certainly not in necessitous circumstances. Besides her jointure and the money settled on her at her marriage, she had succeeded to a property left her, at his death in 1630, by her father, Lord Savile, to whose memory she had—at her own expense—erected a monument in Batley Church, Yorkshire, so she must have had plenty of money at her disposal. She writes to Francis Legh in 1639-40, dwelling much upon Sir John's kindness to her son, whom, as she expresses it—he could not have cared more for had he been his own.

Good Brother, I received your letter this 10th of January, which I thank you for. My son hath been at Mr Aturnis since the Friday before Christmas; his earnest desier is to goe presently to Oxford. Advising with Mr Aturney of it and with his aprobation I am willing to satisfy my sonne, and doe intend within six days he shall goe to Oxford to Oriel College. Dr Tolson by Mr Aturnis means provides his Tutor and intends to see him lodged in his own lodgings. Sr John could not take moor cair for his own sonne, how we shall make him amends Gods knows. I will present your service to Mr Aturney and my Lady, who often remember you. I ley now in Holborne at Mr Hogeshons howse near the Red Lyon, over against the Sword and Buckler. My sonne promises well on his part what he will doe to profitt in learning at the University, so donne I am con-

* The following is from the "Registrum Orielense matric. Oriel," January 25, 1638-9 : " Eboracensis, fil : Peirse de Lime, Lanc. arm. 16."

fident there will be no other cause to frustrate all our desires in that place, the Inns of Court some year or more hence must conclude all. [The obvious reason for her letter appears at the end :] To settle him a fellow-commoner in Oxford and his farewell from Amershom costs me a 100[1]. I must Borowe moine [money] of you when I want for this purpose—the King's payments empties my purse."

We must now return to Francis Legh. In March 1636, after his father's death, he, being then aged about forty-six, bought the estate of Blackley, now part of Manchester, and here he proposed to go and live, much against the wishes of George Bowden, agent or steward and confidential friend of the family, who writes beseeching his master to remain on at Lyme, where the bracing air could not fail to be of benefit to him :

" That ayre and place will best agree with your boddie and if things were a little settled by your absence and a mean wary man the Mr of that house, you will live much more privately then here in Lancashire, for what good fellows in that quarter will not come to you at yor brothers ye Doctors where you are at home, or at Bould with your sister where you wilbe taken to be at home, or at Haydock, whither my good Mr drew the concourse of people though there a sojorner. Good Sir consider of it and leave not Lyme."

He begs that if Francis sell any of the furniture that he may have " the bedd and meane furniture of my chamber at such rate as yourself shall think fitt."

Francis, however, was not much at Lyme after 1637–8. He probably found it very lonely all by himself in the big house where there had always been so much going on, and where he must now have felt sadly desolate, surrounded only by memories of happy days gone by for ever. He seems to have spent most of his time either at Blackley or in paying long visits to his brother and sister-in-law at Walton, or at Oxford, where he still had many friends and interests and where he was always welcome. He was of a gentle and affectionate disposition, devoted to his father and to his brothers and sister, open-handed and generous, and always ready to give largely in the cause of charity. He had all his life been delicate and this weakness and his wife's lingering illness had had a softening

154

effect upon him and made him keenly sympathetic with sickness and suffering. Debarred by his ill-health from taking active exercise (he also suffered much from lameness), he led a somewhat sedentary life; his tastes were cultivated, he was devoted to his books and was a great reader. His old tutor, Ralph Richardson, now parson of Grappenhall, Lancashire, was of considerable help to him in collecting his library.

> " I much mistook myself [he writes to Dr Legh in an undated latter] in sending your brother the Councell of Trent, forgetting hee formerly had it, but for yt lett him dispose of it at his owne pleasure, the truth is I intended the same tyme I sent it him it should not have passed single, but yt Sir Walter Rawlegh's historie should have bore him companie, which I could not then procure, but now have sent it him." *

John Bradshawe was continuing his correspondence with his Legh friends. He writes on April 13, 1636, assuring Francis of his readiness

> " to doe any service for you and the howse of Lyme as there should be occasion. Uppon Saturday next in the afternoone a great Cause stands referred to be heard before the Earl of Derby † and the Judge betwixt the Companie of Brewers (for whom I am) and the Alehouses and Innes of the Citie, so as I cannot stirre that night. But upon Easter Sunday, after evening prayer, I shall post to Warrington and attend you the next morn where you please to appoint."

On September 4, 1637, he writes again to request the favour of

> " As good a Buck as you can procure to be kylled, for I have a sudden and speceyall occasion to use one on behalfe of a ffrynd and my stomache serves me not to make use of any at this tyme but so reall a ffriend as yor self."

He adds that Francis may herein as in many other instances

---

* These three books still form part of the Lyme library. Francis did not dispose of the duplicate copy of the " Council of Trent." The one is a second edition, translated by Nathaniel Brent, folio calf, London, 1629, in the original binding, the letters F L in gold on back and front, and a beautiful bit of tooling in the shape of a cross ; the other copy, translated by Gerard Langbaine, folio calf, 1638, is also in its original binding, and has the initials and same pattern of tooling. " The History of the World," by Sir Walter Raleigh, is a first edition, folio calf, 1614. It has a frontispiece by Elstrach and a portrait of the author by S. Pass on the title-page, with numerous maps. It has also the initials and a beautiful bit of tooling on front and back.

† William, sixth Earl.

discern his boldness with him, but he hopes his true meaning shall excuse it,

"I know your realitie, am bound to you for yor ffavo^{rs}, and ever tyed to be in all bond of gratitude
"Yor ffriend most assured, most readie to serve you
"Jo: BRADSHAWE."

A three-quarter-length portrait of Francis Legh by an unknown artist depicts him as a young man with long chestnut hair, a fair moustache, and short pointed beard. The face has no look of delicate health, the expression is intelligent, and the portrait that of a typical gallant of the period. He wears a short red jacket or doublet with slashed sleeves, a white linen collar trimmed with lace, and linen and lace cuffs. A white embroidered belt crosses his right shoulder and passes round his waist, from the left side of this hangs a sword. His left hand is on his hip, his right hand, on the little finger of which is a ring, rests on a table, where there is also a pair of white gloves with gauntlets. Although gloves became a well-known article of dress in England as early as the fourteenth century and corporations of glovers were in existence in the fifteenth, they seem to have been considered somewhat of a luxury for a very considerable time after their introduction, and frequently figure in portraits of the Elizabethan and Jacobean periods as if the owners were proud of their possession.

The learned doctor and his wife were acquiring property in Liverpool, which was not far from the Rectory of Walton. Dr. Legh was much concerned about the second ship-money writ and complained of being overcharged. The ship-tax had roused great indignation at the time it was first levied in 1635, and at the second writ in 1637 the feeling in the country was extremely high. Dr. Legh, writing to one Chorley, complains of the inequality of the tax, "since which time myself and some more with us have preferred our Complaints to ye King and Councell against the weakness and indiscretion of our Assessors." He begs that Mr. Chorley, who is also aggrieved, may meet him at Bolton, where the matter was to be looked into by the Bishop and Sheriffs, and that he may give his support to the Doctor's complaint by adding an account of his own grievances :

> " which may tend to ye rightinge of your own wrongs as well as mine, Ye Assessors being meane incompetent Taxers of ye Clergy, being such as doe fill their own mouthes and other mens overcredulous ears with lowder reports of our estates then they can bear."

He adds that he made his complaint to the last High Sheriff, who promised a redress, but the obstinate Assessors refused. The amount of the tax for the whole parish appears to have been £69 0s. 7d., the Rector's share being £7 13s. 7d., leaving the sum of £61 7s. to be paid by the parishioners. What the outcome of the petition was does not appear.

In 1637 came the case of John Hampden,* whose refusal 1637 to pay his allotment of 20 shillings caused the matter to come before the Court of Exchequer for judgment, which was given against him. The national spirit was roused. Hampden was acclaimed as a popular hero, and this incident may be said to have been the first signs of the mutiny which culminated in the Civil War.

The crisis, however, came with the policy adopted towards Scotland. The unrest that had followed the partial restoration of Episcopacy, the introduction of a new liturgy, and the exclusion of Presbyterianism reached a climax in 1638. An attempt to read the new service in St. Giles's, Edinburgh, the year before (1637) had produced a riot which spread over the whole North. The outcome of this was the renewal of the former Covenants of 1557 and 1581. In February 1638, at Greyfriars Church, Edinburgh, was signed, by hundreds of people of all classes, the Solemn League and Covenant, in favour of pure religion and against all innovations. A General Assembly met at Glasgow and settled to abolish Episcopacy, the new liturgy, and the canons, and declared the Kirk independent of the State. This rebellious attitude produced what was called the first Bishop's War, which was waged by Charles

* John Hampden (1594–1643), statesman ; resisted second ship-money writ ; most popular member in Short Parliament. Killed in skirmish with Prince Rupert.

against the Scots without any money other than voluntary
contributions. The war was one in which there was no fighting,
only one man being killed and he by accident, and these so-
called hostilities were temporarily brought to an end by the
Treaty of Berwick, in which Charles declared his wish to refer
matters to be decided by a new Parliament.

Life had to go on, however, though a kingdom was rocking
and tottering to its base—ready to fall. We learn very little
of what was happening from the letters of the time. It was
dangerous to write at all, and still more dangerous to express
any views. Dark allusions to " the business that you wot of "
do not enlighten the reader much. Admonitions to burn the
letters at once when read (though these do not seem to contain
anything of special interest) appear in the correspondence.
Cypher was also much resorted to, and many of the letters are
worded in such mysterious and apparently incomprehensible
terms that it is impossible to make anything of the writer's
meaning. There is a tradition that a letter exists among the
Legh archives written from London by one of the family on
the day of Charles I's execution, but not mentioning the fact
at all. I have, however, not come upon it.

Dr. Legh was a great letter-writer. His correspondents,
one of whom was Richard Parr, Bishop of Sodor and Man, were
chiefly old Oxford friends to whom he wrote at great length,
receiving immensely long letters in return. These abound
in Latin quotations, and are full of heavy, obscure, and
somewhat broad jokes chiefly relating to Brasenose and its
officials, some of whom appear to have been extremely unpopular. The following is the description of Ralph Richardson,
who was tutor to Francis and Thomas Legh when they first
went to Oxford, and who afterwards became Vice-Principal,
and was appointed by Francis Legh, in 1636, to the rectory of
Grappenhall, Lancashire. The description, which is rather
uncharitable, is from the pen of Rowland Scudamore, one of the
students, who afterwards became Prebendary of Hereford :

" Indeed he's a good old man and a godly, wonderful devout,
especially when his reverent noddle is well ballasted with a competent

158

portion of nappie * Goulburne. Onely hee bewraies some incogitensie now and then, at Even-songe ; by kneeling downe at ye Creed and Gloria patri ; by standing, as well as he can at ye Paternoster, by sighing and crying Amen in ye wronge place ; but alasse, perhaps hee's meditating on greater matters, as, whether to suppe ith Hall or Spread-Eagle, or how many sorts of liquor to blend for his critical pallate."

Another equally uncharitable description he gives of John Houghton, one of the college officials :

" The greatest part of his time is spent in ye Hall, and Confables ; in ye hall, not at disputations but meales ; for hee's onely verst in that rule of grammar, whose verbes are of filling, emptying, loading and unloading, and knows little but *quod ad ventris victu cum cit.*"

The College was evidently miserably poor and in constant debt, due no doubt to the steady rise in prices during the first half of the century. The debt of the College to its tradesmen alone amounted, in 1638, to the huge sum of over £2000, and this fact had become a great scandal and called for an inquiry.†

" The head and members of our college has beene latelie sicke of a disease [writes John Houghton to Dr. Legh on November 30, 1638] (I believe you knowe it has beene longe possessed with ye white Divill, and yt which is little better, the god of Mammon). These, the members I meane, four of the greatest and most principle, are troubled with an ague (which in winter is somewhat dangerous) for they quiver and quake everie joynt of them ; but I believe (which they feare) the little Man of Lambeth will act ye part of a wise physicon, to purge ym so, yt yt uncouth disease will shortlie leave ym, or they their lives (theire colleges I meane). Ye Archbishop has of late sent downe to inquire after priviledged persons in ye Universitie ; the articles inquired after are these, ye value of theire livinges (pleno valore not in ye Kings bookes), 2, ye distance from ye Universitie ; 3, how longe they have injoyed ym ; 4, what yeares the incumbent hath and what standinge in ye Universitie ; It is to be feared yt they must either (lose ?) their benefices or colledges. . . ."
" Y faith wee are sicke some of us, I am sure, but it is with yt epidemical disease, povertie, ye plague of ye purse—tis true we expect raither feare, another plague (God blesse us as hitherto he hath from yt of pestilence) viz, yt of the Arch-bishop's visitation, for my part and ye rest of my brethren of ye Juniority we feare it little ; for as we have

---

* Strong ale.   † " Brasenose College " (Mr. Wakeling).

little, soe can we lose but little, neither are we sinners (I mean seniors) greate enough to dread such a punishment."

Much building seems to have been going on at Oxford; he speaks of Oriel College :

" There you have new Hall, Chap. and a most brave Quadrangle built, almost all since your last being here. [He goes on to speak of the war still raging abroad :] We hear little save ye takinge prisoners of my Lord Craven* and Duke Rupt by ye Emperor's forces. [He also touches upon matters at home :] For ye news of Scotland wee hear its verie badd, worse then to be reported. Wee hear yt my Lord of Arundle † has called a councell of warre this weeke ; God send us peace and put an end to these troublesome times."

Like his brother Francis, Dr. Legh was a great reader. From the time when he first went to Oxford he had always been collecting books—chiefly those on divinity. By a bill of a Mr. Henry Cripps, stationer, we find that he paid £20 10s. 1638 for books bought in 1638. " Lorinus on the Psalms," " Ainsworth on Canticles." ‡ " Daneus upon . . .," § " Stella upon Luke," are a few of the works named.

A very beautiful miniature of Dr. Legh by Hoskins, painted in 1631, depicts him at the age of thirty-seven. The miniature is full face, showing only the head and shoulders. The hair, which is parted in the middle and worn rather long, with the moustache and short-pointed beard, are of the characteristic family colour—red. The forehead is very high and broad, the features small and regular, and the expression shrewd and full of intelligence, not unmixed with satire. He wears a white ruff, and what one can see of his coat is black, with a small pattern, most minutely and beautifully painted.

A portrait of his wife, Lettice, by an indifferent artist, gives her dark auburn hair, an oval face, a very fair pink and white

---

* William, Earl of Craven (1606-1697), commanded English troops fighting for Gustavus Adolphus ; fought beside Prince Rupert at Limgea. Said to have married Elizabeth, Queen of Bohemia.

† Thomas, second Earl of Arundel and Surrey, general of army against Scots, 1639.   ‡ A leading man in the Brownist Community at Amsterdam.

§ Daneus, Daneau (Lambert), " Orationis Dominicae explicatio," 1583. Name missing in the MS.

LETTICE CALVELEY
Wife of Dr. Thomas Legh. Painted before 1639
From a Portrait at Lyme

complexion and dark grey eyes. The portrait does not indicate the wonderful strength of character possessed by this lady, who was left when still comparatively young, after the death of her husband, to manage her property and bring up her children through part of the darkest and most unhappy period of English history.

Anne Bold, after her husband's death, which it will be remembered took place two days after her father Sir Peter's, in 1635–6, had many difficulties to contend with. Her brothers-in-law were grasping and trying to get all they could out of her ; Henry Bold, particularly, who had been the first to censure her for leaving her husband to go to her father's death-bed, was constantly criticizing her and finding fault. She seems to have 1639 been living in London in 1639, having taken a house in Covent Garden for a year, that her daughters might be " put out to learning." Apparently this course was not approved of by her relations, who considered that she was behaving in an indecorous manner in taking so unusual a step. She had heard of things being said against her and writes to her brother Francis, begging that he will tell her the names of those who " make such a rabble talk of me," assuring him at the same time that she has not been guilty of any misdemeanour since her arrival in London.

> " I have not lived in such a fashion to give anyone just Cause to Censure me of any lewd Carriage or of frequenting any wanton Company, neither have I done anything at all to be a subject for malicious mynds to discourse upon at their tables in the way of derision."

She protests that she is

> " not so much taken with any delights here but for my owne part I could wish myself in the Country again amongst my owne friends, but being I have undertaken this journey for my Children's good, if I should now of a sudden make a removal and return back again without profiting my Children somewhat well, then might the County Censure me of vanitie and Levitie and think me of a fickle and waveringe mynd."

She was having troubles with her servants and begs to know if Francis can recommend her a butler, her own she had had to

dismiss on account of his " prid and sorlines " [pride and surli-
ness], and he showed his annoyance at her having done so by

> " knocking so hard and runged my house dore so I feared he would
> have broke it. I pray if you can help me with a good onist man which
> is not too young nor will not thinke himselfe too proude to do anything
> which I shall appoynt him, which is to buy mee meate and keepe the
> key of that little drinke which I have. I am a stranger here and am
> very loath to make trial of strangers."

Her eldest daughter, Margaret, does not seem to have been
much taken with London life :

1639-40
> " I am exceedinge weary of London [she writes to her uncle Francis on
> February 3, 1639-40], it is a place of great charges and expence, for shee
> [her mother] hath disbersed a good deale above 300¹ scince shee came
> to towne. Indeed I believe if you would please to come up at Easter
> shee needed noe other motiffe to draw her downe into the Countree, for
> I thinke shee begins to bee weary already."

A month later, Anne announces her intention of leaving
London and of engaging a governess for her children : " I will
provide myself of a woman that shall teach my children and
bring her downe if possibly I can." That day being the 23rd
of March, she was beginning to take physic. She was evidently
suffering from some growth which was causing her great pain :
" To-morrow the Doctor intends to let mee blood, by God's
helpe it may prove means to do me good, for he thinks if I
should neglect this means he doubts it would grow to a
Cancer." The doctor's fears were justified, for Anne Bold
must have died very shortly after, though the exact date
does not appear. She is mentioned in her brother Francis's
will in 1642, but probably died the same year and is buried
by her husband in the Bold Chapel in Farnworth Church, near
Bold, where there is a monument to their memory.

This is composed of two figures, life size, beautifully executed in pink veined marble, resembling alabaster, which are
placed upright against the north wall of the Bold Chapel.
Richard Bold is represented as a young and very handsome
man, with the long hair, moustache, and pointed beard of the
cavalier. He wears a ruff and a breast-plate of armour, and

162

armour covers his arms, full trunk hose and high square-toed boots with spurs. His right hand is on his breast, his left hand hangs down by his side and holds a long sword.

Anne is dressed in a plain gown which falls in folds to her feet, a short jacket with tabs and a ribbon round her waist, such as one sees in the portraits of Henrietta Maria, and full sleeves ending in small ruffles at the cuffs. Her hair is dressed in short curls, and over her head and falling to her feet behind is a long cloak. She clasps a Bible to her breast between her hands.

CHAPTER XI

"LITTLE PETER'S" SAD END

1640 WE must now return to " Little Peter." He had spent most of the year 1639 and part of 1640 at Oriel College, Oxford, which he no doubt found a pleasant change from the " supercilous eye of the severe schoolmaster " at Amersham, although nearly as much strict supervision seems to have been exercised over the University undergraduates in the middle of the seventeenth century as was the case at the beginning. He had been entered as a fellow commoner, who, though a privileged person as compared with an ordinary commoner or batteler, was still under a tutor, and had no control over his own affairs or finances.* The expenses of a fellow commoner were about £50 a year or more in the middle of the century. The fees on entering the College were £1 to the Vice-Principal, 10s. to the servants, 13s. 4d. to the Bursar for entering his name, and the same sum to the College for matriculation. His " caution " was £5, and he had to pay his tutor £2 a quarter as tuition fee. He had his own study and bedroom, in contrast to the commoners, who had to share a room with their tutor and several students. The furniture provided for him consisted of a feather bed weighing sixty pounds, and a great box for his linen, the washing and mending of which cost £1 18s. a quarter.

The extraordinary objection of the College authorities to any games still prevailed. One cannot understand their reasons for thus curbing and restraining the natural desire for some outlet for high spirits, and the result was probably something akin to rioting. Mr. G. H. Wakeling, M.A., Fellow of Brasenose, in his History of the College, 1603–1660, writes the following :

* "Brasenose College " (Mr. Wakeling).

164

"LITTLE PETER'S" SAD END

" In 1638, Laud wrote to the Vice-Chancellor on the approach of Lent to warn him that he must prevent disorder in the disputations. There was a game known as ' Coursing,' which consisted first in rival Colleges attempting to outdo each other in the schools, and then a running fight ensued on the way home to reverse, it may be, the verdict of the examination room. Their games were so far forbidden that it is difficult to blame them for thus getting some sport out of life."

Peter Legh can only have remained at Oxford a little over a year, for on the 3rd of November 1640 he is mentioned as being elected M.P. for Newton, Lancashire, having as his colleague Mr. William Ashurst.

Newton-in-Makerfield, to call it by its full designation, was in Saxon times of sufficient importance to give name to one of the hundreds of Lancashire, which distinction was retained in the reign of William the Conqueror. It came into possession of the Legh family—with much of the other Lancashire property —through the marriage of the second Sir Peter with the heiress of the Haydocks, but the barony or lordship of Newton was not acquired till the seventeenth century, when Richard Legh bought it from Sir Thomas Fleetwood, and became, in 1661, first Baron of Newton. In the first year of Elizabeth, 1558–9, Newton was first given the privilege of returning two members to parliament. At that time the members were nominated by the Stewards of the barony and with the assent of the Lord of Newton, and this continued till 1620, when the franchise became vested in the free burgesses, that is to say, persons possessing freehold estates in the borough to the value of 40s. and upwards.* There were sixty of these free burgesses who claimed to vote, but the burgage tenure being chiefly in the lord of the manor, the election was as much in him after the right came into the hands of the burgesses as it was before that time, and he was sometimes suspected of abusing his privileges, and successive Lords of Lyme frequently usurped the right.†

* Baines' "History of Lancashire."
† Newton ranked among the nomination boroughs up to the time of its disfranchisement in 1832, after that time the return of members for South Lancashire was always made from that place.

The young M.P. was only seventeen when he was returned
member for Newton. It seems to have been no unusual thing
for minors to sit in parliament, but they were probably not
allowed to vote, although they seem to have enjoyed all the
other privileges of members.

1641–2 One gathers that Peter Legh must have been intelligent and
cultivated above the average. A letter to his Uncle Francis,
written from London on January 10, 1641–2, shows him to have
had a good handwriting, he expresses himself clearly and well,
and gives a very interesting account of the excitement that was
caused by the impeachment of the Bishops and five members.
The King came down to the House of Commons in person, and
occupying the Speaker's chair demanded the surrender of the
persons of Messrs. Hollis, Pym, Hampden, Strode, and Sir
Arthur Hazelrigge, who, however, had in the meanwhile be-
taken themselves to the City. We learn "that the same is a
high Breach of the Rights and Privileges of Parliament, and
inconsistent with the liberties thereof." *

As a result the House adjourned, to meet again a few days
later at the Guildhall.

Peter Legh's interesting letter begins with excuses for his
long silence, but explains that his reason for not writing was the
fact that it was his

> "ill fortune to lodge in a house where the sicknes [the plague] chanced
> to fall upon now some 3 weeks or a month agoe, but God be thanked
> neither I nor anything concerning mee as yet hath caute anie harme."

He had not written, fearing the danger of infection to his
uncle.

> "For the news ther is but little, but I make noe question but that you
> have heard of glassing [?] betwene the Kinge and us aboute the pr.
> [privileges?] of our hous of impeaching our members of hie Treason and
> coming himselfe in person into the hous to demand them, wheruppon wee
> presently adjourned into the citie and his Maistie his court to hampton
> court and from thence to Winsor where [it] is now. Ther hath been
> divers ialouses [fears] amongst us of divers fals reports of troupes of

* From the " Journals of the House of Commons " for January 4, 1641–2.

horse assembled together by his Matie commanded by my lord Digbie,* Coronell Lunsford † and divers others for surprising, which makes us sitte everie day with a stronge guard uppon us or els adjourn into London, my lord Digbie is gone into Flaunders, hee beinge the supposed man to have framed the accusation against our members, putting it into the Queens hand and so to have put the Kinge uppon it, and some privatly say that her Maistie ere longe will be for France, which I partly believe but cannot affirme it, for truth the Kinge and wee are not so well united together as I could wish but wee receive daylie gratious expressions of his mind and good intentions towards us which makes us hope to see better times then now wee doe, but yett hee doth not desert from his former charge against our members, but saith hee will proceed against them in a tryall way. Wee have voted all the lords in the privie councell voide, but whether his Maiestie will condescend to it or noe God knoweth. Wee have also petitioned his Maiestie to put the kingdom into a posture of defence, the magseens cinqsport and havens into secure hands such as both houses shall thinke fitt, wee have also beene in chousing [choosing] of lords Lieutenants, my lord Strange ‡ is for our countie, but with much adoe, for Sr Ralph Aston sonn and Mr Regbie § did mightily oppose us, for Lord Wharton || and your nechbour did stand neuter till hee saw which was the stronger side. Wee are now in making choice of ministers for a sinode, Mr Hearle ¶ is pitch uppon and our knight, Ashton would put in the warden of Manchester, which shall not bee by my consent and manie more, how it will goe I know not; wee are voting a declaration of heads of grievances of the subjects so to remove away all jealousies between the Kinge and his people. Wee hear of 20 saile of french loaded with armes and amunition. The merchants have made proposition of 50 saile of ships to be readie once in 20 days at what reasonable conditions wee shall thinke fitt for the guard of our seas uppon this day. The 10 Bishopps are to come to triall this day sennet: wee receive almost dayly petitions from severall counties

* George Digby, second Earl of Bristol (1612-1677), succeeded as Baron Digby, 1641; fought for Charles at Edgehill; gave up his command after a quarrel with Prince Rupert.

† Sir Thomas Lunsford (1610-1656), Royalist colonel, made prisoner at Edgehill; died in Virginia.

‡ James Strange, seventh Earl of Derby; married Charlotte de la Trémouille, the defender of Lathom House; he was beheaded in 1651.

§ Alexander Rigby (1594-1650), Parliamentarian colonel and Baron of the Exchequer.

|| Philip Wharton, fourth Baron (1613-1696), champion of the popular party in the Lords; abandoned soldiering on his regiment being defeated at Edgehill.

¶ Charles Herle (1598-1659), Puritan divine. Presented by Stanley family to living of Winwick, Lancashire, in 1626.

accompanied with 2 or 3 thousand a piece against Bishopps and poppish Lords in the hie hous, and that they will maintain the rights and privileges of parlament with their lives and estates ; this most of it is all that is now extante, ther is nothing left now but our prayers to God for you which shall not bee wanting, with my love to my Aunt and cousens I rest   Your most truely honoring and obseruant

"Neaphew PETER LEGH."

1642   An interesting letter from Elias Ashmole,* the great anti-quary and astrologer, addressed to Francis Legh from Clement's Inn, London, on June 24 of this same year, gives hopes of a settlement of the negotiations between the King and his people, but these hopes were unfortunately never to be realized.

" Worthy Sr,

" The Baron [Peter Venables †] hath given me in Comand, to give you many thanks for yor last letter, and to Certifie you that he was not more disconsolate at his first arrival here (when leaving soe many good frends, he encountered with soe many appearances of ruin and Con-fusion) as he is now Joyfull, to perceive some dawnings of a Cleere understanding betwixt the King and Parliam^t ; for yesterday the house fell into debate about the Kings Answer to the 19 Proposicons made by both houses (which is amongst other bookes yt he comanded me to inclose). In wch debate it appeared yt there were many of the other side much afected to Accomodation and Moderation, being infinitely troubled yt such things wch were propounded (and which is by all Confest to have been heretofore sometymes denyed as well as yeilded unto) should by the overpressing of them and standing too much upon them, be the occasion of any Civill warr, and therefore were thought fitter to be declyned. To those things which the King is pleased to give noe answer to, a Comitee is appointed to take Consideration of them and to back them with as good Arguments and Precedents as may be produced, but altogether to declyne their former way of de-manding them. When this vote had passed (in which was included many   other   things   tending   to   Accomodation) Mr Pym ‡ Mr

* Elias Ashmole (1617–1692) held several Government appointments ; presented, in 1677, his collection of curiosities to Oxford University, to which he subsequently bequeathed his library.

† Peter Venables, Baron of Kinderton, a cousin of the Leghs ; married, first, Mary, daughter of Sir R. Wilbraham of Woodley, secondly, Frances, youngest daughter of Sir Robert, afterwards Lord, Cholmondeley.

‡ John Pym (1584–1643), Parliamentary statesman ; impeached with Hampden and others ; buried in Westminster Abbey, whence his body was ejected after the Restoration.

"LITTLE PETER'S" SAD END

Hollis * Mr Stroude † Mr Hampden ‡ and divers others of that side went out of the house in a discontent before the Speaker could reassume his Chaire.

.   .   .   .

" Thus with my due respects to you I remaine
"Yor faithfull servant,
"ELIAS ASHMOLE."

There was no reconciliation possible, things had gone too far and neither side would yield an inch. The tone of both Houses had risen with threats of force, the air was highly charged with electricity, it only required a spark to set everything in a blaze. The King rejected the nineteen propositions of the Parliament, which included the demands for the control of the militia and of all fortresses by officers of its own choosing; the reform of the liturgy and church government; the appointment and dismissal by Parliament of all royal ministers and of guardians for the royal children, and the power of excluding from the House of Lords all peers created after that date, June 1642. Henceforth war was certain.

The Queen fled to Holland to raise money on the Crown jewels, and the King left London never to return again except to die. It was, in short, the beginning of the end.

The sympathies of Peter Legh, belonging as he did to so strongly royalist a family, must certainly have been with the King, but it will be noticed that, following the habit of correspondents of the time, he does not give any expression of his own views, confining himself strictly to a statement of facts.

He was greatly attached to his Uncle Francis, who had always been glad to see as much of him as the jealous guardianship of his mother allowed, and whose sole desire was to supply the place of father to his dead brother's children. The bringing up of the boy had perhaps not been quite judicious. From quite a baby he had been under the care of a tutor at Lyme, with

* Denzil, first Baron Holles of Ifield (1599–1680) ; impeached among the five members. Ambassador at Paris, 1663-6.
† William Strode (1599 ?–1645), politician; after 1640, one of Charles I's bitterest enemies.
‡ John Hampden (1594–1643), statesman: impeached, but escaped attempted arrest; killed in a skirmish with Prince Rupert at Chalgrove Field.

occasional and rare visits to his mother, and Sir Peter, following the example of most grandfathers, had greatly relaxed his stern discipline, and had shown far more indulgence to his grandson than he had ever done to his own children. The boy, in fact, was rather spoilt. After the old man's death he had—as we have seen—returned to the guardianship of a not very judicious mother, who seems to have kept him in leading-strings and to have refused to realize that her son was growing up. High-spirited, headstrong, and wilful, impatient of restraint and control, capable of being led but never driven, he needed the most careful and tactful management, and the severity and harsh discipline of school and college were only calculated to cause him to break out directly he obtained his much-longed-for liberty. His own master at the age of seventeen, beset with all the dangers and temptations of the day, it is not surprising that he should have adopted the life and habits of a fashionable gallant of the period. His handsome face and charming personality made him all the more liable to be assailed by many flatterers, always ready to fawn upon a good-looking and wealthy youth, and to use him for their own ends.*

There had been some project of a marriage between Peter and a daughter of Sir Lewis Watson, afterwards first Baron Rockingham, a friend of George Villiers, Duke of Buckingham. Most unfortunately this came to nothing, or the tragic event which we are about to relate might never have happened.

1641-2 Little more than a fortnight after his letter to his Uncle Francis was written, Peter seems to have been engaged in a duel with one Browne, eldest son of a Sir John Browne † and a nephew of Lord Herbert of Cherbury. What the cause of the duel was

---

* A miniature, possibly by Cooper, represents him as a pale-complexioned, delicate-looking young man, with long fair hair worn in the Cavalier fashion of the time, a small moustache and imperial, and large dark blue eyes. The mouth is beautifully shaped and chiselled but the expression indicates a certain weakness of character. He wears a wide white linen and lace collar tied with a large loose blue ribbon bow, and over the right shoulder a red cloak which partially covers a brown and white doublet. This miniature is painted on the back of the two of hearts ; playing cards were frequently used by miniature painters of the seventeenth century, the smooth surface being very suitable for the purpose.

† Frances, youngest sister of Edward, first Lord Herbert of Cherbury; married Sir John Brown, Kt., of Lincolnshire.

has never been discovered. A hasty word, a fancied slight were
in those days, and even much later, enough to produce a quarrel
ending in a duel, and the senseless sacrifice of a human life.
This was how poor young Peter met his death. He lingered for
six days, succumbing finally to his injuries on February 2, 1641-2.

He made his will on the day before his death in a document
as short as it is pathetic ; it runs as follows :

" Peter Leighe Esq being dangerouslie wounded maketh his desiers and
requests as followeth, viz :

" The Barron of Kinderton to take the moneyes in his trunk wch is
about 70^l. Desired him to speak to his Unckle Ffrannces to be good
to his Mother and Sist^{rs}.

" Sr William Gerrarde to haue his dun nage.

                  " I.   Ffebr. 1641.

" He desireth his Unckle Ffrannces over and aboue his owne
bountie to his Sisters he will for his sake give them c^l. apeece. To
his man Raphe Arnefeilde the xiiii^l. he oweth him to be made up
xi^l, the boy here wth him, Myles Leighe, v^l, his footeboy at Blackley
v^l, and every servant at Blackley xs apeece, Raphe Swindells x^l.

" He giveth his gray Nage he had of Mr Bratherton to Captain
Broughton.

" His Sworde at his lodging in Towne to Mr Carrell Mulineux and
praieth God he may make better Use of it then he hath done, and
his case of Pistolles.

" His watch to his Aunt Lettice Leighe.

" His cloathes to his three servants, the boy at Blackley, Raphe
Arnefeid and Myles Leighe.

" Desireth his father the Barron to see his bodie buried at Winwicke,
and Mr Jones, whom hath beene wth him all his sicknes to preache at
his funerall.

" To his brother Tom,* his Sword at Blackley, and a gray Nage he
bought of the Barron.

" To his father † his whit mare and best sadle.

" Praieth his Unckle Ffrannces to consider the debts he oweth Sr
Wm Gerrarde ‡ and all the debts he oweth to others.

" To his frend Mr Roger Mosten his Caen [cane].

" To his Unckle Ffrannces the Sword that was his grandfathers, his
great seale and his greate fowling peece.

* Probably brother-in-law—he had no brother.
† No doubt godfather.
‡ Sir William Gerard, second son of Sir Thomas, first Baron Gerard.

"Desireth his Unckle to give his Mother c^d ayeare duringe her life, if she give the porcon in money she hath to his Sisters wch if she so otherwaies dispose of, then c^d in money.

"PETER LEGH

"I say my hand.

"Witnesses hereof
"Raphe Assheton.
"John Jones.
"Roger Mostyn.
"Thomas Munckas.
    "1641."

It is impossible to find out exactly where the duel was fought. It was probably somewhere near London as Parliament was sitting at the time. The fact that the dying boy was ministered to in his last hours by a Dr. Featley, author of devotional works, who is described as being the Rector of the parish in which he died, makes it probable that the place was Acton, near London, a Dr. Featley, also a writer, being Rector of that parish at this date.

We get an account of Peter's last hours from a certain Rev. John Jones, who writes a sort of summary of his illness and death and seems to have nursed him with great devotion. None of his near relations were with him. His Uncle Francis was too much of an invalid to undertake so long a journey, and the six days would not have given time enough for his mother to reach London to see her only son die. Peter Venables,* Baron of Kinderton, Mr. Bradshawe (but whether this was Henry or John the regicide judge is not clear), and Mr. Jones appear to have been the only persons present with the dying boy.

He bore his sufferings with much patience, submitting uncomplainingly to the painful dressing of his wounds, and in those days, when palliatives were unknown, this must have been an agonizing process. He faced death with the greatest courage and fortitude, his chief anxiety being for his mother and sisters, whom he left to the care of his Uncle Francis, beseeching

* See note, p. 168.

him that he would be good to them. His assailant he freely forgave, receiving the Holy Communion with him the day after the duel. In the pharisaical spirit of the Puritans of the time it was considered to be "a wicked inconsiderateness" that he should have received the Sacrament at all, it being supposed that he could not be sufficiently prepared after so late an offence as his duel. Mr. Jones, however, considers this

> "overstrictness on the part of some, for [he adds] he was excused by the Minister that gave it him, who assured mee (having had halfe an hours conference with him) hee found him soe richlie quallified with Faith, Repentance, Charitie, and other Graces requisite for such a Condition, that hee could not refuse the delivery of it, knoweing that Mr Legh would receive it with much benefit, and to his great comfort."

Mr. Jones seems to have gone to Peter two days after the duel, which took place on Thursday, January 27, 1641–2.

> "On Saturdaie I came to visit him, and after that was seldome from him; And can witnes thus much, That verie often, everie Night betwixt his slumber (which was but short) Hee would call for Praiers; and therein Joyne with us, going along with us in the words and verie earnestlie, as did appeare by those importunate gestures of lifting up his Eyes, and Hands, and strikeing them on his breast: And verie often hee would call for a Praier-booke, and therein read such Praiers himselfe as were propper for One in his weake state, untill his sight and Spirrits would begin to faile him."

In answer to a question in what faith he died, his answer was that he died in the religion in which he was baptized, that of the Church of England.

> "Hee would often expresse a willingnesse of dying, in respect of the miseries of this world and hope of Heaven, and that nothing retarded that desire, but the prejudice which his death would bee to his Mother and Sisters to whom he desired manie to remember his humble dutie and dearest love.
> "He was free in his good advice to others (whom he conceived not to have been soe strict in their life as they ought) pressing them to have care of their life hereafter, . . . hee would often intimate how he would leave ye companie of those yong Gallants that had abused his too easie and flexile nature; and consulted with Doctor Featley (a

THE HOUSE OF LYME

reverend and Learned Divine, the Parson of the parish where hee died) and myselfe (but the day before his departure when wee had most hopes of him) what Bookes were fittest for him to read . . . Being much taken with a Booke of devotion which Doctor Featley made himselfe and used in his visiting of him. About 4 of the clocke on the Wednesdaie (after his hurt) being his Critical daie, hee began to decline, and the symptomes of Death began to appeare upon him, which increased untill ten, the hower of his death; In all which hee would often call for praier, still joining with us therein (soe long as hee was able) And ever and anon, hee would breath forth sweet ejaculations, as, 'Lord forgive mee my Sinnes : Lord Jesus (for on him onelie would he often expresse himselfe that hee relyed for salvation, renouncing both Saints and Angells) One drop of thy blood is enough to save mee ; Lord Jesus, Lord Jesus,' And theis were the last words hee was heard to speak. I believe his assurance of salvation was verie great, for the night hee died hee tould mee 'Methinkes' (saith hee) 'I see two Angels readie to receive my Soul.' "

His patience, resignation, and courage seem to have filled those about him with admiration, " so that," as Mr. Jones touchingly expresses it

" what teares wee sad spectators did shed in the behoulding of his sufferings, hee wiped away with his patience. [The sufferer thanked God that he never lost consciousness] nor was deprived of the benefit of Reason, whereby hee might reconcile himselfe to God, but his sufferings were soe qualified that noe Sence failed in the discharge of its office, untill hee resigned his expireing Soule into the hands of God that gave it."

He was buried at Winwick, Lancashire, on February 14, 1641-2, where, according to his last wishes, he lies with his forefathers.

The fact of his death was notified in the " Journals of the House of Commons " as follows :

" Feb. 2. 1641-2. Ordered that Mr Speaker shall issue forth his Warrant directed to the Clerk of the Crown in Chancery for the electing of another Burgess for the town of Newton in Com : Lancast^r to serve in this Parliament instead of Mr Peter Leigh formerly returned a Burgess for that town and since deceased."

"LITTLE PETER'S" SAD END

In the Autobiography of Lord Herbert of Cherbury,* he refers to the fact that his nephew " though young sought divers duels, in one of which it was his fortune to kill one Lee of a great family in Lancashire," evidently considering that he had done rather a fine thing and that it was an achievement for the Herbert family to be justly proud of.

There appears to have been some idea of prosecution. 1641-2 Peter Venables, in a letter to Francis Legh, written on March 4, 1641-2, speaks of " the eyes of the kingdom being upon this notorious murder and upon me as prosecutor," and asking if Francis wishes him to undertake the journey to London " to prosecute according as I have begun," but Francis was in such bad health that he was quite incapable of taking the necessary steps and of exerting himself in the matter, and so there it ended.

Francis fulfilled his dying nephew's wishes in paying Anne Legh her £100 a year, but she disappears from this date and we hear little more of her.

The canvassing of the new candidates for the Newton election began immediately after the death of poor Peter. Sir George Booth,† who afterwards headed the Cheshire rising, in 1659, for restoring Charles II, writes on February 11 to beg Francis Legh's assistance " for a kinsman's and a gentleman's sake," assuring himself that Francis " would rather accept of him than any other." Another correspondent writes putting forward the claims of a Mr. Holcroft, Sir Gilbert Gerard was advocating the election of one of his sons, and William Ashurst, Peter Legh's former colleague, was anxious to stand again. In a long letter to Francis Legh he mentions the fact that he has the powerful support of Lady Strange, the famous Charlotte de la Trémouille, Countess of Derby, renowned for her defence of

* Edward, first Lord Herbert of Cherbury (1583–1648). Through the marriage of Lord Herbert's eldest son, Richard, second Baron, with Mary, daughter of John, first Earl of Bridgewater, the families of Herbert and Legh of Lyme became connected.

† Sir George Booth (1622–1684), first Lord Delamere, descended from a younger branch of the Booths of Dunham Massy, Cheshire ; took Parliamentarian side in the Civil War, but entered plot for restoring Charles II ; raised to peerage at the Restoration.

Lathom House against the Parliamentarians. This lady, Ashurst writes, " had freely offered me her assistance which I had thankfully accepted of," he mentions also that Sir Richard Fleetwood —the Lord of the Manor—was supposed to be abusing his privileges and rights, to the great indignation of the free burgesses, who were resolving to oppose whichever candidate Sir Richard should support. Ultimately a Sir Roger Palmer, Knight, was returned with William Ashurst, and both represented Newton until 1646, when they were " disabled to sit," Richard Holland of Heaton and Peter Brooke being then returned.

CHAPTER XII

FRANCIS AND LETTICE LEGH

THE shadow of death had fallen heavily upon the house of Lyme. Within the short space of two years no fewer than four of the family, all in the prime of life, had passed away.

Dr. Thomas Legh's death is recorded as having taken place at Walton on May 27, 1639, at the age of forty-five. We have no details of his last illness, but from the fact that he was buried there the next day one gathers that the illness was probably of a highly infectious nature. His wife Lettice, who was only twenty-nine, was expecting an addition to her family, poor soul, and there were four other children, the eldest of whom could not have been more than seven or eight years of age. Two elder children had died in infancy. Peter Legh of Bruch, Francis's youngest brother, died in 1641, and in February 1641-2 came the tragic death of young Peter, which we have just described, to be followed soon after by that of Francis and his only surviving sister, Anne Bold.

Lettice Legh (widow of Dr. Thomas), after her husband's death, made her home with her brother-in-law Francis, at Blackley, Lancashire, and here her youngest daughter, Francisca Posthuma, was born in December or January 1639–40, her husband having died the previous May. Fortunately for herself and her children she seems to have been a lady of very strong character, clever and businesslike, and capable of managing her own affairs, for the wretched state of Francis's health must have prevented him from being of very much help to her ; he was practically a cripple on two sticks and suffered agonies from acute rheumatism.

Lettice Legh appears to have taken up her life and interests after the birth of her little girl, and to have occupied herself with all the domestic details connected with a large family and household. Her two boys, Richard and Thomas, were in 1642 already at school at Winwick, although they can have been only eight and six years old, and she was writing in May of that year to Francis—then paying one of his visits to Oxford—to know his wishes in certain matters of housekeeping, and was giving him particulars about the brewing, which was always a very important event. Her handwriting shows a great deal of character, but her spelling, even for that of ladies of the time, is exceptionally bad, words are omitted altogether and it is sometimes almost impossible to arrive at her meaning. She was devotedly attached to her brother-in-law, and consulted him on every matter.

1642

> " John Ingam hath brud one bruing at Lim and when the fair is now past, i hop i shall get mor vessell [?] for another bruing, and the therd [third] as soon as can bee shall bee done God willing, and ther shallbee wormwood beer at every place as soon as i can posseble."

She is selling hay :

> " i haue set but littill hay gres [after grass] for unlest in old set the best, the other offer almost nothing for . . . if you will have mee to do any other ways, i pra let me know and i will obay as far forth as i can [subscribing herself] your tru louing sister til deth us part
> " LETTICE LEGH."

One of his servants writes also to tell Francis that he wishes he had the hogshead of beer at Oxford which they have just brewed, " it was excellent good." The old conviviality and hospitality went on at Blackley as at Lyme ; the same correspondent wishes Francis could see

> " Dad Peel, William Wordsworth and Nandie ould Robin, they meet together for the spending of the token you sent them, I heartily wish you a sight of their red noses that will be seen at night when they part."

Although rather better, Francis was beginning to set his house in order, feeling that his health was so precarious that it was as well to be prepared for the worst :

178

" My Physicon has entered me into a course of Physicke agreable to my Body [he writes to Peter Venables from London in May 1642], for I find thereby a new accesse of strength and other good symptoms of re-coverie. I eate my meate with a prettie good appetite and my limbs though still mowldie, are more plyable then when you left me, for with ye alone help of my sticks, I can goe from chamber to chamber, my payne is much easier though it still mind me of its abode with me, (though against my will) I hope ere long I shall be able to undertake a journie, but whether my Doctors intentions are for ye Bath or noe I cannot as yet resolve you, he being not resolved in himselfe how to dispose of mee."

He then proceeds to state his wishes as to the disposal of some of his property, the bulk of which was to go to his heir, his brother Thomas's eldest son, Richard. He begs that Peter Venables and his son will name themselves " feoffies."

On June 11 of this same year he was appointed by the King one of his Commissioners of Array, a kind of deputy-lieutenant for Lancashire, but his duties must have been purely nominal, for he was in far too bad health to undertake any active work.

Hostilities which had so long threatened broke out in August of this same year, 1642. On the 22nd of that month Charles set up his standard at Nottingham as a declaration of war. Almost destitute of money and arms, the great difficulty the King had to contend with was the raising of recruits. He was reduced to the direst straits for want of funds for his new levies, in spite of the gifts of plate from the Universities and Royalists, who willingly gave their all, the women even bringing their wedding-rings in response to a loan opened in the City.

Although only fifty-two years of age, the precarious state of his health and his crippled condition made it out of the question for Francis Legh to take any active part in the Civil War, but he was, of course, expected to contribute his share towards providing men and horses for the service of his King. A very interesting letter from a certain James Bretherton, a Lancashire friend, gives him advice on this matter, and also contains information relating to the Battle of Edgehill, where it appears that Charles himself was present in person, and narrowly escaped death from a cannon-ball, which missed him by only a yard.

" Uppon Thursday last Capten Cornocke from ye Earl of Darbie *
called on mee to give mee notice to bee with the said Earl yesterday,
where I was, and the conference when I came there was to see what
frends, neighbores or gentlemen (for the saftie of the countie) would
furnishe horses for a small tyme, or for laying downe moneyes for
maintaining soldiers or horses for some small tyme, and for that
purpose Mr Frarrington is chosen pursebearer. You were not spoke of
further then inquired after for your health, I tould the Countice † you
were better at your first coming downe then you were nowe, and that I
was not serten whether you were at Lyme or Blackley ; but I thinke
there is an expectation of some furtherance from you, for the safetie
of the countie as afforesaid. I had conferance yesterdaye wth George
Bowden ‡ what was fit to doe (and moneyes being scarce) I thought (yf
it might stand with your likeinge) it were not amisse to give or lend
to the Earl or Ladie your ould whit horse, the little whit horse which
was your nephewes, and what other ould decade [decayed] geldings you
might convenientlie spare, and if you mind any further furtherance
and will not bee seene therein, forecast the business and let it bee my
ackt, it may prevent some further motion that may bee more inconvenient but however my desires are to waite of your pleasure.

" The nuse the Earl received from a gentleman by his Maiestie's
appointment was That the Kinge himselfe was at this bloodie battle §
and Cannon shute miste him but a yard. His Standard bearer ‖ was
slayne and the standard taken by the enemie, but by a private gentleman (one Smith ¶) regayned, the said Smith killinge the enemie. This
Smith is nowe maid Knight Banoret, and is his Maties Standard berer.
Prince Robt [Rupert] with the rest of the regimt bore the other
regimt backe and kild and slue to the number of eyght thousand,
spoyled and tooke all (to anie purpose) of their horse, taken eyght
pieces of ordinance, burst three others, taken most of their ammunicon,
made his excellencie ** to retreat or run awaye, who was said to take
Warwick Castle. And of the Kings partie Toe thousand sleayne and
as it is said noe commander of Lankishere but honest Henrie Byrom,
I desire your lre [letter] of comfort to his mother, for I knowe your

* James, seventh Earl of Derby, husband of Charlotte de la Trémouille, beheaded
1651. Alluding to him, Walpole in his " Royal and Noble Authors " (iii, 37) says :
" Among the sufferers for King Charles I none shed greater lustre on the cause."
† Charlotte de la Trémouille, Countess of Derby.
‡ Francis Legh's agent.
§ Edgehill.
‖ Sir Edmund Verney.
¶ Sir John Smith (1616–1644), Royalist; knighted on the field at Edgehill for
saving the Royal Standard ; killed at Cheriton.
** Probably Essex.

perswesion with her will take deep hold. And soe wishinge you where you thinke your selfe most safe (which I thinke is Hodocke, Bradley or Boulde) doe leaue your Worshipe to the Lord his merciful protection and will ever rest.

"Your servant to command JA : BRETHERTON."

But Francis was soon to be where "beyond these voices there is peace." Within three months after the receipt of this letter he was dead. We get no details of his last illness, nor do we know where the death actually took place, whether at Oxford, where he was staying in November 1642, or at Lyme. The date was February 2, 1642–3, and he was buried with his forefathers at Winwick.

An inventory made about this date has the first page missing; it gives the contents of some of the rooms with the valuation, but it is impossible to say whether this refers to Lyme or Blackley or to any of Francis's other houses :

Each room seems to have contained "Orras." Arras, * was a superior kind of tapestry; some of the rooms also contained pieces of loose or broken "sylinge." † In "the furthest chamber," which must have been one of the best rooms, we find the "vallence and hangings at the standinge bedd wrought upon Velvet with gould and sylke," valued at £4 10s. This bed was composed of one feather-bed, one bolster and two pillows, valued at £3 0s. 4d., one "wolbedd," 10s., 3 blankets, 18s., and one "Cadowes," £1. A truckle-bed in the same room, probably intended for the servant, is priced together with the "Standinge bedd" at £1 6s. 8d. Upon the truckle-bed were 1 feather-bed, one bolster and one pillow, £1 13s. 4d., one "Lynnen and wollen Cou'inge," 3s. 4d., and two blankets, 7s. Other articles in the room are as follows :

one Orras Cou'inge	. . . .	4¹.	
a Darnix ‡ Carpet	. . . .	2s	
One syde table	. . . . .		5d
Half a dozen bedstaves .	. . .		3d
One Chayre .	. . . . .		10d

* Halliwell's "Dictionary of Archaic and Provincial Words."
† Tapestry or hanging (Halliwell).
‡ Darnex was a coarse sort of damask used for carpets, curtains, etc.

One Cou^{red} joyned Stoole . . .	3s	4d
One other Stoole	1s	
One Bill *	1s	

In " a trunke bounde with plate " in one of the rooms we find the following treasures mentioned, with the valuation :

	l	s	d
Itm one greene Cadowes	01–	13	4
Itm one hanginge of Orras worke . .	03	10–	0
Itm 2 greene velvett Cushions, & other 2 of Cloth of gould beanched wth greene and one other beauched [?] Cushion at .	3–	00–	0
Itm a payre of vallence of redd and greene Satten fringed wth Gould . . .	00–	18–	0
Itm one othr payre of vallence of blacke velvett & mingled orrage Coller wth blacke and tany ffrynge . . .	00–	16–	0
Itm a hanginge for a bedds head of greene wth a Cruicifix wrought wth gould .	01–	13–	4
Itm a Carpett of Darnix for a table . .	00–	05	0
Itm 5 Curtaynes of greene and Redd .	01–	10–	0
Itm one Cushion of Orras & twoe pillowes .	00–	05	0
Itm the hangings aboute the Chamber .	01–	06–	8
Itm a trunck bound wth plate, one cheste 2 Chaires & 2 Cushions . . .	02–	00–	0
Itm one leading staffe	00–	02–	0

The prices mentioned seem ridiculously inadequate and would arouse feelings of envy in the breast of a collector. None of the articles can be traced and, alas, the same applies to the following list of plate, to which no prices are attached but which would —at this day—be of fabulous value.

Itm 1 greate bell Salt double gylt, waighing one pound and a half & half an ounce

Itm One bould [bowl] with a Cou^r double gylt, waighing a pound 2 ounces, half an ounce & a dram

Itm One Canne pcell [parcell] gylt waighinge a pound

Itm A silver Canne waighinge one pound, 2 ounce & a half

Itm One other Canne pcell gylt, one pound & 5 ounce

---

* A bill was a kind of pike or halberd, formerly carried by the English infantry, and afterwards the usual weapon of watchmen (Halliwell.)

LYME: CHIMNEYPIECE IN THE STONE PARLOUR

Itm one dozen of Apostle Spoons waighinge one pound and a
halfe & one ounce

Itm One old Salt, waighinge xi ounce & a halfe

Itm xi silver Spoones waighinge one pound 3 ounce & a
quarter of an ounce.

Four muskets and 3 " Calibers " (probably meant for
calivers—a large pistol or blunderbuss), " wth flaxes and tutch-
box," * are priced at £2. The owner's entire wearing apparel
is estimated at £20, " Barlie in the fforreste " at £20, 81
sheep at £14, and " one oxe hyde in the barne " at 16s.

Mistress Lettice had, with her children, taken up her abode
at Lyme after her brother-in-law's death. By an account book
beginning February 2, 1642–3, containing a list of the sums of
money that had passed through her hands, we learn that she
was

" to be imployed by the executors, Henry Legh, Peter Legh, Charles
Herle, Rector of Winwick, Ralph Richardson, Rector of Groppenhall,
and John Houghton, fellow of Brasenose, both for the receivinge and
disbursinge moneys after his decease accordinge to the appoyntments
and direccons of the said Ffrancis Legh."

She was also to be " wholey " trusted to receive the money.

For some six years after the death of Sir Peter Legh, Lyme
had been uninhabited. The old rooms—once the scene of so
much gaiety and merriment—were empty and silent, the garden
with its winding paths and arbours was grass-grown and
neglected, the whole place tenantless and forlorn. In spite of
Francis Legh's desire that his abodes should be maintained and
kept going, the evidences of an absentee landlord must have
been apparent, and signs were not wanting of the lack of the
châtelaine's watchful eye. With the arrival of Mistress Lettice
and her little ones the old place took on a different aspect, and
although the princely hospitality of former days could no longer
be dispensed and the same amount of grandeur could not be
maintained, still there were children's voices once more heard,
and life and movement went on within its walls.

* A touch-box was a receptacle for lighted tinder carried by soldiers for match-
locks (Halliwell).

THE HOUSE OF LYME

Times were sadly changed from the prosperity of Elizabethan days. The Civil War had now begun, and Cheshire suffered as much and perhaps more for its loyalty than most counties. After setting up his standard at Nottingham, Charles, with a numerous train, came to Chester, being received everywhere with the greatest enthusiasm. He was, with all his train, lodged in the episcopal palace, and the next day was entertained by the corporation at the Pentice when £200 was presented to him in the name of the mayor, and £100 was ordered as a present to one of the Princes who accompanied him. Before his departure next day the King ordered the city to be put into a state of defence.*

Of all the events in the history of Chester none is so memorable as that of the protracted siege which the city endured from Sir William Brereton, the Parliamentarian general, which began in 1643. By 1645, the assailants, despairing of taking the town by assault, converted the siege into a blockade, causing the intensest suffering to the citizens, who by 1645–6 were in want of the commonest necessaries of life. Some murmurings and discontents having arisen, Lord Byron † and some of the Commissioners invited the chiefs of the malcontents to dine with them and gave them nothing but boiled wheat to eat and spring water to drink, solemnly assuring them that this had been their only fare for some time past. This had the desired effect upon the citizens, who resolved to hold out to the very last. It was not until after the tenth summons that the intrepid defenders agreed to surrender on the following conditions : (1) the garrison to be allowed to march out with all the honours of war ; (2) the safety of the persons and property of the citizens ; (3) the sanctity of the sacred edifices and title-deeds preserved. Following upon the siege came a most terrible epidemic of the plague, which lasted from June 1648 to April 1649, 2099 persons dying in the several city parishes.

The country was being overrun by hostile armies, plundering

* "Chronological Series of Local Events connected with Chester" (Ormerod's History).

† John, first Lord Byron (d. 1652), a devoted adherent of Charles I ; fought at Edgehill ; was one of the defenders of Chester Castle.

FRANCIS AND LETTICE LEGH

and destroying whatever lay before them. Lyme suffered to a certain extent, but much less than might have been supposed, judging by the fate of neighbouring houses and individuals. " In Ffebruary 1643 " writes the steward in the account book mentioned, " weere tymes of much troble and the horses and mares and much other goods that weere Mr Legh's weere some taken for the use of the publique and some plundred or stoalen . . . goods wastinge by stealth, rottinge wth hydinge from plunder."

From a petition * of one William Burgess of Macclesfield to 1643–4 the Committee for Compositions at Goldsmith's Hall, we learn that the said William Burgess for having (his only crime), in January 1643–4, visited Mr. Legh of Adlington, who was keeping a garrison for the King's party in his house, situated within three miles of where Burgess lived, the latter's whole estate was seized and sequestered. He apologized humbly for his offence, declaring he

> " was never in any other of the enemy's quarters, nor has borne arms or contributed to the King's party, but has always paid his full part in all loans and taxations for the State besides £10, upon the Proposition and has borne the charge of entertainment and free quarter of soldiers far above his ability, whereby his small estate had been much impaired, and the residue now being sequestered he has no means left for himself and family to subsist upon, and begs to be admitted to a favourable composition for what remains to him of his estate."

He must have felt that his friendly visit cost him somewhat dear.

One can imagine the horror and consternation that must have been caused in a peaceful household by the sudden arrival of a troop of rough and often brutal soldiers. One pictures the terrified women herded together, the children clinging round their mother's knees, the hurried collecting and concealment of precious possessions from the looting and destruction of these soldiers, who took complete possession of the houses, demanding the best of what the place afforded, and taking by force all they

* Record Office.

185

could lay their hands on. Nor did they confine themselves only to looting. At a neighbouring house, Poynton, some five miles from Lyme, the wife of the owner, Mr. Edward Warren, died in 1644, after giving birth prematurely to twins, the result, it was said, of rough treatment at the hands of soldiers who came to search Poynton for arms.

Mistress Lettice Legh must have found her hands pretty full. Besides the control of the household and the care and education of her children, the eldest of whom, Richard, was in 1642-3 only nine years of age, she had to assist in the management of the large estates which were left by Francis Legh's will in the hands of the trustees before mentioned. She was, as we have seen, a daughter of Sir George Calveley of Lea, and co-heiress with her sister, Mrs. Thomas Cotton, and must have been aged a little over thirty in 1642. It seems hardly possible for one woman to have attempted, far less accomplished, all that she contrived to do. She showed herself, however, to be possessed of great strength of mind, courage, and resourcefulness, and nothing daunted by a condition of affairs that might well have unnerved most members of her sex, she determined to fight to the uttermost to safeguard the lives and interests of her children.

No sooner had the death of Francis deprived her of a male protector, however feeble, than calls innumerable were made upon the widow and fatherless. Peter Venables, Baron of Kinderton, a distant cousin, came down upon her for a debt owing to him from Francis, wishing her at the same time all happiness and desiring she may be freed from " the troubles of theise tymes, which debarr freinds of enjoying of one another with the same comfort as formerlie," protesting that, were he in the position to do so, " none should be more readie to doe you service. I wish you to esteem of me as an honest man though the fortunes of this world doe not smyle on me, if I would have played the knave I would have climbed first upon others."

There was grumbling and dissatisfaction in the family over Francis's will. The children of Piers and Anne Legh considered they had been badly used. Margaret, the eldest daughter, writes on October 5, 1643, from Blackley, to her Aunt Lettice :

"Honored Aunt,—By your direccons Roger Locke is come to mee for paiment for carrying a Muskit this last year by my Unkel's appointment, to wch I answer ; iff my Unkell had left mee and my sisters the benefit of that estate (wch without offence to God I may call ours) we should willingly discharge those taxations justly imposed upon it, but being wee ar unjustly defrauded of our owen, we rather expected satisfactione for the wronge alredy don us then such quirkes to wringe from us that litell we have left, which I may truly call litell, beinge it will not manteine us wth meate, drinke and clothes, neither do I conceive the lawe to bee so far from conscience and equity as to compell us to undergo such unreasonabell burdens, nor that deceit can so strip us of our birthright but wee shall have competent menteinance."

The burdens imposed upon all were very heavy. In 1644, pecuniary levies upon the citizens of Chester amounted to £200 every fortnight, and towards the assessment for maintaining soldiers the Legh estates paid monthly no less a sum than £19 0s. 7½d., that is, for Warrington, £3 19s. 9d., Haydock, £10 1s. 4½d., Burtonwood, £4. 7s. 6d., and Parr, 12s."

It was almost impossible to obtain any rents, for the tenants suffered so much from the plunder and depredations of the soldiers that they were wellnigh ruined. On the 11th of December 1645 we find in the account book the following notable entry :

Received from William Bankes by the hands of George Bowdon fyve pounds, fourtiene shillings for the Rough Parke wch was paid by Hill, Saunderson and Neiler. In the year 1644, they three undertooke to pay ten pounds for that grounde. But the Prince his armie plundered the cattell and nothinge was made of it, wherefore an agree[t] was made with them and more could not be gott then."

In June 1646 the Steward writes in the same account book :

"The town of Hoole hath beene much impoverished, and untill Lathom House was delivered I coulde not wth safetie send thether, so that the poornes of the people, neglect of callinge uppon them for their rents, together wth these tymes of libertie and distraccon renddered them of that place incredibly forgetfull, and manie would denye to pay anie rent. And since Lathom was delivered to the use of the Parliam[t] I have sent thether three tymes, appoynted Henry Hunt the elder to gather the rents or demand at least. Observe [he writes on March 9th, 1647] that Dickonson's 7[l] is in arrear, and also observe that Henry Hunt senior payes no hennes nor Capons."

Receipts follow to the amount of £37 10s. 7d.

The total receipts that came to Mistress Lettice's hands from the death of Francis to October 1645 amounted to the sum of £1385 1s. 3½d. This statement is duly attested and signed by Ralphe Richardson and three witnesses.

A large quantity of timber seems to have been sold every year. This part of the country consisted principally of vast tracts of forest, providing plenty of timber, and wood being used for the construction of ships made this, of course, valuable ; in 1646 over £500 worth was sold. The average price per tree was from 25s. to 30s.

1646–7   In 1646–7 appears a receipt of £452 4s. for plate sold to a Mr. Vynor * in London—probably Sir Thomas Viner, the noted goldsmith—the following pieces, which were " taken into the hands of Mistress Lettice," being reserved :

	£.	s.	d.
Two Candlesticks—25 ounces one ½ ounce at 4/11d½ the ounce .	6.	6.	6.
One dooble salte 21 ounces one quarter at ye same rate . .	5.	5.	4.
One Tunne & a little cupp 12 : ounces .	8.	19.	6.
One dosen of Spoones 35 ounces 3 quarter .	8.	16.	6.
One Boule 18 onz : & a halfe . .	4.	11.	9.
Totall for plate	33.	19.	7.

Most of the land round the house appears to have been cultivated and sown with oats and corn.

Soon after the death of Francis Legh the Lyme estate, which until then had furnished ten men and one horse for the war, was surcharged to find an extra man and horse, and Mistress Lettice might well have felt intimidated into complying with this demand,

* Sir Thomas Viner, Baronet (1588–1665), Lord Mayor of London ; goldsmith.

however unreasonable, without venturing upon a remonstrance. Such, however, was not the case. She set to work immediately to frame a petition showing that the estate had been already surcharged in another place, although contrary to the advice of her friends and relations, who counselled her to submit without a struggle.

On July 29, 1647, she had drawn up and forwarded her petition :

" To the Lieutenants Councell of Warre for the Countie of Chester and to such to whom the same shall appertaine :

' The umble petition of Letice Legh widdowe, mother of Richard Legh Esqr, an infant of the age of twelve years or thereabout,' "

setting forth plainly that her father-in-law, Sir Peter, had been charged for his Lancashire lands—where the bulk of his property lay—and that having removed his dwelling from Lancashire to Cheshire, he should be charged for the men in Cheshire and be spared from the other charge, and that as the public service is not neglected but is still " supplied and done, seeing the charge that Mr Legh the Infant is at in Lancashire in mayntayning of Souldiers in this service for his Lands, that they sett downe such order for the peticon^{rs} & the Infants releefe as they shall consider just and reasonable." The importunate widow's claims were heard and her petition was successful.

All the worry and anxiety she had undergone must have told seriously upon her health and strength, for on October 14, 1648—her 38th birthday—she died at Lyme and was buried on the 21st in the Legh Chapel in Macclesfield parish church. We have no details of her last illness. By the account book, we learn from one William Bankes that he made his last account to his mistress on the 15th of December 1647, and she was evidently in failing health early the following year, as her will, in which she speaks of the " vncertaintye of this life," is dated March 13th, 1647-8. The executors she appoints are her steward, George Bowden, Mr. John Dunbabin, and her three daughters, which seems curious, as the eldest of them, Lettice,

1648

was only thirteen at the time of her mother's death. The Rev. Charles Herle, Rector of Winwick, Lancashire, chief trustee of Francis Legh's will, seems also to have had a share in the wardship of the children.

Richard, eldest surviving son of Dr. Thomas Legh and his wife Lettice, was born on May 7th, 1634. His elder brother Peter, born in 1632, died in infancy, and Richard then became heir to the Lyme estates. This is the first instance for over 300 years of the heir to the family bearing any other Christian name than Piers or Peter, and there were nine of these in succession. Richard was probably christened after his father's life-long friend, Richard Parr, Bishop of Sodor and Man. Lettice, eldest surviving daughter, comes next, born July 7, 1635; Thomas, second surviving son, born October 6, 1636; Margaret, called after her grandmother and great-great-grandmother, born September 17, 1637; and poor little Francisca Posthuma, goddaughter of Francis, born December 1639 or January 1640, some seven or eight months after her father's death.

A codicil to her will is added on the day of her death in which Lettice Legh desires that " my Cosen Susan Domvile and Mistress Creswell doe stay with my Children and not leave them till they bee of age to have discretion to know how to behave themselves, for I know they will have a care of them for both body and soule."

What pathos is in these words! What anguish of mind must have been hers at the thought of her five children, the eldest, Richard, barely fourteen, the youngest girl but eight years old, left to the mercy of the world, and deprived, at an age when they most required both, of the loving care and guidance of their natural protectors. The state of the country where civil war was raging, the dangers they would be exposed to from both war and pestilence, and the dread of never knowing what each day might bring forth, must have filled her last hours with anguish and misgiving. Just three months before the execution of Charles I, Mistress Lettice Legh closed her eyes upon this world, and " the kind grave shut up the mournful scene." *

* Dryden, "The Spanish Friar," Act V.

CHAPTER XIII

DURING THE COMMONWEALTH

AFTER the death of Mistress Lettice Legh in October 1648, the five children seem to have continued to live at Lyme under the care of Mistress Susan Domvile and Mistress Creswell and with the guardianship of Mr. Charles Herle,* Rector of Winwick, and George Bowdon, the family steward. The former was a great Royalist and always stoutly refused to pray for the Parliament. There is little to tell how the children fared. They must have been a sad little family, for even Francisca Posthuma was old enough to realize what had happened, and no amount of well-meant care and attention from their nurses and guardians could make up to the orphans for the mother they had lost.

The Disley parish registers show no entries whatever from November 10, 1633, to May 27, 1643, nor is there evidence of any religious ceremony having taken place in Disley during those ten years. There are very few letters between the years 1642 and 1659, and in those few there is no mention of the King's fate.

The two boys, Richard and Thomas, had received their early education at the school at Winwick, Lancashire, where they would also have been under the watchful eye of the Rector, Mr. Herle, but after the removal of Mistress Lettice Legh and her family to Lyme, and during the worst part of the Civil War, there was probably small opportunity of much instruction other than that which could be obtained at home. It was perhaps in some ways a fortunate thing that his tender years prevented the possibility of Richard Legh becoming involved in any of the troubles. His youth no doubt saved him from the

* Charles Herle, Puritan divine (1598–1659), was presented by the Stanley family to the rectory of Winwick, Lancashire.

fines and sequestrations that were imposed upon his neighbours, and the friendship of the Legh family with President Bradshawe was also a great protection.

1649   In October 1649 we hear of Richard at St. John's College, Cambridge, where he was admitted in June of that year at the early age of fifteen.   The following is from the book of admissions translated from the original Latin : " Admissions July 1648– July 1649, (36) Richard Legh of Cheshire, son of Thomas Legh Esqr, School Winwig [Winwick], Lancashire, admitted fellow commoner under Mr Creswick 18 June (1649), aet. 15."

But for the Civil War he would probably have been sent to Brasenose, Oxford, where his father and several of his predecessors were educated, but Oxford was the centre of hostilities, the Royalist headquarters, and was, in 1646, in a state of siege. All serious study was impossible, everything had to give way to war. The College was a barrack, every inch of room was required for the garrison, and all the members who remained in it were, if under the age of sixty, compelled to fight.*   Added to the horrors of war came a most terrible outbreak of the plague, combined this time with a virulent form of small-pox.

The effect of the war on the admissions of undergraduates was very great, as we see by the following entries to Brasenose. In 1641 there were nineteen admissions, in 1642 seventeen, in 1643 five, in 1644 one, and in 1645 not a single name appears.   It will therefore be inferred that Mistress Lettice Legh settled some time before her death that Cambridge should be selected as her eldest son's college instead of Oxford.   Writing to him on October 30, 1649, the Rev. Charles Herle says :

" Having heard by your servant Mr Boden that you like well of your College and Company and imploy^t in your studyes I have occasion to signify my gladnes as well as thankfulnes ; as alsoe to encourage you to goe on cheerfully in what I heare you have made soe happy an entrance."

He gives him at the same time some wholesome advice :

" There is nothing more dangerous and dishonourable in a gentleman then to carry his braynes in another mans head."

* " Brasenose College " (Mr. Wakeling).

George Bowdon writes to the boy much in the same strain :

> " I would not have ye Lord B.* nor some other to say that you
> skarted † nor thinke that you hate the benefitt of educacon and
> improvement, that being the only Schoole."

Young as he was, only fifteen, Richard had already taken
upon himself the cares and responsibilities of his position, and
was proving himself to be of a businesslike turn of mind and
a help to his relations. His aunt, Lady Calveley,‡ wife of Sir
Hugh Calveley of Lea, brother of Mistress Lettice Legh, had
not long been left a widow, and was soliciting the help of the
boy Richard in settling her affairs :

> " I have been continuously plyed with letters from my Aunt Calveley
> [he writes in February 1649–50 to Robert Cholmondeley, Earl of
> Leinster,§ his great-uncle], all tending to draw upp my Cosen Cotton
> and mee to London to engage us to assist her with our unkles debts,"

returning his great-uncle at the same time

> " humble and hertie thankes for your loving entertainment when I was
> with you at Cholmondeley and for your large favours shown to mee
> there . . . I have now dispatched my occasions and am returning to
> my studies."

In 1650–51 there was an outbreak of small-pox in his
college, and his tutor, Mr. J. Creswick, writing to his pupil on
March 4, mentions the fact of losing a child :

> " Since you went from Camb : it hath pleased God to take away my
> little Lamb by the small pox. . . . Lumley also dyed a week before
> him wch is about 7 weeks ago, since which tyme no other hath falln
> sick in ye College of that disease. [He speaks of a duel :] The last
> weeke here was a duell fought by Mr Balam fellow comm^r of Trin :
> & one Nicholson of that Colledge who challenged Mr Balam & even
> forced him to ye duell ag^t his mind, but Nicholson was dangerously
> wounded, yet it is now hoped he will recover."

Even at such an early age Richard seems to have taken
keenly to racing and horse-breeding :

---

* Probably Lord Bradshawe, the regicide judge.   † Shirked.
‡ A daughter of Sir Gilbert Hoghton of Hoghton.
§ Created Earl in 1645 ; married Catherine, daughter of Lord Stanhope of
Harrington.

" Yesterday I got up yr Coults, put them and the little bay mare into the meadowe [writes George Bowdon to him in an undated letter of about this date], John Morret hath put yor young geldinge to his stroake, so Mr Thos. his, wch is complained on for dulnes, & was forced to leave them sooner then he would. Dicke Corke hath brought home yr huntinge horse, one of the mares havinge but latly foaled, Sorell brings littel coults, the proofe of them must bee expected after weaninge. The other Norton a larger, but the issue of yr ould horse all over."

Mr. Herle also writes reporting news of the stud ; he finds the mares " extreame fatt, but the Colts as leane." He was evidently a sporting parson :

" Yr Colts are I heare very well att Bradley, soe are not myne, but all extreamely troubled wth the Strangle, yet the Kirke stands in the Kirkyard still, and I remayne tho' exceedingly ill at this tyme, Sr
"Yr most humble and obliged servant
"C. HERLE."

Richard remained at Cambridge until after 1652, when he would have been about eighteen years of age. A farewell letter from his tutor, Mr. Creswick, wishes him all prosperity. From its contents we gather that alterations had already begun at Lyme, and there seems to have been an idea of introducing some of the black-and-white timber-work, so much a feature of Cheshire houses.

" I wish Lyme all white, omnia Albae, all prosperous, successful and happy there, and that your self may know (I do not mean in the phrase but in reality) what Alba Gallinae filius is, The Jewes use to write upon new built houses (having first markt the Wall wth a Black Stick) words that signify Nigrum Super Album and under it they write Recordare Vastationis. I would not have black and white mixt with you or in you, but desyre that for ever it may be a Paradox to say that Lyme is Black or any Nigrum at all in it, and I shall put it in my prayers that it may never know what Vastation means."

After leaving Cambridge Richard probably entered one of the Inns of Court, as there is mention of his intended " studie of ye Lawe." His health was by no means robust, his chest was delicate, and he was frequently laid up with severe colds and cough during the time he spent in London, where we hear

LYME : ENTRANCE

of him at " The Three Tunnes " in King Street, Westminster, and in lodgings in Gray's Inn.

Things had evidently got into a very bad state at Lyme during the long absence of Francis Legh, when the house had been practically unoccupied for some six years. Buildings were falling into ruin, and the enormous extent of park wall had to be repaired and indeed partly rebuilt to prevent the deer escaping.* This was costly work ; the sum of £500 and more seems to have been expended, although, this being a stone district, the materials were close at hand. There are at this day no fewer than four quarries in the park, and all these seem to have been worked at different periods.

> " The wallers are cloase at worke [writes George Bowdon on April 23, 1651], and the getters are getting at the fflood gate and have found a Stone in the browe † [hill], so that a little more then ordinary Cast-inge it, will cast it to the Walle. . . . I am sorie to see these herculean labours to be soe costly to you [adds the careful steward], and the land noe joat better wthin, it hath cost 500¹ and more money that might have beene bestowed of good stuffe, yeeldinge yearely rent. But deere are deare and will bee to you. I drive on yor costly designes, and doe it with eagernes and faithfulnes. [He adds a delightful sentiment :] A man's estate is much his honoʳ, for take that away, and what's a gent more then one man ! "

There were other expenses, the trained soldiers had still to be maintained, George Bowdon complaining that " these soldiers are more and more numerous, onely faire mannered but costly."

Another death occurred at Lyme in February 1651-2,

* Walls are greatly used in this part of the world in the place of hedges. All the enclosures in the park at Lyme are rubble, built of a regular-shaped stone, without mortar or cement of any kind. These have two faces, filled up between with small stones, and are bound together with " throughs " or " binders," which are stones that run through the thickness of the wall binding it together. There is a considerable amount of skill in the construction, the stones require to be built in flat and close together with hardly any space between the interstices, and the art consists in keeping the structure perpendicular and not letting it bulge.

The stone in this part of the county, which is a hard grey sandstone and very much broken, is far older than that found in the plain of Cheshire, the water having receded from this high ground at a much earlier period. That found in the plain is a softer kind of sandstone of a redder hue, due probably to the action of the sea, and is called the " new formation."

† This word is still used for " hill " amongst the Cheshire country people.

namely, that of Lettice, eldest sister of Richard, at the early age of seventeen. There is no mention of the occurrence beyond the record of her burial in the registers at Macclesfield church, where it took place on February 21, 1651–2.

1655   The year 1655 saw two important events in the Legh family, the coming of age of Richard and the marriage of his second sister Margaret with Mr. (afterwards Sir John) Arderne of Harden, near Stockport. According to the Disley parish registers, this took place on February 7, 1654–5, but no other mention of the ceremony occurs in any of the letters. By 1656 little Francisca Posthuma was also married, although aged only sixteen, to Sir Richard Brooke of Norton, Cheshire, but again we have no details, nor does any entry of the marriage appear in the Disley parish registers.

1656   This same year, 1656, Richard Legh was elected M.P. for the county of Cheshire, having as his colleague Sir George Booth, notorious, in 1659, for heading the Cheshire rising in support of Charles II. It was in the Parliament of 1656 that it was proposed to make Cromwell king, but Richard was spared having to vote in favour of what would have been repugnant to his Royalist sentiments, for [says Mr. Beamont, the antiquary] he is reported, on the names of the members being called, as going into the country " dangerously sicke." I have, however, not found any mention of this in the " Journals of the House of Commons " for that date.

People were now beginning to send their letters by post. The first inland post office was established by Charles I in 1635, but for some years none but messengers of the Postmaster General were—with few exceptions—allowed to use it. There were changes made during the Commonwealth, but the post office cannot have been of much general utility, the rate of postage, for one thing, being so high. It cost 2d. to send a single letter a distance not exceeding 80 miles ; for 140 miles 4d. was paid ; and for any greater distance in England, 6d. Letters to Scotland cost 8d.

Mr. Herle writes, in 1657, complaining of the condition in which Richard Legh's letters reach him, the outer leaf being

196

" plundered and unsealed." He finds on inquiry, however, that this damage has not been done by the post office, as he conjectured, but by his daughter, " who did itt because shee knewe that the Post had formerly requyred the Superscriptions to bee sent backe agayne for discharging the officer that (as hee said) requyred itt."

No postmarks appear on the Legh letters before the year 1670.

Signs were not wanting in the country of a desire for change in the government. People were getting anxious to free themselves from the tyranny of Cromwell's rule, and Richard was not behindhand in volunteering his services towards helping to restore the monarchy. " I make no question but that the Royall partie goes clearly on, without any great Rubs or stops," writes Richard Standish, a cousin, on April 17, 1657, " and that Bishop Hiland and his associates are not Able to prevaile against them." On the same day Edward Hyde of Norbury, a friend and neighbour, mentions the fact that " yor Neighbours (must unwilling) * willingly waite the good hower." George Bowdon, who also shared his master's sentiments, expresses his opinion that " manie a Sr will pray for ye Parlt zealously when Maudlin."

The change was not to be effected, however, without a considerable outlay of money. All loyal supporters of the royal cause were expected, and indeed were ready and willing, to show their sympathy in a practical manner, and were subscribing largely. The sum of £600,000 is named as being required to carry out the enterprise, and Richard Standish considers this amount to be excessive :

> " I am verry sorry that our party is soe wordly minded as for to be
> Hyred to let you have your ends [he says on May 8 of this same year],
> for I doe heare that you have noe waies to bring your Royale designe
> About but by Money, for this six hundred Thousand pound may doe
> (perhaps) as Much towards the makeinge up of A.K : As foure hundred
> Thousand pound did with the Scots † in delivering of A.K : I shall
> say noe more but that I love not this honor which is bought so deare.

* Thus in the MS.
† The sum the Scots received in 1647 for betraying Charles I.

". . . I could wishe that you would take care to make your way soe cleare and plane in your K : designs that there be no Knobs in the way."

The Rev. Charles Herle writes on the 15th May of this same year :

"Although it seems we are not like to have King in o^r Israel, yet I beleeve wee must not every one doe what is good in his owne eyes. Wee must leave that to others and bee contented to hewe wood and drawe water."

1658   On March 25, 1658, N. Bowdon writes hoping that Richard will come speedily into the country, where his health will be more secure

"then in a City Fogg or a Scotch Mist, ye last of wch I hope will be dispers'd . . . I hope you will be dismist by ye xth of May or els dismiss yo^{r}selfe, and in ye meane tyme take y^r pleasure of Hyde Parke where you may possibly find as good game as in yor owne. [He addresses to him at] his lodgings over ag^t ye Harp & Ball belowe Chareinge Cross near Wallingford House."

On May 12 we hear of Richard " at his Chamber in Holborne Court, Chisnalls Buildings, Grays Inn," a letter from his brother Thomas begs for tidings of the absent M.P. and expresses concern at hearing of his cough.

"We hard a report [he adds] y^t Jack Booth,* Warburton of Arley,† Leicester of Tabley ‡ should bee in this last plott, but I put it in ye post-script because i am not sure of it."

On September 3, 1658, Oliver Cromwell died, and was buried on November 25 in Westminster Abbey with more pomp and splendour than had been displayed at the funeral of any king. Mr. Herle writes to Richard—back at Lyme—on September 6 :

"I give you thankes for yor fatt Venison. I would you could have sent mee from ye Hills that fed itt as good a Stomache to eat itt. I send you for newes a proclamation for fuller security of the great change lately made of yor namesake instead of his ffather." [This alludes to Richard Cromwell's nomination.]

* Sir George Booth.
† Sir George Warburton of Arley ; knighted 1660.
‡ Sir Peter Leycester, the great antiquary ; married Elizabeth, daughter of Gilbert second Lord Gerard ; died 1678

DURING THE COMMONWEALTH

A new Parliament met in 1659, chosen by the old unreformed constituencies as they had existed in Charles I's time, and in this Parliament Richard Legh was again elected M.P. for the county of Chester, having as his colleague this time the regicide Judge Bradshawe. A great dispute arose over this election, three candidates being proposed for the two seats, Richard Legh, Judge Bradshawe, and a Mr. Brooke, who had sat in the Long Parliament. Richard Legh seems to have been elected without any opposition, but a tremendous fight ensued between the other two candidates. The poll opened at Chester, and after continuing there five days, Richard Legh being elected, it was moved to Congleton for the result of the contest between the other two men. This was, no doubt, arranged by Bradshawe himself, as, Congleton being in his own part of the world, the majority would most probably be in his favour there and would enable him to win the day. Bribery was carried on quite openly. Mr. Brooke offered to spend £1000 and promised to defray the expenses of any who would vote for him. Bradshawe, however, was returned with Richard Legh, who, in spite of the long-established friendship of his family with the regicide, favoured the return of Mr. Brooke.

A long dictated letter written on January 22, 1658–9, by Bradshawe " from my sicke chamber att the Colledge Westminster," addressed to a Mr. Jackson of Nantwich, to be forwarded to Mr. (afterwards Sir Philip) Mainwaring, shows that the judge much resented the objections that were raised to his candidature and subsequent return. The letter is among the Legh papers and was no doubt sent to Richard by Mainwaring

" My condicon at the p^rsent [writes Bradshawe], is not such as makes mee verie fitt either for writeinge or dictateinge of Letters, yet some thinges in yours seeme to mee to require an Answer.

" How the nominatinge of mee should bee anie Just occacon of Annimosities and dissentions in the County or raisinge anie flame there I canot understand ; This I must saie (And noe man will have the Impudence to confront mee in it) that I was not, nor am the cause thereof, And whereas you speake of impartinge my mind before hand touching the Electin ; I must lett you know (whatever the usuall practise is or hath bin to the contrarie) my course hath bin, and ever

199

shall bee otherwise; for by law Elections ought to bee unpreiudced [unprejudiced] and free."

One of the disputed points of this election was whether Quakers should be admitted to vote, by reason of their refusal to take any oath. Bradshawe was in favour of allowing them to do so, it being supposed that they favoured his candidature:

" For the Quakers and their votinge I have not to medle in it; If they were free-holders and acted as the Law prescribes, why should anie bee soe Arbitrarie as to exclude them : or soe simple as to bee offended att them, this Privilidge is a highe p^te of their birthright; If the reception of their votes were contrarie to Law, let them bee iudged for their transgression against it, I have but one rule for them, and for all that come before mee as Judge, And that is the equall iust and impartiall Law of the Land, which directs and Comannds like Justice in like cases to all sortes of psons, And therein Quakers have their share as well as others. . . ."

A petition was framed by Thomas Brooke against this return. It was shown that great irregularities had been committed by Bradshawe's party.

" The hall (at Congleton) is not a fourth parte of the capacity of the great hall at Chester for the takeing of the pole, there being a narrow passage upstaires to the towne-hall, where Colonel Croxton's * souldiers, horse and foote and other hallbeardeirs, to the terrour of the people, obstructed the passage of those that would have voted for P. Brooke Esqr, and forced many, that did passe, upon inquiry who they were for, to pay money; That the Sheriff tooke many votes of those that were not resiants [residents] of the sd County Contrary to a Statute in that Case provided. That when there was not any freehoulder that would appeare for the sd John Bradshawe att Chester: Judgem^t was demanded of & denyed by the Sheriffe, & the Court was adjourned to Congleton twenty miles & upwards distant fro' Chester, when they saw the Countrey Comeing in for Mr Brooke. . . . That Quakers were admitted to vote ffor the sd John Bradshawe wthout oath made as is conceiued of theire sufficiencies to vote: all wch being contrary to Law as wee humbly Conceiue, wee humbly pray that proofes being made of what wee haue p^rsented the sd John Bradshawe may not bee admitted to sitt in parliament."

* A Parliamentarian colonel (1603 ?–1663) who defended Chester Castle against Sir George Booth's troops; arrested for conspiracy, 1663, probably released.

The Committee of Privileges unanimously declared Judge Bradshawe's election void. The Sheriff, one John Legh, thereupon with some of the " Justices, gents and freeholders," framed a counter-petition to the House of Commons setting forth that the Sheriff had received

> " both publique and private provocation affronts and Injuries from Thomas Mainwaring and Peter Brooke, two of the Justices of the Peace of the said County of Cheshire, that they forgot themselves by theire passionate, spleenfull & inconsid^rate expressions & Accons [actions] at the said Eleccon."

Among the complaints against Mr. Mainwaring it was alleged that the night before the election the petitioner

> " offering his endeavour to p^rvent all subsequent differances wch might happen the daie following, Mr. Mainwaring tolde him hee was no Sheriffe, and to the petitioner answering that hee would p^rvent the Writt for eleccon, replyed that itt might cause knocks & blood & by those that coulde not bee discou^red in a rude multitude, whereupon a Justice of Peace then p^rsent said to Mr Mainwaring, ' these are Strange words to proceed from you yt haue taken an Oath to preserve the Peace of the County.' Also that when the voters came to poll they were asked ' what do you Poll for ? The matter is cleare for Mr. Brooke and Mr Legh, onely halfe a dozen or a dozen of inconsid^rable fellowes that vote for Bradshawe ! ' "

Further that at another polling station, the people shouting " a Bradshawe ! a Bradshawe ! " Mr. Brooke retorted with " a Divell ! a Divell ! " That Mr. Brooke and Mr. Mainwaring and

> " divers others of their Complices did at the Election time not onely crowde but thrust, molest and hinder the Petitioner in the execution of his office, and stood between him and the Court so that hee could not many times see such as voted nor they see him, that the County Co^rt beeing upon adjournm^t to Congleton (a Towne of good note in the same County) for conveniency sake and for pfecting [perfecting] of the Ellecon, Mr Brooke w^thout any occasion given, in a menacing way stretched forth his hand towards the Sherriffe and openly said to him, ' if you adjourne to any other place I will follow you to the stilts,' telling him at the same time that he was ' a partiall fellow and no gent.'"

He also sent him a message to tell him that he was a fool, John Arderne (Richard's brother-in-law) adding that he was both a fool and a knave. This Arderne denied in a subsequent letter to Richard, asserting in the forcible language of the period that

> "ye Rotteness of my Accusers Conscience (as well as his Carcase) would not suffer him to dye until he had added yt mischief unto ye reste."

It was further alleged against Mr. Brooke that in the hall at Congleton he did

> "without any cause given, very much abuse John Bradshawe, His Highnes' Attorney General for the sd County, provoking him in these words, ' thou art one of the proudest impudent fellowes that ever I saw,' and stoopeing wth his face neare to the said Mr Bradshawe in a Challengeing way uttered and declared that hee durst Answear him, the said Mr Bradshawe, in any part of England. The said Mr Atturney haueing deserved no ill Language from him and indeed beeing then soe weake and sickly as yt not many daies after hee died."

At the Committee of Parliament for Privileges and Elections it was decided to put off the matter of the election until April 12. Notice of order being given to the parties concerned, we find in the " Journals of the House of Commons " for that day the following notice :

> " Resolved that Mr Leigh—one of the Members of this House—shall have Leave to go into the Country for Ten Days ; Notwithstanding the Order for the Call of the House."

The House reversed the decision of the Committee, and Bradshawe's election was held to be good. He was far too important a person to offend, and party feeling no doubt triumphed over justice.

On April 22 the soldiers forced Richard Cromwell to dissolve Parliament, on May 25 came his abdication and the end of the Protectorate.

In August 1659 took place the famous Cheshire rising of the

"New Royalists," under Sir George Booth,* for restoring 1659
Charles II, and in this rising Richard Legh became involved. The plot, which had been hatching for some months,
actually broke out about August 5. On the 12th, Sir George
Booth issued the following order to Piers Legh of Bruch,†
first cousin of Richard, who raised a regiment of horse in
support of the movement. The order much resembles a
Royal Proclamation :

"To Peires Legh Esqr
"Coll : of a Regiment of Horse
"Whereas the Lords, Gentlemen, Cittizens, Frreeholders and Yeomen
of this nation have taken up armes in defence of themselves and the
knowen Lawes of this Land. These are therefore to Authorize you
Colonell Peirce Legh to receave and enlist all such able and willing
persons as you shall finde for a Troope of Horse, and likewise to receave under yᵣ command five or more other Troopes wth theyr Officers,
and them so receav'd and enlisted to leade and command as Colonell
of the sayd Troopes. and from time to time to obey such Orders as
you shall receive from yr Superior Officers or ye Councell of Warre.
"Given under our hands and dated this twelfe day of August 1659.
"G. BOOTHE :
H : BROOKE.
J : BOOTH."

The insurgents carried all before them for a time, even
succeeding in taking Chester, but their success was of very short
duration, for Lambert,‡ advancing upon them with a large
army, entirely defeated Sir George Booth at Winnington
Bridge, near Northwich, on August 19. In this battle Thomas,
the only brother of Piers Legh of Bruch, was killed fighting
beside him and was buried at Warrington on August 22. Sir
George Booth escaped in woman's dress, but was subse-

* Sir George Booth, first Lord Delamere (1622–1684), entered plot for restoring
Charles II and commanded the King's forces in Cheshire, Lancashire, and North Wales,
1659 ; defeated by Lambert at Northwich.
† Eldest son of Peter (youngest son of Sir Peter Legh), by his second wife, Anne
Birkenhead. He married, first, Margaret, daughter of Edward Hyde of Norbury,
secondly, Abigaile Chetwode.
‡ John Lambert (1619–1683), Parliamentarian general. Took up arms for the
Parliament at the beginning of the Civil War ; at the Restoration was tried for high
treason and imprisoned till death.

quently caught and committed to the Tower on August 24, where, according to the " Journals of the House " he was " kept from hauing the use of Pen, Ink or Paper." He was ultimately released on bail.

What part Richard Legh actually took it is impossible to say, but he was evidently arrested and imprisoned in York Castle some time the previous May, and could therefore have had no share in the fighting. The following undated letter refers to the event and was no doubt sent him during his imprisonment. It is written on Whit-Sunday, which from calculation we gather fell on June 2 in 1659; we can therefore get the approximate date.

> " Knowsley   Whitsunday at 6
> in ye evening.

" Honr^d S^r

" My Lord Derby * rec^d yo^{rs} ab$_t$ an hour agoe and thereupon imediately sent for me, and my L^d being very willing to serve you in w^t you desire, has upon consideration concluded yt twill be ye best and safest way to send your horses to ys [this] place, where his Lords^p will ord^r a stable for y^m, and make use of 'em as his owne. He ordrd me to tell you this is his Lords^{ps} opinion as well as mine, and if you approve of it, you may ord^r y^m to come w^n you please ; Yo^r Groome is to buy his owne corne. My Lord gives his service to you, & is sorry for yor misfortunes, he would have writt himselfe, but was lett blood to-day, and since is not very well.

" I am very much concerned for wt has happened to you for divers and sundry reasons, but it is and like to be ye fate of a great many honest Gent, God Almighty send us a happy and speedy end to these troubles.

> " I am, Honrd S
> " Yor most faithfull humble serv^t
> " E. P. ASHTON."

The address, unfortunately, is missing.

By November, Richard was evidently liberated, as amongst the Legh MS. is the following pass, signed by General Fleetwood :

* Charles, eighth Earl of Derby, son of James, seventh Earl, and Charlotte de la Trémouille ; succeeded to the earldom on the execution of his father in 1651. Married, 1650, Dorothy, daughter of John Kirkhoven, Baron of Rupa, Holland. He supported Sir George Booth's rising, was taken prisoner and attainted by Parliament. He died 1672.

DURING THE COMMONWEALTH

" Permitt the bearer Richard Legh Esqr wth his servants horses and necessaries quiettly to passe to London w^{th}out lett or molestacon ; hee acting noething prejudiciall to the peace of this Comonwealth ; Given under my hand this twentie sixt of November, 1659.

" CHARLES FLEETWOOD.*

" To all Officers, souldiers and others whom these may Concerne."

By a letter from Thomas Bowdon, a son of old George, we gather that he had made application for this pass :

" If you continue y^r resolucon to come up and that passe I sent this day sevenight bee satisfactory to Coll : Crox : [he writes to Richard on December 3] it were better to send y^r money whatever it bee by the Carryer ; bills of Exchange are very slowly p^d and worse will bee."

There was evidently to be some feasting to celebrate the release of the young squire : " I hope on Monday next to hear of the receipt of your wine, cucumbers, oysters and Capons." New clothes were also required after a six months' captivity. Richard was a great dandy and took much pains with his wardrobe : " I hope to heare of the receipt of your cloathes [writes T. Bowdon], alsoe Mr Hunsell [probably a tailor] desires to know how hee hath fitted you, haveing noe better Measure."

A species of anarchy was now existing. The country had been ruled by the soldiers for the best part of a year. Parliaments met and were dissolved every few weeks, and hopeless confusion was the only order that prevailed.

Although Sir George Booth's plot had been a failure, it had undoubtedly something to do with hastening the Restoration. It promoted and encouraged feelings of loyalty in those zealous for the Royal cause, and it stimulated and put backbone into the wavering and fainthearted. The nation was sick of military rule, and a return to a monarchy promised the dawn of a brighter day.

In the midst of the confusion everywhere, Monk, the commander of the forces in Scotland, who was already secretly in communication with the exiled King, saw his opportunity,

* Charles Fleetwood, Parliamentarian soldier, married a daughter of Oliver Cromwell.

and crossed the border with his army, intending to join Fairfax and to advance on London.

> " Yesterday was observ'd a ffast in the Citty by order fro the Ld Major, 'twas very unanimously perform'd, strong Guards were & still are kept wthin the walls ; all businesses almost, except that of Governm^t & manageing Martial affaires, are at a stand, & looke on to see what will bee the Issue of soe great Labour as this Nacon undergoes."

> " The [they] report G : M :* Came into Yorke Friday last with great Joy & acclamations [writes another correspondent on January 18, 1659–60], & som talks of A Declaration by him & my Lord FF : † but nix credo ; the sequestrato^{rs} are more busy in o^r Country then in any County of Engl^d. The Lord in his wisdom order things for the good & peace of this kingdom."

On February 3 Monk entered London, and on the 16th he declared for a free Parliament. The following letter from Sir Robert Booth,‡ written on February 18, 1659–60, gives an interesting account of what was going on in London at the time, and shows that he himself regarded the Restoration, if not with favour, certainly with equanimity :

> " Your Brother (I suppose) gave you an acc^t of the great transactions in the Citty ; & the Gen^{r}alls Lett^r conc^{r}ning the filling up of the Parl^t. The day is past & the writts nott yett issued ; The Qualifications are in a great measure dispatched, whereby all that have borne Armes ag^t the Parliam^t are rendred uncapable of Electing or being Elected, wch some say Extends not onely to Sr Georges § party, butt Lamberts ‖ alsoe, butt others p^{r}tend good ground to beleiue that Sr Georges party (if Elected) will not bee kept out by the Army.
> "Yesterday they went through the Roll of the House, & voted memb^{rs} to bee chosen into eu^{ry} particular place in the Roomes of those secluded. . . . Itt will I conceive concerne y^{r}selfe & the Countrey Exceedingly to bee provided ag^t the coming of these writts, & to pitch upon persons of Integrity, Judgment & Resolution for Cheshyre. I hope y^r

---

* General Monk, afterwards first Duke of Albemarle (1608–1670).

† Lord Fairfax, Parliamentarian general (1612–1671), defeated Charles I at Naseby, where he captured a standard with his own hand.

‡ Sir Robert Booth (1626–1681), Chief Justice of King's Bench in Ireland ; knighted 1668.

§ Sir George Booth.

‖ See note, p. 203.

selfe will not waive that service to yor Country wch this exigency 1659–60 requires from you, which is the advice & desire of y^{or} most cordial & real friends here; yor Interest will carry it against all competitors, whereas if you cast itt upon a weaker Interest it may strengthen the factious party of the Country to the Increase of y^r slavery & oppression. It will likewise concerne you to be active & Instrumental for the setting up fitt persons in other places where either yo^t Interest or advice may take place; wherein it will be of much advantage to prevent the factious party by a timely engagement of yor friends. If the Gentlemen here shall not conclude itt advisable ffor themselves to stand, & y^r cosen Peirces * late Engagements of either sort shall likewise divert his thoughts, Newton will, I hope, give you an opportunity of obligeing yr ffreinds by their Election to that Service, the Gentleman † whoe lately served with y^r cosen ffor that place being not so happy as to receive the approbation of your ffriends here.

"Dunkirk is in some straights, Lockhart ‡ is here wanting men and money, the Spaniards & French being both (said to bee) drawne downe before it. The drums beat for volunteers for that service, but the main weight is wanting."

Another correspondent, who signs himself P.B., writes on the following day, February 19, and speaks of there having been an attempt to poison General Monk and his army:

"I have not much news to impart, but 'tis agreed on all hands that either the House shall be recruited by the old-secluded or new elected members. If it comes to a new Election & that the old members bee not shutt out by any previous Vote, 'tis supposed in most places they will bee pitched on & to that purpose incouragement hath been given by some in power to many of the old members to use their interest, if they go a new way to worke, then many of the burroughs will be deprived of their ancient rights, & then Cheshire will have 3 knights besides Sr William,§ and Lancashire seven. I think yourself and T. M.‖ cannot in conscience deny to serve the country; affaires here

* Piers Legh of Bruch, first cousin of Richard, M.P. for Newton with W. Brereton, 1658–9; fought at Winnington Bridge; married his first wife, Margaret, daughter of Edward Hyde of Norbury, in February of this year, 1659–60.

† William Brereton.

‡ Sir William Lockhart of Lee, soldier and diplomat; commanded English forces at Dunkirk, 1659; made Governor after the town's surrender; deprived of office, 1660.

§ Sir William Brereton of Hondford, Cheshire (1604–1661); Parliamentarian commander; M.P. for Cheshire, 1628–1640.

‖ Sir Thomas Mainwaring of Over Peover, Cheshire, first Baronet (1623–1689); author of "The Defence of Amicia."

are in a hopefull posture, the news comes even now that the court of aldermen have taken oaths that prove the anabaptists' indeavour to poison or destroy Ge : Monk & his Army, he stays in the City where himselfe & soldiers are nobly treated. Many affronts have been offered to divers of the members by the rude multitude & to the Speaker on Saturday night when the Towne made some thousands of bon-fires to congratulate the good accord betwixt the soldiers and the Citty."

Sir Robert Booth writes another letter to Richard from Gray's Inn on February 21 :

" This morning a great Guard attended the Parliament door, & kept back none who owned himself a member ; the business no doubt was privately communicated to the Secluded members, for there were very early a competent Number of them (amongst the Rest Mr Prynne * with a Baskett hilt sword). They have passed several votes to vacate those of their seclusion, & all that have passed against their vote that the King's concessions were satisfactory &c. Monke made General, Lawson † Admiral. The imprisoned Members (Sr Geo: Major Brooke &ct) to appear to-morrow & the L^t to give an account of the grounds of their imprisonment. The vote against the Citty comon Councell vacated, their gates, portcullies &c to bee Erected, with several others of this nature, the Copy whereof you may Expect if itt bee possible to gett them in this hurry. The Bells & Bonfires speake the 2d part of that Acclamation which was on Saturday the 11th Instant. The New Elections are voted to bee suspended & as itt putts a stop to them so I doubt not butt itt will to ye Sequestrations there. The newes booke is now out of doores otherwise I had sent it."

A meeting was called at Preston in March 1659–60, to discuss the nomination of the different knights of the shire, and Richard was invited to attend and to suspend the engaging of his interest until the meeting should be over. His parliamentary colleague, President Bradshawe, had not lived long to enjoy the triumph of his election. He had died of a tertiary ague in the previous October, 1659, and had been buried with much pomp in Westminster Abbey. There had been an idea of Richard Legh's standing again for Cheshire, but a letter from his brother

* William Prynne, Puritan pamphleteer ; forced his way into the House of Commons, which could only get rid of him by adjournment ; readmitted by Monk, 1660.
† Admiral Lawson, in command of ships in Parliamentary service, 1642–1645 ; co-operated with Monk in Restoration.

Thomas, written in March 1659–60, shows that there was some opposition to his candidature :

> "Every day almost I have conference wth ye Herculean Clubb, whose thoughts as for Cheshire are strenuously bent for Sir G. B. [Sir George Booth] now they are put to their wits end who to nominate for ye other, every one of them thinking themselves notorious. Sometimes I have heard them mention G. Warburton before his face, who is so farr from declining ye imployment that he really & seriously expresses his desire for it. Sometimes you are mentioned but I know not heartily wished for."

Although he considers that his brother's candidature would not be popular in Cheshire, he seems to think he would be welcome as a burgess for Newton, Lancashire : " I'me very confident that if you please to express your willingnes for it, there is not any one yt will stand in competition with you."

Mr. Brereton,* afterwards third Lord Brereton of Leighlin, one of the former members for Newton, was anxious to stand again, but apparently was not wanted, and Piers Legh of Bruch, who had been his colleague, was occupied with his wedding and other matters. Ultimately Richard Legh was returned member for Newton in the Convention Parliament, his colleague being a Mr. William Banks; Sir George Booth and Sir Thomas Mainwaring becoming members for Cheshire.

On April 4, 1660, Charles II signed the Declaration of Breda, offering a general pardon and promising to restore all confiscated estates. This was received by the House on May 1, and on the 7th Sir George Booth was elected, with eleven other members, to carry the reply of Parliament to the King. Puritanism was as dead as Oliver Cromwell, and the Restoration was now an accomplished fact.

* Brereton of Brereton, Cheshire, a Royalist family, distinct from the Breretons of Hondford to whom Sir William Brereton, the Parliamentarian general, belonged.

CHAPTER XIV

LYME AT THE RESTORATION

1660 TUMULTUOUS joy was expressed all over the country at the good news. The messenger who brought the King's letter was voted the sum of £500 by the House of Commons, " to buy a jewel as a badge of that honour which is due to a Person whom the King hath honoured to be a Messenger of so gracious a Message." He was voted the thanks of the House, being assured by the Speaker that " our hearts are open to receive Our King—the Glory of England."

Nowhere was there more genuine rejoicing displayed than in loyal Cheshire. We read that the church bells were rung for twenty-four hours without ceasing, thanksgiving services were held, bonfires blazed, the King's health was drunk with acclamation. " Cheshire hearts were never more rejoiced."

John Arderne writes to his brother-in-law, Richard Legh, on May 10, 1660 :

> " I received yours this day, for ye good news I returne you my great and hearty thankes ; from another hand I received the Proclamation of Charles 2d, wch wth all possible Ceremony of Guns Drums, Bells & te Deums in the Church was performed by Ned Hyde, Mr F^Fitton-Zneye [Sneyd ?] and my selfe, accompanied wth ye Mayor & Aldermen of Stockport, by whom afterward we were in their Court house civilly treated . . . wee imagine Sir Geo : [Sir George Booth] maye bee gone upon his hon^ble Embassy, wth whom I heartily wish myself."

> " The pleasing sound of the pleasing Compliance betwixt his Gracious Majesty & Great Councell doth not onely fill our ears but hearts with joy," writes Edward Hyde of Norbury, a connexion of Richard's, on May 12 ; and Peter Venables,* Baron of Kinderton, assures Richard that " Your votes and Proclamation for the King to be

---

* Great-uncle of Richard ; married Frances, youngest daughter of Sir R. Cholmondeley, afterwards Earl of Leinster.

proclaimed was so joyfully taken in Middlewich that the bells rung from Thursday betwixt eight and nyne a Clocke at night until yester night at same time ; many of the Townes hereabout had bonfires, the Bells in severall Churches rung. I caused the Steward to read the Proclamation after he had summoned the towne together. All the inhabitants appeared (excepting Captain Croxton * who never showed his face that day). I desire to know when you thinke his Majesty will be in England and when crowned, and whether Mr Shakerley or any of our Cheshire men bee gone over to wait upon him ? ''

On May 25, 1660, Charles II landed at Dover, and on May 29, his thirtieth birthday, he entered London amid the cheers of a populace frantic with enthusiasm. Richard was one of the Cheshire gentlemen who signed the address to the King congratulating him on his restoration.

The command of the militia was now to be placed by Parliament unreservedly in the King's hands, who was from henceforth to have the supreme government and disposal of that force. The " train bands " which had been substituted for the militia by James I, had sided with the Parliament during the Civil War, and there seems to have been a good deal of grumbling and dissatisfaction at the new arrangements. Peter Venables writes to Richard on June 2, 1660 :

" It rejoyceth me much to heare that his Majesty is safe come to Whitehall and that he was so gallantlie attended ; sure by this the tyme of his coronation is knowne and the place where it shallbe, I suppose he will not come into the house untill after that solempnity be past. . . . The captaine of the militia of the trayned band of Northwich hundred called the freehold & trayned band to Rudheath yesterday, being Friday, but he was not there himselfe but his lieutenant, who after he had spent the day in exercising them gave them notice to come thither again upon Monday by four of the clocke in the morning, and told them they should stay untill Friday night to learne their postures. Soe early an hour was never heard of for people to meete that live nine miles distant from the place, nor soe long a tyme taken to keepe the countrie together without it were in tyme of war or upon the approach of an enemie ; these courses will be very chargeable to the country and cause much grumbling ; the commissioners might doe verie well to set downe some moderate order that the

* See note, p. 200.

captaines and officers might walke by, for none will get good by this but inkeepers and alehouse-keepers who live near to the places of their rendez-vous. Country men that are kept soe long from their families & their employments at home will have little mind to learn postures of war."

1660   In the Disley parish register for October 14, 1660, appears the following notice :

"Oct : 14, 1660.

"The daie and year aboue written an agreement was made in the Chappell of Disley before my Master & patron Richard Legh of Lyme Esqr & others by the inhabitants of Disley, concerninge a trayned soldier to serue the King's Majestie, his heires and successors fro tyme to tyme as followeth."

Five signatures follow, the witness being Samuel Bardsley, minister.

Thomas Legh, brother of Richard, writes on November 21 :

"I have not yet received an answer to my last wch intimated your military charge, wee have att present gott Knapsacks, Bandeleres, & Swords for six men wch shall bee ready when ye word of command comes, for provision for more men we shall stay till wee have orders from your self wch I desire may bee as speedy as possible because they will be forward to call for them."

The troops were to be raised " after the old way " by freehold and train-bands. From a proclamation addressed by Charles II to the Lord-Lieutenants and Deputy-Lieutenants we learn that there were to be eighty foot-soldiers in a company, and fifty horse in a troop. The officers and soldiers were to do fourteen days duty, their pay to be as follows : A captain of horse was to receive 10s. per diem, a lieutenant of horse 6s., a cornet of horse 5s., and a quartermaster of horse 4s. A captain of foot was to be paid 8s. per diem, a lieutenant 4s., an ensign 3s., a sergeant 2s. 6d., and a corporal 2s.

One of the first acts of the new Parliament was the attainting of High Treason of John Bradshawe, Oliver Cromwell, Henry Ireton * and Thomas Pride,† " for the Murther of the late

* Henry Ireton (1611–1651), regicide ; married, 1646, Bridget, Cromwell's daughter. Went to Ireland with Cromwell in 1649 ; died of fever before Limerick.

† Thomas Pride, soldier, entered Parliamentary army as captain; fought at Worcester. He was the instigator of the famous " Pride's Purge " in 1648. He died in 1658.

King." Their bodies, or as an eye-witness, Mr. Edward Sainthill, a Spanish merchant,* expresses it, "their odious carcases" were exhumed and taken to Tyburn, where they were buried beneath the gallows.

The Act of Indemnity—to which there were, however, to be many exceptions—had encouraged hope in those whose consciences were afraid. James Duckenfield, a brother of the 1660 Colonel Duckenfield who fought for the Parliament, writes to his cousin Richard, back at Lyme, on July 28, 1660:

> "Besides this speech of his Majesty there was another made by himselfe this day—alsoe in the House of Lords most of wch was the further pressing of a speedy dispatch of the Act of Indemnity; the Lord Chancellor att the same time seconded him wth another speech differing very little in matter. This hath not a little cheered many drooping spirits such as my brother Duckenfield, Col Bradshaw † &c whose hearing was to have beene yesterday, but was by new order deferred till Monday next. Croxton and my brother keep out of sight yet, though orders are out for takeing them to the blacke rodd. This day His Majesty signed two bills, one for Tunnage & Poundage the other for restoring of lands to the Earle of Ormond ‡ & such of his party as Engaged. wth him against the rebells in Ireland. Many wonder the Commons passed the bill of Tonnage & Poundage & sending to his Majesty to come & sign it before the act of indempnity was passed, but its evident both the King & parliament strive to outdoe one another whether can impose stronger obligations upon the contrary party."

> "There will be a speedy Trial of ye Traitors in ye Tower now ye Judges are returning and come forth of their Circuits [writes Nicholas Bowdon in August], Lambert,§ Axtell ‖ & Vane ¶ are condemned without mercy, I shall not begg their pardons. [He writes again on September 29, 1660:] Coll Worden** was seized upon this morne at his lodgings in St James by 3 of his Majesty's Messengers, ye King last

---

* Quoted in Butler's "Hudibras."
† Brother of the judge.
‡ James Butler, afterwards the great Duke of Ormonde.
§ See note, p. 203.
‖ Daniel Axtell, Parliamentarian; executed 1660.
¶ Sir Henry Vane (1613–1662), statesman; member of Parliamentary Council; distrusted by both parties; executed 1662.
** Robert Werdon or Wordon, soldier; colonel of Horse to Charles I's army; barely escaped with life for joining Sir George Booth's rising in 1659; accused of treason by Royalists, 1660; recovered his estates; died in 1690.

night brought in ye charge against him before ye Privy Councell; after hee was apprehended hee desired Pen & Paper & in ye interval inquired whether ye Chancellor was present at ye Councell, but hearinge hee was there hee laid all aside and submitted & I hope may suffer if he deserve it."

A petition to the King in favour of Piers Legh of Bruch, who had rendered such good service to the royal cause by the raising of a troop of horse in support of what one of Richard's correspondents describes as " Sir George Booth's frolic," was signed by Lord Derby, Lord Kilmorey, Sir George Booth, and others. It states that :

> " Coll : Piers Legh, your Petitioner did appeare the first day in Sr George Booths late Actings with a party of Horse and ffoote in Lancashire, beeing the first in that County, and did after compleate a considerable party both of Horse and ffoote well Armed for yor Ma^{tys} Service. In all which his Deportment was such as became a Loyal Subject, to the great Hazard of his life, his only Brother beeinge slayne neere unto him. This to doe him right wee take the boldnes to certify, humbly recomending the Petitioner to yor Ma^{tys} gratious consideracon."

1660 Piers Legh was apparently made Prothonotary and Custos Bretiam and Clerk of the Assizes within the counties of Chester and Flint, but we do not learn of his receiving any further reward.

Honours were, however, bestowed by the King on others of his loyal Cheshire followers. Sir George Booth was created Lord Delamere, John Arderne and Peter Brooke were both knighted, and it was thought that Richard Legh would be made a Knight of the Bath, the intended order of the Royal Oak. "At his Majesty's coronation, which we expect to be about ye 6th of February," writes Nicholas Bowdon on October 25, 1660, " there are some Kn^{ts} of ye Bath intended to be made, and my Lord (Derby) hath mentioned some desire of having you to be of ye order."

But Richard was of far too modest a nature to be found amongst those clamouring for honours and rewards. His worth was also fully recognized by both Charles II and the Duke of

York. His thoughts were at this time occupied with other matters than with those of aggrandizement and promotion, for he was paying his court to the fair daughter of Mr. (afterwards Sir Thomas) Chicheley, appointed, in 1664, Master of the Ordnance.

Mr. Chicheley, who is described by Pepys in his Diary as " a great high flyer," was a personage in his way. Born in 1618, he married, first, sometime about 1640, Sarah, youngest daughter of Sir William Russell of Chippenham, by whom he had three sons and two daughters, the eldest Elizabeth, becoming, in 1661, Mrs. Richard Legh. Mr. Chicheley was M.P. for Cambridgeshire during the Long Parliament, but was in 1642 disabled to sit, and for his zealously royalist principles was severely punished as a malignant during the Commonwealth, and had to compound heavily for his estates. At the Restoration he was again elected M.P. for Cambridgeshire. His first wife must have died about 1653, and he then married, before 1656, Anne, daughter of Lord Keeper Coventry, and widow of Sir William Savile of Thornhill, by whom she had had with other children George Savile, afterwards Marquis of Halifax.

Lady Savile, who appears to have retained the name of her first husband after her second marriage, was a lady of great strength of character, a devoted adherent of Charles I, and was, in her way, quite as remarkable as Charlotte de la Trémouille, Countess of Derby. Her first husband, Sir William Savile, was governor of Sheffield Castle, and died in 1644, during the time that it was besieged by the Parliamentarians. Although in expectation of the birth of a posthumous child, Lady Savile declared that she would die rather than surrender the castle into the hands of the enemy, only finally consenting to do so on August 11 in consequence of a mutiny having broken out amongst the garrison. On the following day, August 12, her child was born, and it is said that the besiegers barbarously refused to allow her the services of a midwife.

Her marriage with Mr. Chicheley was a very happy one, she seems to have taken his first family entirely to her heart and to have cared for his motherless children as if they had been her own. A portrait of her, painted in the style of Sir Peter Lely, hangs in the dining-room at Lyme. It represents her as a middle-aged lady of homely features, dressed in a grey satin gown, full sleeves slashed with white satin fastened with pearls, and a pearl necklace. A black boy stands beside her with a basket of flowers. A slip of parchment stuck in the frame has her name and parentage written in a contemporary hand. It also states that she was " eminent for her zealous and faithfull services to King Charles the Ist in his greatest troubles."

Wimple or Wimpole in Cambridgeshire, the beautiful place belonging to the Chicheley family, was within reach of Cambridge University, and this was no doubt how Richard Legh and Elizabeth Chicheley first became acquainted. From allusions in the letters we gather that the courtship must have been going on for some little time before their marriage, and the intended bridegroom was the recipient of sundry sly jests on the part of his friends. Messages are sent to " the unparalleled lady in Drury Lane," * and she is alluded to as " the blacke but comelie Doe who is yett (as I suppose) within the lines of communication where you are now."

> " I always thought that providence had a singular mercy for you [writes another correspondent on December 11, 1660], I do not question but you will find it in the completion of your present design ; if once I could see you and that virtuous lady in bed together, I should conclude you the onely happy man, for she is the epitome of all the worth and virtue that can bee in her sex."

1660-61   The marriage, which was destined to be one of unclouded happiness, took place on January 1, 1660-61, probably at Wimpole, Richard being twenty-six years of age, and his bride Elizabeth some eight years younger.

---

* The Chicheleys had a house in Great Queen Street, Covent Garden.

CHAPTER XV

RICHARD AND ELIZABETH

At his entry into public life in 1656, Richard Legh must have been twenty-two years of age—not unusually young for those days, minors being frequently elected Members of Parliament, though probably not entitled to vote before attaining their majority.

About 1660, he bought from Sir Thomas Fleetwood the barony of Newton-in-Makerfield, of which his Haydock property had always been held as a Mesne Manor. He was, as we have seen, elected in 1660 one of the two Members of Parliament returned by that borough, but although possessing the parliamentary privilege, Newton had, up to now, never been incorporated or given any seal. Richard Legh therefore gave the borough as its arms his own crest—"issuing from a ducal coronet, or, a ram's head argent, attired or, holding in its mouth a laurel sprig proper." He was elected M.P. for Newton on June 24, 1661, having as his colleague John Vaughan of the Inner Temple, but this gentleman was transferred to another borough, his place being taken by Sir Philip Mainwaring, and at the latter's death this same year the seat became filled by Richard Gorges, Baron of Dundalk.

The earliest portrait we have of Richard is one painted by Sir Peter Lely in 1660. This represents him as a strikingly handsome man of six and twenty and must have been finished just before his marriage. The prevailing fashion of clean shaving—so trying to coarse irregular features—displays a handsome face, on the other hand, to the best advantage. The eyes in this portrait are large, dark, and dreamy, the nose straight and finely cut the mouth firm and beautifully chiselled, and the chin square and resolute. He wears his own hair—a rich dark brown—long, with the love-lock of the cavalier, and a yellow satin coat, the sleeves very full and slashed to the shoulders. He has a breastplate of armour, and over his right shoulder and across his breast is a broad pink sash tied in a large bow on the left side. His left hand rests on his hip, his right hand grasps a short staff.

" The face the index of the mind," his character might almost be described as faultless. An affectionate husband and father, a staunch and generous friend, a kind and considerate landlord, and a loyal and devoted subject of his king, he possessed all the qualities that go to make a perfect man. His careful and judicious mother's early training had instilled those high principles of religion and morality which were the guiding forces of his life, and her influence had developed in him all that was best and noblest in his character.

He had had practically no youth, for he was little more than a child when circumstances forced him to take his place as head of the family, and all the cares and responsibilities of a man of weight and position fell upon his shoulders. His early training in the school of adversity had taught him patience and forbearance, and had matured him and given him a thoughtfulness far above his years. His intelligence was of no mean order, his judgment was calm and sound, and the high standard of his life at a period of so much dissipation and corruption cannot fail to have shed a purifying influence on all with whom he came in contact.

His character is thus described in a sermon preached at his death by one who knew him well, the Rev. Dr. Shippen, Rector of Stockport :

" He had all the natural charms and graces of a most winning address and a sweet conversation, cheerfulness and delight being as inseparable from him as light from the sun. So that in him, if ever, that saying was really verified, ' that none ever departed sad out of his company, except that they so soon departed.' The natural talents of his mind were above the common order . . . his memory was so faithful as to retain everything it laid hold on but injuries and vanities, he knew no hatred of anything but sin, no fear of anything but God."

RICHARD LEGH OF LYME
1660
By Sir PETER LELY

From a Portrait at Lyme

RICHARD LEGH,
Baron of Newton. 1666.

RICHARD AND ELIZABETH

Richard and Elizabeth seem to have taken up their residence at Lyme immediately after their marriage.

The dark days of the Civil War had barely faded from the memory, and the rejoicings and acclamations of the Restoration had hardly subsided, when Richard brought his fair young bride to the home of his ancestors. There had been no mistress at Lyme for nearly thirteen years, so one can fancy the joyful welcome that greeted the happy pair. The ringing of bells, blazing of bonfires, the feasting and carousing and drinking of healths in the excellent home-brewed ale, were heralds of good times to come, and promised a return to the happy and prosperous days of old Sir Peter.

Though we have no details of their domestic life before 1661–2, Richard and Elizabeth must have started on their housekeeping at Lyme very soon after their marriage. An account book, kept by Thomas Bowdon, a son of the old steward George Bowdon, who died in 1659, beginning on January 10, 1661–2, gives one some idea of the cost of living, but it is unfortunately not nearly so exhaustive as the one kept by the steward of old Sir Peter, and we are unable to arrive at the number of servants.

Though the establishment was probably on a rather smaller scale than that of the Elizabethan days, it seems to have been conducted in a somewhat lavish—not to say extravagant—manner, and the steward probably feathered his nest pretty handsomely.

The young people lived very much " en princes," and entertained largely. Dr. Shippen, in his before-mentioned funeral sermon, speaks of the splendour of Richard's hospitality :

" His Entertainments upon Occasion were very Splendid and Magnificent, and managed with that Decorum, Ease & Stilness as if they had been but their ordinary meals . . . his House might very well be styled a Country Court and Lime the Palace to the County Palatine of Chester."

Richard also appears to have kept a racing stud and hunters, and to have followed all the pursuits of a country gentleman of the period. An order signed by Charles II, bearing also the signature of Sir Edward Nicholas,* Secretary of State, dated March 27, 1661, appoints

> " Our trusty and well beloued Richard Legh to be Gamekeeper about Lyme in Cheshire [and commands him to] haue a speciall care that noe person or persons doe hereafter presume wth Greyhounds, Mongrills, Setting Dogs, guns, trammells, tunnells, netts or other Engines to hurt or kill Our said Game of Hare, Phesant, Partridge, Heron or other wild fowls within Ten miles of Lyme aforesaid."

He was to be authorized to take away and confiscate the said

> " Engines, and to deteyne and certifie unto us or Our Privy Council ye names of any Persons soe offending to the end such further order may be taken for their punishment that Our game may be ye better preserved for Our Sport and recreation at such tymes as we shall resort into those parts."

Lyme being part of a royal forest was within the jurisdiction of the forest laws. Since the earliest times certain districts were set apart for sport to the sovereign, and a series of laws known as " forest laws " were created to reserve his exclusive right to pursue game within the protected areas.

The Legh family had for centuries held posts in connexion with Macclesfield forest, ever since the first Sir Piers had been appointed " equitator " or riding forester of Macclesfield forest, which meant that he was to lead the king (Richard II) when he hunted in the forest. James II visited and hunted at Lyme on an occasion which will be described later, but we have no record of any visit having been paid by Charles.

Elizabeth, who was about eighteen at the time of her marriage, can have had very little of the knowledge required for the control and management of a large establishment, and she and Richard probably bought their experience somewhat dear. But the young châtelaine took much interest in her household, and we find her writing soon after her marriage to one of her cousins : " I'll promise you I shall often remember

---

* Sir Edward Nicholas (1593–1669), Secretary of State to Charles I and Charles II.

you in my dary in Sillabubs and whey, and hope you will not forget me in yours."

A portrait of Elizabeth Legh by Sir Peter Lely shows her to have much resembled other ladies of Charles II's time. She wears a grey satin gown cut extremely low, with large puffed sleeves, and her hands, with long tapering fingers, are clasping a stone vase. She has the same peach-like complexion, languorous eyes, and pouting mouth that one sees in Charles's beauties; her hair is dressed in ringlets round her face in the fashion of the day, and she wears the regulation pearl necklace and large drop pearl ear-rings.

The resemblance, happily, ends there. Nothing could have been more exemplary than her conduct as a wife, she idolized her husband, and their married life was one long honeymoon. " Dearest," he writes to her from Lyme on March 31, 1661, 1661 some three months after their marriage, she being at Wimpole with her father and stepmother,—" Upon Thursday night we gott well home, I can scarce call it home because thou art wanting, for thou art my home." *

He probably attended the coronation of Charles II, which took place on April 23, 1661, but we have no evidence of the fact.

By July 2 the young couple were back at Lyme. The following letter from Lady Savile to her stepdaughter shows the excellent terms she was on with all her stepchildren. She always signs herself " your entirely affectionate mother."

" DEARE DAUGHTER,

" These are to congratulate yr arrival at Lyme, hoping you had no rubb in yr way to deferr it a day. I find by yours which came late to my hands by Sʳ Juc's Carrier, that you purposed to stay at Oxford two days, which I am glad of for my daughter's and my Niece's sakes that would thereby have the satisfaction of seeing you. Besides I thinke 'tis at a season when ye company of friends is more than ordinarily usefull to a poore woman † that's put upon soe sadd a dilemma between a Jamaica voyage & the parting wth her Lord, which

---

* From the Raines Collection in the Library of Chetham's Hospital, Manchester.
† Her daughter, Lady Windsor, whose husband was Governor of Jamaica, 1661–1664.

is one of them to be submitted to without remedy, & being 'tis her Lords desire she should stay till he have first tryed the place, I advise her to it, both in compliance with him & in consideration of her crazie constitution which would, with her own hazard, make her burthensome to a husband that goes upon such an enterprize. . . . Your father came in pity to me to assist me in the entertaining my Son * & his wife, who being gone, he has returned to London, where I hope the Parliament will not sitt long this hot season which is fitter for the Country. I forget how you are upon the entertainment of friends and neighbours whilst I scribble as if you were at leisure to read as I am to write, I shall therefore conclude with my affectionate good wishes & prayers for you & yr husb. being very perfectly Deare Daughter, your affectionate Mother, An Savile.†

"My love to yr bro. & my blessing to yr sister ‡; little fellow § would say something to you all if he could bring it out. Hee showed his fine sister ‖ the same courtshipp you left him possest of, with very little improvement, hee told her hee loved not her Child, hee did soe cry."

A terrible outbreak of smallpox occurred in England during the summer and autumn of 1660, the young Duke of Gloucester ¶ dying of this complaint in September, to the great grief of the Royal family and the whole nation. This outbreak was followed by another in 1661. The household at Lyme seems to have escaped, but two of Mr. Chicheley's sons were attacked, though both recovered. Lady Savile writes on August 5, 1661, to congratulate her stepson Tom on his recovery :

"Deare Sonn,

"I hope by this time I may congratulate yr perfect recovery of a disease that few escape their whole life from, & therefore 'tis a blessing to have past it & it often is a means of better health by clearing the body of those humours that foment distempers, especially where they

---

* Her son by her first marriage, Sir George Savile, afterwards Marquess of Halifax ; he married Dorothy, a daughter of the Countess of Sunderland.

† Raines Collection.

‡ Sarah, youngest sister of Elizabeth Legh ; she spent much of her time at Lyme before her marriage to Andrew Fountaine of Salle in 1672.

§ This may possibly have been a son of Anne, Lady Savile, by her marriage with Mr. Chicheley.

‖ Sir George Savile's wife, afterwards Lady Halifax.

¶ Henry, Duke of Gloucester, third son of Charles I (1639-1660); disowned by his mother for refusing to become a Romanist; died of small-pox in London, buried in same vault at Westminster as Mary, Queen of Scots.

RICHARD AND ELIZABETH

purge well after it as I hope you have done. I ask'd your Father if
he could tell how the face had spedd, who rather laughed att the
querie then resolved [answered] it ; yet in the second place one may
consider that in a man which too oft is in the first for a woman. My
Lady Sunderland * has them at Rufford, which you may believe puts
that house in great disorder, & her Ladyship in noe lesse, who will
consider beauty to her latest day. Here is a sicknes, a sort of Feaver †
that takes whole families, & is begun in our case amongst the servants.
God send it may goe no further but that you may bring and find good
health amongst us, so prays your very affectionate Mother

"A. S." ‡

Lady Savile gives further details of Lady Sunderland's
illness in a letter to her stepdaughter, written also on August 5 :

" My Lady Sunderland has it (the small-pox) at Rufford, & has driven
out her fair daughter my Lady Penn § to inhabit in the Stables. She
tooke the infection from the sound of the word ; one being asked after,
'twas replyed they were now well but had had the Small-Pox. She
presently found herself ill, & they say she is very full of them ; Hinton ||
the Apothecary posted downe from London to her, & yesterday I take
it was her 14th day—the great crisis in that disease." ‡

She writes again on November 26, of this same year :

" Your father ¶ has sent down the Venison and Cheeses, yet with
order to have part sent him up againe, they being too good to spend
wholly here where so few friends can come to partake with us, the
ways being worse than ever, especially about the House. Your
brother is contriving with me how possibly to convey some Apples
to Lyme, for though they were never worse and never scarcer yet if
we can but get them thither before they rott, which they are very apt
to doe, you shall have a taste of them." ‡

* Dorothy Spencer, Countess of Sunderland, Waller's "Sacharissa" (1617–1684),
eldest daughter of Robert Sidney, second Earl of Leicester, by his wife Dorothy,
daughter of Henry Percy, ninth Earl of Northumberland ; married, 1639, Henry, first
Lord Spencer, created Earl of Sunderland ; he was killed at the Battle of Newbury,
1643. She married, secondly, Sir Robert Smythe, and spent much time at
Rufford with her daughter, Lady Halifax, often meeting her old admirer Waller
there.

† The influenza. ‡ Raines Collection.
§ Lady Penelope, eldest daughter of Lady Sunderland ; died unmarried.
|| Sir John Hinton, Royalist physician ; attended Queen Henrietta Maria.
¶ Mr., afterwards Sir Thomas, Chicheley, her husband.

Fruit was a very acceptable present, for in the rigorous climate of Lyme no apples would ripen any more then than they do now.

Sarah Chicheley was a great deal at Lyme with her married sister, who superintended her wardrobe.

> " I put your Father in minde of your Sister when he went up for some Winter Cloathes for her, which I found him willinger to pay for then to choose, so that if you can direct for the one he will doe ye other. I suppose Lyme air makes her suit [shoot] up, though I expect not she should be very tall ; her brother Harry since his Ague is grown much, & I think is the biggest & tallest Child I ever saw of his age—a very Gyant to his little Nephew and Nieces, who most barbarously he despised because he could overlook yem, and cared not to play with them, which little Nan * was sensible of as an indignity to her. I would faine heare you were bringing your husband the most acceptable present, which with all other blessings is prayed for by, Deare Daughter your entyrely loving Mother A. S." †

The Chicheley family was getting seriously anxious about Elizabeth's future prospects. She had now been married ten months without any signs of a baby, and this was causing great distress to her relations. They need not have worried themselves, however, as Elizabeth had thirteen children, her first, a girl, being born in 1663.

The Restoration was marked by a great event in the history of the Church of England, namely, the passing of the Act of Uniformity, which Act enforced the revising of the Prayer Book in its present form, virtually the last settlement of Ecclesiastical affairs in England by the joint action of Church and State. In 1645 the Book of Common Prayer had been forbidden and the Directory of Public Worship substituted for it. Its restitution involved the resignation of many of the clergy admitted to benefices under the Commonwealth.

Among the books at Lyme is one of the first edition of this revised Book. It is folio calf, printed in black letter by H.M.

---

* Anne, sole daughter of Sir George Savile, afterwards Marquess of Halifax, by his wife Dorothy, daughter of the Countess of Sunderland. She married, as his second wife, John, Lord Vaughan.

† Raines Collection.

RICHARD AND ELIZABETH

printers, and bears the date 1662. The following inscription
is written on the front page in Richard Legh's beautiful clear
hand :

> " The first day this Booke was read at Disley was vpon the 28th day of
> September in the yeare of our Lord God 1662: And Mr Bardsley did
> then and there Solemnly read the Declaration and Subscription in the
> Act contained accordingly.
>
> " Witnesse my hand
>
> " RICHARD LEGH.
>
> " A. L :"

The standard of prices had risen with that of the general 1661
comfort in the last fifty years, and it is interesting to compare
the wages of servants and some of the items in 1661 with those
of the opening years of James I's reign.

We find that £20 was paid for servants' wages at Lady Day,
1661 (presumably the quarter), the average of servants' wages
per quarter being approximately the same as in 1607, when they
totalled £20 to £25 the quarter, but the number then was
probably considerably greater. Thus we find that the steward,
whose wages in 1607 were 20s. the quarter, is paid in 1661
£2 10s., " if you please to allow it," the cook—a man—receiving
£3 15s. " For my charges and my horse at Preston last night,
4s. 8d.," the same kind of errand and journey having cost in
former years from 8d. to 1s. 8d.

Besides his Parliamentary duties, which demanded his
presence in London every year, his wife accompanying him
when the state of her health permitted, Richard had to discharge
the office of a Justice of the Peace, and other local matters
took him much about the county. He was appointed, in 1662,
by Charles, eighth Earl of Derby, and William, Lord Brereton,*
joint Lord-Lieutenants, a Deputy-Lieutenant of Cheshire. This
arrangement of having two Lord-Lieutenants of the county was
very unpopular, and Richard was " much importuned by persons
of quality in Cheshire " to request Mr. Secretary Bennet (afterwards first Earl of Arlington, and a member of the Cabal

* William, second Lord Brereton, married Elizabeth. daughter of Lord Goringe,
Earl of Norwich ; Lord Brereton died 1665.

1662 Ministry), who was an intimate friend, that Lord Gerard * might be appointed in their place, the distance at which both Lord Derby and Lord Brereton resided much retarding business. Later on Richard complains to Mr. Godolphin † that he finds it hard to please both his Lord-Lieutenants, and that " Lord Brereton is so wedded to his own humour that nothing else will please him." He adds pathetically that he has " no-one to fly to but Secretary Bennet."

On April 26 following, Richard was appointed Deputy-Lieutenant for Lancashire by special command of the King. He had frequently to visit his Lancashire property, and we find him constantly at Newton, Haydock, or Warrington, besides paying visits to Croxteth, Knowsley, and other friends' houses. These journeys were performed on horseback and occasionally by canal; he was attended by his steward and sometimes by two other servants. The roads were bad, and were not enclosed with hedges, so that it was easy to lose one's way and wander off the track into a bog or river. Travelling was therefore still a matter of difficulty and indeed of some danger. Foot-pads were constantly met with, and it was necessary to be always armed. Guides had to be obtained through the vast woodland; these seem to have been paid small sums, generally not more than 1s., but for what length of time their services were required does not appear.

Here is the bill for the Assize week at Chester in October 1662:

October 29, Att Chester, Powder box and gloves, 15s., hose and socks 15s. 6d.	1^{l}. 10. 6.
Bootes for Matthew	7.
Your bill in the Inn this Assize week . .	2. 19. 6.
Oslers and servants	4.
	5^{l}. 1.

Few particulars are to hand respecting articles of food. Mutton and veal are mentioned in the account book, cod-

* Third Lord Gerard of Bromley.
† Sidney Godolphin (1645–1712), statesman; page of honour to Charles II, 1662; Secretary of State, 1684; created Baron, afterwards Earl.

ELIZABETH CHICHELEY
Wife of Richard Legh of Lyme
1667
By Sir PETER LELY

From a Portrait at Lyme

fish occasionally, anchovies once, also cheese, £5 worth of which 1662
is dispatched to Lyme in May 1662, which looks as if cheesemaking were no longer practised, at any rate in this neighbourhood. The Lyme brawns were famous, and were held to be
very superior to the Wimpole ones, which were prepared in a
different way.

Oysters seem to have been a favourite dish. Two hundred of
these could be purchased for the sum of 2s. 4d. in 1607, but we
do not get the quantity given in the account book of 1661, the
sums paid for these delicacies varying from 1s. 6d. to 4s. ; 3s. 6d.
a barrel for " pickt ones " was the price in 1685. Oranges seem
to have been much appreciated as fruit, as much as 3s. being
paid for them at a time, and for cherries 1s. 6d. Vinegar and oil
are somewhat heavy items, £2 3s. worth being bought on March
25, 1661. " Oyle sent for to London " on April 6 of this same
year, 9s., and " Oyle and Westphalia Bacon—4^1 15." The
large sum in those days of 8s. 6d. is paid for " Hartichoughs "
(artichokes).

On May 19, 1662, Charles II prorogued the Parliament
(which did not meet again until the following February), and
the next day, May 20, he was married to Catherine of Braganza.
There was great excitement everywhere over the arrival of the
new Queen, and many were the conjectures as to her personal
appearance. Elizabeth Legh writes from Lyme to one of her
cousins :

> " I have an earnest request to you that you will give me an account
> when you have seen the Queen whether she is not the handsomest
> creature in the world as I believe by the report she is."

She begs also for Lady Savile's report on Charles's bride :

> " I doubt not but ere these come to you, you will see the Queen, who
> is famed wth us to be the finest creature in the world, I shold be very
> happy to heare your opinion of her."

We gather some particulars of the cost of travelling at this
date from the account book, which gives a few details of a journey
to London in 1663.

The young people appear to have rented a partly furnished

1663 house from Sir Charles Waldegrave * for some ten weeks, for
which they paid a rent of £32 10s., averaging therefore the sum
of £3 per week. An inventory was taken by the steward,
" giving an account of goods in your Lodgeings," for the modest
sum of 1s. 6d. We do not learn the locality of the house; it
was most probably somewhere in the neighbourhood of Great
Queen Street, Covent Garden, where Mr. Chicheley lived,
whose house is thus described by Pepys :

> "March 11th, 1667-8 ; By and by comes Sir W. Coventry † and with
> him Mr Chicheley and Mr Andrew Newport,‡ I to dinner with them to
> Mr Chicheley's in Gt Queen Street, Covent Garden. A very fine house,
> and a man that lives in mighty great fashion, with all things in a most
> extraordinary manner noble and rich about him, and eats in the
> French fashion all ; and mighty nobly served with his servants and
> very civilly ; that I was mighty pleased with it, and good discourse.
> He is a great defender of the Church of England and against the Act for
> Comprehension, which is the work of this day, about which the House is
> like to sit till night. "

As far as one can make out, beds seem to have been the sole
articles of furniture provided in the house rented by Richard
and Elizabeth. Plate, linen, hangings, and chairs were hired,
a maid was also let with the house, her wages being included
in the hire of linen, at £2 18s. a month. The hire of hangings
and chairs came to £3 15s. 6d., and there is an upholsterer's bill
of £46 besides.

The sum of £197 6s. was paid to a Mr. Whitehead for silver
plate, but this was no doubt bought ; 10s. was also spent on
snuffers and tinned plates.

The distance from Cheshire to London is about 180 miles,
and the journey took six or seven days. Stoppages of from
one to two nights were made at different places, the entire
cost of the travelling being from £20 to £25, an average
of £4 being spent at each halting-place. Servants and

* Third baronet, an ancestor of the present Earl Waldegrave.
† Sir William Coventry, brother-in-law of Mr. Chicheley, was secretary to the
Duke of York.
‡ A Commissioner of Customs, younger son of Lord Newport of High Ercall,
Salop.

228

ostlers were generally tipped 2s. 6d. each, and it was customary to leave some small sum, about 1s. 6d., for the poor of each town or village.

Richard himself seems to have ridden the entire way on horseback, attended by the steward and two other servants ; Elizabeth and her maids travelling in Richard's own private coach, with postilions and relays of six horses, as many as eighteen sometimes having to be baited at a time. The heavy luggage went by wagon. Baiting was a very expensive item, the cost of " horse-meat," " rewards " to ostlers, saddlers, etc., almost equals the expenses of the human beings. At Coventry, for instance, the horse-meat came to £2 4s. 6d. ; rewards to ostlers, etc., being extra, the reckoning in the house amounting to £3 8s. 6d.

The first coaches, private or otherwise, must have been extremely cold and uncomfortable. There were no glass windows before the eighteenth century. Curtains and wooden shutters were the only protection against wind and rain, so that in winter the passengers had the choice of being either stifled in the pitch-darkness of the interior, if the shutters were closed, or frozen if they were open. The springs were of a very primitive make, and the excessive jolting and swinging of these vehicles, due partly to their top-heavy condition and the state of the roads, must have been most uncomfortable and fatiguing. The passengers indeed frequently suffered from a nausea resembling sea-sickness. Numerous servants were taken on these journeys, not only to guard the coach, but also to help to extricate it when—as often happened—it stuck fast in a rut or was overturned. Bundles of ropes were carried by the servants for this purpose, and the shoulder-knots that are seen on state liveries of the present day are a survival of this custom.

Starting from Lyme on April 9, 1663, they must have been an imposing cavalcade. The coach with its post-boys and six horses rumbling heavily along, the light luggage strapped on the top, Richard cantering gaily beside it, with his attendants, the wagon and heavy luggage following behind. They seem to have

1663 averaged about twenty-seven to thirty miles a day, which, considering the bad roads and the cumbersome vehicles, was pretty good going.

Their first stop was made at Gawsworth, a village some twelve miles from Lyme. This was probably to breathe or change the horses, as there only appears a charge of 2s. 6d. for servants and poor. Newcastle-under-Lyme must have been reached that night (April 9).

For the discharge of the bill there	.	.	.	2^l. 18.	6.
To servants in the house	.	.	.	3.	
Spent on the roade	.	.	.	.	2.	
To the poore	.	.	.	.	.	6.

3^l. 4.

Travelling all day on the 10th, their next stoppage was at Lichfield, where their expenses were as follows :

Bill in the house .	.	.	.	.	1^l. 18.	6.
Horse-meat	.	.	.	.	1^l. 2.	
Beer in the Cellar afterwards	.	.	.	2.	
Servants in the house .	.	.	.	3.	
Oslers	.	.	.	.	.	2.	6.
Sadler	.	.	.	.	.	1. 2.	
Spent on the roade	.	.	.	.	2. 6.	
Boot-catcher *	.	.	.	.	4.	

3^l. 12.

A stay of two nights, April 11 and 12, was made at Coventry, the bill there totalling £6 6s. They slept on the 13th at Towcester, reaching Dunstable on the 14th, where they also remained the night, arriving at Barnet and London, stiff and weary, on April 15. A charge of eight shillings is here made for washing the horses.

When one thinks of the comfort, not to say luxury, of present-day travelling, it is difficult to imagine the arrival of the weary travellers and the misery of a first night spent in an unoccupied and half-furnished house. They were dependent on what

---

* A " boot-catcher " was a person at an inn who pulled off the boots of travellers.

arrangements could be made for their comfort, on the capacity
of the hired maid, probably a very raw and inexperienced
individual, whose ingenuity must have been taxed to the
uttermost to provide the most ordinary necessaries of life.
What little cleaning there was had probably to be done after
the arrival of the travellers, and the unloading and unpacking
of goods, the noise and shouting of porters, the bustle and confusion in new and strange surroundings, must have tried the
patience and endurance of the most even-tempered.

On April 16, the day after their arrival, we find the sum of
£10 being paid to the housekeeper, "Mistress Jane," "for the use
of the house," and the following articles are procured at once :

April 16.	To a porter and spent this day	.	.	1.	6.
	For Oysters 1s 6 – Paper, Inke &ct, 2s 6		4.		
	ffor glasses	13.	6.		
	ffor white earthenware . . .	2.			
	ffor knives 3s ; Salts & Jugs 2s 4, spent 1s	6.	4.		

There is no mention of tea or coffee. The first advertisement
of tea appears in 1658, at 60s. the pound, so that in 1663
it was probably still expensive. Coffee was much cheaper; it
was sold at one penny the cup.

The housekeeper, Mistress Jane, received sums varying from
£25 to £45 a month "for the use of the house," but this did not
include coals, wine, beer, or groceries. Mr. Cleave, "the
Grosser," is paid £46 3s. 6d. on the last day of their tenancy,
their wine bill totalling £17 4s ; £11 17s. being spent on beer
and ale during the two months of their stay in London.

We do not hear anything about the cook's expenses ; they
were probably no inconsiderable amount.

Arriving from the country after a long stay, the wardrobe
of the young couple would need renewing. Richard was
very particular about his clothes and was always modish
and in the lastest fashion. "Your Coat," writes a correspondent,

" Mr Hornesell hath in hand and the box I have returned with another
petticoat, had the collour of the last been liked as well as your stuff,

they had been of the same piece, but I could not get a sad Canterbury satin neere soe good, and therefore sent this, I hope it will fit for bignes."

We find a bill for £5 19s. 6d. for hats on April 25, and "ribin" is a somewhat extravagant item, £2 12s. 6d. being given for gloves and ribbon about this date. Here is a list of a few of Richard's purchases :

	l.	s.	d.
6 bandes for yourself		16.	6.
Hose and stockings	2.	15.	6.
ffor a white Tabby belt	1.	9.	
A gunsmith for pistolls	5.	12.	6.
For Fustian for waistcoats & holland . .		18.	6.
skowring 4 pair of silk hose			6.
The sword cuttler		17.	
Shoetyes with silver twiste		3.	6.
A pair of hunting bootes		18.	6.
To A. Knowles to buy cloth to line 8 doubletts with flannel	1.	16.	

No less a sum than £18 was spent for boots and shoes. A pair of riding-pantaloons seems cheap at 5s., a pair of riding-gloves 2s. 4d. ; these were, no doubt, more in general use than in the days of James I, and had become cheaper.

The following articles partly provided Elizabeth with a new gown :

	l.	s.	d.
10 yards green buckram at 1s 6 . . .		15.	
2 yards green sarsnet – 17s, silke 3s . .	1.		
green fringe		5.	5
For galoone lace		3.	

The horses had to be kept and fed during their time in London. £12 12s. were paid for oats and beans, and £13 17s. 6d. for hay at £2 10s. the load. The saddler's bill was a heavy one. On April 29 we find £14 paid to the saddler " for your great saddle, holsters, bits, etc," and on June 20, " to the sadler for holster capps, 18s, points 2s, bridle, brest-plate and cropper 6s, bitt 3s 6—total 1¹. 9. 6 "; a further bill of £12 12s. 6d. being paid to Mr. Fletcher—another saddler.

RICHARD AND ELIZABETH

The coal bill for the ten weeks spent in London amounted to £1 14s. this represented 1¾ chaldron at 19s. 6d. the chaldron. The cost of candles was 12s. 6d.

From various entries in the account book we gather that four men in livery must have been kept: "Trimming for Livereys, 7¹ 16ˢ, making of livery Hatts, 8ˢ, and 4 pair of livery stockings, 16ˢ." Swords appear to have been carried by servants on state occasions and when attending ladies; we find four of these bought at 10s. apiece.

The apothecary's bill during their stay amounted to 11s.; this included such items as powder, pills, manna, and troches.

Unfortunately there are few letters about this date, in fact there are none at all between July 1662 and July 1663, so we are unable to learn anything about their life in London. Hospitality was so much the fashion of the day that there is certain to have been entertaining. Richard had many friends at Court and elsewhere, and the house of a young and charming couple was likely to be much frequented. Henry, first Earl of Arlington,* and his sister, Lady Carr, wife of Sir Robert Carr,† were among the Legh's most intimate friends and correspondents, and the intercourse between the house of Derby and that of Legh was still maintained. Richard frequently saw his cousins the Gerards and Molyneux, and there was a constant interchange of visits between the Legh family and that of Lord Bridgewater.‡

The theatre was a very favourite place of amusement, and the occasional entry of tobacco-pipes in the account book suggests many convivial gatherings. These pipes were no doubt of clay, and seem to have cost under a penny each. In spite of its former unpopularity in high quarters, smoking still con-

---

* Henry Bennet, first Earl of Arlington (1618–1685), member of Cabal Ministry; centre of opposition to Clarendon; probably responsible for outbreak of first Dutch War. Unsuccessfully impeached in House of Commons; instrument of King's evil measures.

† Sir Robert Carr of Sleaford, Chancellor of the Duchy of Lancaster; was succeeded in that post at his death, in 1682, by Sir Thomas Chicheley. He married a daughter of Sir John Bennet of Dawley, and a sister of Henry, first Earl of Arlington.

‡ John Egerton, second Earl of Bridgewater, represented the Elder Brother in the first representation of Milton's *Comus* in 1634.

1663 tinued. Charles II derived so large a revenue from the duty on imported tobacco that the home-grown article was very heavily taxed, but its surreptitious growth was continued down to the reign of George III, when it was stopped by Act of Parliament. The price per pound of Spanish tobacco was seven shillings in 1685. Virginia was cheaper, costing only two shillings.

By the end of June 1663 we find Richard and Elizabeth preparing for their return journey. The bill for dilapidations in the house shows the servants to have been unusually careful, as " repairs and losses in the house " do not exceed the modest sum of 12s. A supply of writing paper " for the country " is taken with them, two reams at 8s. the ream, also a pound of wax at 3s. 6d. Writing paper in 1607 cost 4d. the quire; this shows therefore an increase of only 1s. 4d. on the ream in the price. Mention is made of 10s. worth of gold-dust. This was used to sprinkle over the paper to dry the writing, and portions of it may still be seen on the letters. Blotting paper is mentioned in MSS. as early as the fifteenth century, but gold-dust seems to have been more generally used for correspondence.

The return journey, which began on June 25, was by a different route, a visit to Wimpole being made on the way. The first night was spent at Stevenage, and Wimpole was reached next day.

Elizabeth was in an interesting condition, and more time had to be taken over the journey, which we find occupied from June 25 till July 5 or 6. The route followed from Wimpole was by Bedford, Northampton, Daventry, Coleshill, Lichfield, Stone, and a village or inn called Talke o' th' Hill on the borders of Staffordshire and Cheshire, which seems to have been their last halting-place. They must have been glad indeed to get home again, and Lyme in the early days of July would be looking its loveliest.

Richard had probably obtained leave to absent himself from his parliamentary duties, as the House was still sitting in July 1663, in spite of protests from Charles II that there should be a recess, " the season requiring it for health." Although the

234

King named July 16 for the date of the recess, Parliament continued its labours until the 27th, when it was prorogued until March 16 of the following year. This was during part of the Long Parliament, which, summoned to meet in 1661, was not dissolved till January 1678–9.

CHAPTER XVI

DOMESTIC FELICITY

1663 ONE of the excitements of 1663 was the impeachment—ineffectual as it then turned out—by Lord Bristol * of Lord Clarendon,† the Lord Chancellor, whom he accused of various acts of high treason. These included the taking of large sums of money for breaking off the Italian match, converting the public money to his own use, and the selling of Dunkirk :

> " Hee [Lord Bristol] was highly discouraged by the King [writes Nicholas Bowden to Richard Legh on July 11, 1663], who gave him liberty to wave his attendance at the Court, as he hath done formerly to Mr Lacie ‡ for acolding ; I am afraid of losing my place at Court, or I could say more."

Elizabeth Legh's hoped-for baby arrived on December 2, 1663.§ " Let me heare from your husband or somebody how is it with you," writes Mr. Chicheley to his daughter shortly before the event, " for there will not be any newes so joyfull to me as to hear of yr happy deliverance be it either of a boy or a girle." A girl it was, christened Lettice, Mr. Chicheley, Lady Ardern (Richard's elder sister), and a Mrs. Levison being sponsors.

Though no actual declaration of war took place before 1665, there was trouble with the Dutch in 1664, chiefly due to commercial rivalry and a desire on their part to drive the English out of the markets of the world. Hostilities began by the

---

* George Digby, second Earl of Bristol (1612–1677), fought for Charles I at Edgehill; Secretary of State to Charles II; subsequently deprived of seals as a Catholic.

† Edward Hyde, first Earl of Clarendon (1609–1674) ; a consistent supporter of constitutional monarchy, he refused to recognize changed conditions resulting from civil war.

‡ William Lacy, Royalist divine; remonstrated with Charles II on his mode of life.

§ Raines Collection.

REAR-ADMIRAL SIR JOHN CHICHELEY
From a Portrait at Lyme

DOMESTIC FELICITY

English seizing some of the Dutch possessions in the West Indies,
they retaliating by attacking the English forts on the coast of
Guinea. In 1665 war was openly declared, and the enemy
advanced upon the east coast of England. A severe engagement took place off Lowestoft on June 3, resulting in the
complete victory of the English, who defeated the enemy and
destroyed eighteen of their ships.

Elizabeth Legh's second brother, John Chicheley, had entered
the navy and ultimately gained some distinction as an admiral.
He was, on June 3, 1665, commanding the *Antelope*, one of the
ships in the red squadron under the Duke of York, and was
knighted shortly after the engagement.

> " Your father has lately received a letter from your brother John which
> spoke him well [writes Lady Savile to her stepdaughter on October 15,
> 1665], though it having no date & seeming to be writ shortly after
> their encounter with ye Turke making the same relation that we had
> heard before of it, we must conclude 'twas long in coming, but hope
> that he having past the sharpest brunt, hee remaines well and
> pleased with the Sea Service. My bro' Will [Sir William Coventry,*
> secretary to the Duke of York], assures me ye Duke his Master tooke
> particular Notice of him, which is some encouragement to a young
> Sea-man."†

This war continued for nearly three years, and had Louis XIV
supported the Dutch, the consequences would have been
most serious for England. As it was, the Dutch blockaded the
Thames and got within twenty miles of London. The war,
which came to an end with the Peace of Breda in 1667, broke
out again in 1672.

With one exception, the letters of this date contain no
reference either to the Plague or the Great Fire of London.
Lady Savile writes to her stepdaughter on October 16,
1665 : " The general sicklynes of the yeare exempts few places
but Lyme where health and wealth conspire to make you happy." †
This is the only allusion to the terrible scourge which decimated

* Sir William Coventry (1628 ?–1686), politician ; younger son of Thomas, first
Baron Coventry ; Commissioner of the Navy and friend of Pepys.
† Raines Collection.

THE HOUSE OF LYME

London and the whole country for nearly a year.* The Court
had removed from Whitehall to Hampton Court and Syon, and
was transferred to Salisbury in July, the Parliament sitting at
Oxford in September 1665. By 1666 the Plague had greatly
diminished, and the King and Court returned to Whitehall
The Great Fire raged from September 2 till the 6th, two-thirds
of London being destroyed.

1666 appears in margin beside "Oxford".

A second daughter was born to Richard and Elizabeth
on May 22, 1666, to be followed by a third, Frances, the year
after. These events no doubt prevented Elizabeth from
accompanying her husband to London either year. Richard
writes to her on January 3, 1666–7 :

"My dearest Deare
  "Thine was most welcome to me which I received yesterday. . . .
The King does not intend the Parlt. to sitt long, they are as cross
to him as cannot be imagin'd."

The supreme power was gradually being transferred from
the Crown to the Parliament, and this was not to be effected
without a severe struggle. The temper of Parliament had been
roused by the Dutch War, and awkward questions were being
asked in the House as to the expenditure of the money granted
for this purpose to the Crown. There were suspicions as to
whether it was being used to pay for the amusements of the
Court.

"Dearest Hart [writes Richard to his wife a few days later], since my
last to thee the King came to both Houses & (as well he might) tooke
unkindnes att our House that we did soe much distrust him. He
told us we shold sitt noe longer att this Sessions than Monday senight
but (God willing) I intend to be with thee about that time although I
know there will be notice taken on't in the House, yett I care not, there
are three and thirty members of Parl: in the Serjant's hands. Itt is

---

* In the Disley Parish Registers there appears this notice relating to the Plague :

"Sep: 5. 1665
Collected On the ffast then held for the Sicknes
a sume of nyne shillings and eight pence."

"Oct. 4. 1665
Collected on the ffast day for the sickness, the
Sume of ffore shilling and a penny."

238

observed there never was soe angry a House of Commons. I pray 1666-7
God send it ends well." *

He gives his wife details of her brother John, who was
paying his attentions to the lady he afterwards married, a certain
Mistress Norton, a widow, daughter of Admiral Sir John
Lawson † :

> " His affections are lodged with the widow Norton, who went suddenly
> out of town yesterday to my brother's great grief.   He tells me her
> Father proffers to settle a thousand pound a yeare upon him if he
> marries that widow, but then he must take ten thousand pound debt
> upon him ; she hath eight hundred a yeare joynture."

Pepys in his Diary on October 28, 1667, refers to this courtship in somewhat contemptuous terms :

> " To Sir William Pen's‡ to speak with Sir John Chichly, who desired
> my advice about a prize which he had begged of the King, and there
> had a great deal of his foolish talk of ladies and love and I know not
> what."

" Ladies and love " played such a very important part in
Pepys own life that this remark, coming from such a quarter,
seems a trifle inconsistent.

Sir John Chicheley was one of the witnesses examined at the
inquiry into the conduct of Lord Sandwich,§ in countenancing
and abetting the plundering of the prizes taken in the recent
naval engagement.   Pepys in his Diary expresses relief that
Sir John will be able to say little against his patron :

> " November 26, 1667.   This evening comes to me at the office Sir
> John Chicheley of his own accord to tell me what he shall answer to the
> Committee when, as he expects, he shall be examined about my Lord
> Sandwich, which is so little as will not hurt my Lord at all I know.   He
> do profess great generousness towards my Lord, and that this jealousy
> of my Lords of him is without foundation. . . . He will by no means

---

* Raines Collection.
† Sir John Lawson, vice-admiral of the Red Squadron in the war with the Dutch ;
died 1665.
‡ Sir William Penn (1621-1670), admiral, served with the Duke of York in the
Dutch War.
§ Edward Montagu, first Earl of Sandwich (1625-1672), admiral, second in
command of the English Fleet on outbreak of the second Dutch War in 1672 ; blown
up with his ship in Solebay.

crouch to my Lord, but says he hath as good blood in his veins as any man, though not so good a title, but that he will do nothing to wrong or prejudice my Lord, and I hope he will not, nor I believe can."

Richard had been to see some plays. " I have seen one Play since I came, *The Valiant Cidd*," he writes early in January 1666–7, " but methink they seem dull." * This play was a revival of Joseph Rutter's translation of Corneille's *Le Cid*. Pepys mentions it in his Diary on December 1, 1662, and seems to have taken the same idea about it as Richard :

> " I to the Cockpitt, with much crowding and waiting, where I saw *The Valiant Cidd* acted—a play I have read with great delight, but is the most dull thing acted, which I never understood before . . . nor did the King and Queen once smile all the whole play nor any of the whole company seem to take any pleasure but what was in the greatness and gallantry of the Company."

The public of those days was apparently its own censor :

> " There is a new one at the King's House as they say [adds Richard], call'd *The Custome o' th' Country* [by Beaumont and Fletcher] which is soe dam'd bawdy that the Ladyes flung theire peares and fruites att the Actors."

Although he had been married now some seven years, Richard's letters to his wife are still those of an ardent lover :

> " Deare Soule, every instant is two without thee. There is no diversion heere pleasant without thee, thou mayest believe me for I take no satisfaction in them. I was never wearier of this place, especially wanting thee, and ten thousand thousand times wish thee in mine arms. Noe wife breathing has a more true constant loving husband than he that subscribes himselfe
>
> > " Solely thine
> > > " R. Legh."

A few days later, on January 8, 1666–7, he writes again, giving some intimate Court news. The details are somewhat indelicate, but as they show Charles II in the pleasing light of an uxorious and devoted husband, they are here given in full :

> " The Queen is not well. The other night she fell sick when the King was in bed with her. He did rise in his shirt to fetch her a bason, but

* Raines Collection.

240

before he came with itt she had laid all up in the sheets, and then he put on his gowne & slippers & fetch't a towell & dried the sheets cleane about her & laid her on his cleane side, then called her women & went to his owne chamber but came three times before he would goe sleepe to see her. They say it is a fever and she was the other day lett blood." *

Sometime in the spring of 1666–7 Lady Savile died, to the great grief of her husband and stepchildren.

There was an autumn session in 1667, and we hear of the Legh family again in London in September. Mr. Chicheley was a noted tennis player, and Pepys in his Diary on September 2, 1667, reports a match at which the King was present : 1667

" I went to see a great Match at tennis between Prince Rupert and one Captain Cooke † against Bab May‡ and the elder Chicheley, where the King was and the Court, and it seems are the best players at tennis in the nation."

According to Pepys, the King used to weigh himself both before and after a match, sometimes losing as much as 4½ lb.

In 1669 there came to Richard and Elizabeth the long- wished-for son and heir, Peter, born on August 22, Peter Venables, Baron of Kinderton (great-uncle of Richard), Sir John Chicheley, and Richard's youngest sister, Lady Brooke, being sponsors. By the following February, the proud father (back in London, lodging " at the end of Drury Lane ") is seeing about a little " Coach " for the new arrival. This was probably a species of perambulator. 1669

" February 17, 1669–70, This afternoon, I thank God I gott well to Towne, but the beastliest journey for bad travelling that ever was. A deliverance I had that I lay not in Durham Yard, for my Aunt lyes there." *

This undutiful speech refers to his aunt, Lady Calveley, a most tiresome woman, who was always bothering her relations,

---

* Raines Collection.
† Captain Henry Cooke, musician, composer to Charles II ; died 1672.
‡ Baptist May (1629–1696), Keeper of the Privy Purse to Charles II ; Clerk of the Works at Windsor Castle, 1671 ; with Lely and Evelyn recommended Grinling Gibbons to Charles II.

complaining and giving trouble. He goes on to say, " Mr
Rigby hath promised me to send 4 little chaires down by the
Carrier, & I present my son Peter with a little Coach."

On February 19, he writes again : *

> " Dearest, I want nothing this night to compleat the joy I am in but
> thy deare company & the brats. Ever since I saw thee I have not
> eate nor drank before five a clocke except Monday, the House having
> sate these two days so late & this day the King's party therein hath
> overvoted their opposers in every thing & struck so great a stroke into
> his businesse that I hope in God to be with thee in as short a time as
> possible thou canst expect. My father † hath a promise from the
> King to have my Ld Barclay's ‡ place (Master of the Ordnance) who
> goes certainly for Ireland. I have been so tyed to the House that as
> yett I have not soe much as thought of a Play. I saw my Lady Carr
> yesterday, to-morrow, I dine there. My sister tells me the news in
> Towne is the Devill hath fetch't away the Lady Newcastle." §

There was great rejoicing amongst the King's party at the
majority in the House over the Vote of Supply. Charles had
obtained a grant from Parliament of £300,000 a year for eight
years, and in return gave his royal consent to a second Conventicle Act even more stringent than the first. The King
summoned the House to the Banqueting Hall at Whitehall to
convey his thanks in person, and the following description in a
letter * from Richard to his wife gives a vivid account of what
occurred :

> " February 22, 1669-70.
> " Dearest, . . . I told thee in my last what votes were made on
> Friday last. Yesterday the King sent to desire us to come to him into
> the Banquetting House this day, which we did by 9 aClock ; there we
> recd his harty thanks for agreeing soe well & readily with his desires.
> The Speaker then went to the Parlt. House & the Members were soe
> in love with his Maty's gracious Speech that in acknowledgmt thereof

---

* Raines Collection.

† His father-in-law, Mr. Chicheley. Richard always spoke of him as " my
father " and of Sir John Chicheley as " my brother."

‡ First Baron Berkeley of Stratton, one of the Masters of Ordnance. Lord-
Lieutenant of Ireland, 1670.

§ Margaret Cavendish, Duchess of Newcastle (1624-1674), the fantastic poetess.

DOMESTIC FELICITY

they voted they wold wayte upon ye Speaker all on foot which we did 2 & 2 hand in hand, through Kings Street to Whitehall, all the whole House. My Lord Gorges * came running to me & told me he had rather goe with me than any man ith' House, soe we went together through Kings Street all ith' raine into the Banquetting House where the King immediately came, & the Speaker told him the sense that the House had of his Maty's most Gracious Speech did ravish them & he was commanded to return Him their thankes & to acquaint him they had razed Skinner's Case out of their Bookes in obedience to his Gracious Speech when they first mett & did assure him of their affection & loyalty. To which the King replyed he was as joyfull as they & did never doubt their affections nor loyalty. I stood the next but one to him when this was delivered from both King & the Speaker & to this purpose they spoke. All persons there present cold not forbear their acclamations of joy & many did expresse it in teares. The King's Servantes then invited the Speaker & us all into the Cellar. Old & young, grave & madd went, Sr Job Charlton † I led by one hand & Judge Milward on the other, & each man drunke ye King's health soe long that many will want their own tomorrow. We din'd 30 of us by Charing Crosse & gave 30 half Crownes for a bone fire to be before Whitehall. I doubt 'twill be over before I can gett to it. My Father ‡ just now tells me it shines over all the towne. The newes is soe good I cannot abate one tittle on't."

The King and Queen had now been married nearly eight years, so far without any prospect of children. The people were getting seriously anxious, and many hopes were expressed that there might be an heir to the throne. These hopes were frequently expressed even to His Majesty himself, and with that freedom of speech belonging to the period.

"My Father carried me to the King upon Sunday [writes Richard in this same letter, February 22, 1669–70], I kissed his hand & he came to me & gave me very good words. . . . Sir Gilbert Talbott in great joy saluted the King & told him if he would this night begett a Prince of Wales he would make us the happiest people in the world. The King said ' I'll promise you I'll do my best ! ' The Queen I heard say if she saw a man in the Court that had a cheerfull countenance & dart upon his Stockings that was a Parlt man that lov'd the King well. My Father is just come in & hath given orders for a bone-fire before his doore and is gone againe."

* Lord Gorges of Dundalk, his parliamentary colleague.
† Sir Job Charlton, afterwards Speaker.
‡ His father-in-law, Mr. Chicheley.

243

" March 3, 1669–70. . . . Yesterday I din'd with my Lord of Yorke.*
He and his Lady and Daughter expresse great kindnesse for thee."

The House adjourned on April 11, till October 24, 1670,
and Richard set forth on his return to Lyme sometime towards
the end of March. The roads were still in a terrible condition,
and travelling was performed under almost as great difficulty
as ever.

" Ye wayes are soe extreame foule by the breaking of the frost [writes
Richard] that two or three we have seen that ridd Post most terribly
hurt, one I thought had been kill'd. I first came to him and took
him upp. My Lord Derby [Charles, eighth Earl] sent a special Post
this day that overtook us all blood with a fall he gott. There are such
holes that if a horse goes faster than ordinary he comes down." †

Richard's worth was by now fully recognized in Parliament
and elsewhere. His advice was frequently asked for and
followed, and his excellent qualities were being appreciated as
they deserved by every one from the King downwards. At a
solemn debate about a reform of the Deputy-Lieutenants when
the name of Legh of Lyme was mentioned, Charles immediately
declared that he himself would undertake for that gentleman.‡
An undated letter from Sir Edmund Wyndham, a parliamentary
official, addresses him as " a man rightly principled in every
way to the Government, and one who always endeavoured
like a good Patriott and a loyall Subject to preserve a good
understandinge between his Matie and his people." The
writer goes on to say that the King's wishes are for securing
and maintaining the Protestant religion, and that he hopes it will
not be within the power of any person " to make a division
between his Ma^ty and his Parliament." He begs that Richard
will " discourse amongst the worthy persons you converse with
in the Country," and that he will hasten up to London, " where

* Richard Sterne (1596?–1683), Archbishop of York, and alleged author
of " The Whole Duty of Man." Was chaplain to Archbishop Laud, attended him
in the Tower and remained with him until his execution. A zealous adherent of the
Royalist cause, made Bishop of Carlisle in 1660, and in 1664 Archbishop of York.
† Raines Collection.
‡ " Dr. Shippen's funeral sermon on Richard Legh," published 1688.

we may meete at o^r Clubbe and assist with your advice to bringe all things to a happy conclusion."

With one exception, in a letter of 1659, this is the only mention of clubs which occurs in these letters. The word, which is from the same root as " clump," a collection of persons, is illustrated by a " clump of trees " and dates from the seventeenth century. The clubs of the Restoration were chiefly political. They were established in London under the name of " Coffee Houses " about the middle of the seventeenth century. An attempt was made by Charles II to suppress them in 1675, as being the resort of political agitators. Many of them were probably local gatherings, where views were freely exchanged, the discussions occasionally ending in disputes and even blows, resulting in duels. The following description of a brawl occurs in a letter of about this date. The principals were Henry Savile,* half-brother of Mrs. Richard Legh, and a certain Lord Dunbar :

> " Poor Henry Sauill and the Lord Dunbarr, both foule drunke, quarrelled and cuff'd, then drew, Henry could not stand, but fell, then Dunbarr run him through, but 'tis hoped not through the body, though he hath a terrible wound."

Another letter of the same date describes a somewhat similar occurrence—typical of the life of the time :

> " We no sooner alighted at the Crown in Bloomsbury, but two gentlemen came out thence and fought, and one was brought amongst us run 4 times through the body. He dyed in our hands. The other is twice run through—if he recovers he will be hang'd. They are both gentlemen. He that lives hath kill'd 2 or 3 before." †

Members of the House of Commons so far forgot their dignity that such scenes were witnessed even within the precincts of the sacred House itself, as we gather from the following which appears in the " Journals of the House " a few years

* Henry Savile (1642–1687), diplomatist; gentleman of the bedchamber to the Duke of York and afterwards Vice-Chamberlain to Charles II, with whom he had great influence. Envoy in Paris 1679–82. His correspondence was published in 1858.
† Raines Collection.

later, referring to Elizabeth's father, who had become by then Sir Thomas Chicheley :

> "May 10, 1678. The House being informed That upon a division of the House a Quarrel had happened between the Lord O'Brien and Sir Thomas Chicheley and that blows were given
> And Sir Thomas Chicheley being present
> Ordered that Sir Thomas Chicheley be committed to the custody of the Serjeant at Arms
> That the Serjeant at Arms do take the Lord O'Brien into Custody."

1671 To return to 1671. Richard's family was now rapidly increasing. A fourth daughter, Sarah, was born in October 1671.

Mr. Chicheley must have been knighted about this date, after his appointment as Master General of the Ordnance. He writes to Elizabeth Legh on October 28, 1671, speaking of his desire to see his youngest daughter Sarah settled in life, and according to the practice of parents of the time, was trying to arrange a marriage for her. The object of his choice was a son of Richard's neighbour and cousin, Thomas Cholmondeley of Vale Royal.* Such a marriage would, he assures his elder daughter, be very acceptable to him, he feeling that the two sisters would then be near each other " to comfort one another when I am dead and rotten." He adds : " She is very good-natured and has your mother's heart which a flea may master."

This contemplated match did not come off, and Sarah married, soon after this date, Andrew Fountain of Salle, with whom she led a most unhappy life.

A good deal of excitement was being caused in the county by an election for Chester which took place in 1672–3, on the death of one of the two sitting members, John Radcliffe. Two candidates were named, Colonel Werdon, an ardent Royalist, who had barely escaped with life for joining in Sir George Booth's rising in 1659, and who afterwards became comptroller to the Duke of York's household, and a certain

* Thomas Cholmondeley of Vale Royal, Cheshire ; born 1627 ; married, first, Jane, daughter of Sir Lionel Tollemache of Helmingham, Suffolk, by whom he had twelve children ; secondly, 1684, Anne, daughter of Sir Walter St. John of Battersea, by whom he had fours sons and one daughter ; he died 1701–2.

DOMESTIC FELICITY

Mr. William Williams, Recorder of the City of Chester. Colonel Werdon was supported by the King's party and by most of the Cheshire gentlemen. Richard writes to his brother Thomas on January 31, 1672–3 :

> " I am just now come from Whitehall and very opportunely I kiss'd his Ma^ty's hand att Sir Jos : Williamsons * Office.   The Duke of York came to me and very passionately enquired of me what good hopes there was of Colonel Werdons being chosen att Chester ; I told him I hoped well and was the more encouraged to itt since my brother Ardern † told me about 100 of the Citty votes had tendered him their service, and he resigned them all to Colonel Werdon which I assure you pleased him well." ‡

In spite of the most barefaced bribery on the part of Mr. Williams, who promised, if he was returned, to discharge a debt of £40, owing from the City to the King, to lend the corporation £500 gratis for seven years, and " to serve them without salary and to spend his Estate amongst them," Colonel Werdon was returned, Mr. Williams coming in as member on the death of Sir Thomas Smythe in 1675.

Richard reports the taking of some Dutch spies, January 30, 1672–3 :

> " There is two men brought prisoners from Harwich to the Tower, being suspected to be sent from Holland to the Parl^t to endeavor a breach betwixt the K: & them, one of them was sent out of Engl: within this 6 weeks, being suspected for a spy & commanded to return no more ; 'tis thought one of them will be hang'd, as the poore German Princess § was on Wednesday last but one for stealing Aspinwalls watches." ‡

Richard and Elizabeth were back in London in January 1672–3, having taken a good house in Southampton Square, with " stables all convenient." The children were left at Lyme

* Sir Joseph Williamson (1633–1701), statesman and diplomatist ; keeper of Charles II's library at Whitehall.
† Sir John Arderne, his brother-in-law, married to his eldest sister Margaret.
‡ Raines Collection.
§ Mary Moders, alias Carleton, a celebrated impostor, who induced the son of a London citizen to marry her under the pretence that she was a German Princess. Executed at Tyburn for stealing.

under the care of Thomas, Richard's only brother, who kept a watchful eye upon the nursery and managed the property during his brother's absence. Thomas Legh was a capable man. He was given the post of Receiver General for the County of Lancashire, and was in 1685 elected one of the members for Liverpool borough. His letters are graphic and well expressed, and show much business capacity. Long letters are exchanged between the two brothers, who were devotedly attached to each other. Richard writes the news and gossip from London, Thomas replying with all particulars relating to the children and estate. Richard always writes " Dear Brother," Thomas's letters, however, are far more formal, and never have any other beginning than " Dear Sir."

1672-3 On January 29, 1672-3, Richard and Elizabeth arrived at their London house, and on February 4 he writes to Thomas for some of his home-brewed ale :

> " Gett Adam to helpe to brew a load of Derby malt or more into 25 or 26 gallons of stitching ale [strong ale] when itt is clear, let itt be drawne into the sack vessell & another that contains so much to make it a horse load, & send itt I pray by the carrier as soon as possible."

Unless the ale prove strong and " excellent " he begs it may not be sent. He sends some playthings for the children—directed severally, also sweet powder, etc. ; a little magnifying-glass, and an ivory woman in the shape of a frog, as a " Lenton Mistress " for one of his friends.

The ale was sent and proved

> " Exceeding good, if there be any more soe good I cold wish I had itt, for my Father Sʳ John and Sʳ Robert Carr * all admire itt, itt exceeds their Nordowne & Sandbache, the color is soe fine and 'tis very smoothe. It is now a good time to fill the vessells in the further cellar with strong beere ; itt must be stronger than formerly because of keeping. I pray give order about itt."

The baby had been ill, evidently an attack of thrush. " Cousin Downes " is sent for to give medical advice and the

---

* Chancellor of the Duchy of Lancaster ; married to a sister of Henry Bennet, Earl of Arlington.

248

" violence and strong hands " that were laid upon the unfortunate child in the dressing of her mouth, caused her to set up
such a " shrickinge " that it had the most disastrous effects
upon her nurse—a married woman—resulting in the arrival
of an unexpected infant. This is all described in language
more forcible than elegant. Thomas gives a short account of
Peter, the son and heir, now nearly four years old, " who told
me in his dialect he was ' a very little Boy but had a dele Tot '
[small drinking cup]. All conclude as ye Gypseys did when the
Catt was in Swadles, yᵗ 'tis as like Dadd as ere't may looke."

A good deal of local excitement, which, however, also
spread to London, was caused in 1673 by one Jollie,* an
ejected Presbyterian minister and a native of Manchester,
who had been committed to prison on the charge of keeping
a conventicle. Richard got great praise for the manner in
which he had conducted the apprehension of the offender, the
matter being brought before the notice of the King.

> " We shall trounce the rogue Jolly, the Chancellor [Sir Robert Carr] is
> warme agˢᵗ him. I mentioned it to my Lord Arlington & the Treasurer
> who both of them came to salute me whilst the Chancellor and I were
> at Sʳ Joseph Williamson's." †

Jollie was imprisoned ; " the King," says Richard, " wold
not suffer him to come out till he was sufficiently humbled."
He was ultimately, in 1674, fined £20.

A letter from Richard to his brother, written in February
1672-3, speaks of the election of Sir Job Charlton ‡ as Speaker,
recommended by the King. " He made a very coy speech
before he advanced to the Chaire, and another at the Chaire."
Then there appears to have been a motion that none of the
newly elected members should sit until the House was satisfied
that these were duly elected, it being unparliamentary for the
Lord Chancellor to issue writs during a Prorogation. This

* John Jollie the elder (1640 ?–1682), received Presbyterian ordination at
Manchester, 1672.

† Sir Joseph Williamson (1633–1701), statesman and diplomatist; keeper of
Charles II's library at Whitehall.

‡ Sir Job Charlton (1614–1697), judge, son of a London goldsmith; Speaker of the
House of Commons, February 4–18, 1672–3.

occasioned " great heats," but Richard hopes that the King " will heal this."

He mentions dining with the Duke of Ormonde,* when the company consisted wholly of men, who, in the fashion of that time, all wore their hats during a banquet. The dinners of those days were chiefly conspicuous for the enormous number of dishes, quantity not quality being the first consideration. The tables were loaded, all courses being put on together, and with no arrangement for keeping the different dishes warm. Oysters frequently figured in banquets of the period, as they do still, and were evidently greatly appreciated. Although Charles II was supposed to have introduced more refinement into the entertaining, forks were still very rarely seen, and this must have necessitated much use of the fingers. There appears to have been no special arrangement for the seating of the ladies and gentlemen alternately, and they seem to have placed themselves much as they pleased. Mention is made on February 15, 1672-3, of a great supper and masquerade given by Sir John Bennet, a brother of the Earl of Arlington, at which Richard and his wife were present, and which was supposed to have cost £500. " There was 60 Ladyes att one table besides 20 men, soe believe me there was £20,000 worth of plate, & to a miracle none of it was stolen."

672-3

* James Butler, first Duke of Ormonde (1610–1688); Royalist commander in Ireland, 1648; occupied posts in the households of Charles II and James II; Lord-Lieutenant of Ireland.

CHAPTER XVII

THE THIRD DUTCH WAR

THE third Dutch War, long threatened, broke out in 1673.
Sir John Chicheley received a commission as Rear-Admiral to
the Blue in command of the *Charles*. Richard Legh describes
the progress of the war in a series of letters written from London
to his brother Thomas at Lyme.

An eloquent speech in the House of Commons from Sir
William Coventry,* Secretary to the Admiralty, reported in a
letter of February 8, 1672–3, set forth the urgent necessity of
the House voting a sum of money for the purpose of carrying
on the campaign. The speech was so eloquent that the House
resolved itself into a Grand Committee,

> " and did not onely give the King " 1¹260,000, but agreed it shold be
> by a land Tax according to the last Royal aid, 18 months assesmᵗ:
> after ¹70,000, p. mens: and all this was done & passed the House in
> lesse than an houres time 'Tis agreed by all hands that this hath
> given a greater blow to the Dutch than all the guns that hath been agˢᵗ
> them in this war."

This was not to be done for nothing, however, and the
King was forced to withdraw his Declaration of Indulgence.
This act gave complete liberty to both Roman Catholics and
Dissenters, by suspending all penal laws in matters ecclesiastical affecting either one or other. It was disputed that
the King could not interfere with the law, and that the Declaration was a violation of the statutes. The House therefore
passed a resolution that " penal statutes in matters eccle-

* Sir William Coventry (1628 ?–1686), politician; younger son of Lord Keeper
Coventry, and a brother of Lady Savile; Commissioner of the Navy and friend of
Pepys.

251

siastical cannot be suspended except by act of parliament."
1672-3 Writing to his brother on February 15, 1672–3, Richard says :

> " Yesterday the house was somewhat warme, they ordered the house
> with the Speaker to attend the King with that adress I mentioned in
> my last, & that a Bill shold be brought in to give some indulgence to
> his Majesty's Protestant subjects, dissenters from ye Church of Eng-
> land. The heats was occasion'd by some persons that moved in
> behalfe of the Roman Catholics that had faithfully served the King
> in ye late wars, but they are not to partake in this intended act : nor
> wold the house suffer the Lords to be desired to goe along with them
> which to me appeares the worst of anything done yett, for our adress
> is single at present, and we cannot pass itt into an Act without the
> Lords : And truly I know not how we can word that Act."

At length, against the advice of some of his council, the
King gave way, and withdrew his Declaration of Indulgence.
On March 8, 1672–3, Richard writes again :

> " This day, I thanke God, is ye most glorious I have seen this ten
> yeares as to our publique affaires : This morning came the King to ye
> Lords house betimes and gave his speech in writing to our Speaker,
> which we read twice, wherein he doth agree to everything we have
> desired from him, and Secretary Coventry, (after the Speech was twice
> read, ye first that spoke) told us ; ' With myne owne eyes Sir, I saw
> the greate Seale pull'd from the Declaration ! ' So then, most unani-
> mously enter'd (Nemine Contradicente) that the thanks of this house
> be given to ye King for his gracious Answer, And (nemin : contrad :)
> that the Lords be desired to concur with us, which they have done,
> and both houses march this afternoone to meet the King ; I believe itt
> will prove like the last going into the Cellar ; I pray lett the Parson
> give God thankes for itt publiquely. . . . The King told us he was
> sorry any mistake had hapned amongst us, for his part he wold never
> againe be guilty. I believe the money Bill will come speedily out, for
> we have made a great Progress into itt this morning."

More was to be exacted from the King, however, before
Parliament would grant the promised sum. This same year,
1673 1673, was passed the great Test Act, which allowed no person
to hold any office of trust unless he consented to take the Test,
that is to say, unless he renounced the doctrine of transub-
stantiation, and agreed to receive the Sacrament according to
the rites of the Church of England. It was not intended to be a

252

persecuting act, or to interfere with the liberty of the subject, but merely to prevent any person holding certain religious beliefs, whose influence might be damaging to the State, from occupying high office. The fear of a French invasion in support of the English Roman Catholics was ever present with the people, and the knowledge of the Duke of York, the heir to the throne, being a Roman Catholic himself, lent colour to the possibility of this fear becoming a reality. In consequence of the passing of the Test Act, the Duke of York was forced to resign the office of High Admiral.

On March 13, 1672–3, a proposition was put forward in the House, opposed, however, by some of the Court and Church party, to repeal that declaration in the Act of Uniformity which renounced the Covenant :

> " 'Twas most strangely canvas'd [writes Richard to his brother], we debated itt above 6 houres, divided the house twice upon ye reading on't. 1st whether itt shold be read, 2nd time, whether itt shold be read againe, & carried in ye affirmative both times : had it been read the 3d time itt had been part of the Bill for ease of dissenters. Upon the debate the Covenant was rack't & toss'd most bravely, & strange itt was to see some of the old Cavaliers led by the nose by the Presbyt: who were in their colors, they urg'd why this shold passe, that itt only gave ease to about 9 or 10 honest conscientious men, (as they called them) and wold admitt them into ye Church, (this Byrch moved). Honest Mr Secretary Coventry stood up then, & I never heard better nor more honest things said ; amongst the rest he said : ' If you shold allow of this thing desired, and these men shall come in, I for my part will not come to their service, for Sir,' said he, ' I will never receive the blood of my Saviour from that hand that stinks with the guilt of the Blood of my great Master.' Immediately the question was putt & we threw itt out."

A curious incident happened this same day which we suppose Richard himself had witnessed :

> "This morning a strange accident happned about 9 aclock. There came a Fryer into the Palace Yard in the midst of his robes, & an attendant or two brought robes & bookes, & some brought faggots & fire & his beads, & after he had expressed an utter dislike to the Romish Religion, he burn't his beads, then his robes, & though he was an Italian, he expressed his dislike to that Religion in soe high a

nature, that his bookes followed, & he left a heavy curse upon his old father the Pope. This is very true."

He writes again a few days later :

" In the House we have stop'd the money Bill till the Bills for Ease of dissenters which passed our house yesterday & ye Pop : Bill (which hath been some days with the Lords) be both passed, to-morrow we go on the money Bill again."

There were grievances even in those days against the House of Lords :

" Secretary Coventry brought us a message from ye King that upon Thursday we shold have a recess, therefore he desir'd we wold dispatch our Bills, especially the Supply Bill, but (fatally I doubt) the Lords have been very high this day, & have either thrown out or soe mangled the Bill against Popery, that 'tis fear'd the other of Supply will not pass.

" For news 'tis said the Dutch are out with 40 sayle, but I doubt the truth on't, but I fear they will be out before us : some talke as tho' a peace were more att hand, but these are but conjectures."

In an undated letter of about this time Richard says :

" March, 1672–3, The Speaker tooday admonished Col Byrch * publiquely in the Parl house for brushing his whiskers, and said that was not a place to trimme his beard in. We all burst out with laughing att him, but he never blush't for't. Yesterday my father † carried me to Wollage, where we saw 48 great canon proved, & 2 great cast anchors, but those we broke."

1673   Sir John Chicheley was preparing for sea by the end of March, Richard sending him a horse-load of ale as a present with the following letter, dated April 3, 1673 :

" Our fleet is in a better forwardness then I expected, they say we shall have about 50 of our best ships out before this month ends, & the French will send in 40 good sayle besides fireships, & we shall have 40 more of our owne to be ready by the middle of the next month.

" The Dutch sent to desire a cessation for 2 yeares, but the great ones say now is the time to have them humbled. Doubtless they will be hard put to itt to defend themselves att Land & to fitt out att Sea.

* John Birch, Presbyterian colonel ; took prominent part in Restoration.
† His father-in-law, Sir Thomas Chicheley.

254

THE THIRD DUTCH WAR

A gentleman came from Rotterdam that sayd they then had not 300 men in 7 of their greatest men of warr, but I wold not have us to beleeve those things, hitherto they have been too cunning for us. Most think they will come as strong as they can to sea & have one sound brush for itt & then yeld if God send they do not worst us."

He gives glowing accounts of our own ships :

" We have a Company of brave sea Captains goes, & the men come in cheerfully. 10,000 land men goes on board, all expert soldiers. [He obtains a place for one of his cousins.] I have gott my Cos: the Duke's Letter for a Volunteer, & Sir John admitts him into his ship & to his owne table, & sayes he will allow him a midshipman's pay, which will be above 10s a week to him, & if he carries himselfe well, he stands fair for the next Lieutenant's place. Mun Ashton is a Lieutenant in the Gards, he gave 1500¹ for itt."

April 21, 1673 :

" This day I brought Sir John Chicheley to his Pinnace, att ye Temple stairs we parted. Tomorrow I go with my Father * to meet the King and Duke att Sheernesse, who go thither to accompany the Prince [Rupert] : 'Twill be 2 or 3 dayes before we returne. In a fortnight's time the French are expected to be att Portsmouth, there I intend likewise to see the Navies joyne. 'Tis said that Amsterdam will scarce hold out till the Plenipotentiaries meet, ours cannot be ready to go this weeke."

He writes again on April 26, having got back from his expedition to Sheerness :

" On Thursday late in the evening I returned from the Fleet, where we found the Ships in good readiness to sayle, being all of them well arm'd & victualled, but excepting, 7 or 8 of the great ones they are but indifferently mann'd. To helpe that, we expect the Collier Fleet every day, which will advance above 1000 saylors, & the Straits Fleet, they say, are within our Channell with their Convoy, 7 or 8 stout men of warr ; the merchants are above six score sayle, & they will afford 3 or 4000 saylors. Before the French Fleet comes to Portsmouth, 'tis hop'd all will be fitted. The King hath left old Rupert aboard the *St Michaell*, where he will be till he comes about to his *Royall Charles* which is att Portsmouth. The King spent 2 dayes in going aboard all his ships. I parted with Sir John att Sheernesse, that Fort is in a brave posture of defence, so is 4 or 5 more upon Medway, wᶜ will give

* His father-in-law, Sir Thomas Chicheley.

255

May 15, 1673 :

> " The King and Duke intend to go to-morrow morne towards Dover or
> Rye, the 2 Fleets ere this are joyn'd. I doubt I shall not go for my
> Father * does not go, & I shall hardly go without him. 'Tis here
> whisper'd that 10,000 landmen are speedily to be rais'd, & all the land-
> men now on board & all the English soldiers now in the French army
> are to meet the Duke where're he lands. 'Tis thought 'twill be in
> Zeeland, & we have good assurance thence, but God knows how these
> things are. In all probability the Hollander is in a low Condition.
> Some say we shall certainly have an advantagious peace, in the meane
> time the Prince is most impatient to have a bout with them att sea.
> One of our Fireships was accidentally burnt in the Fleet, but no more
> hurt."

May 24, 1673 :

> " My Lord Ossory went with the King to Rye, & Norborough † being
> not yett come in with the Straits fleet, my Lord begged he might go
> Rere Admiral in his roome. The King said My Lord Ossory ‡ had
> but one shirt & 7 guineas in his pockett till he gave him some linnen &
> a bed out of his owne Yacht to ly upon. I had yesterday a letter from
> Sir John Chicheley ; he says they are a brave fleet & well mann'd &
> in good courage, & did expect they shold have a fight within 3 weeks or
> lesse. Ere this the Prince is upon the coast of Holland."

Sir John Chicheley was leaving his wife expecting a baby,
and this caused him great and not unnatural anxiety. His
brother-in-law and sister were to remain in London to look
after Lady Chicheley during her husband's absence. In a
letter to his sister, written " from on board the *Charles* near
Dover," adopting the formal and stilted language of the time,
Sir John addresses her as " Mrs. Legh " :

> " May ye 29, 1673 ; Mrs Legh, Being sensible what 'tis to be absent
> from a neere & deare concerne, makes me the more estime the obliga-
> tion you have done me in resolving to stay with my good woman till
> she's past danger . . . I hope yet, if the Hollanders are as willing as
> we are, to see you ere long at London, ten days being the uttermost in

---

* His father-in-law, Sir Thomas Chicheley.

† Sir John Narborough, admiral of the Red in 1673 ; Commissioner of the Navy ;
died of fever in St. Domingo, 1688.

‡ Thomas, Earl of Ossory, eldest son of the first Duke of Ormonde ; married
Lady Amelia, daughter of Louis de Nassau, son of Maurice, Prince of Orange.

my small judgment before they will beate us or we them. For our
parts we are now makeing all the hast to them we can."

He writes to Richard on the same day :

"Deare Bro: What has occasion'd so long a forbearance was the
hope of seeing you with the King, but now I am disappointed. I
cannot say when it will be since the hazards of war you know are very
uncertain. If it please God I come off well, 'tis probable we may once
more meet either at Lime * or London. We are now dayly making
some little progresse towards our enemy, though but slowly, the winds
being contrary. I hope when we meet a prosperous gaile will attend
both our endeavours & desires. I must confess for the number of
ships we have a very fine fleet to the number of 75 or 6, besides five
or six and twenty fire ships, all well resolved. I doubt not but if you
stay till ye middle of June or the beginning, but we may meet at
Shearnesse, where, ere it be long, I expect to be refitting my ship for a
second encounter.

"I do thinke myself extreamely obliged by Mrs Legh for the resolution she has taken to see my good woman in the straw safely delivered.
I do assure you if I live to returne, upon all occasions I shall be ready
to acknowledge her kindnesse. We are now neere Dover advancing
upon our foes with a faire gaile, so yt I hope one ten days will end this
business for a while till we can fitt our ships againe, which gives me
some hopes of seeing you before you leave London, in case it please
God to spare my life. Adieu dearest Br: Yrs J N CHICHELEY."

This war, which had very doubtful results, came to an end
late in 1673, and we hear of Sir John Chicheley back in London
" looking thin but very harty," in November. " The Dutch
are higher than ever, and have a great Squadron ready to
goe out. We have none, nor any like to have." †

The Duke of York was to set out to meet his Duchess, Mary
of Modena:

Another letter from Richard, dated November 6, says :

"The Modena Duchess comes slowly, she was sick and kept her bed 3
dayes the last week, but the next she is expected. There was such
burning of the Pope last night, Sir Anthony Cope ‡ had a barrell of
Pitch & a Maidment of Straw that had a triple Crowne, Lawne Sleeves

---

* He spells it thus occasionally.　　　　　　† Raines Collection.
‡ Sir Anthony Cope, M.P. for Oxford; married Mary, daughter of Dutton,
Lord Gerard.

& a Cope and several fripperies like to his Holyness att Rome, which was sett in the Barrell of Pitch & a Linke fired & stuck i'th reare of itt which gave fire, & a thousand people I do believe were spectators. My brother Jack * & I walked an houre by the light of itt. Itt was in the higher end of the Square. My Lady Devonshire † & the Lady Southern had each a great fire there."

Peace was signed in February 1673–4, Charles II offering the hand of his niece, Mary, eldest daughter of his brother James, to her cousin William of Orange, afterwards William III.

* Sir John Chicheley.

† Lady Devonshire, widow of second Earl, who died in 1628. She was the daughter of the Earl of Kinloss and a great supporter of the Royal cause.

CHAPTER XVIII

PENDANTS AND PERIWIGS

In 1673 we hear of the Duke of York anxious to buy some of 1673
Richard's young horses, which the latter was as unwilling to sell.
Loyal though he was, Richard had no intention of making a bad
bargain, which he evidently considered he would be doing by
transacting business with His Royal Highness :

> " The Duke of York [he writes to his wife] asked me of them (the
> horses) yesternight, I am soe afraid they shold not prove well in his
> hands, I had rather any had them than he. [A few days later he
> mentions the fact again.] The Duke of York sent to me to bring my
> horses into St. James's Parke this afternoone ; he commended them
> much, soe did all the Courtiers, but the thing called money is not to be
> had amongst them, without it my horses and I do not part." *

Parliament only sat for a few months in 1674, having been 1674
prorogued from February 24 to March 10, and from that day
on to April 1675. The Legh family spent the summer of 1674
at Lyme, Richard delighted to be amongst all his " dear brood."
The relations between parents and children had undergone a
great change. The strict discipline of the Elizabethan age had
been relaxed, children were far more considered and were
treated like rational beings. They still addressed their parents
as " Sir " and " Madam," but there was more freedom of intercourse and a greater amount of confidence was established.
Richard entered into all the amusements and pursuits of his
little ones. They seem to have ridden their ponies, made
expeditions and had their little parties much as do the children
of to-day :

> " The children waer [were] very much made of att Mr

* Raines Collection.

261

Stoperts," writes Elizabeth to her husband before his arrival, she also tells him of an expedition they had made with a neighbour, Colonel Downes to the town of Macclesfield, she herself being unable to accompany them. In each letter their father sends messages to his " dear bantlings," " dear Babes," or " brats," he never mentions them without some such terms of endearment. Sometimes there come presents : " I bought Letty a purse," and for the others " 2 pair of pendants, a pretty silver box, and 2 pair of neat enamald buttons for Pee's sleeves, whether thou wilt dispose of them till I come I leave to thee. Lett me know how thou likest them." Lest Elizabeth should think he has been extravagant, he tells her the price, the pendants cost 7s., the box 3s. 6d., Peter's buttons 1s. 6d., and the purse 1s.; for herself he sends some new play-books. A few days later come pippins and " pear-maines," two dozen of crab oranges, two dozen of lemons and some " Barmoodes "; she is to give " the bratts " some from him. He also sends 400 asparagus, no doubt a very great delicacy; they are to be " sett in wet sand and water awhile before they beboyled "; the Spanish potatoes mentioned in a former chapter and a horse-load of good apples, and " some things for the children," which he begs she will not distribute before his arrival. A jar of fresh capers is presented by Lady Chicheley, with directions to open it and to add fresh vinegar or the contents will be spoilt.

The family now numbered five. Lettice, the eldest girl, aged about twelve at this date, was beginning to be a help to her mother, whose health had never been particularly good, and who was much hampered by her very rapidly increasing family. She also suffered from her eyes. The education of the children seems to have been done principally at home, the boys apparently were not sent to school, and we read of a tutor being engaged, " a Bachelour of Arts, a very good Scholar and of great modesty and sobriety." The children of those days were taught a certain amount of accomplishments. It was considered the right thing to know how to dance, and to play on the viol or mute, " and another thing that is as good to lerne on as the ' mute.' " The " mute " cost 20s., " the other thing " 5s.; if this is not approved of it can be changed for the " mute."

Foreign languages were also part of the education of the youth of the seventeenth century. In 1673 a protégé of Richard's was sent abroad to Saumur, where he was to settle in a French *pension*:

> " He is very well pleased with his adventure, what he learns in French his Tutor puts him to turn into Latin, so hee improves in both Languages at once. [The boy reports himself as being] mightily taken with all the rareties and noble things he hath seene in his journey and the brave Churches with their vast treasures and the Religious houses."

He is also much struck with the fair nuns, and apparently would have been glad of an opportunity of making their acquaintance, " if he had had a message to deliver, hee would have taken it for an honner to have delivered it."

Another relative of Richard's was sent at this date to Christ Church, Oxford. A letter from the Dean, the redoubtable Dr. Fell,* assures Richard that his kinsman is doing well :

> " The discipline of this Place does I know fall under the ill opinion of young People, but it will be a venial fault if we displease them at present, to benefit them for ever hereafter. Those who desire to be debaucht or idle, if they find their life made uneasy are to blame their own choice in coming hither, where licentious practises shall never be encouraged."

The college authorities had the same objection to innocent recreation as those in earlier times, so one can hardly wonder that—in the absence of some outlet for energy and high spirits— the " licentious practices " referred to by the Dean should occasionally have had to be recorded.

Though he took great interest in affairs of State, and never shirked his duty, Richard's heart was always at " sweet Lyme," where he was ever happiest, and where he had to leave his

---

* Dr. John Fell, son of Samuel Fell (1625-1686), Dean of Christ Church and Bishop of Oxford; reluctantly expelled John Locke from Christ Church in 1684; summoned the undergraduates to take arms against Monmouth in 1685.

Elizabeth, who, with a new baby coming almost every year, was seldom able to accompany him to London. There was much entertaining, all the relations were coming and going, and the Leghs kept practically open house. Sir Thomas Chicheley and 1674 his son Sir John, with his wife, paid a visit in June 1674. Lady Chicheley was a good correspondent and her letters are well written and expressed. She writes to her sister-in-law on June 23, after her visit, describing the difficulties that had to be encountered with the stage-coachmen of the day :

> "We had a very prosperous journey home, which we came to on Saturday night last, though pretty late and against one of our Coachman's will, who was very cross on both our journeys. He that drove Sir Thomas's Coach would have even layd us at Barnett all night, though the Sun was above an hour high ; but the other Coachman being better natured, would come on and made him come alsoe, though he threatened and scolded all the way." *

She gives some gossip. Several people, as she expresses it, " catched in the Nouse of Matrimony," Sir Coplestone Bampfylde † to Mrs. Roberts, " the wench hath three thousand pounds a year," Lord Buckhurst ‡ to Lady Falmouth, Sir Michael Wharton to the Lord Treasurer's § eldest daughter (this marriage did not come off), " fat Andrew Newport ‖ is to have Bella Boynton, Maid of Honor to ye Dutchess, and many others which I leave to my Sister Fountain ¶ to remember, and state affairs to Sir John." **

Thrown much upon her own resources for providing a little welcome variety in her cooking, the housewife of the seven-

---

* Raines Collection.

† Sir Coplestone Bampfylde (1656–1691), justice ; active in promoting the Restoration ; married, secondly, Jane, daughter of Sir Courtenay Pole of Shute, a sister of Mrs. Robartes.

‡ Lord Buckhurst, afterwards Earl of Dorset ; married Dorothy, widow of Charles, Earl of Falmouth, who was killed at sea in the Dutch War.

§ The Lord Treasurer, Sir Thomas Osborne, Earl of Danby, afterwards Duke of Leeds.

‖ Andrew Newport (1625–1699), son of the first Baron Newport, a Royalist ; married Isabel, widow of Sir Francis Boynton, who was killed at Wigan in the advance of Charles II towards Worcester.

¶ " Sister Fountain," Sarah, youngest daughter of Sir Thomas Chicheley, married to Andrew Fountaine of Salle.

** Sir John Chicheley, her husband.

teenth century was grateful for recipes of all kinds, and there was a constant interchange of these between Elizabeth Legh and her relations. Mrs. Elizabeth Beaumont, a poor lady relative who acted as housekeeper to the Chicheleys, and who hovered between Lyme and Wimpole, assisting at all the interesting events in both families, sends Elizabeth some directions for making her " Summer Sweetmeats." They would probably be too highly spiced to suit the taste of to-day.

" I have no recept for pudings nor ever had [she writes in 1674], I 1674 make them always by gess [guess], indeed I did teach Mrs Fountain, but it was with letting her see me mingling them, and I wish I was as near your Ladyship that I might doe ye same for you but I'll tell you everything I use to put in them, and give you the best directions I can, and then you must put them together to your own taist. My last white pudings I put all these things in ; grated bread and milk and cream and eggs, mace and cloves and salt Sittern [citron] and Gandy Orange and Lemon peale, rose water and sugar and a little Sack if you please, and a great deal of Marrow, and always very well beaten, and musk and amber, and you may put a little Saffron in through a Tifany into your milk. Mangle your grated bread and your cream, and 8 or 10 eggs with half the whites together as for a boyled puding, but pretty stiff and put Almond in, a matter of half a pound I think will serve, if you find there is not enough, you may put in more next time. There must be a pretty deal of the Sittron and oranges and lemons cut small, for I never put any Currants in these pudings, and so put in all the ingreadents according to your taist and the Marrow in little lumps.

" I have heare sent your Ladysp. the receipt for Drying Goosbery ; tis I am suer a very good way, for noe body in England I am suer doth Sweetmeats better then this Gentlewoman that gave me this, & tis the true way she euse [used] to doe them I dare say ; the way is something tedious but you have soe many paire of hands that will be ready at peeling them, that you will rid a great many in a Little time. I would gladly know how your Goosberys proved that you put up for Tarts, mine proved very good & lookd as fresh as when they was fresh pulled off ye trees & baked, and I have made very good Goosbery Foole with some of them. A Bottle will make a good handsome Creame Glass full, onely you must put the Yolke or two or an Egg more in, because they doe not afford soe much pulp as when they are green, but itt lasts as well every jott, & you must sett them on the fier with a little water & boyle them till they are soe tender that the pulp will rub through a haire Sieve." *

She sends another recipe for what she calls " bread pudings " :

"I mingle these just as I doe the Almond ones, only I leave out the Almonds and put but a little lemon and orange peal, but very small to taste them, and then I put plump currants in and colour them pretty well with saffron. These pudings takes up a deal of marrow, and sometimes when I could not get enough, I have been forced to take some Beef Kidney Suit [suet], and shred it, and soe melt it over a slow fire and soe straine itt into the pudings, for I never lett a bit of Suit [suet] appear in lumps in these pudings, but you cannot make them without some Marrow to lye in lumps in them, for else it will be suspected that it is all Suit."

She begs that Elizabeth will try her hand at these, and in order that she may hit on " these madd directions " she is to " rap two in an owld clout " and send them for her to see. " Be sure you make them fatt enough," she adds, " else they will not be worth a pinn." For Richard she sends " a Sermon, a Play and a Ballet."

1675 By a bill of May 12, 1675, we find that a pound of citron cost 3s., a box of oranges and lemons 13s. 9d., a gallon of oil and a bottle came to 9s. 6d., and " for a Cart to carry ye Grocery ware to ye Carryer " 2s. was paid.

A year or two later oranges and lemons rose to 2s. apiece.

As a return for a " Goos Gibby Pye," which she had received from her father, Mrs. Beaumont begs that Elizabeth will send him some more of the famous Lyme home-brewed ale, which would appear, like audit ale to-day, to have been bottled like wine :

"My Master wished twenty times for some more Cheshire Ale, for ye other day he had a very great Lady and her husband dined with him, and I had kept two bottles of ye Ale that he did not know of and sent it up and bid ye Butler give it him, and when they once tasted of it, they never left whilst there was a drop in the bottles, and all protested there never was such drink drunk in this world of noe sort. [She adds :] If I had had more, in my conscience they would have been fuddled I doubt." *

* Raines Collection.

RICHARD LEGH OF LYME
Painted by Cooper about 1670
From a Miniature at Lyme

MRS. RICHARD LEGH
Painted by Cooper about 1670
From a Miniature at Lyme

PENDANTS AND PERIWIGS

Two beautiful miniatures by Cooper of Richard and his wife were painted somewhere between 1660 and 1670, the first named being especially fine.

It has a dark background and shows him wearing a small periwig and a breastplate of armour. With the introduction of gunpowder in the fourteenth century, armour had declined in importance as being no longer proof against this new weapon; it continued, however, to form part of the dress of the two following centuries, though it was probably only meant to be ornamental. Wigs were becoming the fashion in the middle of the seventeenth century, but these were much smaller and less heavy than the enormous periwigs introduced by Louis XIV, which were not worn in England much before the eighteenth century.

Elizabeth's miniature has a sea-green background; her hair is dressed in curls on her forehead, stiff ringlets standing away from her head. Her dress, a bright blue, contrasting well with the background, is cut very low, and she wears a scarf of some gold tissue over her right shoulder. A brooch in the shape of a cross, formed of five large stones, fastens some pearls to the front of her gown.

Dress played an extremely important part in the days of Charles II, and the costumes of the men seem to have been a matter of even more consideration than those of the ladies. We have it on the authority of Mr. Pepys himself how much he felt his worth increase by the wearing of fine clothes. Richard spent a great deal of time and not a little money on his wardrobe, and took immense pains with every detail of it. One can picture him in his velvet coat with silver buttons, or his " light colored Camelott Coat, with ye breeches," his black satin waistcoat " lyned with persian taffety," and the dimity calico which was to line his sleeves, but we do not read of Elizabeth cutting up her gowns to make his waistcoats, as Mrs. Pepys was in the habit of doing for her lord.*

Elizabeth being so often incapacitated from accompanying her husband to London, he had to buy all her finery

---

* " June 13, 1661 : I went home, and put on my grey cloth suit and faced white coate, made of one of my wife's pettycoates."—Pepys's " Diary."

and fripperies, with clothes for the children in addition to his own. He spares no pains to get her what she likes, going to twenty shops in one afternoon, as he tells her, " to looke out something for the children, thy Mantoe and Petticoat "—then a very important article of dress. Lady Chicheley he took with him to help. " All stuffs were very deare," he complains, " and they all run (that are fashionable) upon those colors in thy last Mantoe, so I thought it best for them to see further lest the new one looke too like." *

A few days later he sends her " Semarr " (a simar, or cloak with long sleeves), and the children's clothes, and he assures her he has not exceeded the price she named.

In a sudden and unwonted fit of economy he tells her :

> " I had ordered my Taylor to come to-morrow to alter some Clothes to be fashionable, but now I will stick to my freeze, which hath not been off my back but when in bed since I saw thee. I have spared from my own back for I have bought neither Suit nor Perriwig, nor shall I buy any as I thinke whilst I stay." *

A few days later, however, he is beguiled by Sir Thomas into purchasing a new suit, " cost me four pound, but my Father † will have another o'th same."

In June 1674 Elizabeth was to be provided with suitable jewellery, presumably diamonds, and the commission to purchase these was entrusted to Lady Chicheley.

> " Sister Fountaine is in a great dispute about your pendants and is advised to persuade you to lay out a little more money, or else they will not be fitt for you to weare. The lesser pattern is as I designed itt at Lyme, but for that you must buy 2 of the corner stones, which will cost 20s apiece, and some small ones to make up the paire, but still they are longish and too little for you to weare." *

1674   Sir Thomas Chicheley was anxious to present his grandson with a new suit, " which will be finer I doubt not than his last," adds his father. The children of those days were dressed very much the same as their parents, the girls wearing the stiff wide skirts, low-neck bodices and elbow sleeves of the period, the boys

---

* Raines Collection.
† His father-in-law, Sir Thomas Chicheley.

with the same velvet coats, embroidered waistcoats, breeches, and even swords. Peter, aged six, was to be fitted out with all the requisites of a man of fashion. His " brave suit," a little velvet coat trimmed with lace, " narrow Pantaloons with ribbonds and lac'd I can assure you," writes the proud father, stockings and buckled shoes, even down to his little periwig, costing £3 5s., and his little sword—a present from his Uncle John. To these were added a case of pistols with holsters and " cads," a strange present for so young a child. The boy was much excited at the prospect of his new clothes. " Deare Cratur [writes Elizabeth to her husband, in acknowledging the gifts], I thanke thee kindly for all thy prasents thou sendest me . . . every day is ten till I see thee, and after a while I shall begin to count the hours for thee as Pe did for the coming of his breeches." He was also given a new saddle " and very fond he is of it." She begs her husband if he sees any new-fashioned cookery at her father's, to ask the housekeeper to give him some recipes.

The four little girls were also to have new clothes in 1675 :   1675

" The children's stuff looks well in the piece and I think will wear well. Mrs B. bought 6 yards and could get no more, by the next or before this is work't out will send more. [Richard buys a remnant for Sarah's and Betty's coats:] but two yards left, a remnant, Mr Rigby [the tailor] hath sent itt and says he will have but little for it. [A pattern shoe of Lettice's and Betty's is to be sent for them to have each] a laced pair, and Fanny and Sarah shall have also. I think to guess big enough for them [he adds with prudent forethought], they will all fit one time or other. [He also sends by the carrier] a trunk with P.L. upon it and the key, they are for my son." *

Thomas Legh, who seldom left the country, had com-missioned his brother to buy him some garments ; these were to be of plain and serviceable material :

" Your clothes I have bought to-day [writes Richard, April 15, 1673], honest plain Serdge, the King wears the very same. You shall have 2 paire of breeches for riding and walking, but they weare no silke wastcotes, what you weare for warmth must be under your halfe shirt. Unless I hear to the contrary I will make you very plain

* Raines Collection.

clothes (which are most modish), at present nothing but mourning is worne nor will any other be till the 29th of May, att Court especially. They wear only coates and breeches very short, just pantaloons, some strait, some wider, the coat very strait to the body. When you have a desire to be in colors, 'tis but putting the blue or philamote as you see the broad black is on the shoulder and sleeves, taking the black away, and then your cuft strings of the same colour. Your hatt is a good one, 'tis most of it beavor, 2 paire of stockings, and 2 pair of breeches, one for riding, the other pantaloons. I wish they prove big enough, they are 4 fingers wider than mine, with garters and silver buckles and a play book. There is a black Spanish lether belt with the silver buckle which you fancied of mine, and a fashionable sword, both which I present you with. [He had evidently been given a specified sum to spend and had overdrawn the amount :] I doubt I have exceeded your instructions of 10^l, but I will give you account ; if you thinke good, send 10^l by Bamford [the carrier] his next returne, for my stock growes low."

Elizabeth writes one of her rare letters about this date. She seldom adds the year, and often puts only the day of the week. Writing was laborious to her, partly on account of her eyes, which were very weak, and partly because she wrote extremely badly, her handwriting and spelling being equally atrocious. Her husband indeed frequently wrote for her, and when she had to write to important relatives, made her rough drafts of what she was to say. She was a great character, and her letters nearly always contain something fresh and original. She gives an amusing account, to her brother-in-law Thomas, of a little money transaction she had with Sir John Bennet, in which she seems to have got decidedly the best of the bargain :

" DEARE BROTHER,
". . . Though I cant return you newes upon soe pleasant a subject as yours is, yet I think you will laugh when I tell you I have sold the old selver minute watch to Sir John Bennet * for 4 gines [guineas] and a new silver watch to boot, but after a weekes triell he found he could not mack [make] the menets and the howers goe together, therefore he desired his Sister Carr † to get his gold and

* Sir John Bennet of Dawling, brother of the Earl of Arlington and Lady Carr; created Baron Ossulston, 1682.
† Wife of Sir Robert Carr, Chancellor of the Duchy of Lancaster.

watch again, and to desire me to tack [take] my own again, but I sad [said] no, if he had spoiled the watch he had no reason to thinke that I should pay for that, for I said he might remember that I told him I would not pass my word for the good going of it, but because it was Aspenall's worke he was fond of it. But now he thinkes he is choust, and everybody tells me that I had great luck to cosen him that has cheated all the indegant [indigent] officers."

This is an allusion to Sir John Bennet's * post of Captain of the Gentlemen Pensioners. The word " choused," which now forms part of schoolboy slang, appears to have been introduced into the language at the beginning of the seventeenth century.

The Dutch War being now over, Van Tromp, the Dutch admiral, was visiting London, much fêted, and ultimately made a Baron by Charles II. This personage had manners the reverse of engaging :

" Van Trump is now at London [writes a correspondent to Lyme in January 1674–5], courted by all the great ones, often drunk, and eminent for nothing more then saying nothing. There was a new play acted last week, the play-house being full, he was conducted over the stage to get to his place, but the whole playhouse did hisse and make such a noise that noe Dutch breeding could have exceeded it, but it was checked as soon as they could by the great ones."

Parliament was sitting again in April 1675. Richard was back in London by the 15th, leaving poor Elizabeth in delicate health at Lyme.   1675

The formation of separate Parliamentary parties, which started in Charles I's reign, may be said to have been completed at this date. The religious strife was still continuing ; on the one side it was Danby and " no toleration," on the other Shaftesbury † and " toleration for Dissenters only." Danby's " non-resistance " Bill, forbidding any one to sit in Parliament unless he would swear that he believed resistance to the Crown to be

* See note, p. 270.

† Anthony Ashley Cooper, first Earl of Shaftesbury (1621–1683) ; attached himself to the Parliamentarians, but was pardoned at the Restoration. Set himself to encourage the popular apprehension of a Romanist revival ; helped to spread the " Popish Plot" illusion as a weapon against the Government ; dismissed from the Privy Council ; ultimately fled to Holland and died there.

1675 illegal, passed the Lords, but provoked a bitter quarrel between them and the Lower House. Commenting on the general situation, Richard writes to his wife on April 15, 1675 :

> " As to the Parlt:, some there carry exceeding high against the King, yett I hope they will settle in a short time . . . we sitt each day till 2 or 3 a clock. The Lords sate this day till 5, and are full as madd as our House. Yesterday we read a Bill wherein 'tis made Treason to levy money without an Act of Parlt : & this Bill is to be read again upon Monday next. As 'tis drawn 'tis of a high concerne & toucheth much upon Prerogative." *

On April 22, he says :

> " 'Tis fear'd we shall breake all in pieces yett. The Divell Presbyterian in both Houses does all he can to force the King to Dissolve us, and the Lords were never higher but in –42. A little term will show how itt will be."

On April 27 comes another letter :

> " I have not had time to write, for the House sate till almost four & we were obliged to be at a Committee before 6. One thing pleaseth me, that I see the House is pretty calme (though severe) & I hope the conclusion may end well, for the malicious party are broke. I have visited the good Lord of York,† who is concerned as deeply in theirs as the youngest in our House, & when yesterday the Lords were soe warme, they moved at 4 in the afternoon to adjourn their Debate, which still continues upon the Test, they believing the Bishops, being old men, wold have been glad of that recesse. The old Lads however, mov'd to stick to itt, & att 9 or 10 att night they voted the Test to be reduced to a Bill. Methinks the violent Presbyterians and Papists goe hand in hand in that house."

He writes again on April 29, sending a parody of the King's Speech which had been found scattered about the benches of the House of Commons on April 13. It is ascribed to Andrew Marvell,‡ who was member for Kingston-on-Hull at that time, and is a triumph of the wit of the period. In sending it to his wife, Richard tells her the paper was the same one which

* Raines Collection.   † The Archbishop.
‡ Andrew Marvell the younger (1621–1678), poet and satirist ; became disgusted at management of public affairs and wrote bitter satires, attacking Charles himself ; advocated a republic.

272

reached the King's own hand : " Sir John Ellois, a Courtier just come from thence, gave me the enclosed Droll, which was presented to the King's owne hand—this very paper " :

"MY LORDS AND GENTLEMEN,

" I told you the last meeting ye winter was fittest for Buisness, & I thought soe till my Ld Treasurer * assured me yt ye Spring is ye best season for sallets and subsidies ; I hope therefore yt April will not prove such an unnaturall month as not to afford some kinde showers to refresh my Parched Exchequer yt gapeth for want of them ; But some of you may perhapes thinke it dangerous to make me too rich ; but doe not fear itt, I promise you faithfully whatever you give me I will allways want, and although in othere things my word may be thought butt slender security, yett in yt you may rely upon me, yt I will not breake itt. My Lords & Gentlemen, I can beare my owne straights with patience, but my Lord Treasurer doth protest to me yt ye revenue as it now standeth will not serve him and me too ; one of us must Pinch for it if you do not help us. I must speake freely to you, I am in incumbrances, for besides my Mistresses in present service my before-made Mistresses lye hard upon me. I have a pretty good estate, I confess, but Odd's fish, I have a great charge upon itt. Here is my Lord Treasurer can tell you yt all the money desired for the next summers good must of necessity be supplyed to the next years cradles & swaddleing cloths, what shall we do for ships then ? I only hint it you, for yt is your Buisenes & not mine. I know by experience I can live without ym [them], I lived above ten years abroad without ships & had never Better health in my life, but how you will live without ym I leave it to your selves to Judge, & therefore mention yt only, by ye by I doe not insist upon it. There is another thing I must press more earnestly, which is yt it seems a good part of my revenue will faile in 2 or 3 years except you will be pleased to contenue it, I have now to say for it, pray why did you give me soe much as you have done except you resolved to give on as fast as I shall ask you ? Ye nation hates you already for haveing given soe much, & I shall hate you now if you will give me no more, soe if you doe not stick to me you will not have a frend leafte in England ; on ye other side, if you will give ye revenue as I desire, I shall be inabled to those things for yr religion & leberty that I have had in my thoughts but cannot efect ym without a little more money to carry me through in it, therefore looke to itt & take notice yt if you doe not make me rich enough to undoe you, it shall ly att your dores, for my part I wash my hands of it ; but yt I may

* Sir Thomas Osborne, Earl of Danby, and afterwards Duke of Leeds; Lord Treasurer of England, 1673-1679.

gaine yr good opinion ye best way is to acquant you with what I have done to deserve it out of my Royall love of yr religion & yr property. For ye first, my late declaration is a true picture of my mind, he that cannot as in a glass see my zeale for ye Church of England, doth not desirve any farthere sattisfaction, for I declare him willfull & not good natured; some may perhaps be startled & say how comes this suden change? To yt I reply in a word, I am a changeling, I thinke that is a full answer; but to convince men farthere yt I mean as I say, there are these arguments; first I will goe toe & you know I never break my word with you, secondly my Lord Treasurer saith soe, & you know he never tould a lye, thirdly my Lord Lautherdaile * will undertake for me, & I should be loth by any act of mine to forphitt [forfeit] the creditt he hath with you; if you desire more instances of my zeale I have ym for you; for example I have converted all my natural sons from popery, & I may say without vanity, it was my owne worke, & much more peculiar to me then the getting of them. It would doe yr hearts good to heare how prettily little George can read allready in his Psalter; they are all fine children, God bless them, & soe like me in their understanding.—But as I was saying, I have to please you given a pension to your favouritte my Lord Lowderdale, not so much that I thought he wanted it, as that I knew you would take it kindely; I have made Carwell † a Dutches, & married her sister to my Lord Pembrook, I have at me Brothers request sent my Lord Inchiquin ‡ to settle ye protestant religion att Tangier; I have made Crew § Bishop of Durham, & at ye first word of my Lady Portsmouth have preferred Prideaux to be Bishop of Chichester. I doe not know for my part what factious men would have, but this I am sure of, yt none of my predecessours ever did any thing like this to gaine ye good will of their subjects. Soe much for your religion; now as for your property, my behaviour to the Banckers for a publique instance, & ye procedings about Mrs Hyde & Mrs Sutton for private ones, are such contenuing evidences yt twill be needles to say any more of it. I must now acquant you yt by my Lord Treasurer's advice I have made a considerable retrenchment upon my expences in candles & Charcoole, & doe not intend to stop there, but will, with your help, looke into ye imbessilment of kitchin stuff, but by the way, upon my conscience, neither my Ld Treasurer nor my Ld Lauderdale are guilty. I speake

* John Maitland, second Earl and first Duke of Lauderdale (1616–1682); aimed at making the Crown absolute in Scotland in Church and State; had complete influence over Charles II, who supported him against attacks of English Parliament.

† Louise de Kérouaille or Quérouaille, Duchess of Portsmouth; her sister Henrietta married Philip, seventh Earl of Pembroke.

‡ William O'Brien, second Earl of Inchiquin, Governor of Tangier.

§ Nathaniel Crew, third Baron Crew of Steyne; Bishop of Durham 1674.

my opinion, but if you finde them dableing in yt bussines, I leave ym to you, I tell you plainly, for I would have ye world to know I am not a man to be cheated. My Lds & Gentlemen, I desire you would believe of me as you have found me, & I doe solemnly promis yt whatsoever you give me shall be esspecially maniged with the same conduct, thrift and prudence that I have ever practised since my happy Restoration. The rest I leave to my Lord Keeper."

Richard was longing to get home, but Sir Thomas Chicheley **1675** was firm about keeping his son-in-law to his duty, although Elizabeth was expecting a baby in June, and her husband was more anxious than ever to get back to her on this account.

> " Dearest [he writes on May 1], Thy last was a great satisfaction to me, though I tell thee truly I am very uneasy to stay thus long from thee & have often mentioned itt to my Father,* who wold hear no discourse of itt till the last night, when he did assure me itt was his great desire we shold be together, & made his request I wold but stay the next weeke. My Father hearing me sometimes say that I wold steale out of Towne & tell nobody, asked me yesterday seriously when I wold goe, so I told him the next weeke. ' I hope,' says he, ' 'twill be the latter end ? ' ' Nay Sir,' said I, ' as soone as I can, God willing.' ' Well,' says he, ' I am loath to part with you, but I will keepe you noe longer then Monday.' In that time he hop'd all wold be right, (as yet there is not a word mentioned of giving the King money). The Lord's House are higher (if possible) each day than other. The Towne is in greate quietness, every body but children & porters are gone to the Parke . . . . . This forenoon Franc : Cholm : Cos : Atherton & I spent in going to the Tower & showing the Lord Mayor of London the bones of the 2 Princes.† I shall stay to receive the answer to this, then write to me noe more. Thence day and night I will trudge itt by God's leave till I come to thee." ‡

He had to wait another few days, however, and did not get away till after May 11.

> " This day I din'd with Cos Chomley at Bawneas [Barnes ?] old Mr Whitmore's who keeps the good house. He drunk thy health & said he wondered thou durst adventure of me. The last time he saw thee

---

* His father-in-law, Sir Thomes Chicheley.
† During some excavations made in the Tower about this date, the coffin containing the bones of the little murdered princes was discovered. This was given into the custody of Sir Thomas Chicheley, Master of the Ordnance, by command of Charles II.—" Secret History of England, by a Person of Honour."
‡ Raines Collection.

was when thou wast very young. I told him if he saw thee now, his wonder would cease. Now I am att the Committee of Privileges & have stole up to the Speaker's Chamber to scribble these, & am never so happy as when I talke of, write to, or thinke of thee, my deare Soule, who am thine

" Whilst I am, R. Legh." *

Parliament had refused the King's supplies, so Charles prorogued it for fifteen months. Richard returned to Lyme, where Thomas, Elizabeth's second son and sixth child, was born on June 13, 1675.

* Raines Collection.

CHAPTER XIX

THE DUKE OF YORK'S VISIT

SUBSTANTIAL alterations had gone on at Lyme during the last twenty years. From the time of its first erection, succeeding generations had made changes in the old house to suit the fashion of the day, and Richard was also anxious to stamp his mark upon its walls. The Elizabethan house had—outwardly at least—practically disappeared. The sloping roof and pointed gables had given place to a flat roof, and the square-headed mullioned windows with their small diamond-shaped panes had, some of them, been replaced by long sash windows with large square panes, similar to those in the banqueting hall at White-hall. These windows are about eight feet high on the first floor. They have five rows of panes, the glass is all bevelled and very thick, the woodwork between the panes is from two to three inches in width and is beautifully moulded. Richard gives the following particulars relating to the contract with the workman :

> "Wilkins asketh 4^s a yard for workmanship of plain wainscot and I find meat, and 2^s a foot for Shass [sash] windows, that is 18^s a square yard and he find timber, which you know is noe great matter."

This alteration in the windows was done very gradually, Richard beginning first with the three windows in the Eliza-bethan drawing-room facing north, and two other rooms which have two windows each, opening out of the drawing-room, pre-sumably those occupied by himself and his wife. From a paint-ing done about the end of the seventeenth century, we find these seven windows are the only ones that had then been altered, Richard dying before the completion of the work, which was finished by his successor.

*

THE HOUSE OF LYME

It is difficult to say when the Elizabethan character of the house was first destroyed. Happily this was only done to the exterior, as much of the sixteenth-century work is still to be found in the interior. The alterations were probably begun about 1652, and continued during practically the whole of Richard's life. One learns with dismay from a letter of Sir John Chicheley, in 1676, that a great deal of the original house had been by then, if not destroyed, at any rate greatly altered and pulled about :

"I am a shearer with you [he writes on February 6 1675-6] in ye satisfaction you have in what is already done at Lime : I cannot but think otherways then that 'twill be extreame fine, and enough to invite you to the pulling down of ye Dary side, but not a word of it till the next broken summe."

One cannot help wishing that " the next broken summe " had been insufficient to provide the means for this vandalism.

The taste of the period, between Wren and Vanbrugh, was all tending towards the classic, the tide of fashion had, already in James I's time, begun to flow in the direction of the Italian, and size and dignity were the first considerations in houses of importance. Nor was this change in the taste of the day confined to the exterior of houses; it was also to be seen in the furniture. Two foreign queen consorts had succeeded one another, each importing some of the taste and fashion of her respective country. Charles II, during his residence abroad, had acquired a liking for the more luxurious furniture of France and Holland, and to this we may attribute the greater luxury and higher degree of comfort that made its appearance in the private houses of the day. The magnificent upholstered four-post beds, hung with embroideries and curtains of Venetian silk and velvet, gold, silver, and even precious stones being sometimes introduced, the tops garnished with plumes, real or in carved wood representations, had replaced the heavy oak beds of the Elizabethan age. English and Irish walnut was being used for chairs and cabinets in place of oak. The increasing degree of comfort and luxury had also meant increasing cleanliness. Chairs were now being made with higher front rails, the idea being that the floor was clean enough for ladies to be able to

LYME : NORTH FRONT

At the end of the seventeenth century.   From an oil-painting at Lyme

place their feet upon it as they sat, without discomfort or inconvenience. Marble was also being much used.

In anticipation, probably, of the visit of the Duke of York to Lyme, Richard was redecorating the two rooms above mentioned, which were intended for the occupation of the royal guest. They are a suite of three, the third room being very small, its windows forming part of the centre portion of the entrance gateway. These rooms are all hung with Mortlake and Flemish tapestries, those in the middle one, which contains the bed, being especially interesting. There are three pieces of tapestry in this room, in which is represented a collection of animals of all kinds, from the lion and ostrich down to the domestic barn-door cock. Whether the subjects are intended for illustrations of the Creation of the World (as has been suggested) or of Æsop's Fables, it is impossible to say. The prevailing colours are the subdued blues and greens that one sees in tapestry of this make, and these form a beautiful and harmonious background. An immensely high bed, the four posts being of fluted wood covered with old English silk of a delicate lemon-yellow colour, the silk being apparently pasted on to the back of the bed as well as on the posts, was possibly made for the projected visit. The Prince of Wales's feathers, carried out in carved woodwork, and covered with the same silk, figure prominently on the back of the bed.

The larger of the two rooms has three panels of Mortlake, with fine borders, and one of very early Flemish tapestry, not particularly interesting, being large figures representing an episode in the life of Solomon. The small room is hung entirely with four pieces of English tapestry of different designs.

The marble chimneypieces in the two larger rooms, which remain there to this day, were ordered to be made in 1675, and we get all the particulars of their purchase from Richard himself :

"April 15, 1675.

"Dearest, ... I have been to look at some Marble Chimney Pieces. They ask 15^l a piece, but then insted of square stones like those in the Dining Roome, they have an whole stone of Marble of the same for the Hearth with the Chimney Piece, which is very fine, and that makes them soe deare, and some have Marble that is cut hollow to sett within the Chimney instead of square tyle, which certainly is very fine, but I doubt with hot fires they are apt to breake. I shall take my Father's * advice therein. I find there is a White Marble veyn'd and a delicate reddish marble full of white and color'd streakes. These are the two colours I intend to fix upon." †

" April 29, 1675 ; . . . The Stone cutter was with me yesterday. I have bid him 30¹ for the two Chimney Pieces of those colours I formerly mentioned, but I thinke it is too little. I am to have halfe rounds of white Marble for the inner sides, for which he had 8¹ a paire at the first when he made them. White marble for them is putt into all coloured chimneys, because thou knowest 'tis whiter then any tyles. I only stay agreeing for them till my Father can see them, but he adviseth me against having window bottoms of Marble for those two Roomes. He sayes they do perpetually cast a moysture, if you lay but a paire of Gloves down they will be wett."

Ultimately he got both chimneypieces for £35. These remain exactly as they are described, the white marble sides have not cracked, as it was feared that they would do, and are as good as the day they were made. That these chimney-pieces were much admired we gather from a letter written by Lord Cholmondeley, ‡ who visited at Lyme a year or so after, and on his departure writes begging his late host will give him advice about purchasing similar ones, intended for some rooms which he is making " something more convenient."

A feature of these rooms, and indeed of all the rooms on the first floor, is their loftiness ; they measure from fifteen to twenty feet in height. How they can have been lit, in the days when rushlights and candles were the only means of lighting, passes comprehension, as even with the electricity of the present day it is difficult enough to obtain sufficient brilliancy.§

* His father-in-law, Sir Thomas Chicheley.

† Raines Collection.

‡ Robert Cholmondeley of Cholmondeley Castle, created Viscount Cholmondeley of Kellis, 1661 ; married Elizabeth, daughter of George Cradock of Caverswall Castle, Stafford. He died in 1681.

§ The idea, formerly prevalent, that electric light was unsuitable in old houses has, happily, quite exploded. Properly treated, adapting, wherever it is possible, all the old fittings, electric light, far from being an eyesore, only serves to show up unknown beauties, and to reveal charms undreamt of in old woodwork and

THE DUKE OF YORK'S VISIT

Richard was evidently looking about him, and adopting ideas from other places. He visits his friends the Carrs :

> " My Lady Carr hath furnisht her house well. She carried me into her best rooms, 'twould swell my paper and tyre thy patience to mention all particulars. [He writes again describing a visit to Arabella Churchill's : *] Peter Hunt and I have been all the morning amongst workmen and fine places. Be not jealous, for I must tell thee I brought him to Mistress Churchill's fine house, where he made his best observacons in the next room where she lay asleepe, where we had free acsesse by the help of a shilling and one of her maids." †

He was buying furniture also about this date. Mention is made of a chest of drawers and a " Scriptore," which was probably a kind of writing-bureau, for which he paid £20, but means of transit being still inadequate, he was unable to " hazard " them during the winter months. He buys a grandfather clock by Knibb, the great clockmaker, in April of this same year, 1675 :

> " I went to the famous Pendulum maker Knibb, and have agreed for one, he having none ready but one dull stager which was at 19¹; for 5¹ more, I have agreed for one finer than my Father's, and is to be better finish'd, with carved capitalls gold, and gold pedestalls with figures of boys and cherubimes all brass gilt. I wold have had itt Olive wood, (the Case I mean), but gold does not agree with that colour, soe took their advice to have it black Ebony, which suits your Cabinett better then Walnutt tree wood, of which they are mostly made. Lett me have thy advice herein by the next." †

In her answer to her husband, the dutiful wife assures him, " My dearest Soule ; as for the Pandelome Case I thinke Blacke suits anything." The clock is still in good working order, and is a prominent object in the " Bright gallery." It has nothing special about it, being quite plain, and considering what clocks of the same kind fetch now, the price (£24) seems to have been rather high. The face is quaint, and it has the two small spiral cornices. The introduction of electric light into the Egyptian tombs has had a wonderful result, and has arrested the further destruction of the paintings by the tourists' torches, to say nothing of its being the means of getting rid of the clouds of bats which infested these temples.

* Arabella Churchill (1648-1730), mistress of James II; eldest daughter of Sir Winston Churchill; maid of honour to Anne, Duchess of York.

† Raines Collection.

pillars at each side, supposed to have been suggested by the ringlets worn by the ladies of the day.

1675 On May 8, 1675, comes mention of a barometer that he is sending down :

> "The Carrier will bring a long deale box with a bottle that hath Quicksilver in itt. Prithee command there be great care of itt, that neither of them—the box nor bottle—be stirred till I come home. 'Tis a device I had of Sir Jonas Moore * to know the weather by." †

Barometers, which had been invented by Torricelli in 1642, must still have been rare, and were evidently considered something very special.

In a letter of about this date he mentions buying " a few of the fine glasses," probably mirrors. It is not known when these were first made. They were in common use amongst the ancient Egyptians, Greeks, and Romans, but these very early types were probably of brass or bronze. Praxiteles taught the use of silver in the manufacture of mirrors in the year 328 B.C. Mirrors of glass were first made at Venice in 1300,‡ and were introduced into England in 1673, so they would probably be still rare and costly in 1675.

The garden was also occupying much attention. We read of " span creepers, red honeysuckle, and seeds for general sorts of flowers," but there is no good gillyflower seed to be had. Two quarts of kidney beans, three or four of " Rouncivall pease," and one quart of " Scarlett Beanes " are sent down with the furniture, also 3 or 4 lb. of wire at 8s. the lb., to finish some hand-screens Elizabeth is making.

The ground on the south-west side of the house falls steeply down and has been built up with walls some twenty feet high, supported by buttresses, which may date from mediæval times, forming a terrace on which the house stands proudly. These hanging gardens are a feature of the place, the walls giving the appearance of battlements, from which a charming view of the

---

* Sir Jonas Moore (1617–1679), mathematical tutor to the Duke of York in 1647; Surveyor-General of the Ordnance in 1663.

† Raines Collection.

‡ Chambers's " Encyclopædia," vol. vii, p. 228.

LYME: VIEW FROM THE DUTCH GARDEN

lower garden is obtained. This was admirably laid out by my father-in-law, the late Lord Newton, as a Dutch garden, with beds bordered in ivy and golden yew, small lead statues of Cupids in between, and a fountain playing in the centre. The terracing was done by my father-in-law about the middle of the nineteenth century.

Richard had some scheme on foot for erecting a statue in the centre of the pond on the south side of the house, which at that time was much larger and must have reached almost under the windows : " The alteration you intend about your Pond must needs be pleasant [writes Sir John Chicheley], and of some use for diversion, which now is none. You must take Care ye Statue be proportionable to ye Bignesse of ye Pond, otherwise 'twill not show well." The pond has since been much reduced in size, and the statue, alas, has disappeared.

In early July 1676 came the Duke of York's visit to Lyme,   1676 for which so much preparation had been made. One can picture the reception that must have been given him. Richard, followed by his retainers, meeting his royal guest (who would come on horseback) at a given spot, and escorting him to the house, where Elizabeth, in her best gown, would be waiting at the entrance to the courtyard, prepared to give him the heartiest of welcomes. No details are to hand, so we are, unfortunately, unable to learn anything about the visit or what amusements were provided for His Royal Highness, beyond that he was taken for a stag hunt. The following appears on a piece of paper in Richard's handwriting, stuck in the first page of the first chapter of the first Book of Kings in the big family Bible :

"The 10th day of July 1676 the Duke of Y: kill'd a stag that was 14 hands 4 inches high, he run soe long a chair [chase] the D: being one of the 1st that came in, who when he was att bay shott him dead with his pistoll, & had 36 miles to ride that night, wch he did, & came home before 8 a clock yt night.   R. LEGH, 1676."

The oak at the bottom of the park, under which tradition states this feat was accomplished, is still standing ; it has been surrounded with a railing, and an inscription recording the fact has been attached.

None of the letters of the time contain any reference to the visit beyond the following, which Sir John Chicheley wrote in August from Montpellier, near the Gulf of Lyons, where he and Lady Chicheley had gone for purposes of health.

> "I take it for granted yt by the time this comes to hand y'l be quitte of yr great Company, wch I do suppose y'l not desire to have often, though a braver worthier man 'tis impossible to meet with. I do expect you shall give me a true & perfect account of wt happens from yr first meeting to yr parting, wch I do suppose will not be at Lime Hall."

Whilst at Montpellier, Sir John visited the French fleet at Toulon in March 1676–7, and appears to have been much struck with its strength. He writes begging his brother-in-law will represent this to the House of Commons, and that no efforts will be spared to "fortifie our Outgards proportionable to w^t it has been to theres; if not, I feare ye scene will be changed, and then they will pretend to ye superiority at Sea, which if so and able to dispute it with us, adieu trade and consequently what makes us subsist."

Lady Chicheley, who apparently did not include a knowledge of the French language among her accomplishments, describes herself as "a body that is deaf and dum, for I nethere understand nor speake." She takes a distinctly British view of foreigners, and her impressions of the French are decidedly unfavourable:

> "The French (especially in this place) are the falsest, cheating lying people in the world, and thinke that English comes on purpose to bring them money, for a Frenchman shall live for a thurd part att most of what an English man shall, and if they have any qarrel or grudging at a man, they make nothing of stabeing him in an evening or pistoleing. 'Tis a kinde of lawlese place and neghbours to the Itallions and Spaniards, so partake some of their qualities."

She is bound, however, to admit the excellence of the figs, grapes, and melons; cherries, too, to be had at 1d. and 1½d. the pound.

1678   We hear of the Legh family suffering from measles and jaundice in 1678, "a very troublesome and faint disease," writes Lady Chicheley, who had had practical experience of it with her husband. She sends the following recipe which she hopes may do good.

"To Cure the Jaundice.

"Take the Roote of Parceley, wild cicory, sorrel, buglose and fennel, of each a handful, wash & pick them clean, & take the pith out & boyle them in 2 quarts of fountaine water to a quart, then put in a few leaves of Sage & let them scalde a while in it, after Stran it, throw a Cloth without pressing it ; when tis cold, put it into a bottle & stope it close, & drink half a Pint or a good draft of it every morning fasting with 3 Spoonfulls of white wine, & fast 2 hours after it, & as much in the Afternoone 2 hours before Supper. Make fresh as you need it.

"Sir John did purge once or twice or thrice with an Infusion of Rhubarbe whilst it was upon him & att its leaving him."

CHAPTER XX

THE POPISH PLOT

1678   A PANIC of distrust had begun, conspiracies were rife, plots, real or pretended, were hatching, and a general suspicion was everywhere in the air. Society was possessed by a moral epidemic as virulent as any physical disease, and for years this state of things continued. There were not wanting adventurous spirits ready to take advantage of the prevailing credulity of the public mind, and bold enough to fabricate conspiracies which they turned very much to their own profit, for this infamous trade was a lucrative business. The year 1678, and the last session of the Parliament which had sat since 1661, witnessed the most memorable of these national delusions, the " Popish Plot," fabricated by Titus Oates, in which hundreds of innocent persons became involved. As early as 1673 the general feeling of distrust had begun, and freedom of speech was an unknown quantity. Writing to his brother-in-law, Richard Legh, from London on February 17, 1673–4, Thomas Chicheley (eldest son of Sir Thomas), says :

> " Here is noe newes more then what is dangerous to write ; if we write of amours, then the next morning comes Captain Bessus, his stile, satisfaction, Reparation &ct, if of the King, a messenger invites you civily to his house immediately after, and takes it extreame ill if you do not goe with him. If of the Parliament, things are remembered that were spoken in jest seven years agone."

In April 1678, Titus Oates,* the perjurer, an adventurer

---

* Titus Oates (1649–1705), perjurer; expelled from Merchant Taylors' School during his first term there, 1665 ; became a naval chaplain, but expelled from the Navy ; fabricated the " Popish Plot " ; tried for perjury, 1685 ; condemned to stand in the pillory annually, to be flogged and imprisoned for life ; sentence revoked and he was set at liberty, 1689.

from his earliest youth, started the idea of the " Popish Plot,"
the planning of which he purported to have overheard in a coffee-
house.   He declared that it had for its object the assassination
of the King, and the setting up of James on the throne as the
agent of the Jesuits.   Oates affirmed this story before Sir
Edmund Berry Godfrey,* a Middlesex magistrate, who not long
afterwards was found dead in a ditch near Primrose Hill.   This
murder caused the greatest excitement all over the country, the
wildest rumours were flying about, a general massacre was pre-
dicted, and every one from the King downwards seemed to have
completely lost all sense of proportion and self-control.   Oates
reaped a rich reward.   Godfrey's murder, supposed to have been
done by Papists, lending support to his testimony, Oates was
lodged in Whitehall, with a salary of £40 a month.

> " Whitehall [we read] is close shutt up, and noe passage to it but
> through the wickett at the greate Gate, and a strict examination of all
> that are suffered to passe in or out."

One of the first to come under suspicion, completely
unfounded, was Sir Robert Carr, Chancellor of the Duchy of
Lancaster, a life-long friend of the Legh family :

> " I thank God I have done nothing to deserve his Majestie's dis-
> pleasure [he writes to Richard on July 2, 1678], and hope I never shall,
> but my enemies have prevailed against me, and I wish they never
> may prevaile in things that will be of more injurie to King and
> Kingdome."

Happily nothing was proved against him, and by November
he was with the King at Newmarket, in favour again, " but
cautious in making use of it."

In October, Sir Thomas Chicheley reports more news to his
son-in-law, back at Lyme after a visit to Bath.

> " We have here a great Alarme of a plot against the person of the
> King, but I hope it will prove noe such thing, for I think noething
> but the Divell who hateth goodnesse can wish him ill, for certainly he

---

* Sir Edmund Berry Godfrey (1621–1678), Justice of the Peace for Westminster;
a zealous Protestant ; received first deposition of Titus Oates ; found dead on Primrose
Hill a month later, believed murdered by Roman Catholics.

is the best of mankind, having ever done evil for good." [The last sentence must either have been ironical, or else a slip of the pen !]

1678   The plot is described by another correspondent as being " as Blacke as can bee, what is said is not fit to be committed to paper." " Never was there greater occation for your presence heere then now," says one Lightbourne to Richard on November 4, 1678, so most unwillingly and in very indifferent health he returned to his Parliamentary duties at the end of the month. Writing to his wife from Coventry on November 26, while on his way, he complains of much pain, and is in evident dread of a further fit of the stone, which illness he had suffered from for years, the excessive horse exercise of the day being, of course, extremely bad for this complaint.

" Coventry, Tuesday night, 1678 ;

" I hope Deare Soul thou hast enjoyed more satisfaction than I have done since I left Lime. For my part I expect none like it till I come there againe. I shall not trouble thee with the dullness of my journey, being I know more melancholy for want of company, but especially the last night, being alarmed with the dread of another fitt of the Stone, which was very afflictive, but I thank my good God itt was more in the apprehension than paine, but made me shorten this days journey which I intended 14 miles further, & just now have eat my Supper very heartily, & my best Dissert is this writing to thee, & this day have pickt up a deal of news.

" First—This morning by 7 a clock came Mr Will Venables post to Lichfield yesterday from London, where things are in a great hurly burly. The great Lord Treasurer * as tis said, sent to the Tower, however he is strongly articled against. You know how & why Montagu † was laid aside for being Envoy in France. He is now chosen for Northampton, & being in danger to be brought in amongst the Plotters for knowing the designe there whilst he was Embassador, & falls now to recriminate upon the Treasurer . . . and now Articles are drawn up to Impeach the Treasurer. . . . but the K. it's said, will release him, tho' he be sent to the Tower." ‡

* Sir Thomas Osborne, Earl of Danby, afterwards Duke of Leeds.

† Ralph, first Duke of Montagu (1638 ?–1709), Ambassador to Louis XIV; denounced by the Duchess of Cleveland and deprived of his post.

‡ Raines Collection.

THE POPISH PLOT

> ". . . The Priests that were condemned are not yett executed, and
> 'tis too plaine that ye K– – said he was weary & wold hang no more
> upon Oates's and Bedloes' * confessions, but God is very good & hath
> brought forth the Murderers of Sir Godfrey by the confession of one
> Prance.† Yesterday we had his Confession read to us which he gave
> to the Members that Examined him. This Prance & the rest were
> all the Qu – – Servants. . . . This morne one Dugdale,‡ servant to the
> Lord Aston, (a Papist) came to the Lords & told them that he saw the
> Lord Stafford § down on's knees in the Chapel taking the Oath of
> Secresy not to discover this Plott. . . . 'Tis said by good hands that
> the K– – – himself said he was now satisfied there was not a con-
> siderable Papist in England but he did believe he was concern'd in itt
> as to his death, & says he, ' I wold rather they were all hang'd.' "

Though Richard speaks of Parliament being prorogued on
December 30, 1678, it continued to sit until well on into January
1678–9. Sir Thomas Chicheley bribed his daughter with a
present of eighteen pies to let her husband remain away from
her a little longer :

> " and hopes [says Richard] thou wilt be friends with him, for it was
> not in the power of him or any to have excused for me, and had I not
> come in as I did, my fees had been double. Many paid as much that
> were out oth' Towne, but hang't lett itt goe ! "

People were beginning to suspect Oates and his confederates,
who were adding fresh lies to those already told : " As for Oates
and Bedloe," says Richard, on January 2, 1678–9, " one is mad
and th'other has been burnt ith' hand." But the mischief
they had manufactured was already done. On January 9 come
more details :

> " For news they say this Dugdale is come up & lays the Plot more
> open than ever, and in the Tower they said the Lord Stafford had a
> stricter guard than ever, in soe much that noe body is suffer'd to come
> to him, or say any thing but what they all heare. The rabble in the

---

* William Bedloe, an adventurer ; supported Oates.

† Miles Prance, a Catholic silversmith ; confessed under torture to have been an
accomplice in the murder.

‡ Stephen Dugdale (1640–1683), informer ; intimate with priests ; pretended to
have knowledge of the plot.

§ William, first Viscount Stafford (1614–1680) ; accused by Oates and others of
persuading them to murder the King ; beheaded 1680.

Citty heard a rumor that the Priests were to be executed the other day, who came in great numbers to Newgate and cried ' bring them out, give them us,' and when they understood itt was a false story they had heard, they went (as they say) to the Recorder's and bid him goe and gett Justice upon them. The Duchess of Yorke they say intercedes for one of them who is her Confessor. Others say he threatens to tell tales upon the Gallowes, but that I believe not. God knows how these things will be, every body is in darknesse." *

Even the Queen herself was not spared, though Charles—to his credit—utterly refused to listen to any of the accusations against her.

A series of what can only be described as judicial murders had now begun. Arrests were made on the slightest suspicion, so-called justice was conducted with the grossest partiality, and the unfortunate victims were sentenced with the merest apology for a trial. There was a veritable lust for blood. Parties were made up to go and hear trials and see the spectacle of an execution, much as people arrange a picnic at the present day. Scaffolding was erected in Westminster Hall, and prices for seats ranged from five to twenty shillings.

1678–9   The impeachment of Danby caused Charles, who favoured his Lord Treasurer, to dissolve the Long Parliament—which had sat for the last seventeen years—on January 24, 1678–9.

Although aged only forty-five, Richard had been in failing health for some time, suffering much from his old malady, the stone. He now determined to give up public life altogether, and to devote his remaining years and energy to his family and the management of his property. The span of life was shorter then than now, due probably to the great strain of those rigorous days, which none but the most robust constitutions was able to withstand. A youth entered upon public life before he was out of his " teens," and cares and responsibilities were thrust upon the shoulders of those who were little more than children; it is not surprising, therefore, that so much wear and tear of body and mind should have aged a delicate man before his time.

Upon his decision not to stand again for Parliament being

* Raines Collection.

made known, Richard was besieged with applications from would-be candidates, eager to take his place in the representation of Newton. Andrew Fountaine,* his brother-in-law, was particularly anxious to enter Parliament, and Sir Thomas Chicheley wrote begging for Richard's help and interest in favour of his youngest daughter's husband.

This gentleman, who married Sarah Chicheley about 1672, was a Hertfordshire squire of unattractive habits and personality. He was addicted to drink, was always in money difficulties, and led his wife a most wretched existence, a great contrast to the happy life of her sister Elizabeth Legh. She was an excellent correspondent, and her letters, though most illiterate in regard to spelling, show a great deal of character and originality, and are full of amusing and piquant accounts of the news and gossip of the day, though in parts somewhat "free." She was blessed with a keen sense of humour, which helped her to rise above her troubles and to make the best of what can have been but a very bad bargain. Owing to money difficulties, it was no doubt important that Andrew Fountaine should secure the advantages enjoyed by a Member of Parliament, the chief of which was immunity from imprisonment for debt.

"I must desire you to help my son Fountain, for he is a most unfortunate man else," writes Sir Thomas in February 1678-9, and Sarah appeals for assistance for her husband in much the same strain :

"February ye 11th.

"DEARE BROTHERE

"I came just now from Sr Thomas who (although he is extreame ill of the gout in his foot) says he is resolved to write to you to-night

---

* Second son of Brigg Fountaine of Salle, Norfolk. In 1666 he bought from Sir William Dudley the manor of Brookmans, Hertfordshire, and built himself a fine house there in 1682. His first wife was Theophila, daughter of Dr. Stubs of Elmham, Kent, and widow of W. Wells of Halvegate, by whom he had no issue. He married Sarah Chicheley about 1672, and by her had, with other children, Andrew, afterwards knighted (1676–1753), who became a famous antiquary, and one of the most celebrated connoisseurs of his day. He succeeded Sir Isaac Newton as Governor of the Mint in 1727, and was Chamberlain to Queen Caroline. His magnificent collection was dispersed by auction in 1885, realizing enormous sums.

about the troublesome busines you have in hand. he writ to you a Saturday last to press thee very much to doe the kindnes we require if you can possible; really itt much concerns me that necessity forcies me to putt thee to all this trouble, but God knows for this seven yeare in all things that wee have proposed any Sattisfaction in, there arises some rouge [rogue] or other out of a corner unexpected to humble us, (butt yett itt will nott bee;) soe that if you cannot doe this thing for us, I am sattisfied within myself 'tis not want of your power, but our misfortune, as publick affaires look dolefully att us, soe doth our own private ones. I writ a Thursday last that Mr Fountaine desires you, if you find it necessary, by all means to lay out money for him, whatever itt is he will return itt with a thousand thanks. . . . For all you are determined to parliament itt noe more, I find all your friends are sattisfied with what you doe; soe wishing for a blessing upon us all, I rest

" Yours

" S: F:

" Methinks I long to hear certainly whethere you can effect the business or noe; for 'tis uneassy to live between hope and feare, though I have been pretty well used to itt since we had to doe with the Law."

1678–9 The new Parliament assembled in March 1678–9. Andrew Fountaine was one of the Members returned for Newton Borough, the other seat being filled by Sir John Chicheley. Richard had to pay the expenses of both candidates, and it is very doubtful whether he ever received his money again; he had not done so in 1681, when Sarah writes announcing the repayment of £30 towards the expenses.

The new Parliament sat but for a few months, the only Act of importance that was passed being the Habeas Corpus. The Exclusion Bill introduced by Shaftesbury, then at the height of his triumph, intended to exclude the succession of James and his children in favour of Monmouth, was read twice but not passed. Richard continued to use his influence, though no longer taking an active part in public affairs, and held fast to his allegiance to the Crown, refusing to recognize the pretensions of Monmouth, and his attitude no doubt decided his two brothers-in-law, the new Members for Newton Borough, to oppose the Bill. He was receiving constant accounts of all that went on in Parliament. A copy was sent him of the arbitrary message dispatched by the House of Commons to the King, in response to His Majesty's request that his faithful Commons would

> "take caire to sett out a ffleet to secure ye ffears of his people from fforraine attempts. By this [says Richard's correspondent] y'll judge ye temper of ye House ; When Mr Powell * had brought into ye House his Majesty's message & had delivered it, ye House was concerned & reflected on Mr Powell for pressing ye Matter of ye Message, saying yt ye aire of ye Court had infected him ; amongst divers others Mr Sacheverill † was pleas'd to say as follows :
>
>> "'Mr Speaker
>> "'When ye Lords in ye Tower are tryed and justice done upon them, when ye Earle of Danby's pardon is declared voyd, when ye Bishops are not to sitt in Judicature upon ye sd Lords, when ye evill councillors Male and Female are removed from his Majesty, when ye Militia is settled in safe hands, and ye land secured, when ye Officers of ye Shipps and Navy are such as ye Nation can confide in, when ye Army is disbanded, when ye books of Mr Bartne (?) are delivered up.
>>> "'Then will be time to consider of Mony to sett out a Fleet.'
>
> "Upon which ye debate was adjourned for almost a fortnight, and yt all persons who were Members do then bring in their previous considerations. Talks there is of another Parliament to be suddenly called, how true 'tis I know not."

Sir John Chicheley reports to his brother-in-law on May 31 :

> "this place affords not much news, only much talke neither fitt to be writ or sayd, but I find now all tongues at liberty to yt degree yt few or none scruples talking treason when they please, what will ye end or Issue of this be none knows or can imagine : affaires has so ill an aspect yt 'tis hard to say what one thinks."

Sir Thomas Chicheley, who had in 1674 resigned the Master-Generalship of the Ordnance, in which post he was succeeded by his son (appointed by special licence from the King), was

---

* Henry Powle (1630–1692). Master of the Rolls and Speaker of the Convention Parliament; identified himself with the opponents of the Court in Charles II's reign.

† William Sacheverell (1638–1691), politician ; M.P. for Derbyshire, 1670 and 1679; opposed Court policy; served on committee which drew up articles for Danby's impeachment.

retiring from being one of the Commissioners of the Navy, and Sir John was hoping to be named in his place, but was apparently not in favour with the King at this moment :

> " This night I intend to discourse his Majesty about my Pattent for ye reversion, which I expect will not be extraordinary pleasing to him ; yet I thinke 'tis not reasonable to lett fall so faire a pretention without knowing where or in what I have offended. In case Sir Thomas goes I do suppose my stay in ye Navy will not be long after ; how I shall dispose of myselfe then God knows, but if I can prevaile with my good woman we'l retire into a quietter Country. By ye next y'll heare more."

He obtained the coveted place, and continued to hold posts in connexion with the Navy until his retirement in 1690.

1679 The King was taken very ill in August 1679. He " was lett blood and his feaver very high," but by September 3 was " in a very good way of recovery, having missed three fits and is very cheerful and talks of going to Newmarket."

Jesuits' powder (quinine) was the remedy administered in fevers. We read that Prince Rupert was cured of ague and fever by taking it every three hours. Sir Thomas Chicheley had also been a sufferer and had taken the same remedy, which cured the distemper, but gave him a " great oppression at his stomacke which made him sigh extremely," writes his daughter-in-law. " God send him now to continue well, but I should have liked it better if he had been soe without the help of the powder." When this and blood-letting failed, there was not much hope left for the patient. The occasional good results of bleeding, however, are shown in an account of an accident to the Duke of York about this date :

> " On Teusday last His Royall Highness being a hunting his horse triped and came over upon him, bruised him a little. He was lett blood neare 12 oz. upon the place and then hunted on for neare three houres and is since Perfectly well, thankes be to God."

A fresh election took place in September of this same year, 1679, and a House of Commons was formed more hostile to the Crown than ever. Both Sir John Chicheley and Andrew Fountaine were returned again, as also in the election of 1680–1, when the Parliament met at Oxford, where it was hoped there would be less interruption from the supporters of Shaftesbury. Party feeling ran higher than ever, and we read of " great doings, fighting and ill words given, and one of the knights pulled by the nose."

The serious illness of the King had brought home to the moderate party the extreme danger of civil war if Monmouth should succeed, and the right of James and his Protestant children be set aside. Charles, therefore, on his recovery, yielded to the representation of his ministers, to send Monmouth out of the country, and dismissed Shaftesbury from his council.

Shaftesbury's revenge was soon to follow. He brought Monmouth back to London in November 1679, and tried to make capital out of another alleged plot, the particulars of which we gather from the following newsletter.

The personages figuring in this pretended conspiracy were a certain Mistress Cellier,* " the Popish midwife," ulti-mately acquitted on a charge of plotting the King's murder, and one Dangerfield,† alias Willoughby, a coiner and per-jurer, befriended by Mistress Cellier, but who eventually turned against her. With these two worthies was connected Lady Powis, a daughter of the Earl of Winchester, and the wife of Lord Powis, afterwards Duke of Powis. One of her daughters was the famous Lady Nithsdale. Other names associated with these were those of Lord Stafford, again accused by one Turberville ‡ of hiring him to kill the King, and Lord Castlemaine,§ who was said to have been seen officiating as a priest. The newsletter, which is dated from London on November 9, 1679, goes on to say :

* Elizabeth Cellier (fl. 1680), *née* Dormer ; married Peter Cellier, a Frenchman ; embraced Romanism ; was a midwife in London.
† Thomas Dangerfield (1650 ?–1685) ; died from a blow inflicted by one Robert Frances.
‡ Edward Turberville (1648 ?–1681), informer; Roman Catholic; served in French army; pretended at Lord Stafford's trial that he had been employed by him to kill Charles II, but gave evidence later against Stephen College and Shaftesbury.
§ Roger Palmer, Earl of Castlemaine (1634–1705), diplomatist and author ; husband of Barbara Villiers, afterwards Duchess of Cleveland ; accused of complicity in the Popish Plot, but acquitted.

" . . . Mistress Cellier, ye Popish Midwife of whom you have often heard, being brought face to face with Willoughby, he charged her to be a Cheife Instigator for ye promoting the Cursed designe, & yt she gave him ye Choyce of 2 daggers to stabb ye Earl of Shaftesbury, which he asseyed twice to doe but was prevented, upon which Mistress Cellier being greatly Enraged, snatched the daggers out of his hand, calling him a whitelivered Cowardly rogue & saying she would see what a woman could doe for ye Catholique Cause, so she went herselfe but was happyly Prevented; shee obstinately denied all she was Charged with, but her maid confessed she carried 2 guinies from her Mistress to Willoughby in Newgate, praying him to remaine stedfast & not discover ye business to any, upon which shee was remanded back to Newgate. Willoughby also Charged all ye Lords in ye Tower, Danby excepted, to be guilty of a fresh contryvance of killing ye King, which hee was to Effect upon the account of breaking out of this pretended presbyterian plott, & was to have 2000[l] reward, & yt hee allready had some of ye money to carry on ye designe & to hire witnesses to sware to ye particulars. He further declared who were ye first contrivers of this Conspiracy, & taxed ye Lady Powis & ye Lord Castlemaine as ye principall promoters thereof, both which being sent for were privately Examined & upon ye whole matter ye Lord Castlemaine was comitted to ye Tower & ye Lady Powis put under an obligation to attend again another time.

1680   " Yesterday being the 5th of November was more then usually observed, the Lord Mayor sending his presepts into every parrish. At night ye people expressed theire dislike to popery by such innumerable bonfiers & burning of Popes as was never seen on ye like occasion, one of them being worth 50[l] was arrested after ye manner of a Pageant, adorned with his usuall accoutterments, having a very rich Canopy over his head with abondance of lights placed round about him & a man dressed up like a devill set behind him which in his Course seemed very lovingly to converse with him; it being carried round about most part of ye Citty, was at last Conveyed to Bridewall where were innumerable spectators to behould his downfall. A great fire being made, this formall divell threw the pope into it, at which ye shouts of ye people echoed ye skies, & yt person yt could get so neer as to give ye Pope a blow thought himselfe happy.

" The Lady Powis hath been againe examined, it was proved point blank against her, & although she denied, ye said Willoughby (alias Dangerfeild for yt is his name) rectyfied her memory by saying yt her ladyshippe could not forgett ye time & place when & where shee admitted him to her private embraces, or words to yt effect, but ye lady was . . . [word missing] committed to ye Tower for high Treason, And directly for conspireing the death of ye King."

The agitation connected with this plot continued for over a year. A correspondent writes on October 23, 1680, that " Mistress Cellier stood this day on ye Pillory at Charing Crosse ye 3d time but her armour was proof ag^t ye great and small shot of ye rabble." The same correspondent, one Richard Sterne,* reports on November 9 that another false witness, Turberville, had brought fresh accusations against Lord and Lady Powis. A few days later he states that

> " Lady Powis and Lady Abergavenny are withdrawn upon some apprehension that Mistress Cellier (who is to be tryed for treason) will rather turn then burn."

Lady Chicheley, writing shortly afterwards, mentions Lord Stafford's trial, in which there was very little done but proving in general the plot, there being hundreds of witnesses to be examined :

> " The parliament house takes up all thoughts and time, tho' under the rose I think they do as little there as in other places, but who knows but I may be called to the bar to receive the sentence of the House for this."

The Powises got off, but Lord Stafford was executed with many others, implicated quite wrongfully in this abominable conspiracy. 1680

It was about this date that the names Whig and Tory were first heard in their application to English political factions. A reaction of horror at the cruelties perpetrated had resulted in a series of addresses from thousands who declared their " abhorrence " of the plot against the Crown. Shaftesbury's party petitioned the King to allow Parliament to meet, their opponents sending up contrary petitions expressing abhorrence at such an attempt to force the King. The two parties became known as the " Abhorrers " and " Petitioners," names which were replaced by those of Whig and Tory.

On November 13, Richard Sterne writes giving information of an address that had been sent to the King in which amongst other things he was desired to adhere to the advice of his Parliament. This message was received with much displeasure

* Richard Sterne, probably a son of Richard Sterne, Archbishop of York ; sat in the Parliaments of 1678, 1679, and 1680–81, as member for Ripon Borough.

by Charles, who sent back word that the House had meddled with what did not concern them : " And ye Lord Privy Seale," adds Sterne, " attended ye King into ye Banqueting house, his Majesty receiving our Address and went his way without giving ONE WORD IN ANSWER." From his own observation Sterne also reports that when the Speaker read that part of the address which mentioned the ill councils that had been given the King for dissolving and proroguing of Parliament, " his Majesty did hastily put on his gloves and take his stick and seemed to sit with some impatience."

1680–1   Personalities mixed with uncouth attempts at humour figure in the Parliamentary discussions of the day. In a news-letter of this date containing mention of a Bill brought in by a Colonel Titus,* for the much-needed repairing of the highways, Sir Nicholas Cary is reported as saying that he " thirded the motion because it was to mend his (Titus's) way to Tyburn," Titus retorting that " he passed by Tyburn and hoped that gentleman would do so too." On December 28, 1680, it was said that " the House thanked Dr. Burnet † for his paines but not Dr. Sprat ‡ who spent most of his powder agst ffanaticks."

Richard Sterne, a very constant correspondent of the Legh family, sends a piece of gossip respecting the Prince of Hanover, afterwards King George I, whom he describes as " a fine young Protestant gent, now come to court the Lady Anne " (afterwards Queen Anne). There had been projects for this marriage but they were abandoned in 1681, the Princess marrying Prince George of Denmark in 1683. A few days later Sterne writes again, evidently elated at receiving recognition from the Duchess of Portsmouth : " To-day we walked ye back way to Whitehall, the Duchess of Portsmouth with her attendants (her windows being open) gave us a low salute as we passed."

---

* John Titus (1616–1691), Presbyterian colonel; took prominent part in Parliamentary investigation of Oates's pretended plot.

† Gilbert Burnet (1643–1715), Bishop of Salisbury; remonstrated with Charles II on his evil life.

‡ Thomas Sprat (1635–1713), Bishop of Rochester and Dean of Westminster.

298

THE POPISH PLOT

The King dissolved Parliament on January 18, 1680–1, and summoned the new Parliament to meet at Oxford the following March.

In August 1682, Monmouth, encouraged by Shaftesbury, started on a series of progresses through the west of England, but nowhere was he received with very great enthusiasm. On the 27th of the month Lord Molyneux * writes to Richard, evidently in jest, that he hopes the hospitality of Lyme may be extended to the rebel Duke :

> " There is great preparations at Chester, and they are in a High Consternation how to treat the Monmouth Duke. Some are for meeting him out of Towne and bearing his Charge, and others are against it : soe it seemes they are variously minded. But you, I hope, are settled in your resolutions of entertaineing him when he comes to Lyme, which I heare will be very shortly. Soe I thought good (like a loving kinsman) to let you know."

But Richard had no such intentions. Monmouth got, however, within twelve miles of Lyme. He made, in September 1682, a stay of some days at Gawsworth, a charming old-world village, which has remained untouched and unspoilt to this day, where he was the guest of Charles Gerard, Earl of Macclesfield.† Sir Leoline Jenkins ‡ writes to Richard, in his capacity of Deputy-Lieutenant and Justice of the Peace, for particulars of this visit, begging him to obtain on oath from the different witnesses answers to the following questions :

1. Where and at whose charges the Duke of Monmouth dined and supped on Monday last ?
2. Where he dined on Tuesday and Wednesday following, and what was observed or did otherwise occurre in that space ?

---

* Caryll, third Viscount Molyneux, cousin of Richard ; was outlawed by the Parliament, but by payment of a huge fine was put in possession of his estates ; married Mary, daughter of Alexander Barlow of Barlow, Lancashire, by whom he had a large family. He died 1698–9.

† Charles Gerard, first Baron Gerard of Brandon and Earl of Macclesfield, great-grandson of Sir Gilbert Gerard, Master of the Rolls ; dismissed from the bedchamber as an adherent of Monmouth ; fled to the Continent and died there, 1694.

‡ Sir Leoline Jenkins (1623–1685), civilian and diplomatist ; led Opposition to Exclusion Bills.

3. What Arts were used at ye severall places he passed through to draw ye Rabble together, and who were the Authors and Abettors of it ?

4. Whether any riott or breach of the Peace was committed in any of the severall places through which the Duke of Monmouth passed ?

He adds that His Majesty desires answers to these questions

"and he is graciously pleased to depend upon your affection and fidelity to him in letting him know everything that is come to your knowledge especially in your own Neighborhood, to the end he may make that use of those Notices as may be most for the preserving of the Peace and for ye satisfaction of his Loving and dutyfull subjects such as you are."

This letter was sent by a special and secret messenger.

Richard accordingly summoned his brother justices and the following facts were obtained from two witnesses examined on September 20, by Sir John Arderne, Richard Legh, and Edward Warren * of Poynton :

That upon Friday, September 15, the Duke of Monmouth came attended by a considerable number of gentlemen to the Earl of Macclesfield's house at Gawsworth, and that the company "called upon ye rabble to shout." The following day, Saturday the 16th, there was buck-shooting in Lord Macclesfield's park, followed by a great banquet, and some sweetmeats were received by one of the witnesses, distributed to him and to others by the Earl's own hand. On the same day, "upon a plaine neare to ye Earl's house a game called a Prison-barr-play was performed by 20 young men," for which a piece of plate was presented by Lord Macclesfield. There were afterwards given five guineas "for making the Duke that sport," another guinea being presented to two kettle-drummers of the Earl's who had assisted on this occasion. Four thousand people were supposed to have been present, and when the Duke came into the field to see the sport, "there seemed to bee great satisfaccon to ye Crowd in his presence, which ye multitude expressed by shouting."

* Edward Warren of Poynton, born 1605, called " Stag Warren " from his great size and strength ; a near neighbour and life-long friend of Richard Legh.

THE POPISH PLOT

Lord Macclesfield desired the householders in the neighbour-hood to wait upon the Duke the Monday following, when he was to resume his journey to Congleton, a town about four miles farther on towards London, and many of " the rabble " were heard to say that they would have no papist to inherit the crown, and that they would venture their lives for the Duke of Monmouth.

The romantic village of Gawsworth, with its fifteenth-century church and rectory, its old cross and quaint tilting-ground, was a fit setting for the little drama that was enacted by the handsome adventurer, whose fascinating manners and charming personality captivated even the unemotional Cheshire yokels. The road that he took on his progress south is no doubt the same which leads to-day from the little village to Congleton. The church, which stands on a knoll above a small lake, is approached on its south side by an avenue of splendid trees ; neither church nor surroundings can have altered much in the last two hundred years.

Mistress Fountaine, in a letter dated September 26, gives 1682 some particulars of the Duke's arrest, which took place at Lichfield :

> " I suppose you hear already that the Serjant att Arms and twelve to gard the great Duck [Duke] met him att Lichfield ; we hard [heard] upon the road he was sent for and that Sir Thomas Armstrong * was gone post to town 2 days before us ; Mrs Langley † said their news from London a Sunday was that the Warrants that was sent for him was drawn up for great Riots and many Misdemeanors committed by him ; soe the Knight rid post before to Judge Raymond ‡ to gett the Duck a Habeascorpus which was granted, at which being done soe soon the King is angry, for hee is extreamely insensed att the D. and 'tis said swore (which is not usual with him) that he and his followers should not find him soe Tame as he had been. I beseech God direct him, and noe doubt his enimies will find 'tis dangerous being ungratefull to soe kind a Prince as he has been to them. 'Tis said he is sent to the Tower, but all reports are yett uncertaine."

* Sir Thomas Armstrong (1624 ?–1684), Royalist ; implicated in Rye House Plot ; after an unfair trial by Judge Jeffreys, was executed 1684.

† Housekeeper to the Chicheleys.

‡ Sir Thomas Raymond (1627–1683), judge ; advanced to the King's Bench 1680.

Sir John Chicheley also writes :

> " I have communicated your letter to Mr Secretary Jenkins who told me he had already written to a dozen or fourteen of ye Justices of ye Peace for farther information in ye affaire, and withall he does intend to write to Sir George Jeffris * to get what he can at ye Assizes and returne it to him, and in case there should be need, he'l send an Officer of ye Crowne, to countenance these enquireys ; this he desired me to write to you. His Grace of Monmouth was this morning (September 23) examined and I finde upon enquire yt he's at liberty upon Baile (of which Mr Lucan Goore † was one) to answer to what shall be against him ye next Terme. I heare he submitted himself very quietly to ye Sargent when he seized him in ye King's name."

Acting upon instructions received, the Justices of the Peace issued warrants to empower them to search the neighbouring houses, and Richard had the painful duty of reporting the seizure of firearms in those of many of his most intimate friends. A quantity of muskets, blunderbuses, carbines, and pistols were discovered at Lord Macclesfield's, he having fled to the Continent, and weapons of all description were found in the houses of Mr. Legh of Adlington, Sir Thomas Mainwaring of Peover, Mr. Bradshawe of Marple, Mr. Legh of High Legh, and Mr. Booth of Mere. A correspondent reports " secret talke among the fanaticks of a wagon loade of Armes having come to Manchester. I hope yt thing is false, however I thinke it my duty in these jealous days to acquaint any one with ye report who may probably inquire after ye truth of it."

1682   The King acknowledged the services rendered by his faithful servant through a letter from Sir Leoline Jenkins ‡ to Richard, written on October 7, 1682 :

> " Your letter was layd before his Matie just as he went to Newmarket, with an Extract of all the Depositions brought from you and others out of Cheshire, and maturely considered of by Himselfe with several of my Lords of the Councill that attended Him.

* The notorious judge.

† Sir William Leveson Gower, fourth Baronet, ancestor of the present Duke of Sutherland.

‡ See note, p. 299.

302

THE POPISH PLOT

" His Matie hath commanded me to give all of you Gentlemen that subscribed that Letter his hearty thanks for your Care and Zeale and to tell you he promised to himselfe, when he commanded me to write to you, (he knowing you all very well either by person or by reputation) that you would use, as you have done, all ye Application that a Service of this kind, which is not only of Importance for ye present but of infinite consequence for the future, could demand from Loyall Gentlemen, true and zealous in their Trust.

" His Matie further commanded me to tell you that he concurs with you perfectly in judgment in what you say, *that there doth yet more lye hid then at present appeares ;* for he knoweth the association to be deep-rooted, and that those that contrived the Rendezvous at Walesea had other designes then those of horse raceing in their heads, which he hopes in Gods good time to be able to discover to the bottome."

Richard and his friends had recommended that the Militia should be called up and this suggestion was approved by the King, who considered it would have " a very ill Aspect upon his Affaires in case of any Insurrections not to have the Militia of those parts in a posture equally advantageous with the very best of his kingdom."

Charles felt his position bitterly. A letter from a correspondent of this date says :

" Sir Thomas Grosvenor * was with the King one day when in discourse he told him his condition was worse than a tinker or cobler, who if their lives were in danger the law would protect them, but he was denyed common justice."

The King dissolved Parliament in 1683, and appealed in a 1683 Royal Proclamation to the justice of the nation. This resulted in a great reaction of loyalty. Shaftesbury, realizing that his case was hopeless, fled to Holland, and Monmouth, who was afterwards implicated, though not seriously, in the Rye House Plot, owed his pardon to his father's tenderness and was sent into honourable exile.

* Married Miss Davis, daughter of a London scrivener, and with her obtained the bulk of the present Westminster estates.

CHAPTER XXI

RACING AND GARDENING

WITH more time to devote to his family and country pursuits, Richard had also greater leisure for his favourite amusements, of which horse-racing was the chief. He had always been fond of horses and had bred them from his earliest youth. Newmarket had been used even before James I's day, but he it was who was supposed to have placed the Turf on a permanent basis, and it is certain that he greatly encouraged this sport, as did also Charles II.

We have no mention of the Newton race-course before 1680 (racing still continues there), when the following rules were laid down, which appear on a paper in Richard's handwriting :

" About the Race at Newton this present year 1680.

" Imp^r That person who brings a horse to ride for ye s^d plate shall be obliged to take thirty pounds for his horse to be tendered to him either by ye Steward or by any other person before ye horse has run for ye s^d plate, & ye Money to be deposited in ye Stewards hands before ye race. The Steward to have ye first refuse of any horse ye rides for ye s^d plate.

That horse which is fourteen hands high or upwards shall carry ten stone, yt horse wch is under fourteen & above thirteen shall carry nine stone, & yt horse wch is under thirteen & above twelve hands shall carry eight stone, yt horse wch is but twelve hands or under may ride as light as he can by the standard, 4 inches to ye hand.

All horses yt are to run must come in 6 dayes before ye day or else they may not ride for ye plate.

All horses that run for ye saddle are to be of 10^l price, that is, before they start they shall be oblig'd to take 10^l as above = to be free without depositing money.

" The Steward to be judge of all differen :"

RACING AND GARDENING

Lord Derby * was a very keen supporter of this local race-meeting, and writes that he is always glad of any opportunity of seeing his friend and neighbour. He makes a few suggestions as to rules :

> " I am desirous the plate shall bee run for again. The enclosed is as fairly drawn for all sides as it could be done, for I am sure I don't desire any advantage neither would I willingly others should. I think if every horse that runs shall put in 20 shillings or 40^{sh} (I leave it to you) may cause more Sporte, and I am the more desirous by reason I would bee glad to run for something more then the bare plate."

He ends begging pardon for a very large blot.

Sir Robert Carr writes from Newmarket, on October 2, 1680, the King and Court having returned to London a few days previously :

> " The King coming soe earlie to Towne before any Matches were to be runn, maketh us have little sport, onlie Tynker I ran befoer his tyme and wonn. I contemn my Lord Rutlands † Horse so much that though I am to runn with him Tuesday sennight, I runn dubb for a Plate last Thursday, which with two other Plates is all the sport wee have had. Tuesday next Darsie runs, Post Boy and Mad Cap not this fortnight, the Scotch Galloway hath the forfeiture paid to him. Cholmlie hath been heer resolving not to bett, but I so provoked him with telling some trew stories of him that I am confident he hath betted two or three hundred pownds."

A letter a few days later gives the news of his horse " Darsie " having been beaten by the King's gelding, " Mouse."

> " Two better horses never were seen run, but ye 12 pound weight Darsie carried above ye other sunk him at last, he was beaten about six lengths."

---

* William, ninth Earl of Derby, succeeded his father in 1672 ; married Lady Elizabeth Butler, daughter of Thomas, Earl of Ossory. This Lord Derby refused to mingle in politics, preferring to lead the life of a private gentleman.

† John Manners, ninth Earl and first Duke of Rutland (1638–1711) ; married, first, 1658, Lady Anne Pierrepoint, daughter of Henry, Marquis of Dorchester ; she was divorced and her children disabled from inheriting by Act of Parliament in 1668. Lord Rutland married, secondly, 1671, Lady Diana Bruce, daughter of Robert, Earl of Ailesbury, and widow of Sir Seymour Shirley ; and thirdly, in 1673, the Hon. Catherine Noel, daughter of Viscount Camden, by whom he had an only son, afterwards the second Duke.

THE HOUSE OF LYME

A series of eighteenth-century paintings of race-horses with their jockeys, executed by an artist named Roper, hang in the gallery at Lyme. Some of these have the names attached, " Old Harlott," " Old Partner," " Regulus," " Lampre," etc., and one very weird-looking creature, with a preternaturally long neck, is said to represent " Black Godolphin," the first Arab horse imported into this country. A picture of Newmarket race-course, painted about the same date by an unknown artist and preserved at Lyme, shows the finish of a race between two horses, ladies and gentlemen following on horseback, the public apparently being allowed to come and go upon the course at will.*

As we have already remarked, a greater degree of refinement was to be noticed after the Restoration ; far more attention was paid to cleanliness and to the care of the person. Tooth-powder is first mentioned in the Legh letters as being used in 1677. The art of dentistry is a very ancient one, dating from the fifth century B.C., and it is said that artificial teeth were made from those of animals, and were found in human skulls among the Etruscans. These artificial aids were, however, not used in England, if one may judge from the portraits of the time. A small and very badly painted portrait of Richard shows the mouth all fallen in, owing to the loss of his front teeth. Hard drinking was apparently going out of fashion. Richard writes to his wife from Lancaster, where he was attending the assizes in September 1680, describing a dinner of forty people, " and not to flatter thee with a false story I cannot say I have seen two gentlemen distempered with drink since we came." He promises her that both he and his companion, Sir Robert Carr, will return to their spouses as safe as they parted from them.

A great sorrow—the first of their lives—came to darken

---

* A coloured print of Newton race-course in 1831, engraved by Charles Hunt from a painting by Charles Towne, represents the winning of the gold cup given by Thomas Legh of Lyme, " Fylde " beating " Halston " and " Recovery." This print has no artistic merit, but from its rarity is of considerable value. Such a sporting centre was Newton that cock-fighting, which had been practised for centuries in the old cock-pit, was not given up until 1831.

306

the happy family at Lyme in the early part of 1681. Two of
the children died, Sarah, aged seven, and Anne, three and a
half, within a month of each other, probably as a result of
neglected colds.

The cradle was never very far removed from the grave
in those early days, and parents bore their bereavements
with a resignation almost approaching to fatalism. Sir
Thomas Chicheley sends his condolences on February 8,
1680-1 :

> " I am confident it was the extraordinary cold that was the cause
> of your Misfortune whereof we are all shairers with you, but that which
> we have to comfort us with is that God of his infinite goodness hath
> been pleased to spaire those great blessings that are, & I doubt not
> but will every day recompense your great losse, I knowing how ready
> both you & yr wife are to make the best use of it."

By April 1681 we find that the girls, who were to be given
new gowns, which Lady Chicheley was commissioned to buy,
were to go out of mourning.

The ordinary rules with regard to this, which were very
strict, had probably been relaxed in consideration of the
extreme youth of the children. After the death of the head
of a family it was the custom for beds, and even whole rooms,
particularly those that had been occupied by the deceased, to
be entirely draped in black, and to be left so for a considerable
period—a habit that must have told seriously on both the
health and nerves of the relatives.

We hear of " stript druged [striped drugget] for ye Nursery
beds " being very dear, and varnish is sent down by Mrs.
Fountaine, " tis dear so I send but a littell for a triall. I forgott
to ask how to lay it on, but if you know not send me word
and I'le write to inquire." This was probably to be used in
connexion with " japanning," an imitation of lacquering, much
practised as a pastime by the ladies of the period. It is
mentioned frequently in letters of this date. With the formation of the East India Company in 1600 began the importation
of Oriental furniture into this country, although the great
rage for " chinoiseries " did not come until much later on, after

the experiments of Sir William Chambers * in Chinese gardening. But lacquer was already very popular at the end of the seventeenth century, and the English imitation of it—which now fetches prohibitive prices—was not restricted only to the cabinet-makers. Mr. Francis Lenygon, in his admirable work on " Furniture in England from 1660 to 1760," mentions that " the art of japanning " was being taught in girls' schools in 1688, but we have evidence in the Legh letters that as early as 1683 it was a recognized fashion, and formed one of the accomplishments of a lady of quality.

Lady Chicheley was helping to do up some of the beds :

> " You say the wrought bed is a good one, therefore will it not deserve a good Lining, I mean a Persian taffity which will not cost much more if anything than a fine Stained Calico ? My Lady Carr hath new lined her White Bed wrought with Fillamote with a Crimson Persian taffity & Chainstitched the counterpain, headcloth & tester diamond ways like Quilting, with white thrid, & trimmed it all with white thrid fringe of her own making, which altogether looks very well & fine being fashionably made up."

1682   A fourth son, Calveley, was born in August 1682. This was Elizabeth's eleventh child, and Mistress Fountaine had been at Lyme assisting in nursing her sister, and writes to Richard after her departure, giving a pathetic picture of her own unhappy domestic life :

> ". . . I protest the joyes and riall sattisfaction I have had att sweet Lime makes all things seeme dull to me here ; for without compliment I thinke itt was the only reall pleasant time I ever knew in my life before. There I found teares hard to approach my eyes, though I thought and descoursed never soe Long of my sorrows, for there I enjoy'd free & easy Conversation with Mankind which I never knew before, nor now must not expect itt till the same oppertunity returns again. Every day after diner & supper methinks I want my two Gentlemen [Richard and his brother Thomas] to take a pipe and drinke a Glasse of wine & Prate without feare of quarills or sencer [censure] for what I said or did, & then to goe up to my dearest Sister's Chamber was an unexpressible pleasure to mee ; but why doe I trouble thee with this tedious repitition of what seemes but now Like

* Sir William Chambers (1726–1796), the famous architect, had spent two years of his early youth in China.

308

RACING AND GARDENING

a pleasant dreame past and gone ; but all things in this world is to be esteem'd noe other, only 'tis a pleasure to tell a pleasant dreame, therefore beg thy excuse, for it diverts mee much att this time, I being extreamely Mallincolly att the Loss of my Lime friends."

A few days later she writes again ; much in the same strain :

" The longer I live the more I dayly find all people have really sorrows or else creates them to themselves, which to me is much more intolerable & continue longer than those God sends himself. I know you will both be glad to find my mind thus composed, but if I writt often perhaps itt may sometimes be now & then clouded, but that's nothing, for our breed you know have the flutters very often upon slight occasions."

She gives a description of a newly engaged couple, Thomas Cholmondeley * of Vale Royal, and Mistress Anne St. John, whom she finds " noe beauty tho' personable."

" I was at Battersea with Potts [a sort of housekeeper to the Chicheley family] to see the Lady St John, Mr Chombley's Mistress, and wee are hand and glove ; really I take her for a mighty good woman, and she is mighty free with us and tells us she doats of Lime already by the Commendation he gives of itt. She has had penny post letters plenty to disuade her from him, and says she believes he is a morral [immoral] for he makes nothing of courting and kissing fine Ladys before her now ; she is indeed a very pleasant companion."

She goes on to give some of the gossip of the day with the freedom of speech belonging to the period :

" Lord Hallifaxes † Daughter ‡ is married to the Lord Vaughan, & 'tis now hotly reported that Lady Henrietta Bartly Lyes Inn in the Strand and the Lord Gray vissits her every day, he being father of the

---

* Thomas Cholmondeley of Vale Royal, Cheshire, born 1627; married, first, Jane, daughter of Sir Lionel Tollemache of Helmingham, by whom he had twelve children ; secondly, 1684, Anne, daughter of Sir Walter St. John of Battersea, by whom he had four sons and one daughter. He died 1701–2.

† George Savile, first Marquess of Halifax (1633–1695), son of Sir William Savile and his wife Anne, who afterwards married Sir Thomas Chicheley. He was the author of " The Character of a Trimmer " and other admirable tracts. He married, first, Dorothy, daughter of the Earl of Sunderland by his wife Dorothy.

‡ Anne, only daughter of Lord Halifax; her father addressed to her his celebrated " Advice to a Daughter." She married as his second wife John, Lord Vaughan, afterwards third Earl of Carbery.

child. 'Tis a sad thing if true (though nothing to be wonder'd att in
that family.)

" 'Tis said Lord Hallifax is to be President of the Councell and
Seymour * Previe Seale."

The hero of the above story was Lord Grey of Werk, married
to Lady Mary Berkeley, daughter of George, first Earl of
Berkeley, a sister of the lady in question. He was convicted
of a conspiracy to carry off his sister-in-law, and fled to Holland
on the discovery of the Rye House Plot.

Richard's coach, which had taken Sarah Fountaine home,
had evidently met with an accident on its return journey,
for which she apologizes :

" Wee are not a little Troubled about your Coach being spoyled, but
I see all things in this world must have an alay [alloy] though sorry itt
Lights upon thee, but God grant thee never worse Luck ; and I am
sure you can truly forgive us who have occasioned this, for I doubt
our Mony burnt in the coachman's Pockitt and he Drunk too much as
he return'd for he drove us very Carefully, soe I hope you forgive this
one time. My Spouse went to town a Sunday and was in a very good
humour all the Time, and never said once ' why staid you soe Long ? '
My welcome was not over kind but that I never expect, soe am Content
if I escape without anger."

She was having an awful time of it, poor thing, from the
following account given by Lady Chicheley :

" Poor Mistress Fountaine hath obtained the favour from her mad husband to goe to Bellbar [the Fountaines' place] but hath to her heart's
grief left her two eldest with him, for he would not let them go, she had
no manner of government over them when here, for he would make them
what he pleased. I doubt not but Mrs Langley † hath told you the
tragicall story of his drunken ill usage of her and he is now robbing her
of what she had left of Jewells or any thing she had. Yesterday she
left the town before I could see her, and glad she was gone, for he
would faine have recanted his leave and had her live under his tyranny
still. His law sutes goe well soe thats no excuse for his passion now,
but he makes himselfe madd with debauchery and drunkenness. She
is a poore miserable creature and wants all our prayers."

* Sir Edward Seymour (1633–1708); Speaker of the House of Commons, 1661
and 1673.
† Housekeeper to the Chicheleys.

RACING AND GARDENING

On the death of Sir Robert Carr in November 1682, Sir
Thomas Chicheley was appointed Chancellor of the Duchy of
Lancaster, which gave much satisfaction to all his family.
Sir John had hoped to receive the post of Master of the Ord-
nance, but to his intense disappointment this was given to
Colonel Legge, first Baron Dartmouth : * " I cannot but think
this a great hardship done me."

Richard, whose health was in a precarious state, was in
great fear of being made High Sheriff; his father-in-law was
doing all he could to prevent this, even speaking to the King
on the subject :

> ". . . I was the other day at Newmarket where I had the good fortune
> to speak with the King who hath promised me you shall not be, but
> that he will take one of those I shall name, and as soon as I come to
> London, I will talke with Sr George Jeffreys [the notorious judge]
> about it & we will resolve who shall be the man before it comes to the
> King."

The appointment was given to Thomas, Richard's brother,
who was sent a quarter-cask of " true Canary " to celebrate
the event.

Sir Thomas Chicheley had been enjoying the society of his
eldest granddaughter Lettice,† now aged nineteen, who was
paying him a visit in London.

> " I thanke you & yr wife for the company of Lettice [he writes to his
> son-in-law], she gaines every day more & more in good opinion so that
> I think she will deserve the best match in towne for she is very good
> & very handsome."

An elderly peer, a widower, twice before married, whose name
never appears, had been paying his addresses to Lettice for
the last three years. He is described by Lady Chicheley as
having an income of £3000 a year,

> " and with 30,000¹ in his pockett, I am confident there can no falt be

* George Legge, first Baron Dartmouth (1648–1691), Admiral and Commander-in-
Chief ; created Baron Dartmouth.

† Lettice, eldest daughter of Richard and Elizabeth Legh, born 1663; married,
first, 1687, William Banks of Winstanley; secondly, Thomas Fleetwood of Bank,
Lancashire.

found in the man except one, which is perhaps you may thinke him too old, he being 2 or 3 years older then my good man, & besides the distance which she will be from you which I always thought would be the greatest difficulty. His person is very well and he lives plentifully."

But Lettice was not at all disposed to listen to the addresses of her elderly admirer.

"Deare Bro: [writes Sir John Chicheley on December 19], I should not have been so long silent could I have given such Newse of ye Love affaire as I wisht; but what ye effects of yr letter together with ye advice of Mrs Potts,* to whom I supose my Neece has with more freedome opened her mind may produce I cannot as yet tell or imagine. I am sure if her objection is not to his age I am certaine the rest is not to be dislikt; but youth sees not with ye Eyes yt age does, and if discretion might have governed I am confident we might have concluded her happyly bistowed. I will not pretend to tell you how it will be yet, more then that my Ld will nott admitte of her being prest beyond her inclination."

Richard's old aunt, Lady Calveley, was also having her say in the matter:

"I hope yt pretty daughter of yours will be persuaded, she is wise and discrete and i hop will not let soch an opertunity as this slip, thow shee cannot Love yet i hope shee may like him so well as to marry him, Love will Com after, i am very Confident many marries yt have noe great Love and yet are infinitely happy in their matches. i Cannot blame ye Lord for being in Love, the vertuous good umour of hers would make all the world in Love with her. i could almost have weeped at reading her letter, the great strat [straight] she is in."

The poor girl was evidently having great pressure put upon her, probably by her mother, who was of a masterful nature, and far more ambitious and worldly minded than her husband. Sir John Chicheley interceded for his niece, who was paying a visit to Southampton Square in January, 1682-3:

"My Neece is well as to health, only melancholy which I do suppose proceeds from ye difficulty she finds in herselfe to love or give herselfe up to be beloved. I hope Sister is so good a Christian as to forgive

* A poor relation and hanger-on of the Chicheleys.

and forget all things in relation to love Matters concerning my Neece
and ye Lord. You must be her advocate."

Lettice held out successfully and got her way. She was   1682-3
far too happy at home, nor did the prospect of making what
her relations considered to be a brilliant marriage, influence
her in the slightest degree, nor cause her to wish to change
her condition. She did not marry for another four years.

The custom of arranging marriages amongst children,
which had prevailed in early days, was continued in the seventeenth century, but not to so great an extent. Richard was
far too adoring a father to wish to coerce his children in any
matter relating to their happiness. His gentle and affectionate
disposition would have revolted against the despotic tyranny
displayed by his grandfather, Sir Peter, towards his unfortunate
son, and he had been too happy in his own marriage not to
wish his children to choose for themselves. But there were
plenty of fortune hunters amongst even his intimate friends.
His eldest son, Peter, had already been marked down at the
age of thirteen. A letter from one of his relations informs
Richard how well he had liked the boy when he saw him at
a bowling-alley, and suggests that he " had thoughts of him
for a husband for Kittie." Another friend writes, offering his
own son, whom he describes as being seventeen years old and
in a " spiritfull age for marriage if you think him worthy for
one of your daughters, which he says is a pretty one." To
both these proposals Richard returned the same answer. To
the first he writes :

> " You cannot forgett how averse I was to marriage untill I found one
> that pleased me, . . . you may remember I told you I was loath to
> engage any of my children untill they came of years to consent, . . .
> I would not engage my son at this time to the best fortune in England
> for fortunes sake, untill he come of riper years to choose for himselfe,
> for therein he will be happy or miserable."

To the second proposal he says :

> " If it please God my Godson lives and my daughter Margaret *

* Margaret, sixth daughter, married, 1712, the Rev. William Denny of Ravening-
ham, Norfolk.

untill they be of years of discretion, I should be as glad to place her in your family as to any Gent : in my neighborhood, but I would not engage either of them till they are of years to consent, because I would not do that to them which I was always unwilling should be done to myself."

1683   Elizabeth Legh went up to London to consult a doctor in the spring of 1683, and was the guest of her brother, Sir John Chicheley, and his wife, in Southampton (now Blooms-bury) Square, her daughter Lettice being with her grandfather on the opposite side of the square. Richard, busy with assizes and other work, was to join them later. He was at this time rebuilding at his own expense the ancient episcopal chapel of St. Peter at Newton, and was contributing himself and collecting from others subscriptions for the better endowment of the living. He gives his wife particulars of this matter in a letter written from Newcastle, describing the miseries of what corresponds to the Judges' Circuit of the present day. After twenty-two years of marriage, his language is still that of a young lover :

" Here I am deare Soule, very weary, but well pleased to write to thee, though I have nothing to say, but my prayers are constant for thee and thine, and lett the distance of place be what it will betwixt us, I am as neare thee and thine in affection as ever and goe as heavily from thee. We are all glad for your good news of y^r D^r. I long for the good time when I shall come, but dare not think of it untill it be nearer. . . . Beds at Lancaster bad enough and fleas a great store."

These, he assures her, were so big they barked like little dogs !

On his return to Lyme, he gives her details of the garden. This had been freshly planned and laid out, and a new gardener engaged, somewhat extortionate in his demands :

" Since my last to thee I have had some discourse with the Gardiner. He asked me at first 80^l a year to keep all the Garden & green plotts in order & to find seeds but noe flower seeds into the bargain. I stood in admiracon att his demand ; then he descended to 60^l a year & there he sticks."

All attempts to beat him down seem to have failed :

" I told him that you & I had computed itt & we thought half that sum

314

enough when all the Gardens were putt in the order we design'd them.
I told him that 50^l a year wold keep 3 men att worke the whole year
round besides himselfe & that I will say for him, he labors as hard as
any of them, & my Lady Devonshire * did not give such rates who has
3 times more Gardening & walks than we have. But under 60^l he will
not meddle."

The present garden covers about thirteen acres of ground.
It was probably larger in the seventeenth century, as remains
of walks have been found in what is now rough ground in the
park. We read of gravel walks that have to be rolled, bowling-
greens, courts, and grass-plots that have to be mown, hotbeds
" in rows," and greenhouses. For this only four regular men,
including the gardener, were kept, weeders and workmen being
brought in occasionally. The three men's united wages appear
to have been under £40 a year ; the gardener's wages and seeds
were not to exceed £80, so the whole garden must have been
run for about £100 a year.

The gardener seems to have been satisfied with his men :
" I fancy the Gardener is well pleas'd with his man Tom
Marsland," writes Richard in 1683 ; " he appeared upon
Easter day in a Sute of Clothes with gold Buttons, better
worth than 2 of my best Sutes." Sometimes, however, they
are careless :

> " Your friend Loll's son served the Gardener but ill upon Sunday—
> shold have cover'd his glasses in the hot-bed when the great thunder
> shower came & truly he was gone into the Parke to find a Stag's horn,
> I advise him to bestow a soft cudgell upon him."

Melons are mentioned in 1683. These were grown exten-
sively in France early in the seventeenth century, but appear
to have been novelties in Cheshire, at any rate, at this period.

The spring of 1683 was very cold and wet. Edward Warren
of Poynton writes to Richard, who had joined his wife in
London in May :

> " The weather heer worse then when you went hence. The price of
> corne much raysed, the best oates at near 40s 2 sacks. The stormy

---

* Wife of William, third Earl of Devonshire, second daughter of William, second
Earl of Salisbury, K.G. She died 1689, leaving issue.

wett weather and lightenings hath killed all fruit with me so that I think there will be neither cherryes, peares, plumbs nor apples in my plantation."

Great efforts were being made to get apples to flourish at Lyme. " 100 Baford Pippens and 20 other trees, Sir Henry Pickering apples," costing £3 3s., including carriage, are sent down, the gardener complaining " what a strange cold place itt is and he cannot have things soe early as his neighbours." He is obliged to admit, however, that other places have neither artichokes nor laurel. Laurels are mentioned as growing in England early in 1600 ; these and Portugal laurels and hollies were almost the only hardy evergreens and shrubs procurable in this country down to the first part of the eighteenth century. A present of " Barberys," rosemary, and vines are sent by a friend to Richard for his new garden, accompanied by the wish, expressed in delicate terms, that the vines may be as fruitful as his lady.

Soon after the return of the Legh family to Lyme in July 1683, the children became attacked with smallpox, probably contracted in London. Frances, the third daughter, was the first to fall ill, and one gets some idea from the following letters of the terror caused by this dread scourge.

Richard's sister, Lady Arderne, condoles with Elizabeth early in August :

"I did soe fully designe to have seene poore Frank as soon as my husband came home, but the news he brings me of my cosen Knight-ley * being come to Utkington, & the invitation I have from my Aunt to see her & the fears my cosen hath of the small pox of her onely son, crosses me in my full intentions & earnest desire of seeing her. . . . I heard from Stopport [Stockport] poor Frank was better, the confirmation of that news Deare Sister will much satisfie me, as of the health of the rest of the Deare Flock, & will not be wanting in my prayers. I would fain think of meeting you to-morrow somewhere neere to you if all was so well as you could leave them, God in Heaven grant mee good news of you a...."

Mistress Langley (Sir Thomas Chicheley's housekeeper) sends,

* Elizabeth Knightley, wife of Mr. Knightley of Fawsley, and daughter of John Crewe, whose wife was a Done of Utkington.

316

LYME : EAST FRONT

on the 19th from Wimpole, in great anxiety, matters being complicated by poor Elizabeth expecting the annual baby :

" MADAM,   1683

" Of Fryday last I rec^d a Letter from Mr Legh which is ye first wee have had from you since wee came to this place. It being above a week that wee was without a letter put us in to great fears and apprehensions of ill news considering ye condition yr family is in ; but God be thankt for ye good news wee have had thus farr. Wee cannot bee without fears every post expecting to heare that more of ye children is downe of ye same distemper . . . I am very glad Mistress Frances * will bee noe more mark't with them, but my great fears is for the boys, not for feare theire faces should be spoyled, for God send them but to scape with life & tis noe matter how theire beautys is, but I hope the saime providence will carry them through it as well as yr Daughters. Your father sends his Blessing to you all and desires to know when your Midwife comes to you, whoe wee hope is not affraide of coming to you because of ye Small pox."

The horrible illness dragged on for two months, Peter, the precious son and heir, being attacked last of all in October :

" Wee both rejoiced over your last letter that Peter was in a good way at the 10th day, which is the time people begin to hope the worst is passed [says Lady Chicheley], and that my Sister had had the satisfaction to be with him soe long."

Elizabeth's twelfth child—a son, John—was born early in October. All the children made good recoveries except Peter, who was longer in picking up than the others.

" We are all in very good health now, thank God [Richard reports to a friend], my son Peter visitts his Mother every day but goes not abroad untill he hath taken some physick to cleare him from that foule distemper which hath been severe with him ; the wise ones say he is not injured, & since itt hath pleased God to spare his life, 'tis that I pray'd for & am very well content."

The following August, 1684, Elizabeth Legh went up to London to stay with her father on her way to drink the waters

---

* Frances, third daughter of Richard and Elizabeth, born 1667 ; married four times, first, Robert Tatton of Wythenshawe ; secondly, Sir Gilbert Clerke ; thirdly, —— Oldfield ; fourthly, Dr. Shippen, Principal of Brazenose, Oxford.

1684 at Tunbridge Wells, taking with her Betty,* her second daughter, who had been in indifferent health since the attack of smallpox. Sir Thomas Chicheley was in a very depressed state. He had always lived above his income, and although after his second wife's, Lady Savile's, death, he had reduced his establishment, and had given up his large house in Great Queen Street and moved into a smaller one in Southampton Square, he was much in want of money. His eldest son, Tom, was unsatisfactory and had given him a lot of trouble, and his application for some court appointment had been rejected. There appeared, therefore, to be nothing for him to do but to sell Wimpole, his beautiful Cambridgeshire home, and the thought of this was breaking his heart. " Wimpole now must go," writes Sir John Chicheley to his brother-in-law in July 1684, " Sir Thomas imputes it to two accidents, ye one my Brother not doing as he would have had him, ye other in his not following my Lady Savile's advice, which was to retire and never looke towards or expect anything from ye Court."

His daughter's visit was, therefore, a great joy to the old man. She and Betty appear to have ridden on horseback as far as Stone, in Staffordshire, where they were to take the coach. A maid and two menservants accompanied them ; these last were to return to Lyme after seeing their mistress and her daughter safely into the coach. Elizabeth sends a letter to her husband from Lichfield :

" MY DEARE SOULE,
" Yesterday we got to Stone before 6 oclock but Jean I belefe lost some leather for she was not able to rid ahorse back this day, and Will Foster and Will Turner confest to Jean that they had some such grefe upon themselves, but I thanke God we are got very safe and well to this place by 11 aclock and I hope we shall have the coch [coach] to ourselves tomorrow."

She gives him directions to reckon up the charges of the garden ; he is to write out a recipe for japanning for her, and to bid Dorothy keep up her recipe book. He is also not to

* Elizabeth, second daughter of Richard and Elizabeth, born 1666, married Sir Strensham Master.

318

forget to go and see Lady Derby,* a visit of condolence on the death of her grandmother. This was the Duchess of Ormonde,† who had just died, it was said, as the result of medicine given her for a cough, to the inexpressible grief of her husband the Duke, who never got over his loss.

Like most mistresses of a household, Elizabeth considered herself indispensable, and was in great anxiety as to how they would get on without her at Lyme, where there was evidently a party which included Lord Derby.‡ Richard tells her, on August 1, of the achievements of Tom, the second boy, then aged only nine, who seems to have figured prominently in a stag hunt, organized for Lord Derby's amusement. In the description of this entertainment, Joseph Watson, the famous keeper (mentioned in a former chapter), now in the tenth year of his service, is spoken of for the first time.

> " DEAREST, This comes to relieve thee from those feares & doubts (I am sure) thou hast had since my last that told thee what company was here. We are all very well & his Lordship kept better hours than thou & I can. He is mightily in love both with Peter & Tom, to the first he lost halfe a crown at Bowles on purpose to try his humour, & he protested he never saw a more equall temper. Tom undertook (if I would give him leave) that nobody but himselfe & his Councellor Joe Keeper, would goe & gather the Stags & bring them to the Gates. My Lord thought it had been a brag, but when he saw Tom upon the little Bay Nag & a long pole of 3 yards in his fist & all the Stags walking at his command, he was very well pleas'd. The next day by 5 a Clock Tom came to my Chamber & askt me leave to call my Lord & the rest to goe hunt the outlying Stagg, which we did, & he proved the fattest & best Venison I ever did eat. The next day I made the Cooke to pott up the remainder & pray tell my Lady (Chicheley) I have 3 or 4 Potts for her against she comes back to her own house ith' Square." §

The melons, he tells her, " come on bravely."‖

* Daughter of Thomas, Earl of Ossory, wife of William, ninth Earl of Derby.
† Lady Elizabeth Preston, daughter of the Earl of Desmond.
‡ See note, p. 305.   § Raines Collection.
‖ Lady Chicheley, in a subsequent letter, sends a recipe for potting venison. " After 'tis boned, parboil it, then press the gravy out with a press, cut it in pieces or slices, season it with pepper and salt only, and so bake it in the Pot from whence 'tis never removed, but covered with butter—indeed 'tis very good."

Here is a delightful picture of Calveley, the ex-baby, then two years old :

> " Your friend Calveley chattles most mightily. Every day he gets new words. He will take poor Jackey (the monkey) about the neck & grin & pull him along till they both stare, & then Nurse chides & he turns quick upon the toe & goes off. Yesterday I tooke a deale of paines to hang up the two Pictures, & my gentlemen had found them out speedily. [He ends hoping the waters agree with her :] For the companies sake I wish myselfe there, but being attained to the age of 50 years I doe find that a mixture of wine does best agree with my constitution."

In a letter to his wife, written about this date, Richard, for the first time, makes mention of spectacles. These had been invented as early as the fourteenth century, and there were spectacle-makers in Nuremberg in 1462. Both lenses and frames were exceedingly heavy and clumsy. The latter were made in horn or tortoiseshell, to which fashion has again recently returned.

> ". . . I have been startled about 2 nights since [writes Richard] being waken'd with a pain in my right eye & a salt humour which hindered my sleep for some time, occation'd I thinke by reading soe much by Candle light, & now I thinke to use my Spectacles for I know not else how to spend my time without thee."

The happy couple were soon to be reunited ; he was to meet her at Norton, his brother-in-law Sir Richard Brooke's place, on her return from Tunbridge Wells. She begs him not to delay :

> " My deare deare Soule, I met thy vary kind letter, I shall trashur [treasure] it up amongst those things I love best, for I am shure [sure] it pleases me better then any Juell in my cabbinet. When I received thy letter I knew not whether to turn to Hadock or Norton, but I hoped thou would come hither to me and therefore I turned hither. Really I have not been warm in bed since thou left me, therefore have what pity thou canst upon her that is intirely thine whilst
>
> " E. L."

Of a headstrong, masterful nature, the one soft spot in the character of Elizabeth Legh was her adoration of her husband.

RACING AND GARDENING

This love, as intense as his for her, shines out through all her ill-spelt and worse-written letters. Her children counted as nothing in comparison with her husband. He was her whole life, the beginning and end of her existence, and through the twenty-six years that their marriage lasted her love grew in depth and intensity, retaining all its romance and early freshness up to the very end.

CHAPTER XXII

POLITICS AND PLOTS

1683 Among the Legh MSS. is a series of newsletters describing the preparations of the French, in 1683, for assuming a fresh offensive against the Algerine pirates, who had for long been a terror and a dread to the European Powers. A squadron of our ships was sent out from England to assist in the work.

There is also an account of the invasion of Austria by the Turks, and a newsletter of the time gives details of the relief of Vienna, after a siege which lasted from July until September. This may not be devoid of interest, as showing the measures adopted by the belligerents of the seventeenth century, not unlike those used in the present great war :

"September 12, 1683 :

" We have had severall Relations from Vienna and all supported with great confidence, but none so particular as that which came yesterday by the French Packquet, which gives advice that Vienna was in a great straight by loss of men and by sickness in the Town and scarcity of amunition, and that the Miners, hearing the Turkes at work and under the Bastion of the Court, they wrought to counter them, but finding the Turkes had given over working and concluding that they were ready to close up the Mine, Count Staremberg * went into the Vault himself and wrought with the Miners till they pierct the Turk's Mine, where they found a prodigious quantity of Barrels of gunpowder ready disposed for the blow. This they took out and filled up the Mine so as to make it unserviceable to the Enemy, in so much that

---

* Count Guido Staremberg (1657–1737), Austrian general took part in the defence of Vienna in 1683 and in many later campaigns.

when the Turkes gave fire to the train and disposed themselves to fall in with the breach, they were in great amazement to find that it took no effect, whereupon the Imperialists sally'd out and did great execution upon the Turks, burnt the ffaggotts they had laid for the advantage of scaling, and by taking this blessed opportunity, saved the towne."

While these stirring events were taking place abroad, the discovery of the Rye House Plot was causing the greatest agitation and excitement in England. A large number of persons were implicated in this conspiracy, Monmouth included. The first mention of this attempt on the life of the King appears in the Legh letters at the end of June 1683, when an anonymous correspondent states that the King had openly expressed greater displeasure towards his son than he had ever been known to do before,

" has forbidden his coming to Whitehall or any part of St. James's, whether His Majesty be in this Towne or not; he has likewise pub- liquely declared that any Servant of his or dependant upon himself or the Courte that shall either goe to him (Monmouth) or howlde any conversation with him shall never serve him an hower after he knows it." Another letter mentions that "His Majesty hath been pleased to order all the Keyes of his Lodgings to bee Altered & yt noe person shall be admited to Lodge in Whitehall but his Mat^{ys} immediate Servants."

Monmouth was supposed to have taken ship from Chichester, but other accounts report his presence still in London.

Sir Richard Brooke, Richard's brother-in-law, had a narrow escape of being involved in the Rye House Plot, but was saved by Sir Thomas Chicheley, a *persona grata* at Court, who proved Brooke's innocence to the King.

Many friends of the Legh family were amongst those who suffered rightly or wrongfully. Charles Gerard, first Earl of Macclesfield,* and his son, Lord Brandon,† were both con- demned to death but pardoned. Others who were arrested

---

* Great-great-grandson of Sir Gilbert Gerard, Master of the Rolls.
† Charles, Viscount Brandon, eldest son of Charles, Earl of Macclesfield.

were Sir John Trenchard,* acquitted; Henry Booth,† afterwards Lord Delamere, committed but released on bail, and
Algernon Sidney,‡ executed in December of this same year.
Piers Legh § of Bruch writes Richard the following account
of the death of the Earl of Essex,‖ which occurred in the Tower
in July 1683, but whether by suicide or by order of the Court
was never known :

" London July ye 14th 1683.

"WORTHY Sʀ

"I make bold to trouble you with ye unexpected news wᶜʰ few
people ever thought of; yesterday morning about 10 ye King and ye
Duke of York went for pleasure to looke through ye Tower; in ye
mean time my Ld of Essex haveing a guilty conscience, which needs
noe other accuser, with a rasor cut his own Throat, yt ye Blood with a
shower of Raine together ran downe to ye Traitor's Gate; ye same
day my Lord Russell, Capt Walcot, Rouse & Hone was tryed at the
old Balife [Bailey] and all brought in guilty of High Treason and this
day I heard sentence pronounc'd against yem but for ye time of execution I can give noe account of. There is every day new discoveries
made, I wish all our Country Gentlemen be free."

A subsequent letter states that the corpse of the unfortunate
Earl of Essex was buried in the vault of his ancestors without
any ceremony, and that the King afterwards received his son
" with all ye marks of love and kindness," bidding him follow
in the steps of his grandfather ¶ (beheaded for loyalty to
Charles I), " and that he would then be a friend to him and
love him."

The Russells were intimate friends of both the Leghs and
Chicheleys, but beyond passing references to the trial in the
Legh letters of the time, no comment is made upon Lord

---

* Sir John Trenchard (1640–1695), Secretary of State, shared in plots.

† Henry Booth, second Baron Delamere and first Earl of Warrington; sentenced
to death, but bribed Jeffreys and was pardoned.

‡ Algernon Sidney (1622–1683), son of second Earl of Leicester; executed
December 1683.

§ Piers Legh of Bruch, only son of Piers Legh (son of old Sir Peter); he fought
at Sedgemoor and died of decline in October of that same year, 1683.

‖ Arthur Capel, first Earl of Essex (1631–1683); associated with Monmouth's
schemes; sent to the Tower, found with his throat cut.

¶ Arthur Capel, first Baron.

POLITICS AND PLOTS

Russell's * fate. The following short account of his execution is sent to Richard in a newsletter dated July 21 :

> " This day about a quarter past 10 ye Lord Russell was brought from 1683 Newgate in his own Coach to Lincoln's Inn Fields, where a Scaffold was Errected for his Execution. As soone as he came upon ye Scaffold he pulled off his hatt & Bowed himself ; The fields & houses were all Crowded with people. After he had walked four Turnes upon ye Scaffold betwene Dr Burnett † & Dr Tillottson ‡ who came from Newgate with him, he pulled out a paper and Read with much Containe about 4 Lines, then he prayed as did all ye people on ye Scaffold with him, after which he walked 2 or 3 Turnes more & there prayed by himself, a Little time after which he pulled off his perruwhigg, Cravatt & Coate himself and gaue it to his Seruant, putting on a white Satten Wast coate, laid his head on ye Block which at 3 Blowes was Severed from his Body by ye hands of ye common Executioner. His head & Body was put into a Black Coffin & then put into a hearse and Carried to Bedford House in ye Strand."

The correspondent allows himself this one comment : " How he lived I know not, but he died bravely and like a Christian."

Two troops of " Granadeers " were now to be raised for the protection of the King. The formation of this regiment (the 1st battalion of the Grenadier Guards) dates from 1656, when Charles II first raised his standard in Flanders. This was followed by a great response in England, Irish and Scotch regiments being also formed. So eager were the officers to join that they willingly accepted a lower rank than that to which they had already risen, in order to form part of the new King's Guard.

Something of the same spirit seems to have animated the youth of the day thirty years later, when we hear in the midst of all the excitement of the plot that " 100 young gentlemen all of very good estates have resolved to forme themselves into a Troop of Horse and to waite on his Majesty as a Guard to

---

* William, Lord Russell, "the patriot," beheaded 1683; married Lady Rachel, daughter of the Earl of Southampton, and widow of Lord Vaughan.
† Gilbert Burnet, Bishop of Salisbury (1643–1715), the historian.
‡ John Tillotson, Archbishop of Canterbury (1630–1694); descended from the Cheshire Tilstons.

325

his person without expecting any Reward." Charles was much pleased with this spontaneous mark of affection, and appointed the Earl of Ossory, son of the Duke of Ormonde, in command of the Troop. The officers were to keep two servants apiece, " well horsed, armed and to be Ready on all occasions."

The marriage of the Princess Anne to Prince George of Denmark took place at the end of July 1683. Lady Chicheley expresses her opinion on the appearance of the bridegroom (whom another correspondent describes as " much an Englishman as to his person ") in a letter of July 26 :

> " Prince George will not be married till Satterday or Sunday. He is noe beauty but well enough, at least for a Prince ; neither doe I heare now nor doth it appear in his face that he drinkes, for that is a quallity will not recommend him to the Duke."

On the 31st, the Lords and Court of Aldermen went in their scarlet robes to Whitehall to wait upon the bride and bridegroom and congratulate them on their marriage.

By December 1683 we hear of the Duke of Monmouth back at Court, and the King and Duke of York " very kind to him." This was within a day or two of the execution of Algernon Sidney.

The Court was spending a good deal of time at Winchester, where Charles II was building himself a palace after designs supplied by Wren. This, it was thought, would become a more popular resort than Newmarket, the King intending to use his new palace during the racing season. He died, however, before the building was completed.

Intriguing for party and place was going on to the same extent as ever. A letter from Sir Peter Shakerley,* dated May 1684, beseeches the help of Richard in obtaining some money due to him from the Crown, assuring him at the same time that the Whig party is capable of any atrocity, even that of " removing the Lord of Lime if it were in their power." In this same letter occurs the expression " taking snuff," as applied to offence given or received.

On February 6, 1684–85, Charles II died, cynical and witty to the last.

* Governor of Chester Castle.

CHAPTER XXIII

AN INFANT LEGISLATOR

THE accession of James II and his promise to preserve the 1684–5
laws and protect the Church was welcomed by the Nation with
enthusiasm. He had always been a good friend to the Legh
family, and Sir Thomas Chicheley was full of admiration of
his character.

> " You see how sudden & great a change we have had [he writes to
> Richard on February 17, 1684–5], I thanke God he hath been mighty
> good to us in blessing of us with such a King that I think all his subjects
> have reason to rejoyce at, for he is full of goodnesse & great justice &
> I doubt not but will make us infinitely happy if we have not a rebellious
> nature amongst us which delights in Mischiefe."

It was necessary to summon a Parliament to obtain money
for the new King, the Royal revenue having ceased with the
death of his predecessor. Richard was much pressed to stand
for Cheshire, the King expressing great desire that he should
do so.

> " It is much desired at Court, you have shown y'self an honest man &
> a good subject, as the King saith & he did it with great kindness to
> you, I dare not say how well he thought of you, for feare I make you
> too proud, for you are in very good esteeme and I would have you
> preserve it [says his worldly-minded father-in-law. Sir John
> Chicheley adds his entreaties :] 'Tis absolutely concluded yt none but
> you and Mr Cholmely can carry it for the county."

But Richard had no desire to take up public life again.
Had he stood anywhere it would have been for his own borough
of Newton, but he was in very indifferent health, so he, therefore, hurried up to London to see the King and explain to His
Majesty how for this reason he was unable to stand again for

Parliament. So lame was he that he had not ridden out of his park all winter :

> " also several worthy gentlemen might take it ill from me & indeed it looks a little vain in me to stand here to put them out when I can with ease come in att my own place (Newton) where I design to put in my own son' with Sir John Chicheley, & his vote is as good as mine. I hope the King will not take it ill at me when I send him one that can serve him better than I can."

He was being pressed to give his support to would-be candidates for Lancashire, amongst others Lord Colchester,* who was most anxious to obtain the good offices of the Baron of Newton. " I hope that you will give me your interest as knight of the shire for Lancashire, where I intend to stand if I have encouragement that my friends think well of me." But Lord Colchester's record was not a satisfactory one. He had been suspected of joining with Lord Macclesfield as an adherent of Monmouth, and Richard was suspicious of him, although he had consented to present him to the King.

1684–5

> " Concerning Lord Colchester standing for Lancashire [he writes from St. James's to an unknown correspondent on February 28], I have by this post intimated privately to my Lord Derby yt his appearing for Lord Colchester [his brother-in-law] in ye Election will by no means be acceptable here, his Lordship [Colchester] must first give some further proofs of his repentance & future good intentions before he have any encouragement or countenance from hence to come into a Parlt. I doe really wish his Lordship well, & do really believe him a convert or I wold not (as I did) have brought him to ye King, but at this time his friends will be kind to him in persuading him not to stand."

It was hoped by some of his friends that Richard would come up to London, specially to take part in the coronation festivities, bringing his family with him. Mistress Fountaine did her best to persuade him to do so, assuring him that it was expected of him, and that he must not let the expense of women's clothes, " usually a terror to Country Gentlemen," prevent his paying his respects to his new sovereign. On

* Viscount Colchester, eldest son of Thomas, Earl Rivers. He married Lady Charlotte Stanley, daughter of Charles, eighth Earl of Derby.

AN INFANT LEGISLATOR

March 8, 1684–5, she sends him one of her quaintly worded epistles :

> " DEAREST BROTHERE ;
> " However the fates have order'd itt of Late I know not, but methinkes 'tis a Long time since you and I did converse with each other, so that the sight of thy sweet fist did rejoyce mee. I heare you are a favorrit att Court and of late have got a place of great honner, soe that I dout [doubt] you will grow proud. Truely I wish heartily itt would exalt you to town suddenly, for sure you ought to Come kiss the King's hand, and bring your wife and children to see the Corronation, and I will meet you and at this time you Cannot plead the expence of women Cloths (which is usually a terror to Country Gentlemen). I am glad to heare Munkey is well."

From a rough copy he had made of his answer to his sister-in-law, Richard gives his reasons for abstaining from attending :

> " Being capable of no honour I can receive none and for the same reason, being old [he was only fifty-one] & useless to the affaires above, I chuse to sitt quiett at home & besteward itt for my children."

He confined himself, therefore, to celebrating the auspicious 1685 event in his own part of the world, directing " bonefires," a huge one being erected in Stockport market-place, and organizing the customary processions, fireworks, and " other triumphs."

The following letter from Piers Legh of Bruch, second cousin of Richard, gives a short account of the coronation of James II and his queen, which took place on April 23, 1685 :

> " DEAR S^R
> " I'm just got home from ye Coronation of our K. and Queen ; all things was performed in ye most splendid manner yt ever was seen or heard of in ye world before. Ye Queen and ladies giving ye greatest splendour to ye whole Matter. Ye whole glory of ye nation appear'd at ye solemnity excepting ye familey at Lime, which I hartely wish't for if it could have suited their convenience ; few bad accidents have hapen'd, onely a Gentleman of Grayes Inn, whose name I cannot informe you of, fell downe from off ye scaffold & broke his necke before ye procession."

Incredible though it sounds, Richard actually contemplated and succeeded in getting his eldest son Peter, aged only *sixteen*, named as a candidate for the borough of Newton, in company with Sir John Chicheley. A Mr. Bretherton, the nominee of the " Free Burgesses," hotly opposed the candidature of the youth, but his objections were overruled, the Legh influence proving too strong, and the baby legislator was duly returned with his uncle on April 25, 1685. His grandfather, highly delighted, sends blessings to the young commoner, who was henceforth to take up his quarters with the Chicheley family in Southampton Square. His Uncle Thomas, who had been returned M.P. for Liverpool Borough, with the Mayor, Sir Richard Atherton, accompanied the boy to London, and reports, on May 14, their safe arrival, " no misfortune nor disaster I thanke God intervening."

There appears to have been some doubt in the mind of Sir John as to the reception that would be accorded to the young statesman, and he seems to have expected that objections might be made by the sitting members to the introduction of so juvenile an addition to their august assembly.

" Deare Bro : [he writes to Richard on May 19]. This morning we met and tooke ye Oathes, after which I carry'd my Nephew into our House, where I found severall Members tooke Notice of his youthfulness, but to keep us ye better in Countenance, ye Lord Plymouth's * son appeared, whose lookes did not so well quallifie him for a law-maker as Peter's. [He mentions also seeing Mr. Bretherton], our antagonist who I am told designs to petition, . . . but what will not a vaine conceited fool doe ! "

A few days later Peter sends his first impressions of the House of Commons in a well-written and well-expressed letter to his father, and with the tone and seriousness of a person twice his age :

" London May 23, 1685.

" DEAR S^R

" Upon Wednesday & Thursday very little was done but Swearing. Then upon Friday wee went to the house of Lords where the King gave us his Speech, with great satisfaction to us all. Immediately we return to our house again where the first thing wee went about was

* Thomas Windsor, first Earl of Plymouth, married a daughter of Lady Savile, Sir Thomas Chicheley's second wife, by her first husband, Sir William Savile.

330

AN INFANT LEGISLATOR

Settling the King's Revenew, which was agreed upon presently and no one took exception against it. After that the Black Rod came in and told us that we must wait upon the King at four a clock in the afternoon at the Banqueting House, where the King gave us thanks for what we had done, and all the Spectators said that they never saw him look so pleasantly before as he did this day. This morning we went to the house again where this bill was agreed upon. That this House will Stand by his Majesty with their lives & Fortunes against Archbold Camoden [Archibald Campbell] the pretended Earle of Argyll * and his adherents and all Rebells, Traitors and others whatsoever shall assist him or them. After that very little else was done but the wrangling petitioners, but Bretherton's petition I do hear nothing of yet. This day the Lord Willoughby stood and desired that the Minors Might be turned out of the house, which Mr Speaker told him it shall be considered upon, but it will come to a debate (I do believe !) and this Willoughby was one himself when he was under age, & he is not very much more. If it be so, then I shall have Company enough . . . here is noe more news as I do know   So I rest

"Yr obedient Son

"P. Legh.

"Pray my duty to my Mother & love to my Sisters."

It will be observed that whereas he ends by sending love to his sisters, his duty is all he ventures to offer to his mother.

A movement was set on foot for ejecting all minors, but the debate was adjourned, "in case they be excluded I wish it be not the means of bringing Bretherton into the House." Opinions differed in Newton itself, where amongst the opposite party the betting was five to one that Bretherton would be a burgess for Newton before the end of the Parliament. Other and weightier matters were, however, occupying the attention of the House, so the question of the exclusion of minors was dropped for the time being, and Peter remained unmolested.

The Monmouth Rebellion was one of the great excitements of the year 1685. The accession of James II had been fatal to Monmouth's hopes, so he now entered upon a desperate attempt to stir up the spirit of fanaticism in Scotland and the West of England, in which enterprise he was assisted by

* Archibald Campbell, ninth Earl of Argyll, opposed James II's arbitrary measures; joined in Monmouth rebellion; executed after Sedgemoor at Edinburgh without trial.

the Earl of Argyll. They sailed from Holland within a few days of each other, Argyll undertaking the Northern expedition, the rebel Duke the other.

The militia was called out, the Deputy-Lieutenants were all given strict injunctions to " be watchfull and employ your utmost care, to agree amongst yourselves to have 2 at least of your number constantly together in some convenient and certain place in the County . . . to oppose all villanous designes," and to disarm all dangerous and suspected persons. The searching for arms was to be left to them to use their own discretion in as they should think fit. Richard made himself very active in looking up those of his neighbours whom he feared were of doubtful loyalty, and in seeking to inspire in lukewarm spirits a sense of their duty to King and country.

Monmouth meantime landed at Lyme Regis, on June 11 ; the following extract is from a letter of Sir John Chicheley's, written on the 13th :

> " The Duke of Monmouth landed at Lime Thirsday night last about ten of ye clocke with about two hundred jentlemen all well armed. They tooke possession of ye Towne and pitcht his colours in a place called ye Bowlingreene, and declared he comes against Popery and Arbitrary Power ; the partys who gives this information was this morning with us at ye Barre of ye House, and came from thence Thirsday night, they heard the Duke tell a man who came to offer his service yt he would take care of them all, and yt as for Armes he had enough for all yt would come to him."

Monk, Duke of Albemarle, who was Colonel of First Horse and Captain of all the King's Guards, was meantime raising the militia of Devon and Cornwall, and was waiting in readiness for the advance of the rebels ; Sir John goes on to say :

> " The Duke of Monmouth is within two miles of Tauntondeane, one of ye most factious Townes in all England, and where ye Duke without all doubt does expect ye considerablest part of his forces ; the Duke of Albemarle is not farre from them ; there's orderd to March some of ye Standing forces both Horse, Foot and Dragoons, but tis not possible for them to reach his Grace these five days at soonest, it being above a hundred Miles thither."

AN INFANT LEGISLATOR

He adds a postscript to the effect that Monmouth was sup- posed to have returned to Lyme Regis "in order to reembark himselfe and all his forces in case he's prest by ye Duke of Albemarle, who they say has four thousand horse and foot not far off ye place where Monmouth is."

Peter, still in London, writes to his mother an undated letter early in July, giving interesting details of what was going on :

> " Dear Madam,
>
> ". . . the last post I writ my Father word that the Monmouth was landed at Lime in Dorsetshire and had two hundred men, now he has very near three thousand with him. Yesterday in the Parliament house wee had his declaration read, wherein he said that the Duke of York had no right to the Crown & yt wee had Murdered his Father, and withall said wee was a Pack Parliament, but if he was King he would have a free Parliament, and a great deal more to this purpose. After it was read we ordered it Should be burnt by the Common hangman before the Royal Exchange, & wee have ordered that 1000 Ps be set upon his head for any man that will bring him alive or dead. Wee expect every hour to hear when the Duke of Albemarle has ingaged him, wee are all up in Arms here for fear of the worst. My Lord Brandon has kist the Kings hand & likewise my Lord Delamere . . .
>
> " Pray my duty to my Father & love to my Sisters
> " So Dear Madam
>   " Your Affectionate Son P : Legh."

With reference to Peter's statement concerning Lord Delamere's kissing the King's hand, Lord Derby had, in a letter to Richard dated June 24, stated that he was " absolutely of opinion that Lord Delamere should be secured, and I think Stockport is as fit a place as any, but I leave it to you."

If Lord Delamere was apprehended, he must have been released soon after. He was thoroughly untrustworthy, for he had been concerned in the Rye House Plot and released on bail, was then mixed up in the Monmouth Rebellion, but acquitted, and finally went over to the Prince of Orange in 1688.

A proclamation from the King to Lord Derby and the

Deputy-Lieutenants of Cheshire and Lancashire commanded them to seize and apprehend " all disaffected and suspicious persons, particularly all Nonconformist ministers and such persons, as have served against our Royal Father or Royal Brother of blessed memory, and send them in safe Custody to Chester to be secured there."

The rounding up of all suspected persons was, therefore, proceeded with. The Deputy-Lieutenants, whose signatures include that of Richard Legh—with Lord Derby's at the head—sent an answer to His Majesty that many leading men in the country had been secured, Sir Thomas Mainwaring,* Sir Robert Duckenfield,† Mr. Legh of Booths,‡ etc. They begged, how-ever, for instructions as to how to deal with " those who are old and decrepit, not well able to goe to Chester, we keep them all under a gard & their horses, most of them are for the Coach & troublesome for us to keep, having no horse meat in our Country to keep them in ye house." How this difficulty was overcome history does not state.

A haul of twenty-five rapiers and fourteen guns was the result of search made through the neighbouring townships, the list containing such weird implements as " a simeter, a little short tucke, a gun without a Locke," etc.

An interesting, undated letter from Piers Legh of Bruch, who had enlisted in Lord Feversham's § army, written just before the Battle of Sedgemoor, probably on July 5, the battle taking place on the 6th, gives an account of the plundering and outrages committed by Monmouth's followers, much resembling those of the Germans at the present day :

"DEAR S^R

" As I thought it ye Duty of all yong idle fellowes as I am to serve his King against all rebellious villans, I came volantere into my Lord

---

* Sir Thomas Mainwaring, of Over Peover, M.P. for Chester, 1660.

† Sir Robert Duckenfield, son of the Colonel Duckenfield who was in the service of the Parliament.

‡ Peter Legh of Booths, married a daughter of Robert Barcroft of Barcroft, Lancashire.

§ Louis Duras, second Earl of Feversham (1640–1709), General; commanded James II's troops at Sedgemoor, 1685.

Feversham's Army; about 10 days agoe (we had) a very little scirmage 1685
at Philips Norton where we thought to have made sure of the Enemy.
He deceived us in ye night time & marcht all his army to a towne ye
call Frome, & has still been a days march before us. We are now got
to ye County Towne in Somersetshire 10 miles from ye Enemy who is
making what fortification he can to a towne called Bridgwater, & if he
stayes there we shall certainly make an end of this troublesome
business in a few dayes time. In ye enemies late marches they have
been forced to plunder townes for subsistance, he giving them noe pay.
Ye last town they pillaged was Wells in Somersetshire, where they got
some little amunition tho' not much. Ye traitorous villains have
defaced most Churches they come near, as shaving [?] thro ye orgaines,
feeding their horses upon ye Comunion table, & such like revengefull
tricks they have put upon God's house, which they are to smart for
in a little time. To-morrow if ye enemy stayes us we are to encamp
as near them as possible we can, soe we shall force them to Battle or
Starve them out."

The official account of the Battle of Sedgemoor, details
of which were supplied by Colonel Oglethorpe,* was sent
from Whitehall to Lyme on July 7. From this document
we learn that Lord Feversham's army, about 2500 strong,
took up a position on Sedgemoor Plain, near the village of
Weston, having in front of it a deep ditch or drain which
traversed the moor. The rebels, who numbered between
5000 and 6000, attempted a surprise on the night of the
5th, but Lord Feversham having received notice of this,
was prepared for them when they advanced " with a great
volley of shott and shouts which was returned by ours
in ye same manner." Checked by the deep drain, the
rebel forces were completely broken by the Royal Horse;
" 3 pieces of cannon, all they had " were taken with about
400 killed, " the rest being pursued into ditches & Inclosures
& great Slaughter was made of them, in all about 2000 men."

The Duke of Monmouth's " vale de Chamber " was captured
with his master's coat, " which he usually wore, and 200
Guineys, all ye moneys he had Left."

Lord Churchill, afterwards the great Duke of Marlborough,

* Sir Theophilus Oglethorpe (1650–1702), Brigadier-General; served in
Charles II's Life Guards; led the charge at Sedgemoor.

much distinguished himself, as did also the Duke of Grafton *
(second son of Charles II by Barbara Villiers); while Lord
Colchester entirely recovered his reputation, and is reported
as having "behaved himself in all the businesse as well
as any Man could possibly have done." Of the King's
forces 200 were returned as killed, "none of them of any
note."

The following letter from Colonel Werdon, the noted
Royalist, Comptroller to the King when Duke of York, was
also sent to Lyme the day after the battle :

> "This morning early, Oglethorpe came Expresse with the happie
> Newes of the Totall defeat of the Rebells in the West. Above 2000
> of them were left deade upon the place, the rest all dispersed and
> pursued, and not one man of Note of the King's syde kild that wee
> heare of. Capt Sands is hurt; Lord Dunblane shott in the shoulder,
> one Chevalier Dangerously wounded and Col Finch of ye bed-chamber
> slightly hurt, and these are all that Oglethorpe or Mr May (who was
> prisoner with them untill they were routed) can tell us of. More
> particulars wee are expecting from Lord Feversham this Night or in
> the Morning. . . . The rebells marcht out of Bridgwater in the night
> and at peep of day fired over a bank many round vollies into the King's
> Campe, but as soon as the Horse & ffoot began to charge them they
> broake & routed, their Horse first with Lord Gray † in the Head of
> them, at which Monmouth cried out Aloud 'That Cowardly Rascall
> hath undon us all,' and soe itt seemed, for his Army stood not at all,
> unless some particular obstinate Syth-men [scythemen] & Clubb men,
> most of which dyed for it as all did, until the Souldiers were weary of
> killing.
>
> "The King knighted Oglethorpe by the Queen's bed syde after
> hee had told all hee could in her hearing."

Monmouth escaped, but was captured shortly after the
battle and beheaded on Tower Hill on July 15. The following

---

* Henry Fitzroy, first Duke of Grafton, married a daughter of Henry Bennet,
Earl of Arlington.

† Forde, third Lord Grey of Werk, afterwards Earl of Tankerville ; was convicted of a conspiracy to carry off his sister-in-law, Lady Henrietta Berkeley ;
escaped to Holland. From there he accompanied Monmouth on his attempted invasion of England ; he was at the Battle of Sedgemoor, where, owing to his cowardice,
his troops were routed. He was captured, turned King's evidence, revealed all he
knew of the plot and the names of his accomplices. After the accession of William III
he was created Earl of Tankerville. He died in 1701.

letter from Piers Legh of Bruch describes the execution, of which he himself was witness :

" London July 16, 1685.

" HonRD S_R

"Yesterday ye Duke of Monmouth was executed on Tower Hill. He behaved himself verry soldier like uppon ye scaffold. He had with him all ye night before he died ye Bishop of Bathenwells & ye Bishop of Ely, who both waited on him to ye place of execution, he has made noe speech yt I hear of, but ye say he did disown his mariage with ye Dutches,* being it was a forced marriage, & yt he was precontracted before he knew his Duchess to my Lady Henrietta Wentworth,† whom he has lived with for this two last years, as he called it very Chastely, & yt they had committed no sin together because they were man & wife. As he went out of ye Tower he took little notice of his Duches, but gave his Children his blessing and bid them be dutyfull to ye King. Severall carriages of prisoners are brought to town this day, who are to be sent as fast as possible after their leader."

It is generally supposed that Monmouth died craven and supplicating to the last. The above letter, however, disposes of this idea, and shows that, whatever cowardice he may have displayed during his last interview with James II, when the supreme moment came he met his fate with both courage and dignity.

* Lady Anne Scott, Countess of Buccleuch.

† Lady Henrietta, Baroness Wentworth, mistress of the Duke of Monmouth, lived with him in Holland.

CHAPTER XXIV

DEATH OF RICHARD LEGH

1685 PARLIAMENT adjourned in the summer of 1685 to enable Judge Jeffreys to hold in the Western Counties what will always be known as the Bloody Assizes. Hundreds of persons, some quite old women, were condemned to death on the merest suspicion of high treason, others suffered for harbouring or sheltering so-called rebels. A newsletter written to Lyme in October 1685 gives a list of many condemned to be hanged, drawn, and quartered, " and Mistress Gaunt to be burnt." This unfortunate woman, the last of her sex to be executed for a political offence, was burnt at Tyburn for sheltering Burton, a Rye House conspirator and an adherent of Monmouth. Whether James II was entirely responsible for all these outrages it is hard to say, but we may give him the benefit of the doubt. A letter from Judge Jeffreys—a copy of which is among the Legh papers—apologizes to Sir Roger Bradshaigh of Haigh for

> " the impudent behaviour of the King's soldiers at Wigan, which I dare assure you gave as great a disturbance to him as anything that ever happened since he came to the Crown, that he will have them recompense the injury they have suffered under the pretence of his authority, and has commanded me to let you know that if they are not able to make sattisfaction, that he will do it out of his own purse."

Happily for the Legh family, Richard was in high favour with the King, and appears even to have won the respect of the infamous judge himself, a letter of the time speaking of the admiration the Lord Chancellor felt for him.

Young Peter Legh was in London all through the spring and early summer, attending assiduously to his Parliamentary duties under the watchful eyes of his grandfather and uncles. He had been enrolled in some form of militia, and we hear of him " following his exercises " amongst other young men of " ye Blade."

> " I have lent my nephew ye Coach this morning [writes Sir John Chicheley on March 6, 1685–6] to goe to High Parke to see ye three troups of Gards and two Regiments of foot exercise before his Majesty which 'tis said will be very fine. Y^r son has now begun to learne ye Exercise of his Armes according to ye New Moode, as is now in ye Gards and abroad in ye French Army. I hope before he leaves this place he'l be expert in them . . . y^t I may put him into a Garbe proper for a young Cavalier to appear in coming home after so long an absence."

Peter was a delicate boy, constantly suffering from colds and " agues " and threatened with lung trouble ; his relations were very anxious about him on this account, more so even than were his parents. Both Sir John and Lady Chicheley write reporting a serious illness in May of this same year, 1686 : " he goes not abroad yet, the weather is too churlish."

By the end of July the boy was back at Lyme, accompanied 1686 by his Uncle Thomas, and it must have been intense relief to the fond parents, in times of such peril and danger, to get him back to the safe shelter of Lyme. He brought with him many injunctions from his relatives that he was to be well taken care of, above all things he was not to be allowed to go nutting, " nothing being more unwholesome then Nutts, especially for the lungs." The boy had won golden opinions from his grandfather, who reports him as " good in all respects and I misse him." A beautifully written and charmingly worded letter of thanks from Peter to his grandfather assures the latter that he shall make it the study of his whole life to " deserve that character of me which you are sure to give."

Legible writing was considered to be of great importance in the seventeenth century. Richard wrote a beautiful hand himself and expected his children to do the same. At the age of sixteen, and not very long before his entry into Parliament, Peter was still being made to write copies. Amongst the

Legh MSS. is a small scrap of paper ornamented with a pattern of elaborate flourishes in red and green ink, and the following sentence is written six times over in a neat copperplate hand : " Prayer wings the pious Soul and makes her fly, P Legh."

His handwriting compares very favourably with the untidy scrawl of the schoolboy of to-day.

By November we hear of him back in London with his Uncle Thomas. The journey seems to have been performed on horseback, " the roads very plashy and dirty, but good accoutrements secures our healths."

Mistress Fountaine, writing from Wimpole, where she had been escorted by her father, whom she disrespectfully designates as " ye old blade," talks of taking a house near the Temple at £5 a month, and hopes to see something of her nephew : "Dear Peter sends me word he thinks the town a dull place without me which I assure him I take for a great honner from such a pritty fellow, for 'tis strange he should think an old woman & an Ant a diversion, but on my conscience if I live to a hundred I shall love Lads & Lasses company." She is more than ever " out of conceit " with matrimony, and speaks doubtfully of some companion of her good-for-nothing husband, " men are cattle I always am fearfull of."

In a letter of about this date we read of fox-hunting for the first time in the Legh correspondence. It is mentioned in English records as early as the fourteenth century, but until the seventeenth the fox was hunted for purposes of extermination only, and not for sport. The animal was driven into nets or hunted to earth and dug out. By the middle or end of the seventeenth century, however, the sport attained greater dignity ; packs of hounds were kept by private individuals, including, it is said, the Duke of Monmouth. By 1686, therefore, it was becoming universally popular, and Sir John Chicheley, writing to Richard in the early part of that year, mentions the fact that Peter " has pretensions to fox-hunting, tho' as yet his hands are so tender he cannot hold his Reins nor governe his horse." Later on in life Peter became himself the owner of hounds as well as of race-horses.

340

LYME: ENTRANCE TO THE COURTYARD

LYME: WEST SIDE OF THE COURTYARD

DEATH OF RICHARD LEGH

Meantime, building and alteration to the house was still going on at Lyme. Richard had been making changes in the kitchen (which faces due south, as is the case in so many old houses) and other offices, and was planning the beautiful saloon, which was to be hung with carvings by Grinling Gibbons. This room is on the first floor facing due south, and is one of the most charming and livable in the house. It has been found difficult to establish its exact date within thirty years, and this has been a subject of much dispute, as has also the authenticity of the Gibbons carving. In a letter of Sir John Chicheley, bearing date November 9, 1684, there appears the only mention among all the Legh letters of the Grinling Gibbons carving : " I shall talke Mr Gibbons concerned a peece of carved worke." Dr. Pococke, in his " Tour in England in 1750 " (which will be quoted again later), speaks of Lyme and mentions the carvings in the house as being by Grinling Gibbons. This is very good (though not quite contemporary) evidence. We know that most of the house, during the previous thirty-five years, had been completely altered and Italianized in accordance with the fashion of the day, and it is more than probable, therefore, that Richard, having given the order for the carving, which tradition states took seven years to execute, began the room, but died before its completion.

The room, which is 23 feet by 33, with a height of 16 feet 6 inches, has three windows facing south, looking on to the great balcony under the portico which was built by Giacomo Leoni * in 1726. The whole room is composed of six great panels of oak (alternating with double fluted Corinthian pilasters) which form the background to the carving. This is treated in the most original way, and is laid on in the centre of each panel from the cornice to within about a foot and a half of the dado, instead of being used as a framework, as is most of the Grinling Gibbons carving that one sees. Another instance of the carving occupying the centre of the panel is seen, I believe, in one of the Oxford colleges. Each piece of carving is 8 feet 8 inches in

---

* Giacomo Leoni (1686–1764), a Venetian architect, who settled in England early in the eighteenth century.

length, and all are different. The subjects are believed to represent the four seasons, music, and painting. They are composed
of trophies, flowers, and fruit, delicately carved in pearwood,
the softest of woods, and executed in the highest relief. All
contain the pumpkin, melon, and sunflower, so characteristic
of Gibbons, and all have the split pea-pod, generally accepted
as his signature. One panel has the lace handkerchief or
cravat, another a classical-shaped beaker, beautifully executed,
while cherubs' heads and wings, baskets of flowers, fish, fruit and
nuts, musical instruments, palettes and paint-brushes, all heaped
together in artistic confusion, make up a form of decoration
as harmonious in colour as it is exquisite in design. Two other
small square panels have, one, the ram's head crest, the other, a
centre bouquet of flowers with a small palm-leaf at each end.

There were orignially two fire-places, one on the east
and the other on the west side of the room, the door being
placed where the fire-place now is, on the north side opposite
the windows. The present doorway opens from the grand
staircase vestibule on the east side of the room, where one of
the fire-places was originally; this alteration was no doubt
effected by Leoni. Above the chimneypiece is a looking-
glass, with a frame of Grinling Gibbons carving. The gilt and
plaster ceiling, of Italian design, has in each corner, executed
in similar material, the hand and banner, the shield of augmentation granted to the Legh family in 1574.

Leoni undoubtedly had a great deal to do with the decoration of the room in 1726. We have his letters written at the
time, showing that he intended raising the ceiling and building
the great portico outside, but this does not alter the probability
of the carving having been made for this particular room,
which may well have been planned and begun before 1687,
the year of Richard Legh's death, although he never lived to
finish it. An inventory made after his death mentions, with
other things, three pairs of curtains for the three windows in
the " New Parlour." *

* Lyme has suffered—like many other beautiful places—from visits of numerous
so-called experts, who each in turn have given their opinion as to the period, date, or
authenticity of different parts of the building or works of art, refusing to listen to any

LYME: PART OF THE SALOON SHOWING CARVING BY
GRINLING GIBBONS

DEATH OF RICHARD LEGH

A thirteenth child, a boy, christened Francis, was born at Lyme in March 1685-6, and congratulatory letters were received on the arrival of the " brave boy," with the hopes of Sir John Chicheley that this may be the last, " especially as it has pleased God to continue so many of them to you." Poor Elizabeth made a very slow recovery, and was indeed for a time in considerable danger. There was great difficulty in obtaining medical aid. Dr. Hollings, a noted physician of the day, suffering from " an impostumacon in one of his eyes," and thereby forced to keep his room, and another equally eminent practitioner being also indisposed.

Elizabeth's strong constitution triumphed, but she was a very fractious and difficult patient, and many references are made to her " ungovernableness " and " melancholy fancies," which must have severely tried the patience of her devoted husband. The cares of the household were now left entirely in his hands, and we hear of his difficulties in connexion with the engaging of a butler. Various friends whom he appealed to were endeavouring to find him a suitable man, and it is amusing to hear of the qualifications for such a post, the chief of which seems to have been that the butler should be a musician ; the efficient discharging of his other duties was a matter apparently of quite secondary importance. Sir John Chicheley recommends a man who plays both violin and harpsichord, but he won't pass for his honesty, nor is he an expert in shaving nor " laying of a cloth, but is ingenious at many other things." He is described also as being " civil and drinking no manner of strong drink," and (what was supposed to tell very much in his favour), he possessed an elder brother with an estate of £100 a year. We do not learn whether or no this paragon was engaged for the post.

In June 1686 began the negotiations for the marriage of young Peter, then aged seventeen, with Frances Legh of Bruch, a daughter of the late Piers Legh of Bruch by his

argument but their own, or to draw a logical sequence from testimony or tradition unsupported by documentary evidence. I listen to their strictures, which do no harm, and keep my own counsel.—E.N.

second wife, Abigail Chetwode, and a great-granddaughter of
old Sir Peter Legh. The young people had a liking for
each other, and the match was desirable in every way. The
lady, besides being attractive, was also an heiress, her only
half-brother, Piers, having died of decline after fighting in the
Battle of Sedgemoor. There was much gossip and discussion
over the proposed marriage, for the pair were cousins, though
distant, and it was doubted whether they came within the
proscribed degree of relationship. This gave opportunity for
the tongues of scandalmongers to be set wagging. The opinion
of Dr. Fogg,* Dean of Chester, was taken in the matter, and
he most emphatically gave it as his verdict that there was
not the slightest reason against the match.

> " He wonders [writes a family friend, one Mistress Hester Dod, who had
> undertaken to obtain the advice of the reverend gentleman], at the
> ignorance of those that raises such scruples, for sence [since] the 2d
> degree is lawfull, the 3d must be, so I hope you will be fully satisfied
> and noe more give eare to those that talke without books. If the
> young ones have a free affection for each other, in God's name let them
> goe on to increase it dayly."

Frances and her mother were, therefore, invited to Lyme ;
a long letter from Richard to the latter assures her of a hearty
welcome, and expresses his hopes that

> " no damage may be done to her reputation by coming at this time ;
> . . . it is not her fortune I so much regard as the sweetness &
> goodness of her temper. . . . I doe expect God's blessing will follow
> and that is and shall be my chiefest aim in marrying all my children."

This invitation was sent by special messenger, and we gather
that Peter would gladly have been the bearer of the missive.
" My young Master," adds his father, " offered his services
very freely to that end, but not knowing how convenient that
might be to you, I did advise him to desist," the poor boy being
taken to the Assizes instead, as a compensation for his disappointment. Mistress Abigail Legh returns answer that she
would willingly come to Lyme, " but loath I am to give the

* Laurence Fogg (1623–1718), Dean of Chester; much admired as a preacher;
author of various works on theology.

County occasion to talke, therefore to avoid that, I do not thinke it convenient to bring Franke [her daughter] with me."

Peter's constancy was, however, rewarded, for all obstacles being finally removed, the marriage took place the following April (1687), that of Lettice (eldest daughter of Richard) with William Bankes of Winstanley, a Lancashire magnate, being celebrated some three months earlier. 1687

The ringing of joy-bells was to be followed ere long by the wringing of hands, for the angel of death was spreading his sable wings over the house of Lyme, which was soon to mourn its lord, struck down by a painful disease when scarcely past the prime of life. That he had for some years past felt his end approaching is evident from his later letters, and portions of prayers scattered about amongst his papers and written on the backs of letters are mute testimony that he was preparing himself for the great change. For him Death had no terrors. His daily life was an example of all that an upright, honourable man should be ; he served his God, obeyed his King, and carried out to the letter all the duties of his position. There were no bitter memories to sadden his last hours ; there was nothing in his blameless life of which he need repent ; his marriage had been one of cloudless happiness, and his only regret was that of leaving all too soon a world which held so much for him.

The work so near his heart—the consecration of the chapel at Newton, which he had rebuilt, was, after many delays, finally to take place, and the first week in July was named as a possible date. The Bishop of Chester was to perform the ceremony, but again there were delays, and Richard was to die without seeing the desire of his heart accomplished.

The King (James II) was expected to pay a visit to Chester about the end of August 1687, in order, it was said, to persuade some of the leading gentlemen of the City and County to approve of the repeal of the Penal Laws and Test Act. Lord Derby, writing to Richard on the 5th of that month, proposes

THE HOUSE OF LYME

himself for a visit to Lyme, preparatory to setting out from thence with his host to attend the King:

> "I should be glad to go straight from your house hoping to have the favour of your company, yr advice in this affair would be very acceptable, wᵗ manner we should meet his Majesty, for I suppose it must be at his entrance into the County, & whether we all meet in a body at such a place & what part of the militia must be up."

But Richard was by this time far too ill to receive visitors or to undertake public work of any kind. His illness was probably an aggravated form of gout complicated with a severe fit of the stone, which disease he had suffered from at different times for many years. A letter from Phineas Fowke,* the celebrated doctor, written on August 19, gives a list of suggested remedies, as fearsome in sound as they were drastic in nature. Turpentine water, 2 spoonfuls in a draught of ale to be taken in the morning, "lucatedlas balsom yᵗ is fresh and not rancid," morning and night, salt prunella, chalybeate waters, nitrous salt—recommended as "a fine worker"—white wine posset with a little liquorice and syrup of althea; while if the pain were excessive, diacodion in cowslip or mallow water, or 10 grains of "Matthews pills" are suggested as opiates. The patient is also to avoid violent exertion, such as that caused by hunting, etc., but is to take gentle walking or riding exercise, or to recreate himself with playing bowls.

1687 The remedies, it is perhaps not surprising to learn, proving of no avail, the sufferer died on August 31, 1687, in the fifty-fourth year of his age, and with the death of her beloved husband the light of Elizabeth Legh's life went out for evermore.

The grief occasioned by his death reached far beyond his immediate family circle, and widespread was the sorrow and regret expressed by all who knew him, from the King downwards. His Majesty, on hearing of his fatal illness, "gave an evident Testimony of his great value and kindness for him in a free Commendation of his person and a Pathetical Con-

---

* Phineas Fowke, M.D. (1638–1710), physician to Charles II and to St. Bartholomew's Hospital; was learned in theology as well as medicine.

346

dolance for his Sickness." * His sorrowing wife mourned the loss of the tenderest of husbands, his children that of the kindest and most indulgent of fathers, while his friends lost in him a wise and sage counsellor, and the poor a generous benefactor. Though he might have held high office in the government of his country, he was content to discharge the simpler duties of his position as a country gentleman, respected and looked up to by all. Under his beneficent rule his property had increased in value and extent, his tenants had prospered, and all who came in contact with him had felt the ennobling influence of a good man, the keynote of whose life was honour, and duty his watchword.

On September 6, 1687, Richard Legh was buried in the Legh **1687** chapel of Winwick Church, where he rests amongst his forefathers. The funeral sermon, which was published at Oxford the following year, was preached by the Rev. William Shippen, D.D., Rector of Stockport, in which he gave a long and eloquent appreciation of the great qualities of his departed friend.

A very elaborate and rather inartistic monument to her husband was erected by Elizabeth Legh, and is still to be seen in the Legh chapel in Winwick Church. Upon it are two busts of herself and Richard, and below are the arms of Legh and Chicheley with the following inscription :

> " Here lyeth the body of Richard Legh Esqr of Lime in Cheshire, who dyed upon ye last day of August in ye year of our Lord 1687, and in the 54th year of his age."

> " Cruel and senseless death thou dost thyselfe deceive,
> In snatching him thou art more death to them yt live,
> Hapless and destitute distracted are they grown.
> Lost with their loss for he that was their life is gone,
> Pious and brave, just, noble all that could wonder move,
> Softened with honest husband's father's friendly love,
> These and all excellences were in him exprest,
> Peaceful and sacred then let his loved ashes rest,

* Dr. Shippen's " Funeral Sermon on Richard Legh of Lyme."

Till reinformed with light immortal he shall rise
A welcome glorious ornament of Paradise."

The following touching lines conclude this epitaph :

" His most affectionate Wife (who wanted no
monument to Remember him by) Erected this
that others should not forget him."

CHAPTER XXV

PETER AND FRANCES LEGH

An inventory of the contents of Lyme was taken the January 1687–8 following Richard's death. It was obviously very incomplete, as many of the rooms are spoken of as if they contained only chairs and cushions. In each room, however, at least one " easie chair " is mentioned. Some of the furniture it has been found possible to identify. The following is, for example, a description of the contents of the " Greate Dining Room," which probably corresponds to what is now the Hall. The total valuation of this room is placed at £60 ! Curiously enough, there is no mention of any table, an indispensable article of furniture, one would imagine, in any dining-room.

> " 2 great Chairs with Armes
> 18 Chairs with backs, all velvett & Red Cloth cases upon them
> 6 black turned Chairs [these are Jacobean chairs still existing] and
> 6 Damask cushions with Red Cloth Cases
> 1 Squab [a long seat or sofa] and cushion with a Red Cloth case on it
> Two large Crimson Curtains lined with Persian silk tyed back with large Red Tassells, 4 Dimity Curtains for windows
> 1 large blue Jar
> Andirons of brass."

These last still exist ; they are very fine specimens of pierced and engraved brasswork, *circa* 1670.

> " A foot Cloth."

Carpets were not generally used as coverings for the floor before the middle of the eighteenth century. " Foot-cloths," says Halliwell, " were housings of cloth hung on horses, generally considered a mark of dignity or state," but here, I imagine, the foot-cloth mentioned must have been a species of carpet.

Two beautiful specimens of needlework carpets are preserved at Lyme : one has the Legh coat of arms in the centre, worked in cross-stitch ; the other has a basket of flowers with a floral pattern worked in bright colours running round.

" The Withdrawing Room "—no doubt the present drawing-room—has mention of the following pieces :

" 6 Chairs, all Walnut tree and carved."

Seven fine Charles II carved walnut high-backed chairs are still prominent objects in this room. They have the original Venetian cut velvet, and are no doubt identical with those mentioned in the inventory.

" 12 blue Damask Cushions
A large glasse, Table and Stands, Blue Tapestry hangings."

These might be some blue and green needlework of the Elizabethan period, still existing.

" a blue Jar
2 large Diaper Dimity window Curtains
Andirons."

The contents of the " Bed Chamber," possibly the Yellow State Room containing James II's bed, with those of two other smaller rooms, are priced in the inventory at £500.

All the rooms have " diaper dimity " window curtains. Dimity was a coarse white cotton fabric, chiefly used for bed-hangings and window curtains.

The habitual custom of hanging whole rooms with black after a death seems to have been followed on this occasion. This terrible practice was not confined only to the apartments of the widow, but was here extended to the nurseries and " Madam Bettie's (the eldest unmarried daughter) Chamber," which were similarly draped. " Madam Legh's Mourning Chamber " (which is named separately from her usual bedroom) is described as having black hangings for the bed, a black counterpane, two large Spanish blankets of the same sombre hue, and four black chairs. One can scarcely imagine anything more shattering to both nerves and health.

PETER AND FRANCES LEGH

The contents of the chapel, "a pulpit Cloth, Cushions, velvet cloths for the Seat where the Decedent and Madam Legh his Lady used to sit," together with a surplice are returned at £22. This chapel is situated under the Elizabethan drawing-room, and is approached by a charming old Jacobean staircase opening out of the hall. It is probably of the same date as the saloon; one side of it is occupied entirely by the family pew.

The plate is valued at £1000. The list contains pegged tankards, salvers, dishes, spoons, porringers, and plates, with a large Water Bason, but there is no special mention of the rose-water dish and ewer.

Thirty-seven horses are valued at £195 11s.; 706 sheep at £124 13s.; 18 swine and 12 pigs at £7 10s.; 14 draught oxen are also specified; the total valuation of the contents of house, farm, and stables is put at £4179 14s. 4d.

Richard Legh's will, which calls for no special mention, was made in 1677. In it he makes what was then considered to be ample provision for his widow and children.

Their many relations were doing their best to comfort and sustain the sorrowing family at Lyme. Sir Thomas Chicheley was prevented by illness from attending the funeral of his son-in-law, as was Sir John Chicheley, but both the latter and Lady Chicheley paid a visit to Lyme in September to try and cheer the drooping spirits of the mourners.

Peter Legh of Lyme, second * Baron of Newton, was aged only eighteen at the time of his father's death. He was already

---

* Baronies, now called manors, were manorial and hereditary rights arising out of land, and denote the land held under one seignory or lordship. The Lord or Baron had powers with reference to trading privileges and municipal government of certain burghs, deriving his right from the King or some superior Lord. The reputed barony fee or liberty of Newton-in-Makerfield comprises twenty-four townships. This liberty is almost conterminous with the Domesday hundred of Newton. Robert Banastre, the first grantee, received it from Henry II. This reputed barony of Newton "with the members" was bought by Richard Legh of Lyme from Sir Thomas Fleetwood in 1660 for £3500. From Richard Legh the barony has descended to its present representative, Thomas Wodehouse Legh, second Baron Newton (cr. 1892), who is the twenty-fourth reputed Baron of Newton-in-Makerfield in succession from Robert Banastre, the first grantee.—"The Victoria History of the County of Lancaster," edited by William Farrer and J. Brownbill, M.A.

a married man, his wedding with his cousin, Frances Legh
of Bruch, who was just one year his junior, having taken place
in the spring of 1687, about four months before the death of
Richard. Peter came into his inheritance at a very trying
and critical period, and it was no easy matter for one so young,
with judgment immature and no experience to guide him, to
steer a just course between loyalty to his sovereign and the
satisfying of his own conscience.

1688   The country was distracted by James II's arbitrary measures,
which were estranging from him even the most devoted of his
adherents. He began his attack on the Church by issuing
a fresh Declaration of Indulgence in April 1688, ordering every
clergyman to read it during the service on two successive
Sundays. The clergy refused almost to a man, and seven of
the bishops who petitioned against the Act were arrested and
tried, but were acquitted. The country might possibly have
decided to let matters rest until James's death, realizing that
this would mean the accession of a Protestant Queen in his
daughter Mary, but an event which occurred in June 1688
at once changed the whole situation.

This was the birth of a son to James II, on June 10, 1688.
The event threatened the establishing of a Roman Catholic
dynasty, since the boy would most certainly be educated in the
religion of his father. An attempt was made to suggest—
without a shadow of foundation—that this was a supposititious
child, introduced into the palace in a warming-pan, and this
theory was advanced, and the rumour spread far and wide,
although letters of the time all speak of the Queen's approaching
confinement. Mrs. Langley, the housekeeper and old family
friend of the Chicheleys, writes from London in February
1687–8 : " God be praised the Queen goes on very prosperously.
God send it proves not a daughter, but all people has Girles
this yeare."

Whether the Prince was supposititious or not, there
was no doubt amongst the English people that he would
be considered James's heir, and as such would succeed
to the throne in due course and establish the Roman

352

Catholic religion. It was, therefore, decided by a small committee of important personages to invite William of Orange to land with an armed force to defend the liberties of England.

A compromise was attempted, the Tories suggesting that the country should be governed by a Regent, James remaining nominally King, but this proposal was rejected and the invitation was dispatched to Holland.

The menacing danger of war with France, against which almost every European country—with the exception of England —was allied, and his own frontier being threatened, decided William of Orange to accept the invitation of the English throne.

On December 1, 1688, Sir John Chicheley writes from London to his nephew, Peter Legh, at Lyme :

> " By this Proclamation all will be satisfied of his Majesty's intention to have a Parl^t. . . . I am told ye P. of O. is now about Shaftesbury moving this way with his Army and Artillery; ye ways & weather are so bad he cannot but move very slowly. 'Tis to be supposed he increases dayly both by ye people of ye severall Counties yt dayly come in, & some few deserters from ye Army."

He ends hoping for " a happy Conclusion without Bloodshed."

On December 11 he writes again, speaking of the flight of the King and Queen with the baby Prince of Wales, aged only six months :

> " Friday last 'tis sayd Ld Sunderland,* Saturday Lord Peterborough †
> and Bishop of Chester, and Moonday at two or three in ye Morning y^e
> Queen wth ye Prince of Wales, & this Morning His Majesty with y^e
> Duke of Barwicke ‡ & two or three more, all supposed to be gone for
> France. I am also told ye Chancell^{or} is gone with y^t Seales he being
> not to be heard off at neither of his Lodgings. [This was Jeffreys,
> arrested in disguise at Wapping and sent to the Tower, where he died.]
> Some of ye Scotch forces are gone over to ye Pr of Or : he advances this
> way dayly as his Cannon & Carriages will permitte ; 'tis sayd ye Town

---

* Robert Spencer, second Earl of Sunderland, only son of Henry, first Earl, by his wife Dorothy ; fled in female disguise to Rotterdam.

† Henry Mordaunt, second Earl of Peterborough (1624 ?–1697), served in Parliamentarian army, but deserted to Charles I.

‡ James FitzJames, Duke of Berwick, natural son of James II by Arabella Churchill.

z

will be putt into ye hands of ye Citty. Queen Dowager stays as yet at Somerset House. All writts for a Parl^t are stopt, the R. Cath. are all leaving this place, but whither to goe I thinke they scarce kno'. Tis sayd considerable quantitys of Powder wth Arms has been found in severall private houses. The rabble is now defacing all ye Popish Chapels, as yet we are not got over ye great question who we shall place in ye throne now we are all agreed y^t K^g James ye 2^d has forfeited it."

1689   William and Mary were crowned in April 1689, but the Legh family did not attend the ceremony. A copy of the Coronation Oath was, however, forwarded to Lyme.

Although at heart a Jacobite, as were his predecessors, it is hardly likely that Peter Legh could have approved of James's arbitrary measures and his attack on the Protestant religion and liberties of the people of England. Peter certainly had no sympathy with the new régime, but realizing the futility of attempting to stem the tide, he found it best to bow to the inevitable, though he persistently refused to take the oath of allegiance to his new sovereigns.

The new régime was none too popular, and William, recognizing this fact, sought to combat it by a system of terrorism and coercion, causing the people to wonder whether after all they had benefited by the change. A correspondent writes to Peter in 1690, alluding disrespectfully to His Majesty : " Billy's so quick home again and has complimented halfe the Kingdom with a Proclamation against them which some calls the disaffected."

The following year we hear of the clerk of Stockport Church being put in the stocks for giving out the 137th Psalm : " By the waters of Babylon we sat down and wept : when we remembered thee, O Sion."

Without either his father's great beauty or personal charm, Peter Legh had many qualities. He was a devoted son and husband, was endowed with good judgment and much shrewd common sense, and had a high sense of his duties and responsibilities. He and Frances undertook the care and charge of all his little brothers and sisters, who were left by their mother to make their home at Lyme.

Some six months after her husband's death, Elizabeth

PETER AND FRANCES LEGH

Legh decided to settle in London with her two eldest un-married daughters, leaving her younger children to the care of her son and daughter-in-law. She took a house on a lease in Devonshire Street, Bloomsbury, and here she gathered around her the principal people in the society of the day. The Duke of Ormonde, Lord and Lady Derby, Lord Colchester, Lord Cholmondeley, were all intimate friends and habitués of the house, which became a sort of centre for the leading lights in the political and social world. Elizabeth was only forty-three or forty-four at the time of her husband's death, and her youngest child barely a year old, but she became henceforth " old Madam Legh," and this appellation stuck to her for the remainder of her very long life. Her masterful nature seems to have asserted itself more than ever after her husband's death, and, deprived of his restraining influence and guiding hand, she became somewhat of a thorn in the flesh of her children, whom she petted and thwarted by turns. Although she was only a visitor at Lyme, for long or short periods, as the case might be, she continued to keep a watchful eye on the young couple, and was never behindhand with criticism and advice : " I would desire you to be very careful what company you invite to the howes or give any encouragement to be hangers on," she writes to her son, " for you will find you cannot be quit of them when you would," naming several people whom she disapproves of, " neither of them ever lodged one night at Lime whilst your father and I were Master and Mistress there." She also counsels economy : " I fear by the years end so much company will be found to be chargeable, but my prayers and best advice shall never be wanting to you."

Some time in 1688 a terrible tragedy occurred at Lyme. John, Elizabeth's fourth son, five years old, was drowned in the water in front of the house. The fact is recorded in the family Bible, but no mention of the disaster occurs elsewhere. Mrs. Langley, writing to Frances Legh in September of that year, begging for news, speaks of having had a letter from Madam Legh, in which she tells her " something has lately befallen her that troubles her extremely but doth not name what it is. I dare not write to know." This may possibly refer to the tragedy, which must have been a heavy blow to the poor stricken Elizabeth.

Peter and Frances kept up the same amount of state at Lyme, and the establishment was run much on the same lines as those of former days. A contemporary speaks of the splendour of their entertainments, and there were constant visitors to the house. We read of a new " calash " being made to order. The price of this was to be £48, and was to include six sets of harness, the " hammock cloaths " to be extra.

The saddles of those days were very elaborately embroidered in gold and silver, and this work was generally done by the ladies of the family. Frances, who was a beautiful worker, was anxious to try her hand at one, but was assured that the materials would be very expensive, " 10s. is nothing for the twist and gold."

Amongst the outdoor amusements of the day, bowling, hawking, and racing continued to be as popular as ever, and Peter, though he himself preferred fox-hunting, still maintained the racing stud which had been started by his father. He kept his own pack of hounds, but his hunting must have been chiefly in Lancashire, where the flat country gave better opportunity than north-east Cheshire for a good gallop.

From a list of thirty-six hounds kept in Lancashire in 1688 we get the following names :

" Little Thunder," " Greate Thunder," " Juell," " Sweet lippes," " Truelove," " Courtier," " Madam," " Wellcome," " Wonder," " Suregate," and " Wagg "—a Spaniel.

The annual deer drives, attended by all the neighbours, took place as usual at Lyme. One is disposed to wonder whether there can have been the same number of rabbit-holes in the park then as there are now, where in places riding is extremely dangerous. The following extract describes a run that took place at a hunt in Lancashire, and is a graphic description of the habits of the period :

" On Saturday last we had a hearty Chace after a fox but lost him among ye Rabbit holes in ye Rough Parks, but yesterday we found

PETER LEGH OF LYME

1702

By Sir GODFREY KNELLER

From a Portrait at Lyme

P. Legh

him again & were just able to kill him fairly above ground after Hounds, Horses & Men were sufficiently tir'd ; it happen'd just below Garswood, when Sr Willm (Gerard *) was in a perfect Extasie att our Good fortune, & would have us to dine with him, but I was engag'd with some Company at home, but return'd with him to drink a bowle of Hott Punch with ye fox's foot stew'd in it. Sr Willm drank pretty plentifully, & just at last perceiv'd he should be fuddled, ' but,' quoth he, ' I care not if I am, I have kill'd a fox to-day.' I herewith send you one of his feet with Sr Will's service who says we shall kill 'em all for you."

The indoor amusements were chiefly cards and backgammon, 1689 but in 1689 we hear of a billiard-table mentioned for the first time. Billiards was brought into fashion in France about the middle of the seventeenth century by Louis XIV, whose physician recommended him exercise after meals. A correspondent writes to Peter in December 1689 :

" I received a letter from Will Aston to send down furniture for your Billiard Table, but not knowing how to buy them myself, I have been forced to stay so long. I spoke to Sr John to have the directions off some players, and we will send the best that can be got."

A portrait of Peter Legh at the age of thirty-three, painted by Sir Godfrey Kneller in 1702, shows him wearing the huge wig of the period. He has a brown velvet coat, opening at the neck, over a white silk shirt with a ruffle. Round his waist is an embroidered sword-belt, from which hangs a sword. His left hand is tucked into the front of his coat, his right rests on a table beside him, and shows long tapering fingers, characteristic of the race. The chief feature of his somewhat uninteresting face is a long nose.

Frances Legh, painted about the same date by the same artist, must have been charmingly pretty. She has dark eyes, regular features, and a beautiful fair skin, contrasting well with her luxuriant dark hair, which is piled high above her forehead and hangs down her back in curls. She wears a sort of loose pale yellow wrapper, opening over a soft white chemisette. Her character was as charming as her face. She was a cultivated, clever woman, far in advance of her contem-

* Ancestor of the present Lord Gerard.

357

poraries, and a great reader ; many of the books in the Lyme
library, particularly those dealing with heraldry or family
history, have her name written in her own beautiful clear
hand. Her letters are well expressed and are full of originality
and humour. She rivalled her mother-in-law in her wifely
devotion, and the one cloud in her very blue sky was the fact
that she had no children.

This was the sorrow of her life, and it was also a cause of
much trouble and distress amongst her friends and relations,
who offered many hints and suggestions, and sent different
recipes supposed to be infallible in similar cases. One of these
is accompanied by many apologies from the sender, " who is
timorous of rendering himself under the figure of an unwarrantable presumption," but who states that the medicine here
prescribed is

> " an infallible encourager of the internal instruments of the body, soe
> as in process of time will undoubtedly produce an external issue to the
> intent thereof that the person he soe much honours may be blest with
> innumerable offspring."

These remedies, alas, proved futile, and poor Frances
resigned herself to a childless existence, and became a second
mother to her little brothers- and sisters-in-law, whom she took
to her heart and treated like her own children.

It was no easy task to keep on good terms with her mother-in-
law, but that she succeeded in doing so, and in winning the love
and respect of that imperious dame, there is ample evidence.

> " Deare Daughter [writes Madam Legh in an undated letter in which
> she describes some wonderful presents given by Queen Mary to her
> Groom o' the Stole,* the Countess of Derby †], I fear I can give you
> but small hopes of seeing me this winter, the somer being far gone &
> winter approaching fast, I am afraid to ventur in the dorty [dirty]
> lanes, but at the Spring of the year I hope in God to be with you.
> Queen Dowager is going for Portugal. This Queen Mary has made
> my Lady Derby a noble present against her lying in. In the first

* Queen Mary conferred this post upon Lady Derby. It carried with it £1000
a year, and gave precedence over Duchesses.
† The wife of William, ninth Earl of Derby ; she was a granddaughter of the Duke
of Ormonde.

PETER AND FRANCES LEGH

place there was a brafe Japan Cabenet & in this Cabenet there was 12 peeces of Damask to make a bed and chares, & 7 peeces of white Damask to make baby Cloaths & 2 imbroidered night gownes with gold and a very rich gold & crimson stof to make her a Manto and paletot, & 2 very fine quilts for her bed of 3 score genes [guineas] a quilt, all these things were Indian of the richest sort that comes from that place, and 30 peces of Cheney to set a-top of the Cabenet and these things was all packt up in the Cabenet, Cheney and all, that you may imagine it was a very large one. Pray give my blessing to all mine and service to my Sister Legh [Frances' mother] I am Deare Daughter

"Your ever affactinet Mother E.L."

Peter was not so great a dandy as his father and had apparently fewer clothes. Frances was particular about hers and always anxious to hear about the new London fashions. She writes to a friend, describing a garment which she has seen,

"the prittylest y^t ever was seen; a broad plain plate over the sholder but not rufled only stands hollow and plaited in the top of the back & gethered at the bottom like a nightgown, & the plaits sits very huffling."

In another letter she sends for her yellow "nightgown" This was a kind of loose wrapper, no doubt the garment she wears in her picture.

"If Cos Betty thinks hee [the carrier] will bring my yellow nightgown safe & not scrumpled shee may send it by him, if she thinks it will be crushed let it alone. I hope my things will be handsome—I am goeing a walking."

The broad dialect of the Elizabethan period had given place to a more mincing form of speech. Gentility was the order of the day, and a sort of reaction from the free and easy manners of Charles II's period had set in. The following sentence, constructed from words in the phonetic spelling of the time, will give some idea of the pronunciation of ladies and gentlemen of the upper classes:

"Railey, Marm, I a bin maining to sind the yaller cheney sarvis and writ you a latter a porpos to tall you so." [Really, Ma'am, I have been meaning to send the yellow china service and wrote you a letter on purpose to tell you so.]

CHAPTER XXVI

IMPRISONMENT OF PETER LEGH

1689   ABOUT this period the gentlemen of Cheshire were in the habit of holding meetings at each other's houses, forming themselves into a sort of club, where they held discussions on the leading topics of the day. Peter Legh is said to have been its originator, and the first gathering of the " Cheshire Club " took place in the Stag Parlour at Lyme somewhere about the year 1689.

At a time when every man's hand was against his neighbour and the air was charged with distrust and suspicion it is not surprising that this assemblage should have been viewed with disfavour by the Government of the day, or that Peter Legh, with his well-known Jacobite sympathies, should fall a victim to the many spies and miscreants who follow in the wake of every revolution. Repeated warnings were sent him of what might be his fate if he still persisted in his refusal to swear
1690   allegiance to the new King and Queen. His Uncle Thomas writes to him on July 26, 1690, telling him plainly of the threats uttered against him :

> " I suppose now Elijah brings a Letter to you from yr Mother wch directs you wch way to steer, God send it prosperous and successfull to you. . . . At Nantwich Session yrself and Jacobite acquaintance were indicted as such, yt have obstinately refused ye Oaths. That Bench ordered that if within a month at most yrself and sociates did not come in and swear, Process shold come out & impower Bailiffs to distrain upon yr goods respectively to pay £10 a Man, . . . these indirect practises are used to draw vexation & greater Charge upon you, O Almighty God reward them in thy good time as they deserve."

Disregarding these warnings, however, Peter became, in

IMPRISONMENT OF PETER LEGH

July 1694, involved in what was called the " Lancashire Plot," one of a series of Jacobite conspiracies, having for its object the restoration of the exiled King. On July 19 he was arrested on a charge of treason, and was accused of conspiring against William III in the interests of James II. A wretch named Lunt was one of the chief witnesses against Peter, who was probably fastened on as being rich and influential, and, as such, a fit subject for blood-money. Lunt, a mercenary, whose one object was blackmail, deposed before Sir John Trenchard * that he had been in France in 1689, and had brought with him from St. Germain commissions for various Cheshire and Lancashire gentlemen, and that one of these—a Colonel's commission, with blanks left to insert the names of inferior officers—was to be for Peter Legh of Lyme. He was also to be given power to raise foot, horse, or dragoons.

On July 19, 1694, between the hours of 6 and 7 A.M., there 1694 appeared at Lyme a King's messenger with Lunt the informer, who was provided with a warrant, and fourteen Dutch troopers armed with pistols, who are also described as wearing blue cloaks. They all entered the house and proceeded up the great staircase to Peter's dressing-room, where they found him attired only in his night-gown. He is described as " a young gentleman, little of stature." † They took him, just as he was, into his " closet," where they left him under a guard, whilst Lunt searched through all his papers, calmly putting into his pocket anything he chose. This occupied some five hours. About noon, having been unsuccessful in discovering anything incriminating, they allowed their victim to dress himself, and they then carried him downstairs into the parlour and set two Dutch troopers to guard him whilst they searched through the entire house for arms. All they succeeded in finding, however, were a case of pistols and a carbine, which they carried off. Having discovered nothing

---

* Secretary of State (1640–1695) ; took prominent part in Exclusion debates and shared in plots.

† " The Jacobite Trials at Manchester in 1694," from an unpublished MS. edited by W. Beamont.

to satisfy their suspicions, Lunt and his followers took the unfortunate Peter off to Knutsford under the guard of twelve troopers, Lunt appropriating the best horse in the Lyme stables (the legacy of a dying kinsman) to his own use. From Knutsford the poor prisoner was taken to Chester Castle, where he remained under a close guard until about September, when he was removed to the Tower of London in pursuance of a warrant to the Governor, signed by the Earl of Shrewsbury.* This states that

> " the body of Peter Leigh of Lyme, herewith sent you, being Charged before me for high Treason in Levying War against their Majesties and Adhering to their Majesties Enemys, and you are to keep him safe and close Until he shall be delivered by due Course of Law, and for so doing this shall be your Warrant
> " Given at the Court at Whitehall the 12th day of September, 1694.
> " Signed SHREWSBURY."

He was here lodged in the worst room, and was most harshly treated, no one being allowed to see him.

One can fancy the agony of mind of poor Frances and all Peter's other relatives, for scant was the justice of the day. Even if he was lucky enough to escape with his life, the unfortunate victim, arrested on a political charge, was in many cases kept imprisoned in a loathsome gaol, in some instances for a period of forty years. It was nothing that no proof could be found against him, it was only necessary to obtain an Act of Parliament (very similar to the terrible French *lettre de cachet*), which left him to His Majesty's pleasure, the decree expiring only on His Majesty's demise.

His friends were all much concerned and wrote in guarded tones, offering condolences and prayers, but nothing else. Lord Cholmondeley † assures him that

* Charles Talbot, twelfth Earl and only Duke of Shrewsbury (1660–1718), was given places and employments by Charles II and James II, but nevertheless was prominent in bringing about the revolution ; became K.G., Duke, and head of the Administration, 1694.
† Hugh, first Earl of Cholmondeley, succeeded his father as second Viscount Cholmondeley of Kells in 1681 ; Treasurer of the Household. He died unmarried in 1724.

362

IMPRISONMENT OF PETER LEGH

" I should have bin most unhappy and very unsatisfy'd with my self if I had not ere I left London and upon the first news of the unfortunate accident of your being seized, done all that was in my power towards the serving you, which I am very sorry has proved so ineffectuall. . . ."

His Uncle Thomas writes also, begging him to arm himself 1694 with patience, offering prayers and earnest desires that he may be delivered from " wicked men who are the offspring of Belial and filled with diabolicall malice."

It was left to his devoted wife and mother to find the practical means of rescuing Peter from his fate, and to this end they left no stone unturned. So anxious was she about her son that old Madame Legh came and stood under the window of the room in the Tower where he was confined,* hoping to be able to catch a glimpse of him or just to hear his voice. She was roughly treated by one of the sentries, who levelled his gun at her, and threatened to shoot her if she did not go away.

By dint of petitioning and through powerful influence Frances Legh obtained permission to be with her husband. Madame Legh writes to Mr. Kenyon, a lawyer and family friend, on September 14, and gives in the following letter a graphic description of the sufferings of her son, who was confined in a room four yards square :

". . . I thank God my son is in good health, but so close confined that his wife and sisters was at the Tower to have seen him, and they would not so much as permet him to loock out of the window to speke to them, nor his footman to tell them he was well, and he is put in the worst lodging in all the Tower, and in a room but four yards square, and a warder lyes by him ; but the pore warder is so sorry for him that he cannot speke of him without tears in his eyes. We are petitioning the Queen that his wife may goe to him, but Lord Lucas hinders it all he can, to see if by that means he can get his fees out of them. I think the prayers of our friends were never more necessary then now to preserve the innocent from fals wetnesses, and sure, the parliment will think it hard to give money to maintain such a pack of hellhounds that hunts after the lifes and estates of innosent men. I pray God open the

* " The Jacobite Trials at Manchester in 1694."

eyes of the King and Queen that they may deserne their fiends from their foes." *

On September 17 came the permit from the Queen, who, herself a devoted wife, probably sympathized with her unfortunate subject :

" To Lord Lucas, Governor of the Tower,
   " My Lord, Her Majesty would have you permitt Mrs Leigh and a Maid Servant to be with her husband Mr. Leigh of Lyme in Case she shall be Willing to be Confined with him."

The fond wife was only too happy to take advantage of the permission, and was in such haste to rejoin her husband that she commissioned one of her sisters-in-law to send after her some clothes and necessaries. The following is a small account of money laid out by Lettice Fleetwood, Peter's eldest sister, in connexion with his imprisonment :

	l.	s.	d.
Paid for the Carriage of 2 Boxes from Chester and the Porters		9	6
Pd my Sister for Coach hire from Mrs Beaks & Mrs Beaks going back		2	
To a porter that went one day to the Tower with drink		2	
pd. my sister one day in the Tower		1	
pd. for a black hood for her		4	
for drawing a petition		2	
Mr Beaks' Bill	4		
Mrs Chetwode's Cabbinet	3	7	
To Mr Rigby ffor Allamode for Lts. wife	1	5	
an order ffor Councell	2	5	
Layd down for Sweetmeats in the Spring	7	1	
ffor Crevatts	1	6	
ffor Shirts	1	12	

Money was sent at different times to the amount of £180, with 24s. worth of worsted. Frances was very fond of needlework, and this must have helped to while away many a weary hour.

A further concession was granted by the Queen on Septem-

* Kenyon MS., p. 305.

FRANCES LEGH OF BRUCH
Wife of Peter Legh of Lyme
1705
By Sir GODFREY KNELLER

From a Portrait at Lyme

Fra: Legh

ber 24 for Peter to obtain some fresh air and exercise under certain restrictions, his health suffering from the continued confinement in so small a space. This took the form of an order from Lord Shrewsbury to Lord Lucas :

> " Whitehall, 24th Sept. 1694.
> " Her Majesty commands me to acquaint your Lordship with her pleasure that you allow Mr Leigh of Lyme such liberty of Walking Within the Tower at Convenient times as you shall Judge Consistant with his safe Keeping, and that care be taken he do not enter into Conversation at that time."

On the 27th came another order allowing old Madam Legh and her two daughters to visit the prisoner, and by October the severity was so far relaxed that having been told to prepare for his trial his counsel were to be permitted to confer with him.

> " Mr Leigh, one of the Prisoners in the Tower, having Notice given him to prepare for his Tryall, in Order thereunto it is Her Majestys pleasure that your Lordship permit Sir Thomas Powis, Sir Bartholo-mew Shore, and Mr Upton to have Access to the said Mr Leigh as his Councill, to advise him, and to be with him from time to time in private either singly or together, and Her Majesty is pleased to direct further, that Sir Thomas Chicheley, Mr Banks, Mr Masters,* and The Lady Chicheley,† Mrs Abigail Leigh‡ be permitted to see him from time to time at Convenient hours either Singly or so Many of them together as your Lordship shall think fit provided it be in the presence of a Warder or such person as you shall Appoint."

This act of kindness was probably one of the last of Queen Mary's life, as she was attacked with smallpox and died in December of this same year.

Peter was to be tried for his life at the Assizes at Chester some time during October. He was taken from the Tower with other prisoners and a numerous guard, " exposed as a show through the streets of London and through the several

---

* Afterwards Sir Streynsham Masters; married Elizabeth, second daughter of Richard and Elizabeth Legh.

† Isabella, daughter of Sir John Lawson, and widow of —— Norton, wife of Sir John Chicheley, uncle of Peter Legh.

‡ Abigaile Chetwode, second wife of Piers Legh of Bruch, mother of Frances, wife of Peter Legh.

countys and towns in the road from thence to Chester."*
Here, after awaiting in the common gaol the coming of the
judges, he with Sir Thomas Stanley was brought to the Bar,
and, there being no witnesses forthcoming against them, they
were discharged, " the cryer's proclamation being far from so
loud as the acclamations of the people." *

The same authority (probably Mr. Roger Kenyon) in stating
Peter's case protests indignantly at the treatment he received,
and inveighs against the law of England for authorizing a
Minister of State to impower

> " any common person that hee will style the King's messenger, to
> break and enter into any man's house to search for and seize arms . . .
> Can this his case and usuage, were the laws of England had in due
> execution, lye long unremembered, or when remembered, remain
> unresented ? "

1696 But although they may have resented—and rightly too—
the iniquitous treatment to which he had been subjected,
Peter's relatives were so thankful to get him back that there
was no thought of obtaining redress. They only asked that
he should be allowed to live in peace and quietness and enjoy
his beautiful home, far removed from the strife and turmoil
of public life. He was, however, not left long undisturbed,
for he was again, in 1696, apprehended and committed to Chester
Castle, charged with high treason, and was again discharged
as before, no evidence being found against him.

He never received compensation in any shape or form for
the gross injustice done him, and this warped and soured his
character. So thoroughly disgusted was he with the harsh
and unjust treatment he had suffered that he never sat in
Parliament or sought to obtain office as a magistrate or Deputy-
Lieutenant under a Government which had behaved so shame-
fully to him. In his will, which he drew up many years before
his death, for he lived to a great old age, he says :

> " I would have no monument over me, only a plain brass nailed to the
> wall to express my innocency in that wicked conspiracy by false wit-
> nesses, imprisonments and trials in 1694 and 1696, and I die a member

* " The Case of Peter Legh of Lyme," Kenyon MS., pp. 363-366.

366

of the Church of England, looking upon it to be the best and purest of Churches, and do most sincerely wish it may continue for ever."

The death of James II at St. Germain in 1701 and his son being proclaimed King of England by Louis XIV caused great excitement and a certain amount of indignation in this country, the people resenting what they considered to be the unwarrantable interference of the French King. Lord Derby,* writing to Peter Legh, begs him to meet him at Preston to join with him in an address, " declaring frankly that the French King never pretended before, and now has a right no more than formerly to name us a King, for whatever gloss may be put, this is the true state of the case." With the recollection of his former experiences, Peter viewed with dismay the possibility of being further involved in the subsequent Jacobite rising. A letter from his friend and legal adviser, John Ward of Capesthorne,† strongly counsels him to come up to London and put himself under the protection of a Secretary of State, as he had done at a ticklish time before.

Whether he followed this advice or no, Peter certainly realized that his conduct at so critical a period could scarcely be too circumspect, and that gatherings like the " Cheshire Club " were undesirable at such a time. It met together once more in 1715, this time it is said at Ashley Hall, to decide whether or no its members should espouse the Chevalier's cause. Peter Legh's is supposed to have been the casting-vote against taking part in the revolt, and the club was dissolved. Its members unanimously resolved to commemorate the occasion by having their portraits painted and hung in the room in which they had held their last meeting. This was done, and the portraits, ten in number and all full length, with the name and date attached, were painted in 1720 by an unknown artist. They now hang on the staircase at Tatton, having been removed from Ashley Hall in 1860 by Lord Egerton of

* William, ninth Earl.
† John Ward of Capesthorne (1670–1748–9) and of the Inner Temple; an eminent lawyer; was M.P. for Newton, Co. Lancashire, in 1712. His eldest daughter and co-heiress married at Kensington, in 1721, Davies Davenport, of Woodford and Marton, ancestor of Brigadier-General W. Bromley Davenport, D.S.O.

1720 Tatton. Their names are given in the order in which they are placed on the staircase, and are as follows : Thomas Assheton, Constable of Chester Castle ; Sir Richard Grosvenor of Eaton ; James, Earl of Barrymore ; Charles Hurleston of Newton ; Amos Meredith of Henbury ; Alexander Radclyff of Fox Denton ; Robert Cholmondeley of Holford ; John Warren of Poynton ; Henry Legh of High Legh ; and Peter Legh of Lyme.

These representatives of the Cheshire gentry of the eighteenth century all wear the same pattern of long coats of different coloured velvet, with knee-breeches and silk stockings, square-toed shoes with buckles, and huge wigs. The portrait of Peter Legh is an exact copy as to dress and position (except that it is full length instead of three-quarter) of the one painted by Kneller in 1702, the wig differing slightly, as does the face, which shows that of an older man.*

The secret clubs, such as the one we have just described, were partly responsible for bringing into existence the Jacobite glasses, a few beautiful specimens of which are still carefully preserved at Lyme. These include six of the " Fiat " wine-glasses. Five have the graceful air-twisted stems with the six-petalled Stewart rose and two buds—said to typify James II, the Chevalier, and Prince Charles Edward—the oak-leaf, emblematic of the Restoration, and the word " Fiat " engraved on the bowl. The sixth wineglass is straight-sided and has a plain stem with the tear-drop, the Prince of Wales's feathers engraved on the foot, and the rose with two buds, the oak-leaf, and the word " Fiat " engraved on the bowl.

These glasses were used for toasts at the clubs when the health of " the King over the water " was drunk in silence, and often by the old Cavaliers on their knees, each member holding his glass over the finger-bowl placed before him. The adherents of the exiled Royal Family derived a melancholy satisfaction from these ceremonies, which continued with loyal sympathizers well on into the reigns of the Georges, and the

* The particulars of these portraits are taken from an interesting account of the Cheshire Club written by the late Earl Egerton of Tatton, which by the kind permission of the Duchess of Buckingham and Chandos and Lord Egerton of Tatton I am allowed to publish.—E.N.

custom must have prevailed at Lyme if one may judge by these silent evidences of the politics of its owners.

There are other specimens at Lyme of straight-sided glasses with knopped and bulbed air-twisted stems, engraved with the rose and two buds, also some charming old sweetmeat and preserve glasses in rock crystal, shaped like shells, others in cut glass on tall faceted stems. A number of footless, "no heel-tap" wine-glasses (the toast having to be drunk straight off without putting down the glass) are probably of a rather later date. These have a faceted boss at the end of the stem, the bowl engraved with a toast. Finger-bowls with a lip at each side have the corresponding toast running round. No doubt these were used to rinse the glasses before a change of wine. These toasts are many and varied; some are political and some relate to the Legh family, but the majority are of a sporting character.

Here are some of those connected with politics : " May Aristocracy Rise on the Ashes of Democracy," " Blood o'er the Face of the Earth," " The Standing Forces of Great Britain " ; while the sporting ones include " Falconers Hall," " The Five-and-Twenty Couple," " The Stagg well Rouzed," " A Fresh Earth and a High Metaled Terrier," " The Vermin Blood," " Bear-Baiting," " Bull-Baiting," " Falconry," " The Merry Harriers," and " Sans Quarter." Those relating to the family comprise " Lime House For Ever," " Long Life to the House of Lime," and the quaint and original one of " Mrs. Legh's Delight."

The following are rather ambiguous and the meaning seems somewhat obscure : " Daming and Sinking," " The Otters Potter," " Maria and the Otters Potter," and " Death and the Devil " ; while we may complete the list with " The Agreeable Ups and Downs of Life," " Bear a Bob wherever you Go," " Any Toast but a Dry One," " Long Life and Long Corks," " A Flatt Decanter and a Sprightly Landlord," " A Cellar Well Filled and a House Full of Friends," which suggest many happy and convivial gatherings and a keen appreciation of the good things of life.

CHAPTER XXVII

LEONI'S ALTERATIONS

1720 THE building and alteration at Lyme, begun by Richard in 1652, was still going on. Peter became obsessed by the fever of bricks and mortar, and had evidently settled matters with the great Italian architect, Giacomo Leoni, who, by 1720, was hard at work. Old Madame Legh, in a letter to her son in September 1721, speaks of taking a message to " Mr. Leone," and talks hopefully of the building being finished by Michaelmas. It continued, however, during the whole of Peter's long life and that of his nephew and successor, the orangery, designed also by Leoni, not being completed before the middle of the nineteenth century.

The grand staircase, situated between the library and the saloon, was probably finished about this date—1720. It is in the Palladian style with large balusters of the Italian type. Four massive square Corinthian columns support a short gallery, leading from the top of the staircase to the Long Gallery and bachelor wing. The ceiling is of plaster-work in a fine Italian design, the hand and banner crest figuring prominently in it, as it does in so much of the decoration all over the house.

The Hall was also probably completed about this period. This is a splendid room, 40 feet by 45, and is approached from the courtyard by a double flight of steps. Four massive Late Ionic columns support an immense beam which runs the whole length of the entrance portion of the room, and divides it from the fire-place end, which is used as a sitting-room. The floor was originally on the same level as that of the drawing-room and library, but was sunk some 12 feet by Leoni. A short

370

LYME : SOUTH FRONT

staircase at either end leads up to the galleries (from which open the principal bedrooms) over the arcades which surround the courtyard. These were added by Leoni. The gallery on the north side gives access to the Elizabethan drawing-room, which communicates with the Hall by the secret opening in the panelling described in a former chapter. That on the south side leads to the grand staircase and library.

The Hall, redecorated a few years ago, was disfigured by a hideous Early Victorian wall-paper, which has been replaced by three pieces of Mortlake tapestry which formerly hung in bed-rooms, with the fine borders tucked in. These three pieces are part of the well-known Hero and Leander series, and have the wide or grotesque borders. Complete, they are a set of six, and are known to have been woven between the years 1623 and 1636, from the cartoons of Francis Clein or Cleyn (who died in 1658), a native of Rostock, who was employed for years as a designer for the Mortlake factory. Each panel is about 14 by 15 feet, and each is signed with the initials F. C., which are those of Sir Francis Crane, who died in 1636, the first director of the Mortlake factory. The borders measure from 2 to 3 feet in width. The panels comprise—reading from right to left :

1. The meeting of Hero and Leander outside the Temple, Cupid hovering in mid-air, aiming an arrow at the lovers. This is perhaps the most exquisite of the series. The details of Hero's gown are carried out in a most elaborate pattern, and the colours, as also those of Leander's cloak, though no doubt far less bright than when first executed, are harmonious and not too subdued or faded.
2. The arrival of Leander after swimming the Hellespont.
3. The departure of Leander, Hero standing with clasped hands watching him swim away.

The borders of these tapestries are especially fine. In these, which are complete and frame the four sides, figure Cupids threading garlands of flowers through a trellis or balustrade. Six medallions, three on each side, supported by Cupids, have within them scenes connected with the subject of the panel. A plain medallion, probably intended to contain a coat of arms, is in the centre of each panel at the top, while the corresponding medallion at the bottom has a couplet in Latin verse applicable to the subject. The inscription under the first-named panel runs as follows :

> ARDET . HERO . PARI
> LIQ : ACCENDITVR .
> IGNE . LEANDER .
> QVAEQ : FVIT VENERIS
> SERVA CVPIDO
> TVA EST.

That under Leander's arrival has :

> ECCE . FRETVM . TRA
> NAT . FLVCTV . IAC
> TATUS . ET . EVRO .
> TENDIT . ET . AD .
> THALAMOS . FES
> TA . PVELLA TVOS.

while the panel representing the departing lover has this inscription, very much faded and partly obliterated :

> HIC . SOROR . INCAER .
> TO . FRUSTRA . DEI EF
> RET AMANTEM .
> NON . ME . . . . TV
> DAS . . . . NIS . AMORIS
> AQVAS.

No record exists as to when these tapestries were acquired or how they came to Lyme. The house is especially rich in tapestry, Flemish and English. There are in all twenty-three pieces, filling seven rooms. One piece is signed with the initials S. C., which are those of Sackville Crowe, who, during the reign of Charles II, was director of the Mortlake works, which, inaugurated by James I, existed for about eighty years.

Three panels with large figures somewhat resembling the Raphael cartoons are descriptive of Biblical subjects, the

LYME: THE HALL, SHOWING MORTLAKE TAPESTRIES

angel ministering to Elijah under the juniper-tree, Elijah and
the priests of Baal, and Elijah being carried up to Heaven in
the chariot of fire. Some of these pieces have been sadly cut
about to fit the different rooms, the work being treated with
no more respect than if it had been wall-paper. One lovely
little piece of English tapestry hangs at the back of the portrait
of the Black Prince in the secret panel between the drawing-
room and the hall. This is probably a portion of the tapestry
that hangs in the yellow state dressing-room, but it has been
pieced together, as the top has a portion of the same border
as that in the Hall, the Cupids threading the garlands of
flowers. The portrait of the Black Prince was bought about
this date and was converted to its present use by Leoni.

There appears to have been a sale of pictures at St. James's
Palace. The portrait of the Black Prince and one of Edward III
—also a full-length—were acquired by an emissary of Peter
Legh for £16 16s. apiece. The fact of a tip of £1 1s. being
given to the groom of the chambers at St. James's, and the
same emissary stating that he had saved his patron £7, " for
the price of a warrant from the Lord Chamberlain is £4 for
each picture," looks as though the transaction had been conducted in a back-stairs way and without the knowledge of the
new King. The sale list includes, however, some full lengths
of the Stuart family, " which will come cheap," so it is possible
that George I may have wished to part with some of the portraits of his Stuart predecessors, and that he may have desired
these to be included in the sale.

From letters which speak, in 1723, of the house being partly
ready to receive visitors, it is probable that most of the interior
work was completed before Leoni began upon the south front,
for it was not until October 1725 that he submitted his plans
for this and the great portico.

His original plans are still preserved at Lyme. They were
carried out exactly as he intended, with the exception of some
statues, which he meant to be put over the great entrance door
and in the niches at each side. These were omitted, no doubt
on account of the considerable extra expense they would have

entailed. The library, which faces south with a bay window to the east, containing now some Greek stelæ of the fifth century B.C. and antique bronzes, was finished in 1728. The dining-room, a well-proportioned room approached from the library by a small anteroom hung with English tapestry, is 33 by 39 feet, and about 19 feet in height, and has a large bay window facing east. It was built by Sir J. Wyattville in 1818, and has a very fine Italian ceiling.

Much furniture was acquired about this date. Some pieces of tapestry—unfortunately not described—were bought at 37s. the ell at a sale of Lord Cadogan's * goods in 1726–27. A Venetian silk bed was also secured at a cost of £69, " one of the finest I have seen, very noble and as fine as any in England." This must be the remnants of a bed, now, alas, all dismantled and in pieces almost beyond redemption, in carved wood, covered with red Venetian silk. Sarah, Duchess of Marlborough, seems to have attended this same sale, and is reported as having bought most of the china and fine glass.

Amongst some of the most interesting pieces of furniture at Lyme is a set of eight Queen Anne walnut-wood chairs, and a settee of the same in the shape of double chairs, all covered in yellow damask, sent from Croome to her Uncle Peter by Lady Coventry.† She writes him a delightful letter, in which she apologizes for sending them without his leave and being forced by her circumstances to demand payment for them.

" I am ashamed to say there is a price to them (25 guineas) and that I am not able to say they are at your Service, but as the Lord of Lyme is so farr a richer & potent person then me, poor Widow ! am forced to name the sum, but you are as free to send them back & no harm done. For fashion I do assure you they are as Modern as if only made to-day. They were my Dear Lords present to me and I am loath to part with

* William, first Baron and Earl of Cadogan (1675–1726), General; served under William III in Ireland; Quartermaster-General to Marlborough; negotiated Quadruple Alliance, 1720.

† Anne, Countess of Coventry, daughter of Sir Streynsham Master by his second wife Elizabeth, second daughter of Richard Legh of Lyme; married, in 1715, Gilbert, fifth Earl of Coventry, who died in 1719, leaving no issue.

them, but it would please me better to think they were at Lyme then anywhere else. The chairs with the damask cost my Lord better then 4¹ a chair and the Sattee more then double that without the damask, but I would rather be that money out of pocket rather then disoblige you."

The damask has lately had to be restored, but the suite is otherwise in perfect condition. Among other things acquired about this date are three very fine carved wood and gilt chandeliers.

Much was being done in the garden at this time. "The plat of your garden will be best laid out in a green walk and gravell walks and a border in between," writes a careful friend, who suggests that the quantity of seeds proposed by Peter's gardener are "sufficient to sow Hampstead Heath or set up a shop." He sends some plants, begging for some box and some cuttings of silver fir in exchange, also "40 or 50 of those young whakings (?) but I won't ask for any of your red pinks, you have so very few." Old Madam Legh contributes also spire hollies and yews, with directions to set them in baskets in the ground; she recommends laurustinus as being hardy and making handsome heads, laurels, bay-trees, and "philarays." She sends likewise some golden pippins, fruit being always a welcome present, and some seeds, "the seeds man thinks that the seed which is writ Convolvolis is that flower which your wife calls 'chiny dishes.'"

With these she contributes also some rather malevolent London gossip relating to Sarah, Duchess of Marlborough (recently widowed), and Lady Cowper, whose husband, William, first Earl, had just died : "The Duchess of Molbear is certainly going to be married to the Duck of Somerset, and her reasons for marrying is that shee may take place of her Daughters." The Duchess had received several offers of marriage, amongst others, one from "the proud Duke of Somerset," to whom she recommended another lady as a substitute.

"Wise Lord Kuper (Cowper) suffered his heart to be broke by a Imperious Wife, for he would not suffer her to be brought into the room for some few hours afore he died. He only left her 800 pounds a year and no Legacy and all her jewells to be sold." *

The letters of this date contain references to the various lotteries which were so much the fashion of the time. These had been established in 1693, and for more than 130 years they yielded a large annual income to the Crown. In 1709 a Bill was actually brought into the House to increase the infamous window tax (taxing air and light), the money to go towards making a fund for a lottery. This was opposed, but was carried by 132 votes to 111, " but I believe it will not be carried further against yᵉ poorer sort." Old Madam Legh was somewhat of a gambler and dabbled a good deal in these doubtful speculations. We read of her paying £80 for tickets and being anxious to get rid of blanks. She writes to her son on the subject of the " Lottery business," regretting that (perhaps fortunately for her) she was too much in debt to tradesmen to indulge her appetite for more of these ventures.

Having abandoned all hopes of a son being born to him, Peter made a formal settlement of his estates upon his four nephews (sons of his brother Thomas), who in the event of his own death were to take the estates in succession in tail male. The year 1723 saw an important event in the Legh family, namely, the marriage of Fleetwood, the eldest of these, and heir to the Lyme estates, with Meriel, daughter and heiress of Sir Francis Leycester of Tabley.† Both Thomas Legh and Henrietta his wife were dead, the former dying about 1715, the latter in 1722, when their ten children all came to Lyme to be under the care of Peter and Frances.

Fleetwood Legh was twenty-two years old at the time of his marriage. He had been educated at Westminster School and Brasenose College, Oxford, where he was under the control

* William, first Earl Cowper, Lord Chancellor of England; married as his second wife the lady in question, a daughter of John Clavering of Chepwell, Durham.

† Sir Francis Leycester of Tabley (grandson of Sir Peter Leycester, the noted antiquary), born 1674, married Frances, daughter and heiress of Joshua Wilson of Colton, Yorkshire, and widow of Bryan Thornhill, by whom he had an only daughter, Meriel, born in 1705. She married, first, 1723, Fleetwood Legh of Bank, who died in 1725; secondly, 1728, Sir John Byrne.

of his uncle, Robert Shippen,* the Principal. We hear of his having dancing and fencing lessons, and being taught arithmetic : "He constantly rises to 6 o'clock prayers and lodges in his uncle's apartment and eats with him, so that he always has his eye upon him."

In spite of all this care and watching, however, the young 1723 man seems to have been rather wild and unsatisfactory, and to have contracted a good many debts. It was, therefore, a great relief to his devoted grandmother, and no less so to his uncle and aunt, when his marriage was settled and arranged in the summer of 1723.

Sir Francis Leycester and Peter Legh were lifelong friends. Seldom did a week go by without some communication passing between Lyme and Tabley. Messengers were constantly sent from one house to the other with a "how do" and a haunch of venison or other token of goodwill, although the distance between the two places is fully twenty-five miles by road. "Dear Sir," writes Sir Francis to Peter Legh in an undated letter, "Your nephew is now returning to you ; I think his London journey has been no diskindness. Wee have drunk tea and played at Cards and this morning he speaked it to her so I hope in God if they goe together perfect happiness and harmony may attend them."

No more romantic place for a courtship than Tabley Old Hall could possibly be conceived. It stands on a small island within the circuit of the upper part of a large lake, and is a perfect specimen of a Jacobean manor house, untouched and unspoilt, and maintained by its late owner, Lady Leighton Warren, in its original condition with all the furniture belonging to the period.† This is carried out even to the rushes on the floor of the great central hall. The garden, with its flagged paths and aromatic herbs, where Fleetwood and Meriel wandered in the early days of their courtship, remains much

---

* Fourth husband of Frances, third daughter of Richard Legh.

† Owing to its damp situation, the Old Hall was abandoned as a residence in the latter part of the eighteenth century, and the present handsome Georgian house was built on higher ground, about a quarter of a mile distant. It was the home of the poet, the third and last Lord de Tabley (1835–1895).

as it was two hundred years ago, and retains all its old-world charm and fragrance. Here one can be transported from the bustle and noise of the hurrying present to the poetry and romance of other days long past and gone.

Great preparations were being made for the wedding, which was to take place at Tabley. Fleetwood's eldest sister Elizabeth,* who had lived after her mother's death with her grandmother, old Madam Legh, in Devonshire Street, was deputed to buy all the material for Frances's gown, her cousin, Lady Coventry,† being called in to help in the selection.

> "We have been to look at the silk to-day, there is but six yards and three quarters which would be too scanty a pattern and too slight a thing for you Madam, and for the money you allow, me Lady thinks she can get something of the price much better."

She promises to send a pattern of Cousin Fountaine's "huckaback," which is to be sent down in a box with a book of "Sacremental Devotions." Peter's clothes are also selected. She chooses the prettiest silk to be found in Mr. Gorderill's shop, "but indeed it is a poor furnished shop to what Mr. Binks's is"; she adds a true feminine touch: "I love to go where there is most choice and the newest fashions." These goods are all sent down to Lyme by the carrier, who is given special instructions to deliver them safely.

Jewels were showered upon the bride-to-be. Her future aunt and uncle presented her with a beautiful diamond necklace, Frances's own, which was to be reset upon a "white file," the jeweller undertaking to make the alteration for 2d. a "soakit." "Your parting with your diamond necklace is the kindest thing that ever was done," Elizabeth assures her aunt, who also adds a pair of diamond drop ear-rings, to be made after a special design of Lady Coventry's, "so that the tope [top] stones look much larger than settin of 'em lengthways."

---

* Elizabeth, daughter of Thomas (second son of Richard) Legh by his wife Henrietta Fleetwood; married, 1731 Rev. John Holt, LL.D. of Hartlebury, Co. Worcester.

† See note, p. 374.

To these is added " a very handsome Brylon [brilliant] hoop ring," made at a cost of £16 16s.

Old Madam Legh was to have a new gown " against the wedding," which evidently made quite a stir, " everybody talks of it in London." There was to be a great gathering of relations, and many invitations were issued. One poor lady, in writing to decline, gives as her reason for doing so that she is suffering from a " twisting of the gutes." There was to be a ball at Lyme ; a book of country dances is sent down with the clothes, and much rejoicing, carousing and merry-making was to celebrate the union of the houses of Legh and Leycester.

The wedding took place on November 24, and the young people started their married life on an income of £1000 a year. Although this sum should have been ample, representing as it does a great deal more then than the same amount would do at the present day, it was evidently not considered sufficient by Sir Francis, who writes that he loves to have young people struggle with difficulties, " it makes them mind the world much sooner and better."

The bride and bridegroom took up their abode at Bank, Lancashire, the property which Fleetwood had inherited from his mother. It is near Southport and close to the sea, and in 1778 the house is described as " a venerable pile since demolished." Here one little daughter was born to them. Meriel seems to have won the heart of her Uncle Peter, who writes to Sir Francis : " You do not need to compliment me on my late entertaining your daughter at Lyme, being fully recompensed by an inward satisfaction I received from her behaviour and the great hopes there is of the young couple's happiness."

Frances was devoted to her niece, and a constant corre-1725 spondence was kept up between Bank and Lyme. Frances wrote excellent letters, giving graphic descriptions of the life at Lyme, where there was a constant stream of visitors. She writes in 1725 in great apprehension of a projected visit to London, the roads being infested with highwaymen, but determined to brave the dangers with her Peter rather than let him go alone :

> " This London journey affects me above all things. Mr Legh had soe ill a winter of the Gout, and is but just patched up, and travelling and change of beds is very troublesome, and above all things I'me frighted. There is soe much robbing & murthers about both upon the Roads & in London streets, that I shall have noe ease till hee's at home againe ; and to goe myselfe I dont love stirring of all things, & a very great fatigue & charge it will be, whether I goe or noe. All that I propose if I goe is if a fit of the Gout takes him, I shall be with him."

1725-6   In January 1725–6 there was a terrific fall of snow in the north of England, and she mentions the fact of the interruption of the post caused by this, and the casualties resulting therefrom.

> " I received yours, dearest neice, & from yr uncle and myself return you both our humble service and many thanks for your kind wishes, which though your letter lay several posts, occasioned by the sad snow and weather, yet came not out of season. . . . I thank God wee have escaped better than expectation, tho' many poor sheep & deer are dead in Snowdrifts, abundance of poor people have in Derbyshire bin lost, in particular two poor gentlemen as they came from a Funerall and was benighted. Parson Raynes went as far as he could, then took leave of his friend, kissed him & laid himself down & died. Mr Rossington had the good fortune to goe a little further & was relieved by a man that was fetching sheep ; hee had lost his senses & one of his legs they had much adoe to preserve from mortifieing . . . indeed I never knew such a storm in my life . . . we couldn't till yesterday either see or goe into the gardens for snow."

Later comes another letter in which she speaks of being very busy, " a great deal of company . . . two grave ladies that have bin some time with me and are but gone this day, I was obliged to attend more than the young ones." She speaks also of having " a great deal of fine singing and music," of which she was very fond. She gives an amusing account of the delinquencies of her butler—an old servant—whom she complains of her husband being far too lenient with :

> " Since I have writ this I'me tould yt Worthington [the butler] is gone to Bank & had not the civility to let me know and enquire if I would have anything ; indeed hee is the most sacy impertinent servant that

ever was, & far from a good one. I'me sure no master but his would keep him. I was lately tould how abominable rude he is, that when he speaks of my nephew Legh hee calls him Fleetwood Legh, and the rest [her other nephews and nieces] all by their Xtian names, without Master or Miss joyn'd to it, as Molly & Sally &c, and the same time his bratts must be Master & Miss Worthington. I've really no patience; hee grows so rich & proud. I onely hope when hee has rope enough he'el hang himself. I'me sorry I have noe better a subject to entertain you with."

But these old retainers were faithful and devoted. Those were the days of long service, when generations of servants remained in the same family, bequeathing their heritage of love and loyalty to their successors. Carefully preserved among the plate at Lyme is a beautiful George II silver tankard which bears this inscription :

> Samuel Parepoint
> Legacy to his Master
> Cook at Lyme 64 years
> Died 31st December, 1757 in His 75 year
> of his Age.

This wonderful old cook must, therefore, have begun his duties at the age of eleven !

Amongst the letters of this date is one from Peter Legh to the son of the old keeper, Joseph Watson, in which Peter suggests that it might be as well for the old man, being now aged about seventy-nine, to relegate his duties to a more youthful successor and retire on a competence. Being somewhat addicted to drink

> " he has more opportunities for indulging when the season comes to send out venison, and raily he had another tussle for his life last winter occasioned by his old misfortunes, Fr^{ds} & Bottle . . . and I'me afraid for the consequences."

He outlived his master, however, dying only in 1753, as we have seen, at the age of one hundred and four.

The happy married life of Fleetwood and Meriel was very short. He was taken ill with a violent attack of pleurisy very soon after Frances's letter describing the severe cold

1726 weather, and died on January 21, 1725–6, aged only twenty-five. The news was received with the greatest sorrow and consternation at Lyme. Peter was incapacitated by a severe attack of gout—an illness he suffered much from all his life—and was, therefore, unable to be of any practical assistance to the poor little widow, who, to add to her grief and distress, was in expectation of the birth of a child. The funeral took place at Bank, but Peter was too ill to attend.

The arrival of the coming child was awaited with the greatest anxiety, but the ardent hopes of its being a son were not destined to be fulfilled, and Meriel gave birth to a second daughter in the summer of 1726. Later Meriel married an Irishman, Sir John Byrne, and the Bank estate passed ultimately from the Legh family and is now in the possession of Lord Lilford.

CHAPTER XXVIII

DEATH OF OLD MADAM LEGH

HARDLY had Peter Legh begun to recover somewhat from the 1727 shock of his nephew Fleetwood's sudden death than he was to suffer another far severer bereavement in the loss of his beloved wife. Frances had been in indifferent health for some time and was undergoing medical treatment of the usual drastic kind, against which, poor lady, she was evidently protesting. Dr. Leacon, a Manchester physician, writes to Peter on April 6, 1727 :

> " I do not wonder at Mrs Legh's being angry when she takes physick, for it is a little rough, but that very roughness will be of service to her I assure you ; but she complains so much of it, that I have agreed to let her leave it off at present. I am glad to hear she is better."

The roughness of this treatment probably hastened her 1727-8 end, for she succumbed to her illness, and died somewhat suddenly at Lyme on February 17, 1727-8, in her fifty-eighth year, to the inexpressible sorrow of her husband, who was never the same man again. So prostrated was he with grief that he was confined to his room for many days after her death, being quite unable even to stand. In answer to a letter of condolence from his old and dear friend, Sir Francis Leycester, he writes that he thanks him for his kind advice, which he is endeavouring to put into practice, " but I am struggling under the severest loss that I ever received."

He was indeed in a sad position, for apart from the deep affection he had for his wife, Peter was so dependent upon her for help and guidance in the management and upbringing of his dead brother's children, some of whom were at school and some being educated at Lyme. One of the last acts of Frances's life had been making all arrangements for her nieces going to a school in Derbyshire, kept by a gentlewoman, who undertook the education of her pupils and to provide their "table" for £20 a year.

His mother, to whom he had always been devoted, was a great age, besides being in failing health, so she was not able to be of much assistance to poor Peter. Her eyesight, which all her life had been defective, was now seriously threatened, and she writes pathetically to her son, deploring the loss of the sight of one of her eyes :

"... And now I must tell you of a great afflicktion I am in, I have lost the sight of one of my eyes, and I am much afread of my tother eye, I desire your prayers that God would give me sight while he gives me life."

1728　　In the May following Frances's death, old Madam Legh died somewhat suddenly at her house in Devonshire Street, having reached the age of eighty-five, and Peter had to deplore the loss of wife and mother within the space of three short months. Writing to Sir Francis Leycester, he speaks of his mother :

"who has been for forty years last past [his father died in 1687] so tender and beneficial unto all her children, especially to her sons and to me in particular, that notwithstanding her great age, I can't at present throw off affliction, and always to her memory must be gratefull."

Her powerful will and dominating personality had made her more feared than loved, but Peter recognized her great qualities and appreciated them at their full worth, so that her loss—coming as it did so soon after that of his beloved wife—was a severe and crushing blow.

Old Madam Legh outlived eight of her thirteen children. In the course of her long life she witnessed many changes, both social and political. Born in the reign of Charles I, she saw England under six different sovereigns, dying just before the accession of the seventh. At heart a staunch Jacobite,

384

her sympathies were always with the Stuart cause, and she never became reconciled to the rule of the House of Hanover.

Her funeral took place in the family burying-place at Winwick, Lancashire, where she rests by her beloved husband. Her sensible character shows itself in the expression of her last wishes, that the ceremony should be as private and quiet as possible, the cost not to exceed £100, and that there were to be "no escutcheons, no gloves nor hatbands nor drink." Only six of her nearest relatives were to be present; Peter was too ill to attend, so the office of chief mourner was undertaken by his next surviving brother, Richard. 1728

In her will, which was drawn up in January 1724-5, she appoints her granddaughter, Elizabeth Legh, her executor, and to her she leaves the lease of her house in Devonshire Street, and her pew, No. 48, in St. George the Martyr Church, Queen Square (still existing), for which she paid a rent of £2 5s. a year. To her granddaughter Elizabeth she also bequeathes her great diamond buckle, " my great Tortoishell Cabbepot," all her plate, china, clothes, linen and household linen, her " repeating Pendulam," and lacquer cabinets, worked beds and curtains. Sundry heirlooms are to return to Lyme, the portraits of herself and Richard by Lely, all the miniatures, two big lacquer corner cupboards, "a great Japan cabinet," and "a great Japan screen," all these can be traced; also the flower-pots and statues in her London garden; these are no doubt the little lead Cupids now in the Dutch garden. Various worked chairs and beds are also mentioned, one a copy of a bed sent by the Duke of Modena to James II, the pattern given to Madam Legh by the Dowager Lady Derby, but these are not described definitely enough to be traceable.

Two " great diamond rings," a lodestone ring, and a purple velvet Bible, formerly the property of Lord Keeper Coventry, have, alas, disappeared. " A black Ebaney Cabinet inlaid with juery," which has fortunately been restored to Lyme, is a beautiful little Italian cabinet inlaid with jewels, having several secret drawers, and in perfect preservation. This has remained ever since in the sitting-room of the reigning lady of the house.

Elizabeth Legh found the house in Devonshire Street somewhat of an encumbrance, and it ended in Peter taking it off her hands, though he writes to Sir Francis that he would as soon take a house in Gomorrah as in Sodom. He offers it to his friend for £600, twenty years' lease, and " good conveniences in house and garden." How the transaction terminated history does not say.

1729　As a distraction from his grief Peter endeavoured to absorb himself more and more in his building schemes—a very costly occupation—which increased with growing years : " 16 Carts loaded with Billinge slate—4 horses apiece, 2 men to each Cart, pray do you think I shall want company this night ? " he writes to Sir Francis in 1729, and again in 1730, he alludes to Lyme as " this dirty place," as if it was still very much in workmen's hands.

He was also much interested and absorbed in the education and development of his nephew and heir Peter, who, from being heir presumptive, passed, on the death of his elder brother Fleetwood in 1725-6, to the greater dignity of heir apparent. Peter was born in 1707-8, and was educated at Westminster and Cambridge, where he was sent in October 1728, to St. John's College, accompanied by a divine and a servant, and was admitted Fellow-Commoner on the 7th of that month, his tutor being a Dr. Newcome. His uncle writes of him as creating a good impression, " passed his examination to satisfaction, so I hope with God's Blessing he will do well."

The two Peters seem to have got on very well together. The boy made himself useful to his uncle and helped him considerably with his voluminous correspondence when he was incapacitated by gout—as was often the case—from even holding a pen. The older man, in his turn, showed sympathy and consideration for his young namesake, entering into all his pursuits, so that their life together was happy and harmonious.

The choice of a suitable wife for his nephew was now the

386

chief object of the elder Peter, and for some years he searched in vain for a lady answering in all respects to his demands. Parents still continued to exercise a considerable amount of control over their children in matters connected with their marriage, though not to so great an extent as formerly, and Peter was consulting his nephew's wishes, while still endeavouring to influence him in what he conceived to be the right direction.

> "As I have no one I respect more than yourself [he writes to Sir **1733** Francis Leycester in November 1733], I desire your advice how & to whom I should make an application for the disposal of my nephew. I have reason to believe he's entire at liberty from any engagements . . . my desire is more for a good woman & an honest family (no lover of London) than for money."

Several suggested brides were rejected for different reasons. **1737** One was considered to be too fat and, therefore, not likely to answer the purpose for which she was intended, and there were objections to various others. The choice finally fell upon Martha, sole daughter and heiress of Thomas Bennet of Salthrop, Wilts, probably "no lover of London," worthy, but exceedingly plain, to whom Peter was married in December 1737.

Two very beautiful Chippendale chairs with a large ram's head carved on each, and the Legh and Bennet arms, and a pair of glass goblets engraved with the crest and the same arms, are probably commemorative of this event.

Peter had the joy and satisfaction of living to see his great-nephew, the little son—their first child—born to Peter and Martha in October 1741, but he was spared from sharing in their grief at the loss of the child a year or two later. Peter **1743-4** died at Lyme in January 1743-4, and was buried at Winwick, where, according to his own wishes expressed in his will, drawn up many years before, there is neither monument nor inscription to his memory.

CHAPTER XXIX

THE SHADOWS CLOSE

THERE is little of very special interest to mark the lives of Peter and Martha Legh, and a few pages will suffice to dispose of their history. They were a somewhat dull, uninteresting couple, neither of them possessing any great charm or attraction. No portrait exists of Peter except a small crayon drawing done of him when quite an old man. He wears a white wig and a three-cornered hat, a plain coat buttoned down the front, and a white "choker." There is little character in the face, which is weak and inexpressive. A portrait of Martha depicts her as a singularly unattractive-looking female with a large thick nose. An earlier portrait is more flattering and shows her as a sort of Amazon armed with a spear and shield, and suggests the possibility that she may have served as a model for the lead figure of Britannia which Leoni erected on the north front of the house; if this is so, it must have been a special compliment paid her by her husband's uncle.

1745   The troubles of '45 passed lightly over the house of Lyme. Peter avoided being drawn into the rising, although Charles Edward with his Highland army reached Manchester, and must have passed close to Lyme on his way to Derby. There was a faint attempt on the part of the more adventurous Cheshire squires to rally to the Standard of the Prince, whom they still looked upon as their rightful king. A meeting of the famous Cheshire Club—dissolved in 1720—was called together again, it is said once more at Lyme, where it assembled—as it had done at its inauguration—in the Stag Parlour. But it was Peter's voice, as it had been that of his uncle's, that gave the

388

A VIEW IN THE PARK AT LYME SHOWING "THE CAGE"

Driving the Stags across the pond. From an oil-painting at Lyme by T. Smith, 1745

deciding vote against any action being taken. John Ward of Capesthorne * writes to him on December 21, 1745 :

> " I am glad to hear that you escaped ye Scots better than some of your neighbours. My poor tenants at Capesthorne have lost 17 horses out of 18, besides great charges in going to Preston both with them & after them, & some will be ruined, having no horses nor money to buy more. Teams were taken to draw ye Chevalier's Carriages & ye Carts wch were left in Peter's yard he has used to ye Coalpits & now demands 10s for each towards his damages & calls 'em Rebell carts. I'me glad to hear ye King's forces are come up with ye Scotch."

The peace and prosperity of the country under the rule of the stodgy Georges had, in England at any rate, dimmed part of the glamour and dispelled much of the romance of the Stuart cause, although such as came in contact with the Prince were captivated by his gallant bearing and fascinated by his great personal charm. But the country as a whole was disinclined for any change, and was content to let the present state of things continue and not to embark on any doubtful venture. Although his army had increased to 6000 men, Charles Edward realized that his gallant Highlanders were insufficient to cope with numbers twice as great, so he fell back again to the North, and Culloden settled for ever the fortunes of " Bonnie Prince Charlie."

Among the prints at Lyme is one of Charles Edward, executed by Sir Robert Strange, the famous Jacobite engraver, who fought on the Stuart side at Prestonpans, Falkirk, and Culloden. Few examples of this print exist. It represents the Prince as a very young man, dressed in a velvet coat, with a small wig and queue, wearing the ribbon and star of the Order of the Garter. Inscribed beneath the portrait is the motto

EVERSO MISSUS
SUCCURRERE SECLO

and it is signed " A Paris chez Chevreau rue St. Jacques.— C.P.R.," which letters it is suggested may stand for " Cum

---

* John Ward of Capesthorne and of the Inner Temple (1670-1748-9), an eminent lawyer. He was M.P. for Newton, Co. Lancaster, in 1712. His eldest daughter married at Kensington, in 1721, Davies Davenport of Woodford and Marton, ancestor of Brigadier-General W. Bromley Davenport, D.S.O.

Privilegio Regis." A branch of oak-leaves, one of the Jacobite emblems, and a sword and shield, the latter embellished with the head of Medusa, also figure as accessories to the print, which has no great artistic merit.

1748 Peter, who had always been interested in politics, was returned Member of Parliament for Newton Borough in 1748, and sat in each of the Parliaments called for the next twenty-five years. This necessitated his being a good deal in London, where he and Martha occupied for many years a house in Greek Street, Soho.

1750 A description of Lyme house and park, as they existed in 1750, is given by Dr. Richard Pococke.* He appears to have found Lyme a sort of enchanted castle, equally impossible to get in or out of :

". . . I went to the park and house of Mr Legh of Lyme ; the situation is extraordinary, the park being on a declivity up the side of those hills on which are the bounds of Cheshire and Derbyshire, it extends also to the west on the other side of the other valley at the foot of the hills. The house is situated on a plain spot a little above the vale. The north side was built in the last age, but the other three round the court by the last possessor on the model of a Roman palace, having a colonnade on the sides within, and the front to the garden consists of a grand Ionick portico, and the whole front is adorned with pilasters. There are fifteen windows on a floor every way, and over the door at the entrance is a statue of Britannia with a star on her head and in one hand the arms, if I mistake not, of the family quartered with the Union flag. The ascent to the saloon is by a flight of steps, it is a good room, but not grand enough for the house ; in it at one end is the picture of the Black Prince, another of his father. There is much good room in the house, a fine old chimney piece in a dineing room in the old part, several pieces of Gibbons carvings in wood, and an old gallery with ordinary pictures in it. There is one picture in the house of Watson, a park keeper who is 104 years old and now alive, having been in that office ever since 1674, and has seen five generations hunt in the park. Behind the house is a large piece of black water with wood behind it, and to the west is a hanging garden, now neglected, which goes down to the vale ; but the great curiosity of this place are the red deer. The stags are brought together before the house and being drove

* Dr. Richard Pococke, " Travels through England during 1750, 1751, and later Years," vol. i, p. 211.

390

gently up to the pond they swim through it, and it is an extraordinary sight to see their horns like a wood moving along the water; in the hot weather they often stand in the water, and many of them remained in it after they had swam through. There are no buildings in the park except one, which at a distance has the appearance of an obelisk * and an old castle whited up which is seen at a great distance. All the avenues in the park are lock'd and no one is admitted but with somebody that is known, unless they have the weekly watchword, and it is the same to those who would go out, tho' one would imagine any person might be permitted to go out who had been let in. I went near two miles up and down hill in a very hot day, and not having the word was obliged to ride back and bring the keeper with me to get out of the park."

This ancient ceremony of deer-driving was continued at Lyme long after the death of the famous old keeper, Joseph Watson, in 1753.† A MS. book in the possession of Miss Fanny Richmond of Blackheath ‡ has an account of this curious custom, which was witnessed by her grandfather § about the year 1780 while on a visit with his parents to Peter and Martha Legh at Lyme.

The letters of this date are with few exceptions rather uninteresting. They contain chiefly directions to servants, and are full of business details with scarcely any reference to the current topics.

The following account of Queen Charlotte's arrival in London, and the candid and not altogether flattering report of her personal appearance, written to a member of the Master ‖ family, is worth reproducing :

"Now I must acquaint you that our Queen arrived Safe a Tuesday Afternoon at half an hour after three; they came through St James' Parke, the Coach set her down at the Garden Door, the King came to meet her. Her Majesty fell on her knees & his Majesty took her up in his Arms and led her into the Palace. She is not tall, thin & not

---

* The Cage.

† It continued up to 1810.

‡ A descendant of Posthuma Brooke, sister of Richard Legh.

§ Rev. Legh Richmond, born in 1772, chaplain to the Duke of Kent, father of Queen Victoria. He died in 1827.

‖ A descendant of Elizabeth Legh, wife of Sir Streynsham Master.

handsome, but agreeable. Her complexion is pale, a little on the yellow.

" Her travelling dress was pink with Gold & Silver. At ten that Evening they was married ; her Dress then was white & silver with a Purple Velvet Robe, a very long Train almost covered with Silver Fringes, a Diamond Crown & Stomacher. The King in white & Gold. Her Bride Maids in White Sattin, their Sleeves made very close to their Arms, no ruffle cuffs for it's said they are a going out of Fashion.

" I am pleased to hear of this Character of her Majesty—that she ever was a religious, sensible good natured Lady, so that I hope they will be happy & set good Examples, which pray God may be followed." *

Peter and Martha kept up a good deal of state ; there was plenty of entertaining, and Lyme maintained its reputation for hospitality. Among the papers are some interesting old bills of fare, written with an attempt at French, and a plan of the dinner-table, which must have groaned under the weight of the solid food piled upon it. All the dishes were put on together—as in former times—and no regard was paid, apparently, to keeping the food warm. (See page 393.)

The following paper of directions for a journey to Lancashire gives one some idea how an establishment was moved in the latter part of the eighteenth century :

Family to Haydock, Jany. 13. 1783.
Master & Mrs Anne Legh in Masters Coach past Macclesfield.
With my Master
Mrs A. Legh's Man on the Mule
Under Butler on the Dun Horse
Coach Stable Helper on the spare Coach horse to meet Coach at Knutsford
Cook in my Masters Chair
Butler on the Chesnut Mare
Baker on the Brown Mare
Kitchin Man on the old Wafe Mare
John Butterworth ride the Stone Horse and lead my Masters little Horse.

* Raines Collection.

THE SHADOWS CLOSE

MENU OF A DINNER AT LYME

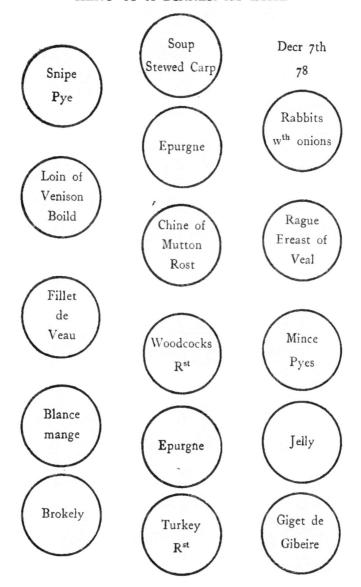

Snipe Pye

Soup Stewed Carp

Decr 7th

78

Loin of Venison Boild

Epurgne

Rabbits wth onions

Fillet de Veau

Chine of Mutton Rost

Rague Ereast of Veal

Blance mange

Woodcocks Rst

Mince Pyes

Brokely

Epurgne

Jelly

Turkey Rst

Giget de Gibeire

No one went any distance in a coach without four horses; indeed, the old approach to Lyme, which went right over the Cage hill, is so steep that no conveyance could have attempted it without four or even six horses. In those days the way to get to a place was by the shortest route, quite irrespective of the lie of the country.

Five children were born to Peter and Martha Legh, two sons and three daughters. The eldest son, Peter, died an infant, but a second son, Bennet, born in 1748, came as a 1756 consolation to the bereaved parents. They were, however, destined to lose this child also, for he died in 1756, at the age of eight. A very badly painted miniature of a beautiful boy with golden hair and dark eyes hangs under the crayon drawing of the last Peter Legh of Lyme, in what was his own sitting-room. Although there is no name attached, it is more than probable that this was the beloved son whose loss was an abiding sorrow, the bitterness of which time might soften, but could never heal.

With this little life all joy and peace departed from the house of Lyme. His parents, whose future at the time of their marriage had seemed so bright, now fell utterly apart. Martha, warped and soured by excessive grief, became more exacting and difficult as time went on, and Peter's weak and shallow nature sought distraction in a vortex of dissipation which ultimately caused the wreck of both their lives. The couple lived together under the same roof, but at opposite ends of the house, and led a cat-and-dog existence.

A skit on the leading members of society in Cheshire, written about the year 1779, presenting the characters in the form of a series of portraits, gives a picture of the unhappy family life at Lyme. How different and how sadly altered from that of former years! This rather scurrilous production runs as follows :

" Peter L--- Esqr   L-me.

. . . .

A house divided against itself.

. . . .

394

INDEX

INDEX

INDEX

BOLD, Margaret, letter from, 162

BOLD, near Prescot, Lancashire, 97

BOLD, Richard:
marriage to Anne Legh, 97, 98
monument in Farnworth Church, 162–63
references, 44, 132

BOOTH, Sir R., letters from, 206–7, 208

BOOTHE, Sir G.:
created Lord Delamere, 214
implicated in Monmouth Rebellion, 333
Royalist rising in Cheshire led by, 203–4
reference, 175

BOWDEN, George:
co-guardian of Legh estates, 1648, 189–90, 191
letter from, 127

BRADLEY HOUSE, Cheshire, 7

BRADLEY HOUSE, Lancashire:
building at, during Elizabethan and Jacobean periods, 65
described, 1465, 9
inscription at, 1598, 65
Legh ownership of, 7
Piers Legh and his wife reside at, 106–7
reference, 126
Richard III's visit to, " The King's Bed," 11–12

BRADSHAIGH, Sir Roger, of Haigh, letter from, 125

BRADSHAWE, Henry, 119

BRADSHAWE, John:
behaviour as President at trial of Charles I, 123
Chester election, 199–202
correspondence with Francis Legh, 1636–37, 155–56
death, 208
descent and birthplace, 119–20
letters from 120–23, 135–36
marriage, 123
references, 115, 172

BRAMSHILL, Hampshire, 83

BRASENOSE COLLEGE, Oxford:
affairs at, 1638, 159–60
appearance of, in 1608, and students' life at, 86–87
during Civil War, 192
Francis and Thomas Legh at, 86–95
plague outbreak at, 88
Richard Parr at, 1635, 135

" BRASENOSE QUATERCENTENARY MONOGRAPHS," by G. H. Wakeling, references, 87, 88

BRERETON, Dorothy, 2nd wife of Sir P. Legh (9th):
attitude towards her stepchildren, 107
death of, and will, 150
letters to, 78–79, 118
marriage, 77–81
portraits of, 81–82

BRERETON, Sir William:
letter from, 145
siege of Chester by, 184

BRIDGEWATER, John, 1st Earl of, letter from, 102

BROADWOOD, L., letters to and from, 128, 129

BROOKE, Sir R., 196

BROOKE, Thos., Chester election petition brought by, 200–2

BRUCH, property of, 127

BUCKINGHAM, George Villiers, 1st Duke of, letter from, 84–85

BULLINGE, John, letter from, 82

BURGESS, William, petition of, 185

CADIZ BAY, battle of, 49

CAEN, battle before the gates of, 1346, 1–4

CALLENDER OF STATE PAPERS, 1580, 34

CALVELEY, Lady:
letter from, 312
references, 193, 241

402

INDEX

CALVELEY, Lettice, wife of Thos. Legh:
death, 189
life at Blackley after her husband's death, 177–83
life at Lyme until her death, 183, 186–90
marriage, 128
petition *re* surcharges on Lyme during Civil War, 188–89
portrait, 160–61
will, 189–90

CARMELITES of Chester, interment of Sir Piers Legh's remains by, 4

CARR, Lady, 233, 281, 308

CARR, Sir R, letters from, 287, 305

CAUDLE CUP, 98

CAVENDISH, Henry, friendship with Sir P. Legh, 85

CAXTON, Sarum Missal printed by, 1487, at Lyme, 69

CELLIER, Elizabeth, 295–97

CHARLES I:
at Edgehill, his narrow escape, 179
political affairs, 1632, 136–37
political affairs, 1641–42, 166–69
portraits at Lyme, 56, 57
ship-money writs and Scottish policy, 156–58
trial of, 123
visits House of Commons to demand surrender of five members, 166–68

CHARLES II:
appreciation of R. Legh, 244
death, 326
a devoted husband, 240–41
illness of, 1679, 294
marriage to Catherine of Braganza, 227
Parliamentary distrust of, 238
parody of speech of, 272–75
popular anxiety for heir, 243
portrait at Lyme, 56

restoration of, 209–14
Third Dutch War, 251–60
Vote of Supply, 1670, 242–43

CHARLES EDWARD, Prince, portrait of, 389–90

CHARLOTTE, Queen, account of arrival of, 391–92

CHARLTON, Sir Job, 243, 249

CHATSWORTH, formation of deer park, 85

CHESHIRE:
Legh estates in, 7
loyalty of, to Richard II, 5–6
Royalist rising in, 202–3

"CHESHIRE CLUB":
dissolution of, and portraits of members, 367–68, 388
origin, 360–68

CHESTER:
parliamentary elections, 199–202, 208–9, 246–47
siege of, 184
Sir Piers Legh beheaded at, 1400, 2–5

CHETHAM SOCIETY publications, 5–6, 150

CHICHELEY, Elizabeth, wife of Richard Legh:
death of, and will, 384–85
fondness for lotteries, 376
illness of, after birth of thirteenth child, 343
letters from, 63, 227, 270–71, 318, 320, 358–59, 375
as a letter-writer, 270
love for her husband, 321
marriage, 215, 216, 219
miniature of, 267
portrait, 221
removal from Lyme, after her husband's death, 354–55
visit to London, 1683, 314
visit to Tunbridge Wells, 318–20
visits her son in the Tower, 363–64

INDEX

INDEX

INDEX

INDEX

INDEX

INDEX

INDEX

INDEX

INDEX

INDEX

INDEX

INDEX

INDEX

416

INDEX

INDEX

INDEX

INDEX

INDEX

INDEX

PRINTED AT THE COMPLETE PRESS
WEST NORWOOD
LONDON

Milton Keynes UK
Ingram Content Group UK Ltd.
UKHW041323081024
2071UKWH00035B/460

9 789353 977573